The Wisconsin Frontier

A History of the Trans-Appalachian Frontier

Walter Nugent and Malcolm Rohrbough, general editors

Andrew L. Cayton. *Frontier Indiana*

R. Douglas Hurt. *The Ohio Frontier: Crucible of the Old Northwest, 1720–1830*

The Wisconsin Frontier

Mark Wyman

Indiana University Press   Bloomington & Indianapolis

Library of Congress Cataloging-in-Publication Data
Wyman, Mark.
The Wisconsin frontier / Mark Wyman.
p.   cm. — (A history of the Trans-Appalachian
frontier)
Includes bibliographical references and index.
ISBN 0-253-33414-4 (alk. paper)
1. Frontier and pioneer life—Wisconsin. 2. Wisconsin—
History.   I. Title   II. Series.
F581.W96 1998
977.5'03—dc21   97-50165
1   2   3   4   5   03   02   01   00   99   98

for

River Falls

—from Kinnickinnic to Clifton Hollow,
Glover Station to Cherma,
Mann Valley to Randall School—
and every person and place therein,
where my dreams and memories began.

⬚ Contents

Foreword   xiii

Preface   xvii

Acknowledgments   xix

I. ——————————————————————————— 1

THE FRENCH OPEN A FRONTIER

2. ——————————————————————————— 18

BEFORE THE EUROPEANS

3. ——————————————————————————— 38

FRENCHMEN AND INDIANS

4. ——————————————————————————— 66

AN ARENA FOR INTERNATIONAL COMPETITION

5. ——————————————————————————— 97

STRUGGLE OVER THE UPPER LAKES

6. ——————————————————————————— 127

MINERS, INDIAN WARS, AND A FRONTIER TRANSFORMED

7. ——————————————————————————— 157

RUSH TO THE LAND

8. ——————————————————————————— 185

AN ETHNIC AND RELIGIOUS JUMBLE

9. ———————————————— 215

RESTRICTING THE INDIAN DOMAIN

10. ———————————————— 246

LOGGING THE PINERIES

11. ———————————————— 279

LEGACIES

Essay on Sources 298

Index 327

☙ Illustrations

Nicolet landing at Green Bay, 1634	13
Effigy mounds at the Mendota Asylum grounds, Madison	30
Traces of early nineteenth century Indian agriculture	33
Indian village on the Wolf River	43
Gathering wild rice	46
Juliet Kinzie	129
Fort Howard in 1818	133
Black Hawk	154
Gustaf Unonius	186
Log cabin	199
Jacob Spaulding	219
Chief Oshkosh of the Menominees	222
Oneida Indians in school, circa 1900	232
Winnebagos picking cranberries	242
Louis Blanchard	253
Sawyers cutting a felled tree	255
Logs on sleigh, circa 1905	257
Logs floating down the Black River	260
Log raft on the Mississippi	265
Men sorting logs at Beef Slough	270
Devastation left by logging, circa 1915	276
Passenger pigeon	280

☙ List of Maps

Major river systems and bays   23

Indian tribes of the Western Great Lakes   35

The French in the Great Lakes country   68

Changes in territorial boundaries   131

Indian cessions, 1829–1842   162

Indian reservations and Winnebago settlements   227

Logging rivers and sawmill towns   248

Advancing frontier line, 1840–1880   295

Foreword

For most Americans, the phrase "the American West" conjures up the western half of the nation. From the Great Plains across the Rockies and the Intermontane Plateaus to the Pacific Ocean came a flood of popular images, from trappers, cowboys, miners, and homesteading families to the "Marlboro Man" and country-western music. This has been "the West" since the California Gold Rush and the migration of '49ers propelled this region into the national consciousness.

But it was not always so. There was an earlier American West, no less vivid and dramatic. Here the fabled figures were not John Charles Fremont but Daniel Boone, not Geronimo but Tecumseh, not Calamity Jane but Rachel Jackson, not "Buffalo Bill" Cody but Davy Crockett. This earlier West ran, geographically, from the crest of the Appalachian Mountains to the Mississippi River, from the border with Canada to the Gulf of Mexico. It was the West of Euro-American expansion from before the American Revolution until the middle of the nineteenth century, when the line of frontier settlement moved through it toward that next, farther West.

In its initial terms, the story of the First American West involved two basic sets of characters: first, the white people of European origin (and south of the Ohio River, many African American slaves), who spread relentlessly westward; second, the original settlers, the Native Americans, who retreated grudgingly before this flood. These first Europeans, French and Spanish, appeared on this landscape in the 1600s and early 1700s, where their interactions with the original native peoples involved both cooperation and conflict. The English arrived a half-century later. In numbers, the Europeans were almost always a minority, and so both sides sought not conquest or annihilation but mutual accommodation, a joint occupation of the land and joint use of its resources, a system of contact allowing both sides to survive and even to benefit from one another's presence. Trade developed and intermarriage followed; so did misunderstandings and violence. But a delicate balance, supported by mutual interests, often characterized relations among Europeans and native peoples.

When Anglo-Americans began moving through the Cumberland Gap from Virginia into what hunters called the Kentucky country in the 1750s, they soon tilted the balance between the two cultures, occupying large portions of Kentucky and pressing against native groups from Ohio south to Georgia. By 1780, the Anglo-Americans had also occupied the former French settlements of Cahokia in Illinois and Vincennes in Indiana. Despite strong resistance by several native groups, the seemingly unending reinforcements of white families made their gradual occupation of the trans-Appalachian frontier inevitable.

In the 1780s the infant American government issued ordinances spelling out how the land between the Great Lakes and the Ohio River was to be acquired, subdivided, and sold to the citizens of the new republic, and how a form of government organization would lead to statehood and equal membership in the Union. A parallel process was soon set up for Kentucky, Tennessee, and the lands south to the Gulf.

In the 1830s and 1840s, the remaining native groups east of the Mississippi were removed to the West. The expansion of settlement into the trans-Appalachian frontier now continued unchecked into Illinois, Wisconsin, Michigan, and the great cotton lands and hill country of Alabama, Mississippi, and Florida. The frontier period had been completed—as early as the 1820s in Kentucky, and within the next twenty years over much of the Old Northwest and in the Old Southwest.

In brief terms, this is the story of the trans-Appalachian frontier. Over scarcely three generations, the trickle of settler families across the mountains had become more than four million, both white and black. Beginning with Kentucky in 1792 and running through Florida in 1845 and Wisconsin in 1848, a dozen new states had entered the American Union. Each territory/state had its own story, and it is appropriate that each should have a separate volume in this series. The variations are large. Florida's first European arrived in 1513, and this future state had both Spanish and American frontier experiences over 350 years. Missouri had a long French and Spanish history before the arrival of American settlers. Kentucky and Ohio did not, and Americans in large numbers came there quickly through the Cumberland Gap.

The opening and closing of the settlement frontier is the subject of each of these volumes. Each begins with the world that existed when Europeans made contact with native peoples. Each describes and analyzes the themes associated with the special circumstances of the individual territories/states. And each concludes with the closing of the frontier.

The editors have selected these authors because of their reputations as scholars and interpreters of their individual territories/states. We believe that you will find this history informative and lively, and we are confident that you will enjoy this and other volumes in the Trans-Appalachian Frontier series.

In this volume, Mark Wyman describes for us the vast panorama of varied peoples and diverse landscapes that would come to be known as Wisconsin. Set at the intersection of crucial waterways that connected the central and north-central parts of the continent, this place became a center of trade and human contact. Indian peoples met and interacted with an assortment of French traders, trappers, missionaries, and government officials. As imperial fortunes changed over a century and a half, the British replaced the French, and then within a generation came the Americans.

The citizens of the new, independent American nation only slowly established a presence within what would become Wisconsin. Until the peace with Great Britain in 1814, the great forest and waters remained the domain of the fur trade and a meeting place of native peoples and Europeans, but quickly thereafter, the impulse to agricultural settlement began to be felt in the north country. Yet even then it was not until the decade of the 1830s that farming families poured into the newly organized territory. Along with fertile lands in the southern half of the territory/state, Wisconsin developed a massive lumber industry in the north, which along with mining and fishing gave it one of the most diverse of frontier economies on the trans-Appalachian frontier. The heavy influx of European immigrants in the 1840s gave the State of Wisconsin's population a variety not heretofore seen on the trans-Appalachian frontier. All these threads come together here in a compelling story told by an expert historian.

Mark Wyman, born and educated in Wisconsin, has written on the far West and more recently on immigration in the Midwest. Among his best known works are *Hard-Rock Epic: Western Miners and the Industrial Revolution, 1860–1910* (1979), *Immigrants in the Valley: Irish, Germans, and Americans in the Upper Mississippi Country, 1830–1860* (1984), *DP: Europe's Displaced Persons, 1945–1951* (1989), and *Round-Trip to America: The Immigrants Return to Europe, 1880–1930* (1993). He is Professor of History at Illinois State University in Normal, Illinois.

WALTER NUGENT
University of Notre Dame

MALCOLM J. ROHRBOUGH
University of Iowa

Preface

The past is ever-present in Wisconsin, where even the name of the state represents an English interpretation of a French interpretation of what some Indians called their major river. Many other place names today hark back to earlier times, and archeologists continue to find relics of Indian wars, fur trade posts, and logging camps, from islands in Chequamegon Bay in the north to the Rock River's shores in the south.

Its location and natural wealth were crucial in placing Wisconsin at the center of many important developments of North American history. Bordered by two Great Lakes and the Mississippi, astride the major route between the St. Lawrence and the Gulf of Mexico, it was visited for nearly two centuries by Europeans who sought furs and a Northwest Passage, then fought for control of the ground itself. Indians were early partners in most of these endeavors, and were recruited as allies by the French, British, and Americans. These colonial era struggles were carried on without extensive settlement by outsiders, but this changed in the nineteenth century when mineral, farming, and logging frontiers appeared in waves that eventually lapped against the twentieth century and the modern world.

To tell this story of almost three hundred years in a single volume is to risk oversimplification; it also chances the danger of concentrating on the dramatic and exciting and ignoring the everyday existence of men and women who saw life mainly as survival. The author has sought to draw important themes of this history together, while presenting an honest understanding of all major groups who participated in the Wisconsin frontier down to 1900. The governmental story has been slighted except where it bore heavily on what happened on the frontier.

Lincoln's statement, "We cannot escape history," was delivered in the context of the slavery debate but applies equally to modern America. That history in Wisconsin included displacement of Indians, destruction of forests and wildlife, and the defacing of many of nature's proudest monuments. The modern world will dismiss that history to its peril. But the Wisconsin frontier also gave birth to a hope for betterment for peoples long condemned to overcrowded, war-torn Europe; and it presented thousands of Americans arriving from the east and south with a chance to start over in a new territory and state whose natural riches, opportunities, democratic government, and leadership in conservation led to international renown. This mixing of peoples, in turn, became another of Wisconsin's major characteristics.

Lincoln was right: we cannot escape history—especially that rich, varied, and sometimes tormented history of the frontier past, an era which really began when reports first arrived in the French settlements along the St. Lawrence of a distant land of abundant wealth beyond the lakes, a land eventually called Wisconsin.

Acknowledgments

To be asked, in middle age, to write a frontier history of one's native state is an honor indeed. I am thankful to my two editors, Malcolm Rohrbough of the University of Iowa and Walter Nugent of Notre Dame, for offering me this opportunity. They and John Gallman, director of the Indiana University Press, have been both helpful and congenial.

Many persons assisted me in gaining familiarity with materials, while correcting my wanderings and directing me to both new sources and insights. Chief among these was Father Francis Paul Prucha, S.J., of Marquette University. Others who helped by reading sections of the manuscript were Charles E. Orser, Jr., and Frederick Kohlmeyer (ret.), both of Illinois State University; Jack and Ella Woodbury, of Elkhorn, Wis. (who accompanied me on some of my Wisconsin trips); and my former colleague Arlan Helgeson, now of Prescott, Ariz.

Personnel of the State Historical Society of Wisconsin were always helpful. These include Harry Miller, manuscripts; Jack Holzhueter, associate editor of the *Wisconsin Magazine of History*; archeologist Robert Birmingham; and Andy Kraushaar, visual and sound archives. At the Milwaukee Public Museum, Head Librarian Judith Campbell Turner and Photographic Collection Coordinator Susan Otto gave their attention to my wants. Dave Snyder, Park Historian for the Apostle Islands National Lakeshore in Bayfield, helped me learn of Chequamegon Bay's past.

Archivists at several of the Area Research Centers on campuses of the University of Wisconsin system deserve my accolades, both for the diligence they have shown in assembling collections on their regions, and for the attention they gave to my requests: Stephanie Zeman, UW–River Falls; Ed Hill, UW–La

Crosse; Lawrence Lynch, UW–Eau Claire; and Michael Klawitter, UW–Green Bay. In Green Bay, I was also helped by Louise Pfotenhauer at the Neville Public Museum, and Diane Perkofski at the Brown County Library. Wally Capper of the Jackson County Historical Society, Black River Falls, aided my hunt for photos and information, as did Janice Terrill at the Mineral Point Public Library. Eldbjorg Tobin provided help during my work at the Chippewa Valley Museum in Eau Claire.

As usual, the staff of Milner Library, Illinois State University, went out of their way to assist my research. Seven who were extremely helpful were Carol Ruyle, Joan Winters, Michael Lovell, Connie Bass, Pat Werdell, Garold Cole, and Vanette Schwartz. Several Illinois State University colleagues helped me locate information: Lauren Brown and Roger Anderson in Biological Sciences, and Carl Ekberg and Gerlof Homan in History. I also worked extensively at the Minnesota History Center, St. Paul, and at the Main Library and Biology Library of the University of Illinois at Urbana–Champaign, and was aided by their staffs.

Vernon Carstensen no longer walks the earth, prodding his students and friends on to greater accomplishments, but I could still feel his influence as I studied the state he had grown to love during his years at the University of Wisconsin; he never lost that love after his move to the University of Washington.

Family members have always been my strongest supporters, and this held true for the Wisconsin Frontier project also. It was especially true because I could lean heavily upon my parents, Walker and Helen Bryant Wyman of River Falls, for so much help regarding the state they know and love—and which they have worked long and hard to protect and improve.

The Wisconsin Frontier

I.

THE FRENCH OPEN A FRONTIER

Autumn had begun before the canoes passed up the *sault* to enter *Lac supérieur*, the Upper Lake, and October was underway when the weary group of six French traders and a priest, with their Indian escorts, finally crossed the long sandspit angling out from the mainland and entered Chequamegon Bay. It had been a difficult trip, pushing off from Trois Rivières in the company of Indians from the upper country who had come down to Montreal to trade; heading up the Ottawa while dealing with leaking canoes, bad weather, rotten food, and contemptuous tribesmen. But finally they entered the cold waters of the Upper Lake; soon Keweenaw Point was at their backs, and now the long-sought bay the Indians called Chagoüamigong lay before them. For Father Claude Jean Allouez, the picture that unfolded that autumn day of 1665 was almost beyond belief, a missionary's dream.

"It is a beautiful Bay, at the head of which is situated the great village of the savages," he wrote. His initial count was 800 Huron and Ottawa warriors, indicating that the total in that single village may have reached more than 2,000 with women, children, and elderly included. But Father Allouez soon realized also that the Bay "forms a sort of center for all the nations of these regions": in addition to the Hurons and Ottawas, the French priest encountered the Petun or Tobacco Hurons, Potawatomis, Foxes, Chippewas, Illinois, Sacs, Miamis, and eventually the Nipissings who arrived from Lake Nipigon far to the north. Other tribes eventually arrived, providing the missionary with an opportunity few religious leaders would ever encounter again in Wisconsin. As the Jesuit account explained,

> It is assuredly a very great consolation to a poor missionary, after a journey of five hundred leagues amid weariness, dangers, famines, and hardships of all sorts, to find himself listened to by so many different peoples, while he proclaims the Gospel and gives out to them the words of salvation, whereof they have never heard mention.

This multitude gathered around Chequamegon Bay represented tribal groups drawn from an enormous swath of the continent, as the turmoil of the eastern fur trade and ongoing Indian wars scattered Indians toward Lake Superior: they came from the St. Lawrence River country far to the east; from the shores of Lake Huron; from the Nipigon country to the north of the lake; from both the Upper and Lower Peninsula of Michigan, and even from the fertile prairies of Illinois and Iowa in the Mississippi Valley. They represented eastern tribes of the Algonquian language grouping as well as Iroquoian groups.[1]

This coming together of tribes from distant regions, along with Frenchmen paddling westward from their base along the St. Lawrence, helped mark the French expeditions of the seventeenth century as the real beginning of the frontier era in Wisconsin, the start of Wisconsin's frontier story. Soon there would be many more Frenchmen, some working for the government, some for the Roman Catholic Church, others traveling independently and leaving few records. And because these men—Indians and whites—were pushing westward, wars and diplomacy conducted in far-off regions would cast a shadow over events around the Great Lakes, and soon British, and eventually Americans, would arrive as well.

These people from outside would change Wisconsin, and would

---

1. Modern geographical designations will be used throughout, although in most cases these were not affixed until after the events described.

in turn be changed by it. Indians would initially benefit by sales of their furs and other items of less value to them than the wonderful iron knives and kettles which the Europeans brought; but eventually their way of life would be transformed as well. Such was the reality of European and American settlement across North America.

The focus of this story is therefore on the events, changes, and transformations that took place on the Wisconsin and Great Lakes frontier. *Frontier* is a term which has been used in a variety of ways, usually referring to the contact area between settlement and wilderness, or between a more complex, technologically developed society and a less developed one. The term is elastic, however, and also means the adaptations and adjustments which take place among those coming to reside in such an area. Issues identified with the frontier era elsewhere would be confronted in Wisconsin: Indians would be subdued, removed, or assimilated; land would be parceled out and distributed to incoming men, women, and families; local governments would be installed and the sovereignty of an outside regime established; distant political and religious leaders would seek to guide the new societies forming in the wilderness. And throughout this process, exploitation would proceed of what has been called the "primary windfalls of the frontier"—in Wisconsin, furs, minerals, wild game and fish, timber, virgin soil. The natural world itself would be sharply modified. All this was part of Wisconsin's frontier story that began with the arrival of the French in the early seventeenth century. It was a story that would not be finished until the frontier era closed at the end of the nineteenth century.

Roots of the French Thrust Inland

Incidents involving the French at Chequamegon Bay and elsewhere were not the first seeds, not the true embryonic beginnings of Wisconsin's frontier story, however. Nor does that saga properly commence with the French settlement at Quebec in 1608 that eventually dispatched men westward to Wisconsin. Much earlier lies this genesis, generations before in the murky past of Europe's late Middle Ages, as adventurers and scholars and fishermen began to question the truths about the world handed to them from earlier generations.

These challenges to tradition finally brought Columbus westward in 1492, and, five years later, John Cabot—coasting along Newfoundland as he sought a route for his English sponsors to reach Japan and its spices. Two ships from a Portuguese expedition to eastern Canada's rocky coasts in 1501 returned to Lisbon with fifty-seven Indians; another Portuguese mariner entered the Gulf of St. Lawrence in 1520, and the Italian Giovanni da Verrazzano—sailing for France—went along the East Coast as far north as Newfoundland in 1524. And so while the Spanish were exploring and exploiting the Caribbean, knowledge of the north coast grew and began to appear on European maps and publications.

But others came without government sanction: European fishermen who began working the codfish-rich Grand Banks, at least by 1504 and probably earlier. Reports of their activities were numerous during the century, and when England's Sir Humphrey Gilbert dropped anchor in the harbor at St. John's, Newfoundland, in 1583 he discovered sailors from thirty-six Spanish, Portuguese, French, and English ships partying together in blissful ignorance of—or disdain for—their own nations' maritime competition. In another twenty-five years the number of European fishing ships coming to summer around the Grand Banks would reach a thousand. They left few records; they were after fish, not glory.

Tales of the new world of eastern Canada were already in the air, therefore, when an official French explorer, Jacques Cartier, began investigating the northern route into the interior in 1534. In his next voyage of 1535–36, Cartier went up the St. Lawrence as far as the rapids at Montreal, then spent the winter downstream at Quebec; he came back again in 1541–42. In these voyages—where he met Indians, heard stories of abounding wealth, and learned of threats from other European powers—Cartier became aware of the possibilities of that inland river highway that in short decades would become France's great axis of penetration into the continent: up the St. Lawrence into the Great Lakes and Mississippi Valley.

While official French explorers were noting geographic, topo-
graphic, and religious features of inland North America, fishermen
along the coasts made a significant contribution of their own to
future developments: they discovered they could trade knives and
trinkets for Indian furs—furs which would bring immense profits
back in Europe. This stimulated the search for peltry that would
eventually lure thousands of Frenchmen up the St. Lawrence
like a surging tide, and would draw Englishmen, Dutchmen, and
profit-seekers of other nations to the interior regions as well. The
Indians' eagerness to participate in the fur trade was evident by
July 1534, when Cartier's ship, tacking along the shores of the
Gaspé Peninsula, was suddenly surrounded by Micmacs in forty
or more canoes, waving pelts on sticks and shouting wildly to
attract attention. Cartier was chary of their intentions, but the
Micmacs rowed determinedly after the Frenchmen like eager
merchants. Trading finally got underway the following day, and
furs from the Indians were exchanged for such French items as a
red cap for their chief and knives and other cutlery for the rest.
Some of the Micmac women sold the furs off their very backs
and went away naked. If the Europeans had now learned something about the local residents they encountered along these coasts,
the Indians also received a lesson about Europeans: the visitors
would trade metal goods and other exotic items for furs. It was a
good bargain for both sides: the Micmacs, who had acquired the
pelts easily, and the Europeans, who had an abundance of metal
items to carry along as they crossed the Atlantic to the fishing
regions.

The potential for wealth of another kind also drew the Europeans on, and this quickly steered them in the direction of the
Great Lakes. Copper, traded by Indians throughout the continent and noticed by early explorers, impressed the Frenchmen
with the possibilities inland. Cartier encountered Indians with
copper ornaments during his second journey; asked about their
source, these Hurons could only point to the west. The general
direction to Lake Superior had been given and the French would
soon follow it.

They had yet another goal, common to all European explorers. This was a route to Asia, and like Columbus earlier, Cabot in

his 1497–98 expedition up the northern coast had sought a route to Cathay and thought he had found it. Others had the same objective as they struggled into the North American interior, and the dream was still alive when missionaries reached Chequamegon Bay. Father Allouez heard the Sioux at the head of Lake Superior describe a land "farther toward the setting Sun," where dwelt the Karezi nations—"beyond whom, they maintain, the earth is cut off, and nothing is to be seen but a great Lake whose waters are ill-smelling, for so they designate the Sea." Hopes remained when Father Claude Dablon, who came after Allouez, wanted to go to Hudson's Bay to see whether "a passage could be made by this route to the Japan Sea." Father Jacques Marquette, passing on some late 1660s tales told to him by the Illinois about the Mississippi and the tribes living along it, could not believe "that that great River discharges its waters in Virginia, and we think rather that it has its mouth in California." His hopes for a continental water connection were also stimulated by news of the Assiniboines, northwest of Lake Superior: "I heard that there was in their Country a great River leading to the Western Sea; and a Savage told me that, being at its mouth, he had seen Frenchmen and four large Canoes with sails."

Pressure to find the Northwest Passage was so great, and the failures so frequent, that some began to despair. One frustrated visitor was René Robert Cavelier, sieur de La Salle, who left a name on one of the many obstacles encountered in that search. Years later, people were still talking about his problems getting men to accompany him beyond the St. Lawrence rapids above Montreal—a boiling stretch of water ever after called *la Chine*, China. Francis Parkman quoted a respected French source who affirmed that the name was attached to the rapids in derision after some of La Salle's men returned there from one of his ventures inland. A Swedish naturalist visiting a century later heard another origin for the name:

> When the unfortunate M. Salée [La Salle] was here, . . . he was very intent upon discovering a shorter road to China by means of the St. Lawrence River. He talked of nothing at that time but this new short way to China. But as his project of undertaking the journey

in order to make this discovery was stopped by an accident which happened to him here, and he did not at that time come any nearer China, this place got its name, as it were, by way of a joke.

Champlain and the West

The search for the Northwest Passage, like the hunt for wealth and the efforts to bring Christianity to the Indians, was pushed most forcefully by another Frenchman, Samuel de Champlain. In his voyages beginning in 1603, Champlain demonstrated a curiosity about the unknown that is always present with great explorers. He carefully questioned the denizens of each new area he entered, and from their stories and drawings began to produce reports and maps for his royal sponsors. This curiosity, combined with Champlain's other aspirations for the New World, would ultimately lead the French under his direction to reach Wisconsin in 1634 in an official expedition, and earlier in at least one unofficial visit.

Thus Champlain, at the site of Montreal, wondered what lay in the world above the rapids: "When we saw we could do no more, we returned to our long-boat, where we questioned the savages we had with us about the end of the river, which I made them draw by hand, and [show] whence was its source." And again, in his 1615 expedition, the French explorer gave an Ottawa chief a hatchet, after which "I asked him about his country, which he drew for me with charcoal on a piece of tree-bark."

Champlain's interest in the West was whetted by a foot-long piece of copper given to him by Indians, and by the copper bracelets they wore; he questioned them "whether they had knowledge of any mines?" Hurons, he was told, reported a mine of pure copper "toward the north." The copper mines along Lake Superior were gaining notoriety.

The French also discovered they were in the midst of the natives' ongoing wars, and that they would be sought as allies by one side or the other for battles stretching far into the future. It was an activity that would remain throughout the frontier era, and Champlain encountered it dramatically in 1609 when he yielded to Huron and Algonquin requests that his men join them to fight the Mohawks, one of the Iroquois cultures. It was the Iroquois' first battle against anyone carrying firearms, and after losing three members, with more slain during their escape, the Iroquois began to realize the enormity of the changes brought by these Europeans. Tribal alliances with the newcomers now became crucial. Similarly, alliances with Indians would be an ongoing goal of European diplomacy as European kingdoms sought entry into the wealthy lands of the North American interior.

This fact led the Europeans to the Hurons, middlemen in the developing interior fur trade, dealing with the French, the Dutch, and occasionally the English. In 1635 a French missionary described the Hurons as people "who have not a single beaver, going elsewhere to buy the skins they bring to the storehouse." The fur trade center in Champlain's time was Quebec, where the first large fur shipment from the *pays d'en haut*—the "upper country"—arrived in 1633 in the canoes of the Ottawa. Trade fairs moved upriver to Trois Rivières in 1634, then in 1642 to Montreal. That city remained a major rendezvous point for years as the Indians arrived with furs in vast canoe flotillas and the French presented an intoxicating array of goods, ranging from the always-popular knives and hatchets to agricultural produce and even cakes. Since each side grew to covet the other's items so strongly, neither could afford to alienate those with whom they traded, at least in the early decades when alternate sources were unknown.

The First European Visitors

Many eager young Frenchmen got caught up in the search for furs, and some combined this with a religious quest to carry Christ to the interior peoples. One of these adventurers was a protegé of Champlain, Etienne Brûlé.

Traditional accounts have given little importance to Brûlé in the exploration of Wisconsin and the region, but more recent studies have concluded that he may have earned the title "Columbus of the Great Lakes." Brûlé emigrated from France in 1608 to Champlain's new Quebec settlement, and in 1610 was sent to live with Algonquian Indians along the Ottawa River that angles down to the St. Lawrence just above Montreal. In July 1615, Champlain and Brûlé went together up the Ottawa River in two canoes with ten Indians and a white servant, taking what would become the French bypass into the upper lakes—paddling into a branch of the Mattawa, portaging into Lake Nipissing, then connecting to the French River flowing southwest into Georgian Bay on Lake Huron.

This Champlain-Brûlé expedition brought further hints, and some factual information, about the land beyond. Spending the winter along Lake Huron's eastern shore, Champlain learned from Indians of a "great river" which passed through a lake "nearly thirty days' canoe journey in extent." Champlain returned to Quebec in the spring of 1616, but Brûlé apparently stayed in the Great Lakes region. Knowledge of his activities over the next several years rests solely upon the report of Gabriel Sagard, a Recollet[2] brother who in 1623 joined a mission group journeying to the Huron country with Brûlé and another Frenchman as interpreters. Brûlé told Sagard of a trip by canoe through Georgian Bay and evidently into the body of water that the French would soon name *Lac supérieur.* Sagard recorded this account of Brûlé's entry into the lake through Sault Ste. Marie:

> The interpreter Brûlé assured us that beyond the Freshwater Sea, there was another very large lake which empties into it by a waterfall, which has been called *"Saut de Gaston,"* of a width of almost two leagues, which lake and the Freshwater Sea have almost thirty days journey by canoe in length, according to the account of the savages, but according to the interpreter Brûlé's account, they are four hundred leagues in length.[3]

2. The Recollet order was a branch of the Franciscans. They came to the New World in 1615 with Champlain, and in 1625 invited the Society of Jesus, or Jesuits, to help Christianize the Indians. However, in 1632 missionary work in Canada was officially placed under Jesuit control. Another famous Recollet friar who explored in the interior was Louis Hennepin, captured briefly by the Sioux in 1679.

3. A French league was 2.76 miles; therefore, Lake Superior was some 1,100 miles long by this reckoning. Today's maps show its longest dimension at 400 miles.

Brûlé also carried back a large piece of copper, which he said came from a mine about eighty or a hundred leagues beyond the land of the Hurons.

Although Champlain's reports to France contain no mention of Brûlé's unofficial expedition, the map which Champlain made in 1632 clearly and accurately shows Lake Superior to the west of Lake Huron, the two connected by a long *sault*, or rapids. Since Champlain had never reached the *sault*, someone had informed the French governor of what lay beyond Lake Huron. And this was someone with enough details to even mention *la Nation des Puans*—later known as the Winnebagos—the tribe then living on the west side of Lake Michigan near Green Bay. Although the map misplaced the Winnebagos, locating them north of Lake Superior, this could be explained if the person providing the information was not on hand at creation of the eventual map.

Etienne Brûlé, it seems likely, had entered Lake Superior, and should be considered the first European to reach Wisconsin. He had seen Indian copper mining activity along Superior's shores, and he reported the information to his chief. Personal animosity between Champlain and Brûlé may be behind the lack of credit for the latter's findings; the record shows that Champlain was angry at Brûlé for aiding the English during their short-lived takeover of Quebec in 1629. Brûlé was killed—and eaten—by Hurons in 1632, and so could never contest, correct, or even comment upon the amazingly accurate map Champlain prepared that year back in France, apparently from Brûlé's information.

Nicolet at Green Bay

Champlain was preparing another Frenchman to carry on the nation's mission to the west. This was Jean Nicolet, a Cherbourg native who arrived in Canada in 1618 at the age of twenty. Two years later Champlain dispatched him up the Ottawa River to live on Allumette Island among Algonquins. Over the next two years Nicolet learned to speak Algonquin, essential in dealing with many northern tribes. Later he lived for eight or nine years among the Nipissings, arriving back at the French settlements with the fur flotilla in 1633. Nicolet promptly signed on as clerk and interpreter for France's Company of the Hundred Associates.

Because the Nipissings and Ottawas traded to the west, Nicolet likely heard references to Wisconsin tribes then. It is known that Champlain, during his contacts with the Huron and Ottawa, had learned of a "Tribe of the Men of the Sea" to the west, possibly the Winnebagos near the head of Green Bay. Champlain placed *la Nation des Puans* (Winnebago) on his 1632 map, near a lake connected to Lake Huron, and Sagard learned during a Michigan trip that the Ottawas traveled as far as 400 leagues away, to trade goods "for furs, pigments, wampum, and other rubbish." This information, Sagard argued, might be useful for future trips by French missionaries to the *Puans* or *Puants*, a name he likely heard from his Huron or Ottawa contacts.

Puans or *Puants*, like so many names fastened onto Wisconsin's people and places during the frontier era, was a French interpretation of an Indian word; many such terms would later be modified and twisted in both spelling and meaning as the arriving English and Americans added their own interpretations. In this case the word came from attempting to understand the Algonquian term which the French wrote as *Ouenibegous*, used both to refer to salty, brackish water (therefore, possibly to the distant ocean, the French hoped) and to a tribe of non-Algonquian Indians there; the English would later call them the Winnebagos.[4] Green Bay, around whose borders these Indians lived, was called *la Baye des Puants* by the French. The bay was known as being brackish, and a later missionary commented that "the water of this bay and of the rivers is like stagnant ditch-water." Distant Algonquian tribes referred to this quality in describing tribes inhabiting its shores, i.e., those who lived around the "bay of the stinkards" were called "stinkards." This translation bothered the missionaries; Father Marquette later wrote that the *Baye des Puants* "bears a name that has not so bad a meaning in the In-

---

4. Today the tribe has rejected "Winnebago," a name always assigned by other groups, and made its name officially "Ho-Chunk."

dian language, as they call it Salt Bay rather than Fetid Bay, although among them it is about the same."

These early references to salt water, tenuous as they were, stimulated interest in a possible ocean connection through Wisconsin, and in 1634 Champlain dispatched Nicolet to the Baye des Puants, both to get to know these people in the West and to bring peace between them and the Hurons. Any fighting with the fur middlemen upset trade.

Traveling first to the Huron country in July, Nicolet pushed on to Ottawa villages on Manitoulin Island, touched the Lake Superior outlet below Sault Ste. Marie, then headed south and west through the Straits of Mackinac. With seven Indians as companions he made his way along the western shore of Lake Michigan and entered Green Bay. The canoe journey from Quebec would have taken ten weeks if conducted without breaks, but stops at French missions and Indian villages added weeks; it is likely he did not enter the waters of Green Bay until September. A Jesuit account published eight years later by Father Barthélemy Vimont reports that as they neared the Indian villages—possibly at Red Banks, some eight miles from the head of the bay on the Door Peninsula—Nicolet sent one of his companions ahead to announce his coming to the tribesmen. The Winnebagos responded enthusiastically:

> They meet him; they escort him, and carry all his baggage. He wore a grand robe of China damask, all strewn with flowers and birds of many colors. No sooner did they perceive him than the women and children fled, at the sight of a man who carried thunder in both hands—for thus they called the two pistols that he held. The news of his coming quickly spread to the places round about, and there assembled four or five thousand men.

Winnebago accounts of this encounter, passed down in tribal folklore and recorded by Paul Radin early in the twentieth century, also indicate the impact of Nicolet firing his guns:

> Once something appeared in the middle of the lake (Green Bay). They were the French; they were the first to come to the Winnebago. The ship came nearer and the Winnebago went to the edge of the lake with offerings of tobacco and white deerskins. There they stood.

Jean Nicolet was dispatched westward to Green Bay in 1634, to patch up a dispute between the Winnebagos and the Hurons as well as to expand French knowledge of the interior. When Nicolet stepped ashore at *la Baye des Puants* he wore a Chinese robe, demonstrating French hopes that they had crossed the continent and might meet Oriental peoples. "LANDFALL OF JEAN NICOLLET," BY DEMING. COURTESY STATE HISTORICAL SOCIETY OF WISCONSIN, WHI (X3) 30553.

When the French were about to come ashore they fired their guns off in the air as a salute to the Indians. The Indians said, "They are thunderbirds." . . .

Then the French landed their boats and came ashore and extended their hands to the Winnebago, and the Indians put tobacco in their hands. The French, of course, wanted to shake hands with the Indians. They did not know what tobacco was, and therefore did not know what to do with it. . . . The French tried to speak to them, but they could not, of course, make themselves understood. After a while they discovered that they were without tools, so they taught the Indians how to use an ax and chop a tree down.

After rounds of banquets "the peace was concluded," Father Vimont wrote, and Jean Nicolet "returned to the Hurons." Champlain had likely provided him with the Chinese mandarin outfit he wore, for Nicolet would not have had access to such materials. Whatever its source, the "grand robe of China damask" spoke dramatically of French hopes that these people were in some way the key to reaching the Orient. Perhaps they knew the Northwest Passage. But like the Montreal rapids called *la Chine*, the incongruity of a Frenchman unfurling a Chinese robe before Winnebagos on Green Bay's shores in 1634 stands in frontier history as another case where European eagerness led to an error of enormous magnitude.

Nicolet's other activities in Wisconsin in 1634–35 remain largely unknown, but there are clues. In 1640, a Jesuit reported that "Sieur Nicolet, who has advanced farthest into these so distant countries, has assured me that if he had sailed three days' journey farther upon a great river which issues from this lake he would have found the sea." And the Jesuit reporter adds his "strong suspicion that this is the sea which answers to that north of new Mexico, and that from this sea there would be an outlet towards Japan and China." This was obviously a reference to the Fox-Wisconsin route; however, the "sea" was likely the Mississippi, misunderstood by Nicolet because his Algonquian language skills did not aid him with the Winnebago, who spoke a Siouan tongue.

A "Shatter Zone" of Tribes

Most of the basic patterns of succeeding generations of European activity in the Upper Lakes were laid down by the time these early explorers had played their roles in the opening scenes of the region's recorded history. Routes to the interior were now established: as New France's Intendant explained in 1665, "The country is laid out in such a way that by means of the St. Lawrence one can go everywhere inland, thanks to the lakes which lead to its source in the West and to the rivers that flow into it along its shores, opening the way to the North and the South." The French entered the region as explorers seeking imperial expansion, religious conversions, the natural resources of an untapped frontier, a route to greater wealth beyond. Later Europeans and Americans would seldom deviate from these goals; some modifications would appear as dictated by diplomatic maneuvering, the realization that the Northwest Passage did not exist, or the discovery of other opportunities in the wilderness.

As they ventured inland the Europeans would eventually bring major changes to accustomed ways of life among the Indians. Even the migration of tribes, a tradition that long preceded the arrival of the French, now accelerated under the stimulus of the fur trade to the east, and Wisconsin became a "shatter zone" with tribes fleeing distant regions and confronting Indians who had occupied the area for generations. The French would learn much later that shortly before Nicolet's visit, Winnebagos had refused attempts by the Ottawas to draw them into the developing trade, rejecting offers of French goods for Winnebago furs. Attacks followed by several tribes—the Ottawas, the Foxes, the Illinois, and possibly others—which nearly decimated the Winnebagos in this early war centered on fur trade connections.

With the Winnebagos weakened, eastern Wisconsin was now more open to new arrivals. Visiting with the Foxes in 1670, Father Allouez could report that "these Savages withdrew to those regions to escape the persecution of the Iroquois, and settled in an excellent country." Because of Iroquois pressures, the Green Bay area eventually received influxes of Foxes, Sacs, Mascoutins, Potawatomis, Kickapoos, Noquets, Miamis, Weas, and Ottawas, as well as some refugee Petuns and Hurons. As Frenchmen traveled the Upper Lakes they encountered some strange combinations, constituting what a later historian called "a hodgepodge of peoples": one Wisconsin village had Kiskakon Ottawas, Petun Hurons, and a band identified as the Negaouichiriniouek; another village nearby was occupied by Menominees, Winnebagos, Noquets, and Ottawas. After his transfer to the Fox River Valley and Green Bay area, Father Allouez visited a village of 600 Sacs, Potawatamis, Foxes, and Winnebagos. He also encountered many Indians he had known short years earlier at Chequamegon Bay, all of which meant that the migration both into and within Wisconsin was continuing, perhaps increasing.

But Iroquois pressure was not constant, and as it lessened some tribes moved out. Northern Wisconsin then lost population and began to attract large numbers of Chippewas, whose large fishing villages near Lake Superior's outflow at Sault Ste. Marie had earlier attracted the French who called them the *Saulteurs.* These incoming Chippewas became strongly identified with northern Wisconsin from that era to the present.

A Frontier Spanning Three Centuries

Thus the mix that would make up the Wisconsin frontier story for several generations was present in the seventeenth century: Indian migrations, alliances, and warfare; French explorers, traders, and missionaries; travel routes opened by the Great Lakes and the array of interlinking river systems. All went into creating this early Wisconsin frontier. Wisconsin became one of those points where European civilization met the world of the Indians, where two radically different ways of life would clash, compromise, accommodate. It was not a frontier where one would immediately overwhelm the other; rather, Indians and Europeans (and eventually Americans) would meet in conditions where each was frequently dependent upon the other for at least some goods, support, information, or advice. They influenced each other, and a large part of the frontier story consists of the give and take in that relationship.

From the European perspective, Wisconsin for several generations would mark the outer reach of imperial expansion, the farthest grasp of a movement that had begun centuries earlier and would continue long into the nineteenth century, as nations rushed to occupy what they considered the unoccupied or unclaimed spaces of the globe. Wisconsin was such a place.

For the native population, the frontier experience would be a one-way path to defeat only if viewed in retrospect, looking back nearly three centuries from modern times. But human beings of every age look to the future as well as the past, and often the Indians' condition would not be one of defeat and despair. Indians were eager for European trade goods precisely because these made their lives easier and, they thought, better. They would soon learn that not all of the Europeans' gifts were beneficial.

As it neared its end, the frontier era would be recognized for what it was: a vastly different world, but only an interlude in human development. People would look back on it, recalling old times, studying documents and artifacts, trying to discern its lessons. But that would be the reaction of another day, and it lay far in the future as the French turned their boats up the St. Lawrence in the early seventeenth century and heard the Indians describe a land to the west, beyond the freshwater seas, its shores lapped by a great body of water they came to call *Lac supérieur.* Drawn by these dreams they dipped their paddles into the current and headed westward.

2.

BEFORE THE EUROPEANS

Settlers moving inland from Lake Michigan in the opening decades of the nineteenth century encountered a strange sight on the banks of the Crawfish River. It seemed to be an ancient city, with pyramids like those they had read about which existed in Mexico. A stockade had been there once, too, with what seemed to be bricks encrusted onto its walls. In all, the stockade and ancient city enclosed twenty-one acres, with ruins of fifty buildings; outside the walls were forty-four conical mounds. It first received public notice in an 1837 newspaper account which affixed the name Aztalan because of a tale that Mexico's original peoples had come from a distant land in the north with that name.

More recent visits by archeologists to this Jefferson County site in the rolling ridge country near Lake Mills have discounted the possibility that the inhabitants came from Mexico. And they have rejected fanciful suggestions that the builders were a mysterious race of giants, refugees from Atlantis, or one of the lost tribes of Israel. Instead, results of their digging and the use of radio-carbon dating have convinced researchers that the occupants of Aztalan were ancestors of the American Indians. Their residence at Aztalan has been placed within the general period from A.D. 900 to 1300, and they were well advanced in using bones, shells, antlers, stones, sheet copper, and making pottery.

Their pyramids stood some fifteen feet high, and one contained a crematorium. But these people who built pyramids and worked with copper were also afraid of attack, as demonstrated by their elaborate efforts to erect fortifications—stockades with posts a foot in diameter, rising twelve feet above ground, with special gates providing the only entry. Away from the river, on the landward side of Aztalan, a triple stockade gave further evidence of the importance of defense.

It was the pottery, however, which has proven especially significant to those digging today into Aztalan's secrets. For in fitting together pottery sherds, jigsaw-puzzle pieces from a millennium ago, archeologists have discovered two separate styles of ceramics: one simple and representative of northern Indian cultures, the other elaborate and intricate and speaking of origins in lands to the south.

S. A. Barrett, who led a 1919 excavation of the site, found that much of the pottery was tempered through mixing the clay with pieces of shells; it had angular shoulders and rolled rims, similar to pottery unearthed some 300 miles to the south at the contemporary massive Indian settlement at Cahokia, located just east of St. Louis in western Illinois. Cahokia may have had a population of 40,000 in A.D. 1000, with enormous pyramid mounds, a highly stratified society apparently under strong religious control, heavy reliance on agriculture, and numerous "suburbs" or outlying communities providing support. Cahokians used a specific side-notched arrowhead also, similar to those found at Aztalan; this type is absent from other Wisconsin sites of the period. Some of Aztalan's pots, however, are like those being made elsewhere in Wisconsin in the years around A.D. 1000—vessels with rounded shoulders and short necks, with definite collars on the rims. Tempering, to keep the clay from falling apart, was of grit, pieces of crushed rock.

Barrett commented that the first type of pottery, the Cahokia style, "is found almost nowhere else in Wisconsin and vicinity," which would not have been true if Aztalan's residents had lived there over a long period. Rather, the Aztalan people had apparently migrated from the south, probably from Cahokia or a Cahokia outgrowth, and either were killed or made their exit after a relatively short residence; Aztalan was burned and destroyed. But archeological evidence also shows that other people were nearby, trading or perhaps watching, influencing and being influenced by the people who had come from the south.

A Distant Past

With mysteries still unsolved and questions still unanswered, Aztalan opens the door for us today to the fact that ancient peoples once trod the land, coursed through the rivers, tramped the forests of the Great Lakes region. Like the pioneers who encountered "ancient monuments" in southeastern Wisconsin, those curious today about Wisconsin's past can enter into that prehistoric period through the doorway of archeology, examining what the early peoples left—spearpoints lodged in a mastodon's bones, copper ornaments buried with a corpse, discarded tools strewn about the edges of what was once an early Indian settlement.

From such scattered, seemingly insignificant objects we can gain understanding of the inhabitants the Europeans encountered as the frontier era opened across the Midwest. For if it is crucial to know what lay behind European desires to explore the world—desires driven by intellectual curiosity, technological advances, and imperial dreams—it is equally important to understand the backgrounds of the Indians who met these visitors from afar.[1]

European explorers, especially missionaries, were interested in learning about the Indians they encountered, but they generally did not confront the issue of the length of the Indian residence. Perhaps the native peoples were far ahead of the visitors in being aware they were inheritors of lengthy traditions, for it seems likely that in the course of their own hunting and migrating the Indians would have come across enough clues to the past— cave paintings, ancient mining operations—to suspect that the land they trod had been occupied for many generations. But the newcomers, they soon realized, were ignorant of this. When Fa-

---

1. Modern political boundaries were meaningless in prehistory, of course, but will be used in this discussion to orient the reader to geographic locations.

ther Louis Hennepin, touring to Green Bay and beyond in the early 1680s, warned an Indian that he was clinging too stubbornly to traditions, the Indian turned on him and demanded:

> How old are you? You are only thirty or forty and you think you know more about things than our old men. What nonsense! You do not know what you are saying. You might know what is happening in your country because your old men have told you, but you do not know what happened in ours before the coming of the French.

When the priest responded that he learned from books, the Indian shot back: "Before you came to this place where we live, did you know we were here?" Hennepin answered that he did not. The Indian asserted, "Then you do not know everything from writing and it has not told you all."

Geography and Geology

The early Indians arrived in the Upper Lakes after the glaciers had finished most of their work. As the glaciers were overriding millions of years of ocean sediment and lava, grinding and spreading, compressing and leveling mountains, they also blocked waterways so that Lake Michigan was lowered drastically, leaving behind beaches many miles wide. But later other receding glaciers blocked Great Lakes exit channels, raising their waters hundreds of feet. Shifts in terrain once sent Lake Michigan draining south through the Illinois and Mississippi rivers; only later did it move to its present outlet into the Straits of Mackinac and through Lakes Huron, Erie, Ontario, and into the St. Lawrence. The geologists' Rule of Uniformity continues: all the forces that shaped the land over millions of years are still operating. The land is still changing—rising a few inches each century on Lake Superior's north shore, but sinking on the south shore where tree stumps that were above lake level short decades ago are now submerged. As the land continues to change, rapids on streams flowing into the lake from the south have been overtaken by Superior's rising waters within the lifetimes of people now living.

The last episode of the Wisconsin glaciation period—beginning some 70,000 years ago and completely ending only 9,000 years ago—helped create something else that would leave behind diversity. The glacial era created, in effect, two Wisconsins: northern Wisconsin is part of the Canadian plant and animal province, cool and wet, with acidic soils, where most of the state's nearly 15,000 lakes are located today. It is home to some trees common to the boreal forest of northern Canada, but also contains large quantities of cedar, white and red pine, alder, yellow birch, beech, elm, hemlock, aspen, basswood, and sugar maple. Southern Wisconsin is warmer, in contrast, dominated by savannas (settlers called them "oak openings") and oak forests, for other trees were kept out by frequent prairie fires. One recent estimate puts half of southern Wisconsin in oak savannas and prairies before European settlement, part of a soil and plant region that includes central portions of the Midwest.

Wisconsin's shape, topographically, is akin to a dome, its highest area in the north-central region, sloping downward toward the east, south, and west. One result is that major river systems arise in the upper levels of that dome—the Menominee flowing into Lake Michigan, the Ontonagon and Montreal into Lake Superior, and the Wisconsin, Chippewa, and the Black to the Mississippi.

The differences between these north and south regions are often extreme: Ashland harbor on Lake Superior is usually closed with ice from early December until the end of April, approximately 145 days; on Lake Michigan, meanwhile, Green Bay's harbor is blocked by ice some 130 days; but Milwaukee's—130 miles farther south—is usually closed on average only from February 24 to March 10, around two weeks each year.

The glaciers also decreed that the boundary between these two regions does not create northern and southern halves, but runs closer to a northwest and southeast separation, the dividing line making approximately an "S" shape. Where these overlap, a broad "transition zone" or "tension zone" contains some features of each. This combined forest-savanna overlap or ecotone in central and western Wisconsin became home to a wide diversity of plants and animals, an area of joint occupation for the northern and southern natural environments that merged there.

Because the southwestern quarter of the state was missed by

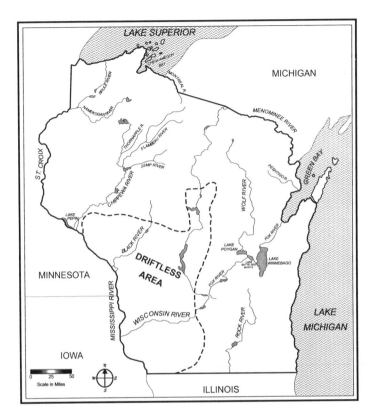

1. Wisconsin's terrain is marked by many rivers, lakes, and bays. The Driftless Area, missed by the last period of glaciation some 9,000 years ago, features deep valleys and large rock formations. Northern portions of the Driftless Area take in the so-called "transition zone" or "tension zone," where the northern forest environment overlaps with that of the southern savannas and oak openings. MAP BY JILL FREUND THOMAS AND MICHAEL MAST.

the final glacial lobes 9,000 years ago, sharp landform differences exist within Wisconsin. Known as the "driftless area," the 15,000 square miles of the southwest retained deep valleys and high hills by avoiding the leveling effects of the final glacial sweep. Southwestern Wisconsin is a remnant, almost a museum exhibit, of what all of Wisconsin had once been. But elsewhere, where that final glacier scraped over the landscape in the remaining three-quarters of Wisconsin, lakes, swamps, bogs, moraines, drumlins, kames, kettles, and eskers were left behind. The result is a heterogeneous conglomeration of surface types.

Sharp climatic changes followed the glacial retreat, warmer weather opening the way to the arrivals of new plant and animal life. The spruce forest, intermixed with tamarack and fir, pushed northward, initially replaced as it left southern Wisconsin by a heavily pine forest, which in turn gave way to a drier, deciduous forest.

Animals struggled to cope with these changes. The mammoths which had thrived after the glaciers receded saw their prime grazing areas gone, occupied now by invading plants and trees. Then came mastodons, which were browsers, eating leaves and twigs. Mastodons and mammoths were but two of the large mammals—including woodland musk-ox, giant moose-elk, giant beaver, native American horse, giant ground-sloth, among others—that became extinct in Wisconsin over only a thousand-year period, before 8500 B.C. The extinctions of prehistory are another mystery waiting to be solved, and the blame may belong with the other living creature moving in as the glaciers departed: humans.

Humans Arrive

Paleo-Indians

Humans arrived in Wisconsin as the glaciers retreated. Anthropologists today call them the Paleo-Indians; they entered the Upper Lakes in the 8000–11000 B.C. period, and lived by hunting the large mammals that grazed the open spots scattered throughout the spruce-fir areas. Paleo-Indians attacked their prey with spears possessing a specific kind of point: spearheads chipped from stone with "flutes" or grooves extending upward in the middle from the base, making it easier to attach to a spearpole. The Paleo-Indians' fluted spearheads also had jutting corners or "ears," which served as barbs—probably to keep them jabbed within a mastodon's hide despite its shaking and stomping.

Few bits of evidence of the Paleo-Indians have been unearthed in Wisconsin, but archeologists have reconstructed the 1897 discovery of a mastodon skeleton near Boaz, Richland County, that indicates a spearpoint was stuck into the animal. Two boys discovered the mastodon skeleton eroding from a stream bank, the fluted spearpoint with it. Other spearheads found in Wisconsin show that Paleo-Indian groups were scarcely isolated; instead, they either traveled or traded widely, bringing in points of Upper Mercer flint from eastern Ohio, northwestern Illinois chert, dark grey Indiana hornstone, and Knife River chalcedony from North Dakota. Their burial sites reveal that they had special beliefs about their dead, the corpses interred with skillfully crafted blades and spearpoints.

These humans whose ancestors had crossed the continents from Asia to North America, then trekked south and east and now north, were passing from the scene as the Ice Age finally drew to a close across the region. The fluted-point makers, believed to have been the first to inhabit the world left by the glaciers, now gave way to others called the Archaic peoples.

Archaic

These new inhabitants were entering the warming Great Lakes environment in the period from 6000–8500 B.C. as pines spread north and a forest dominated by hardwoods began its occupation of southern Wisconsin. Archaic peoples could no longer rely on mastodon meat for their sustenance, for the mastodon and many other large mammals were gone. The new deciduous forest contained a wide variety of fruits and nuts, however, and these forest dwellers turned to them. By 3000 B.C. they were using plant foods extensively: nuts of hickory, butternut, walnut, and oak, as well as berries and the edible seeds of smartweed, marsh elder, goosefoot chenopod, sumpweed, sunflower, Jerusalem artichoke, and maygrass. Archaic peoples also ate wild grapes and in some districts apparently wild rice as well. Garbage areas at their sites across the region reveal not only axes and spear pieces, but also the remains of plant foods and the tools used to crack, grind, and mill them.

Their meat came increasingly from elk and, especially, white-tailed deer, then expanding in numbers across southern areas; moose and caribou dominated the north. Smaller animals such as rabbits, muskrat, and beaver were taken as well, as were fish, waterfowl, wild turkey, and passenger pigeons.

As their tool-making became more skillful, Archaic groups began to employ something else that sharply improved their fishing success and, in the process, enabled their populations to increase. This was copper, exploited in the period 3000 to 500 B.C. to such an extent in the Upper Great Lakes region that this era is termed the Old Copper Culture. Copper was abundant: the glaciers dragged masses of native copper into the Upper Peninsula and northern Wisconsin, including a famous boulder near Ontonagon, Michigan, that attracted early explorers (and wound up in the Smithsonian Institution), and an 800-pound chunk found on Wisconsin's Bayfield Peninsula in the early colonial era. The Jesuits reported in 1669 that Indian women planting corn on the Apostle Islands often encountered pieces of copper weighing from 20 to 30 pounds. Evidence on Isle Royal shows that ancient miners lit fires to heat the rocks, chilled them with cold water to cause splits, then broke out the imprisoned copper particles with stone hammers.

Many of the copper tools created after 3000 B.C. by these Archaic peoples—including fishhooks, awls, gouges, punches, pikes, adzes, wedges, beads, knives, eyed needles, hatchet blades, and spearpoints—were like those made of stone in the East during the same era. Wisconsin's Indians encountered native copper and simply used existing skills to turn it into tools they already knew, then used these tools to carve wooden bowls, fashion frames for dwellings, make hair pipes, or tailor clothing and footware. Many of these items are found in their burials.

Eventually this Old Copper Culture largely disappeared from Great Lakes tribes, its tool-making skills surviving only in regions far to the north beyond Lake Superior. Later groups used copper mainly for ornamental items, a practice that would endure for centuries. Copper was at the Atlantic shore when the Europeans arrived in the early sixteenth century, and not only among the French entering the St. Lawrence: the Spaniard Cabeza de Vaca in 1536 received a copper bell from Indians in Florida who said it came from the north.

With the decline of the Old Copper Culture, several Indian cultures developed, distinguished by different forms of burial. By then these groups were coming into contact with other Indian cultures whose traits distinguished them from Old Copper and other Archaic cultures: these new Woodland Indians made ceramic bowls, buried their dead in mounds, and—a fundamental shift—actually cultivated specific plants for food.

Woodland Indians

The Woodland Culture spread unevenly over Wisconsin as the Archaic era was ending. Because of high rates of mobility among most of Wisconsin's Woodland peoples, gourds were often used for storage instead of the more fragile ceramic pots, and the use of pottery spread slowly. This was especially true in the north, where thick-walled pottery (the first stage of pottery development) did not appear until the Middle Woodland era, A.D. 100–500, and northern Wisconsin's Indians apparently picked up on Woodland ceramic styles only after those to the south had been using them for generations. With these, new designs were made on the surfaces of grit-tempered clay, and ceramic pots began to be used to store plant foods.

Woodland peoples of southern Wisconsin were within the reach of another important development, which spread out of the Ohio Valley and southern Illinois: Hopewell Culture. Hopewellians, whose period is generally placed from 100 B.C. to A.D. 500, have been called the Midwest's first farmers. Corn, their major crop, arrived after centuries of travel as it was carried from its origins in Meso-America in one of the dramatic stories of world food history. Archeologists digging in Mexican caves have traced the beginnings of corn from wild plants that were eventually domesticated by people who learned to eat, and then to plant, its kernels. Corn growing spread into the the U.S. Southwest by 2000 B.C., then was carried northward over succeeding centuries as it evolved to thrive in cooler and wetter climates. By the time it reached the Great Lakes region it was producing flinty, hard kernels that could germinate in a typically cool and rainy Midwestern spring.

Wisconsin's Indians who were part of the Hopewell Culture lived predominantly south of the "transition zone," that is, well within the limits of corn production. Corn shared mealtime offerings with squash and beans, believed to have spread from the Illinois River Valley into Upper Great Lakes Indian villages after 100 B.C. Tobacco arrived also, and the first Wisconsin evidence of pipes for smoking is at Hopewell sites. Hopewell Indians in the Great Lakes region, however, continued to be mainly hunter-gatherers, relying heavily upon taking deer. In this they apparently used dogs which they had domesticated by this time (and which were occasionally eaten and even given structured burials). The Hopewell peoples developed ceramic and artisan skills extensively, and some anthropologists today consider their products unsurpassed by later Indians across the region, demonstrated by surviving examples of woven cloth, elaborate pipes for smoking, and panpipes.

Hopewell peoples are best known, however, for burial mounds, the most visible remnant today of their occupation of Wisconsin and other areas of the Middle West. Conical or dome-shaped, these were usually concentrated in groupings of up to twenty-five; most average ten feet in height and reach up to sixty feet in length. Log tombs within the mounds contain one or more skeletons as well as "grave furniture," that is, special items placed with burials which are believed to indicate higher status. This social stratification, their use of burial mounds, and production of items only for use in burials are among the defining characteristics of Hopewell culture.

Trempealeau County, along the Mississippi River in west-central Wisconsin, stands out among Wisconsin Hopewell sites. Destruction by farming has meant that the 396 historically mapped mounds at Diamond Bluff have declined to thirty-four in less than a century; aerial photos and other studies put the county's original total at more than 1,000 burial mounds. The area was apparently linked to the Southern Illinois Hopewell culture by means of the Mississippi.

Trade is evident in most Wisconsin Hopewell sites. Archeologists have concluded that trading networks reached their greatest prehistoric development during the Middle Woodland period of Hopewellian culture, up to approximately A.D. 500:

> Gulf coast conch shells are found in Michigan and Wisconsin. Sharks' teeth are found in Middle Woodland mounds in Illinois and an effigy alligator pipe dating to this period has been recovered from

western Michigan. Copper from the Lake Superior region is traded far to the south. Obsidian and grizzly bear teeth from the far west find their way to Illinois and Ohio. Mica and special types of flint, such as that from Flint Ridge in Ohio, are also traded and carried over long distances and find their way into village and burial sites over much of eastern North America. The distribution of these goods makes it clear that some network, either social or religious, must have existed for this exchange to take place.

What else was transferred?—philosophies, languages, ceramic designs, religious beliefs, styles of warfare? Once the networks were in place the possibilities appear endless, and the evidence of such connections across a large section of the continent offers tantalizing hints at reasons for the Hopewell peoples' outstanding artwork and burial mounds. But their skills did not help them avoid destruction of their culture, and by A.D. 700 the Hopewell Culture, too, had passed from the scene.

Perhaps the collapse of trading networks was part of the Hopewell peoples' demise, for archeological sites of the next major culture group in Wisconsin—the Late Woodland peoples, from A.D. 800 to 1600—show little in the way of exotic items from distant corners of the continent. These peoples appear to have drawn on Hopewell's skills and traditions in some ways, such as pottery types and the use of burial mounds, but in others their development took different, much more limited routes.

Mound-building continued among Late Woodland Indians, however, and provided one of the few occasions in prehistory when Wisconsin developed separately from neighboring areas. Effigy mounds were built in many districts of southern Wisconsin from A.D. 800 up to 1300, overlapping only slightly into neighboring Minnesota, Iowa, and Illinois. A 1911 survey found some 20,000 conical, linear, and effigy mounds in Wisconsin. These Indians, probably semi-nomadic, may have wandered much of the time, returning sporadically to the same spot to build burial mounds, then starting other mounds elsewhere when their search for food drew them away.

Surviving mounds are low, only a few feet in height, but their length often runs to several hundred feet; they are usually built in the form of animals. Increase Lapham, writing in 1846, reported on several mound groupings he had examined:

Effigy mounds, usually in the shape of animals or humans, were built across southern Wisconsin from A.D. 800 to 1300 by Indians of the Late Woodland Period. This mound in the shape of a deer, on the grounds of the Mendota Asylum, was outlined for this early twentieth century photo. COURTESY MILWAUKEE PUBLIC MUSEUM, 108152.

Some have a resemblance to the buffalo, the eagle, or crane, or to the turtle or lizard. One representing the human form, near the Blue Mounds, is . . . one hundred twenty feet in length; it lies in an east and west direction, the head toward the west, with the arms and legs extended. The body or trunk is thirty feet in breadth, the head twenty-five, and its elevation above the general surface of the prairie is about six feet. Its conformation is so distinct that there can be no possibility of mistake in assigning it to the human figure.

Mound-building eventually spread north of the "transition zone," and several major sites have been located in northwestern Wisconsin.

As the effigy mound people passed on, other Late Woodland peoples spread across Wisconsin and eventually took a fateful turn toward increased warfare, one of the most obvious facts of Indian life to the Europeans who arrived several centuries later. These struggles developed in part from rising population totals accompanying the abundance of food linked to the spread of

agriculture, placing greater pressures on territory used for hunting. The bow and arrow were known earlier, but by the Late
Woodland era after A.D. 800 these weapons of war became ubiq-
uitous across the region. Village sites of the period are awash
with small arrowheads, which replaced the large stone points
used for many centuries on spears. Arrows with smaller points
were more accurate to shoot, easier to carry, and could be transported to battles in large numbers. As further evidence of growing warfare, stockades began to be constructed around villages,
built by people who had reason to fear attack.

By the close of the first millennium A.D., Wisconsin's residents
represented several cultural groupings, increasingly competing
with each other. The effigy mound culture, considered part of
the Late Woodland period, shared the region with Middle Mississippian Culture[2] groups coming out of Cahokia and southern Illinois, as well as a new Upper Mississippi group known to archeologists as Oneota. Aztalan, discussed at the beginning of this
chapter, may have been an isolated outpost of Middle Mississippian Culture thrust among other Indian groups of southern Wisconsin.

Oneota became the major representative of Upper Mississippian cultures in Wisconsin. As a distinct culture it ran from perhaps A.D. 900 to 1500 (and even overlapped the Europeans' arrival, as can be discerned at a few sites). Differences between
Oneota and others were mainly in degree, and some archeologists believe Oneota represents Effigy Mound people adapting
new methods. Wisconsin Oneota settlements were primarily along
the Mississippi River and from Door County running south and
west from Green Bay and Lake Winnebago. These Indians fished
heavily, and their agriculture was highly developed. Corn and
other plants were grown in fields and stored in pits; the Oneota
Indians expected to stay awhile, rather than rushing off soon on
lengthy hunting or gathering expeditions. Women tended the
elaborate gardens and fields, a lifestyle that would remain
identified with their gender; men were the hunters and warriors.

---

2. The term Middle Mississippian can be confusing, since the "middle"
refers here not to a time period but to a geographical area, the middle-Missis-
sippi Valley. This is in contrast to Middle Woodland, in which "middle" refers
to a chronological time span.

Corn was becoming the crucial crop for the Oneota because it could now be grown across much of southern Wisconsin. A new variety had evolved, Northern Flint, with a growing season which had fallen to 140 days by A.D. 1000 and to 120 days by A.D. 1600; it also resisted insects well and had extremely high yields compared to earlier varieties. It spread east as well, and Northern Flint helped feed the Pilgrims after their 1620 arrival at Massachusetts Bay. Beans appeared after A.D. 1000 in Upper Midwest sites, and proved to be complementary: corn removes nitrogen from the soil but beans replace it. Further, corn and beans satisfy normal protein needs for all except nursing mothers. Squash was also planted in Middle Mississippian fields, and while beans climbed the cornstalks, the leaves of squash vines shaded the soil to reduce evaporation while slowing weed growth. The Sand Lake archeological site in La Crosse County reveals that all three plants were sowed along raised ridges by the Oneota, who then ran water through adjacent ditches for irrigation. Carbon dating shows the site was used as late as the fifteenth century; the ridged fields may have covered 200 acres. Traces of other ridged fields from the period are abundant across southern Wisconsin.

The Oneotas were also prolific potters. They created round-based jars topped by broad mouths with flaring rims, and then—unlike most previous groups—they smoothed the surfaces before firing the vessels, rather than marking them extensively with impressions of cords or paddles. Frequently their ceramic vessels had handles, and often Oneota potters would push down repeatedly with a finger, as if to measure the distance around the rim. Like Middle Mississippian groups along the Rock River and farther south, they often tempered their clay with finely crushed clamshells rather than grit; this reduced the weight, made possible thinner walls, and increased conductivity of heat.

Separate Tribes at Contact

It was this final offshoot, the Oneota culture with its main strength along the Mississippi and Lake Michigan, that persisted as the dominant way of Indian life in much of Wisconsin during

Ridged fields left by earlier generations of Indian
farmers greeted settlers arriving in the early nineteenth
century; frequently these same fields were then used for
the newcomers' crops. These remains of curved garden
beds, photographed after a 1915 snowfall along the
west shore of Lake Winnebago, were testimony to the
Indians' extensive agriculture. COURTESY STATE HISTORICAL
SOCIETY OF WISCONSIN, WHI (X3) 44500.

the remaining few centuries before the arrival of the French. A
basic north-south division remained, however, with lifestyles of
the agricultural Indian groups in southern and eastern Wisconsin contrasting with the growing numbers in the north who pursued fishing and hunting. However, direct links between prehistoric groups and later tribes are difficult for anthropologists to
trace, and no tribes have been definitely identified as descendants of Wisconsin's mound-builders.

There seems general agreement, however, that the Winnebagos
encountered near Green Bay by the French in 1634 were closely
related to the Middle Mississippian groups who had arrived centuries earlier. They had broken off from western regions of the
central Mississippi Valley, and were linked to such tribes there as
the Iowas, Otos, and Missouris. Winnebagos also had distant lin-
guistic ties to the Dakota Sioux. Since Santee Sioux occupied
parts of northwestern Wisconsin, and Iowa tribesmen came into
the southwestern part of the state, it is apparent that this Siouan

Winnebago intrusion belonged to Indian movements late in the prehistoric period and did not represent a brief visit or invasion.

The Winnebagos encountered by early French visitors had already adapted well to the northern forest, and made a determined pursuit of hunting and fishing like the Algonquian tribes nearby. But their agricultural expertise continued, and tribal stories tell of gardens "several arrow-shots in length and breadth," supporting settlements of several thousand people.

Other tribes of the late prehistoric era whose descendants would become deeply involved in the Wisconsin frontier story were all Algonquian groups, however. Most resulted from splits in the East which created progenitors of such tribes as the Menominees, Chippewas, Ottawas, Potawatomis, Sacs,[3] Foxes, Kickapoos, Miamis, and Illinois.

Menominees were located just north of the Winnebagos when the French arrived, along the Menominee River that divides Wisconsin and the Upper Peninsula. They were known for their reliance on wild rice as well as their hunting and fishing. Chippewas may have been visitors to northern Wisconsin before European contact, journeying from their homes north and east of lakes Huron and Superior. They were relatives of the Potawatomis and Ottawas, who also entered Wisconsin from Michigan in the early colonial era. Chippewas lived in small bands, were nomadic, and developed their hunting-fishing-gathering culture to a degree that made them experts with birchbark canoes, sugar maple, and wild rice. They also did some gardening, but the northern climate precluded extensive agriculture; as Father Hennepin reported from the Upper Peninsula in 1679, the "Saulteurs" did not plant corn "because their land is unsuitable and the frequent fogs of Lake Superior would smother it."

As the colonial era advanced, the Sacs and Foxes gathered inland from Green Bay, settling just north of the Miamis who ranged around the southern end of Lake Michigan. Far to the west of these tribes, various bands of Sioux occupied areas of western and northwestern Wisconsin. The total Indian population around the Upper Lakes in the year 1600, just before the

---

3. "Sacs" have been known as "Sauks" at various periods; to avoid confusion, the former name will be used throughout this study.

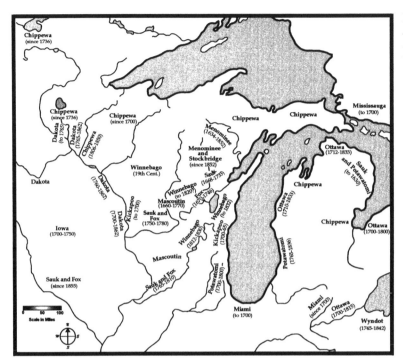

Indian tribes changed locations frequently, both before and after arrival of the Europeans. This map notes locations of tribes at different times after contact in the Upper Lakes. ADAPTED BY JILL FREUND THOMAS AND MICHAEL MAST FROM ALICE E. SMITH, *The History of Wisconsin. Volume I: From Exploration to Statehood* (STATE HISTORICAL SOCIETY OF WISCONSIN, 1973), AND EMMA H. BLAIR, ED., *Indian Tribes of the Upper Mississipi Valley and the Region of the Great Lakes* (ARTHUR H. CLARK, 1912).

French arrival, has been estimated at 100,000; perhaps 20,000 were in Wisconsin.

Indians at Contact

The Indians who met the French as they entered the Upper Lakes in the early seventeenth century had demonstrated a high degree of adaptability over the years. Without the Europeans' arrival—without the diseases, the fur trade disruptions, the challenges to native religions—it is possible that another Golden Era similar to that of the Hopewellians or the Cahokians might have developed. Five major points regarding their lives and impact upon the frontier era emerge from the long centuries of Wisconsin's prehistory:

1. Trade networks were extensive and brought items from far and wide to the Great Lakes region; they undoubtedly also brought ideas. When Samuel de Champlain found a foot-long piece of copper in the hands of an Indian visiting him at Quebec, he was only viewing the latest outward evidence of a trading system that had been developing for hundreds of years.

2. Agriculture's slow but steady development forms another chapter. The arrival of Northern Flint corn stimulated the spread of extensive gardening as a new factor of Indian subsistence in the region, and brought increases in Indian populations. Although northern Wisconsin remained inhospitable to most agricultural pursuits, it is believed that Menominees and Chippewas raised small amounts of food in their gardens, in addition to harvesting wild rice. In the southern half of Wisconsin, however, planting and harvesting became crucial to Indian existence, and cornfields of up to 400 acres were encountered by early European visitors. Such prime farming areas, however, were targets of the waves of white settlers arriving in the early nineteenth century; these groups were less interested in the forested north country, at least until after mid-century. The French fur traders, however, were not interested in obtaining either farmland or timberland, only furs.

3. Warfare was an accepted part of life. The shift to small arrowheads and better arrows occurred at the same time that friction between groups was worsening as populations increased. Soon stockades began to appear around settlements, sometimes— as at Aztalan—triple stockades. Warfare was unending, integrated into the whole fabric of Indian life. The rounds of attack and revenge helped assure that incoming Europeans could be viewed by some tribes as potential allies against other Indians, rather than as invaders. And the fur trade, introduced by the Europeans, heightened the possibilities for competition and, frequently, for war; the new guns and other metal items soon added new dimensions to battles. But the earlier pre-contact trends make it clear there is no clear evidence to assume that without the arrival of the Europeans there would have been no large-scale battles.

4. Prehistoric peoples brought great changes to the North

American and Wisconsin landscapes, through fires, mound-building, hunting, gardening, and the sheer fact of settlement. Recent research has shown that Indians were altering forests and landscape, often in significant ways. These changes included modifications of forest size and composition, the expansion of grasslands, and erection of earthworks, causeways, and sunken features. Burning of grasslands by Indians, over a period of some 5,000 years, helped develop and perpetuate Midwestern prairies. It was not a pristine world the Europeans entered.

5. And finally, the human story before the seventeenth century in Wisconsin is remarkably similar to what came later in one other way: ideas in people's minds were important in directing their activities. For in addition to reacting to climate, soils, forestation, animal abundance, and the availability of water, the humans of prehistory acted also on the basis of what they believed—regarding migration to other areas, burial practices, status within the group, attitudes toward others, threats of war or desires for peace. While struggles for survival formed the backdrop to human activity, what was in their minds was crucial in determining the paths they followed.

These developments lay in the background as the prehistoric peoples ended their 9,000-year adaptation to the Wisconsin environment and confronted the new people canoeing up their waterways—men with whiskers and pale skins, speaking strange tongues and dressed in clothing never before seen. It was the start of a new period of human existence in the Upper Lakes, the era of the frontier.

3.

FRENCHMEN AND INDIANS

Beside the rushing waters of Lake Superior's outlet a large throng gathered one day in the spring of 1671. It was a collection of striking contrasts: French officials in their hauteur, several roughly garbed fur traders, Indians whose greased bodies were draped with furs and feathers, and black-robed Jesuits who challenged the roar of the nearby Sault—and the wilderness—with their singing of *Vexilla Regis Prodeunt* and the *Exaudiat*.

The date was June 14. The ceremony in 1671 came about with the convergence on Sault Ste. Marie of men drawn from many locations and stations: there was Simon François Daumont, Sieur de St. Lusson, sent by New France's intendant;[1] Nicolas Perrot, the roving explorer who had already gained familiarity with much of the *pays d'en haut;* Father Claude Allouez, whose recent past included a stay at Chequamegon Bay as well as visits to tribes in the Green Bay region.

And there were Indians—from fourteen tribes, listed in the official report, but actually representing several more according

---

1. The intendant ranked second to the governor in command of New France. While the governor commanded troops and was in charge of foreign relations, the intendant was drawn from the legal class and generally handled civil and economic matters.

to references in other accounts. Perrot had gone earlier to Green Bay to enlist tribes there to attend the event at the Sault, and returned in late spring with delegations of Sacs, Winnebagos, Potawatomis, and Menominees; these agreed to speak for the Kickapoos, Mascoutins, Foxes, and Illinois, who stayed behind. Chippewa bands who resided nearby were on hand as well, as were other tribes and clans from the shores of Lake Huron and adjacent regions.

All had been summoned to witness France's declaration that it was claiming for itself the entire North American interior, including Wisconsin as well as other lands north, west, and south. St. Lusson's proclamation that day was scarcely original; such claims were heard often from 1492 onward as Europeans rushed to exert dominion over newly discovered lands in the western hemisphere. After the French leader explained his king's greatness, the Indians signed the proclamation for their tribes—drawing on the sheet a beaver, otter, sturgeon, deer, elk, and other symbols of their respective clans.

However, soon after the crowd had dispersed, Indians showed that their feelings at the ceremony involved more than awe. Perrot recalled years later that Frenchmen had placed one of their documents, signed only by themselves, behind the iron plate attached to the cedar post. But the Indians removed this: ". . . they drew out the nails from the plate, flung the document into the fire, and again fastened up the arms of the king—fearing that the written paper was a spell, which would cause the deaths of all those who dwelt in or should visit that district."

The events at Sault Ste. Marie in 1671 held many elements that would dominate the frontier era in Wisconsin and the Great Lakes region over the next two centuries. There was European arrogance, yet with recognition of the need to win the Indians' support while seeking their conversion to Roman Catholicism; there was the fur trade, represented by the French traders standing by, already the underpinning of the vast French endeavor in North America; and there was the Indian presence—apparently mingled with wonder or mystification, doubt, fear, perhaps anger, and filtered (as with the Europeans) through layers of belief and tradition. Through it all the fact remained that these two groups were far, far apart in their comprehension of what was taking place before their eyes at the Sault on June 14, 1671.

With all these elements, this pageant at the outset of the French era on the Upper Lakes marked an essential step in the Wisconsin frontier story. And while the event seemed controlled by the French who explained, exhorted, and sang, it was also true that each of the outside interests represented—imperial expansion, religious concern, and trade—was affected in crucial ways by the presence of the Indians. Soon, in fact, French policies would face challenges from these same tribes, and also from independent French traders who were learning to live like Indians in a region largely beyond the grasp of French law. This complex record of an outside power moving with technological superiority into a new region was a story that would be repeated often on the frontier of the North America.

Beginnings of the Fur Trade

The fur trade was the magnet for French expansion in the region. As the French initially moved up the St. Lawrence they carried dreams of gold and expectations of finding the Northwest Passage. But the new territory held other riches: "It was a Peru for them," wrote the contemporary La Potherie, a friend of Nicolas Perrot. Their wealth was to be in furs, and furs became their money; pelts were used in place of coins not only around Green Bay but also in French settlements far to the east along the St. Lawrence. There, furs went to the tax collector as well as into church collections.

This was so because the seventeenth century saw an exploding popularity in Europe of the broad-brimmed felt hat, made from beaver pelts. Extinct in much of Europe, beavers were still trapped in Scandinavia and Russia but soon the flow from North America overwhelmed these other sources. Beavers' barbed hairs interlocked to form high-quality felt, and beaver pelts accordingly brought top prices. Before the Iroquois wars, Montreal exulted in fur profits—250,000 *livres* in profits by 1648, a fantastic sum. To the south, New Yorkers had begun pushing into the trade also, and the colony's Collector of Customs warned in 1687 "that if the Indian Trade bee disturbed or distroyed it will be Impossible for the Inhabitants of this Province to provide themselfs with Clothinge and other nessisaries from England their beinge Little else then furrs Sutable to make returnes."

Enormous profits drove this expansion. Reports of 1,200 percent profit were heard in the early years, and when the English began to compete openly with the French, they soon realized they could pay the Indians more and still manage a good return: a French memoir lamented that one beaver skin brought eight pounds of gunpowder at Albany, but only two pounds at Montreal; forty pounds of lead were paid for beaver skins at Albany but only thirteen pounds in the French trade center. But the French were first into the Upper Lakes and it was estimated that most of New France's 12,000 non-Indian population were involved in the fur trade in some way by 1688. Three hundred years later, archeologists digging at the site of Fort Michilimackinac concluded that "fur trading permeated almost all other activities" at that outpost of the Upper Lakes.

The Europeans' desire for beaver hats stimulated many activities in Wisconsin and adjacent territory; gradually the newcomers would seek also the pelts of otter, muskrat, marten, bear, lynx, fisher, mink, wolf, and buffalo. Exploration was often only another approach to acquiring furs. The 1634 visit to Green Bay by Jean Nicolet was made at the behest of the Company of the Hundred Associates, with the aim of making peace between tribes so that the growing trade in peltry would not be blocked. Montreal became the eastern center of the trade and its trade fairs drew Indians, traders, and local folk with goods to barter. The expeditions westward of Medard Chouart de Groseilliers and Pierre Esprit Radisson, in the 1650s, and by Daniel Greysolon Dulhut (Duluth) and Robert Cavelier de la Salle, in the 1670s, were motivated by the fur trade. And the fur trade was never far from the thoughts of Nicolas Perrot as he worked to bring peace to competing western tribes, especially when he stood by his newly built fort on Lake Pepin in 1689 and took possession of the Upper Mississippi for the Crown. By then the fur trade, and with it the French regime, had crossed Wisconsin and was in the process of enveloping it.

The Native Inhabitants

Indians were crucial at every stage of the fur trade's expansion. The French—unlike the Spanish, Portuguese, and English, who relied on Indian and African slaves in the Caribbean and South America—had no need of forced labor in the fur trade. Under their system, furs were trapped by Indians, who then bartered them to Frenchmen for European goods of iron, porcelain, and cloth, or for alcohol. This relationship was not one of slaveholder to slave; rather, it was usually that of two sides who each relied upon the other to supply something they desired. The arrangement could tilt sharply in favor of one side or the other, but the underlying truth was that the Indians entered into the fur trade era not as slaves but as free people, restricted—to be sure—by competing tribes at times, but generally held back only by the forces of nature and their own beliefs.

The vast numbers of Indians from eastern and Upper Lakes tribes who poured into Wisconsin in the mid-seventeenth century began to decrease after the 1667 Iroquois peace with the French. The Sacs and Foxes remained, however. The Sacs had left the Saginaw district of Michigan and settled near Green Bay around mid-century. Decades later, in 1733, they would join the Foxes in a formal alliance. But long before they arrived in Wisconsin the two tribes were linked by both language and customs, which were also close to those of the Mascoutin and Kickapoo, two other tribes arriving in eastern Wisconsin during the seventeenth century. The pre-contact location of the Foxes remains shrouded in mystery, although tribal memories indicate residence along the St. Lawrence near Montreal before moving into Michigan near the Sacs. After fleeing into Wisconsin they first settled along the Wolf River, moving to the upper Fox River by 1677.

To the north, the Chippewas were entering in bands from the Upper Peninsula, a movement underway for some time and emerging from an earlier division in which the Ottawa grouping split into Chippewa, Potawatomi, and Ottawa tribes. The Chippewas'

This Menominee Village on the Wolf River, from a mid-nineteenth century drawing, reveals customs that were unchanged for centuries. Mats of reeds and other plants, along with bark and skins, covered wigwams in summer communities, where hunting and fishing complemented the annual harvest of wild rice.
COURTESY STATE HISTORICAL SOCIETY OF WISCONSIN, WHi (X3) 20034.

Algonquian language dialect eventually replaced Huron as the *lingua franca* around the Upper Lakes.

To the west, the Issati (or Santee) Sioux, or Dakotas,[2] who had long dominated much of the rest of Wisconsin, yielded only grudgingly to the incoming Chippewas. In 1679, however, Duluth brought the Chippewas and Sioux together in a peace agreement that would last until 1736. (Perrot reported that the the Sioux cooperated because it was only through the Chippewas, to the east, that they could obtain French goods.) Pierre le Sueur, an active trader who had traveled with Perrot, pushed this alliance further and in 1695 brought a Sioux headman and a Chippewa leader down the St. Lawrence to cement their pact with the governor of New France, Count de Frontenac. Although it was an

2. The French called the Dakotas the *Nadouessis*, corrupting the Chippewas' term for them. The French word, in turn, was eventually corrupted further to Sioux.

uneasy alliance, the Chippewas now had western and northern Wisconsin opened to them and they continued their western spread, becoming the dominant Indian group across most of northern Wisconsin.

It all meant that Wisconsin remained a conglomeration of Indians, a meeting place of tribes, in many ways a contested area. French reports suggest the population of Wisconsin in 1650, before large-scale Chippewa arrivals, to have included 3,000 Menominees; 3,800 Winnebagos; 25,000 Dakotas; 1,200 Iowas, and 6,000 Illinois. More recently, historians have offered 12,000 or 17,000 as the total in the broad region centered on Green Bay.

Food

This concentration of population in eastern Wisconsin was possible because food supplies were abundant. Indians lived off the land, of course, but the types of food sought also determined many fundamentals of their existence.

Winnebagos, as noted earlier, were farmers, impressing Nicolet in 1634 with their large fields of corn, melons, pumpkins, beans, tobacco, and other plants. Although other Wisconsin tribes grew corn and collected wild onions and wild potatoes along with nuts and fruits, and although the Winnebagos also hunted for game, the Winnebagos were the region's prime horticulturists, and this fact had two major results: it let them exist as mainly a sedentary tribe and it brought development of large communities. They were not a tribe always on the move, in temporary, portable housing. To the contrary: Winnebago villages featured solid, large lodges, round or rectangular, covered either with cedar bark or reed matting or both; usually poles of ironwood were bent together to form the underlying round frame. The permanence of these structures and villages rested on the Winnebagos' success as farmers, and they looked down on the Chippewas' over-reliance on hunting and uncertain harvests of wild rice.

Other tribes also grew crops—Sac cornfields were reported at 400 acres, with enough production to supply an extensive trade network. Larger villages were typical of the Sacs also, and a visitor told of Sac summer lodges that were square houses covered with elm bark, the roofs ridged, running up to fifty feet long and thirty-five feet wide. In winter, however, the Sacs often used the typical Algonquian round wigwam covered with cattail mats. All this was fine for the Winnebagos, Sacs, and other tribes relying on corn; but for those north of the 140-day growing season, other types of organization and housing were required because of their dependence on hunting, fishing, and upon one other plant: wild rice.

Wild rice was the staff of life for the Menominees, Chippewas, and several other northern groups. The French called it *folle avoine*—"fool oats" or "wild oats"—and the Chippewas termed it *manoomin*. Both names were then fastened on the wild rice–dependent tribe on the north side of Green Bay, although today only the Chippewas' word, Menominee, survives. The plant itself is not a rice but a grass which grows in lakes and rivers over much of the upper Great Lakes region, especially in northern Wisconsin and Minnesota. Father Ménard reported that Indians he encountered in Wisconsin in 1660–61 harvested "a certain plant, four feet or thereabout in height, which grows in marshy places." Radisson went into some detail in his fourth voyage at approximately the same time, when he was with the Menominees:

> We had there a kinde of rice, much like oats. It growes in the watter in 3 or 4 foote deepe. . . . They have a particular way to gather up that graine. Two takes a boat and two sticks, by which they gett ye eare downe and gett the corne out of it. Their boat being full, they bring it to a fitt place to dry it, and that is their food for the most part of the winter, and doe dresse it thus: ffor each man a handfull of that they putt in the pott, that swells so much that it can suffice a man.

Wild rice was sometimes so abundant in shallow lakes and rivers that canoes maneuvered among it only with difficulty. But crop failures were not uncommon, and a trader reported from the head of Lake Superior in 1783 that he was told "there was no wild rice because the rainfall had been too abundant." Indeed, evidence indicates that the Chippewas' wild rice crop was only successful about one year in three, due to flood, drought, wind, hail. Much of the harvest was dried and stored, making it

Wild rice was the staff of life for northern tribes,
especially the Menominees and the Chippewas. Harvest
time—little changed today—meant pushing canoes
amid the beds of wild rice and bending the stalks so the
heads could be beaten loose into the canoe. Women
usually did the harvest in earlier times, as shown in
this lithograph from the 1830–40 period. COURTESY STATE
HISTORICAL SOCIETY OF WISCONSIN, WHI (X3) 13608.

a year-round food and one that could be brought forth when
other foods failed. Wild rice was rich in protein and carbohy-
drates, easy to digest, and provided thiamin, riboflavin, and vi-
tamin B; scientists today report that it outranks oats, barley,
wheat, and rye in total nutritional value. Visitors told of wild rice
being eaten at every meal, sometimes with meat or berries, at
other times cooked like modern oatmeal or with grease. (Later
these tribes would use wild rice as a reference point in naming
the new grains imported by the Europeans: "wild rice with a
tail" described barley; "horse rice" was oats.)

Relying upon wild rice could have a dual impact upon northern tribes: it encouraged a near-sedentary existence for those,
like the Menominees, who had abundant wild rice beds nearby.

Their "gardens" were provided by nature. And for hunting tribes such as the Chippewas and Sioux, wild rice could offer a food source that was often found near their hunting areas. As such, wild rice entered into Sioux-Chippewa struggles, for each knew locations of prime rice beds, and each harvested extensively for sustenance and increasingly for trade. As European metal pots came into wide use, maple sugaring became an important activity for Indians as well.

But it was fishing and hunting that were most closely identified with the Chippewas and Sioux. Parts of Green Bay and Chequamegon Bay were prime fisheries, though not as famous as those of upper lakes Michigan and Huron. Tribes fishing in these waters relied upon gill nets to catch the whitefish and lake trout in November and December, which could then be preserved to last through the starving time of late winter and early spring. Father Henry Nouvel wrote of the Indians spreading their nets in the Fox River and coming up with ducks, teal, and other wild fowl as well as fish; they also drove stakes to form underwater fences on the river bottoms and speared fish passing through. The nearby Menominees, moreover, speared sturgeons through winter ice, again aiding the tribe's ability to remain in the same location through most of the year. For many Wisconsin Indians, fishing became a frenzied early winter activity involving all members. Father Louis André noted one November that Indian women and girls around the Green Bay mission were smoking the fish while men worked on their nets—making it impossible for the priest to have them pray in their cabins, "because these were so littered with nets, and so full of fish, that I could hardly enter or kneel in them without inconvenience."

Hunting-fishing bands moved frequently: some groups headed inland from the coastal waters of the Great Lakes in late winter, while others hunted and trapped in large family groups through much of the winter as they sought moose, elk, deer, and smaller animals. Then they would converge on the sugar bush in larger groups for the early spring festival of maple sugaring. Women smoked the meat during the hunt, and at sugaring time they tapped the trees and boiled down the sap, while men brought

firewood. Next came the move to summer quarters, usually located along a river, where large numbers gathered to catch fish
and pick berries and do some gardening. Dome-shaped wigwams
were typical of the Chippewas and other groups that moved frequently, similar in general structure although smaller than the
more permanent dwellings of the Winnebagos and Menominees.
Birchbark, cattail mats, hides and, later, even blankets provided
the outside covering on these homes. The Chippewa equivalent
of a hunting shack was an A-frame lodge, formed by bark draped
over poles.

Religion

Religious beliefs among Wisconsin tribes, both Algonquian and
Siouan, were similar. Controlling the Indians' journey through
life, whether Sioux or Winnebago, Sac or Chippewa, was a mystical spirit world that touched all events and objects, all people,
plants, animals, and fish. These beliefs yielded—if at all—only
in fits and starts to European theology, although a hereafter, a
place where souls went after death, was also an integral part of
the cosmology of Great Lakes tribes. Father Hennepin explained
the Indians' belief in life after death as "a very delightful land
toward the sunset where there is good hunting." Visitors were
often perplexed by the contrast between the Indians' intense religious life (including belief in an unending number of spirits)
and their deep understanding of the materialistic basis of existence. The answer for this seeming paradox, one anthropologist
has argued, lay in the fact that Indians did not interpret life in
terms of religion, but found religious meaning in life—exalting
the real world around them until it took on religious significance.
Missionaries challenged Indian beliefs. Father Claude Allouez,
like many French missionaries, was bothered by their doctrines
but sought to comprehend just what the Indians were thinking:

> The Savages of these regions recognize no sovereign master of
> Heaven and Earth, but believe there are many spirits—some of whom
> are beneficent, as the Sun, the Moon, the Lake, Rivers, and Woods;
> others malevolent, as the adder, the dragon, cold, and storms. And,
> in general, whatever seems to them either helpful or hurtful they

call a Manitou, and pay it the worship and veneration which we render only to the true God.

These divinities they invoke whenever they go out hunting, fishing, to war, or on a journey—offering them sacrifices, with ceremonies appropriate only for Sacrificial priests.

Dreams were crucial. Dreams came from the manitous and could direct hunting, fishing, crop growing, warfare; they were the Indians' "Prophecy, Inspiration, Laws, Commandments, and Rules," the missionary Father Hennepin concluded. When a group of young Indians near Green Bay dreamed of bear, they quite predictably then headed to the woods for a ten-day bear hunt. A boy dreamed he was female, and from then on dressed and worked as a woman. Dreams could instruct an Indian to kill someone, or to have sex. Boys and girls were sent at puberty on a dream fast, seeking through starvation to induce visions. The sweat lodge, the manitou bundles or medicine bundles, and various charms were used to bring on dreams.

Role of Women

Women were important in most tribal activities, although it is clear in their general absence from most reports written by Europeans that their work was often overlooked by male visitors. Traditional divisions of labor had women cooking and managing households; collecting berries and fishing and hunting small game near camp; handling all gardening; harvesting wild rice through all stages of production; carrying items when traveling; making utensils for the home; weaving mats; making clothing, and dressing skins. As such, Indian women became crucial in the developing fur trade. They also made nets for the extensive Great Lakes fishing operations, twisting the string from nettles or wild hemp, tying the nets together with cords of basswood bark or leather and repairing these. Father Hennepin was impressed by the work done by Indian women, carrying goods in such amounts that few European men could match them.

Efforts of men and women seldom overlapped: men killed the moose, elk, bear, buffalo, and deer, but it was women who did the butchering and controlled distribution of the meat. Nicolas

Perrot discovered some of these labor customs when he presented gifts to the Mascoutins at Green Bay, handing a dozen awls and knives to the women: "Throw aside your bone bodkins," he told them; "these French awls will be much easier to use. These knives will be more useful to you in killing beavers and in cutting your meat than are the pieces of stone that you use."

Records of the colonial era contain occasional accounts of women serving as tribal leaders, as when Jonathan Carver met a female Winnebago chief in 1766. However, it is not clear whether these women were actual office-holders or were simply being recognized and respected for their abilities; the Europeans may not have understood the difference.

Warfare

The longstanding tradition of tribal warfare provided another complication for the early fur trade. Warfare often stemmed from feuds over hunting territory; even agricultural groups like the Winnebagos and Sacs still followed the hunt. Competition for hunting grounds became even more tangled when the Sioux threat from the West virtually closed off much of western and northern Wisconsin for lengthy periods; arrivals of refugee tribes added to the possibilities for conflict over hunting grounds.

There were, however, no basic differences between Indians and Europeans on this point. Their religions and customs were sharply divergent, but on the issue of the frequency of warfare the two groups were remarkably similar. To look at Europe then was to view a continent frequently at war, and when peace broke out it was all the more beautiful and memorable because it was so rare. The same could be said, of course, for the rest of the world and for the entire human race, in all ages.

The question is no different when considering torture of war's captives: when Champlain berated an Indian for cutting the finger off a woman captive, the Indian told him "that their enemies treated them in like fashion: but that since this method displeased me he would do nothing further to the women, since that was not agreeable to us, but only to the men." It was only a generation prior to Champlain's, however, that French Catholics and Protestants went at each other in the ferocious religious wars climaxed by the Massacre of St. Bartholomew in 1572; and a generation before that the German states were in upheaval in the Peasants' War and the Anabaptist revolt, where bodies were smashed and torn asunder over the question of whether infants could be baptized. In truth, neither side of the Atlantic could learn much from the other regarding war and torture. Only in technology could the Europeans instruct, while Indians were teachers in battle methods on American terrain. Neither possessed an advantage in inflicting cruelties.

The near-decimation of the Winnebagos rose from these truths. Seeds were planted early in the seventeenth century in the failure of French missionaries—and later the governments of France, England, and The Netherlands—to keep muskets from the Indians. The Iroquois purchased guns from the Dutch at Fort Orange (Albany), then passed them on to the Neutrals, who attacked tribes in lower Michigan and drove many Indians westward into Wisconsin.

When the Foxes relocated near Green Bay they launched war against the Winnebagos, who had been weakened already by disease but nevertheless raised a force of 500 warriors. But the Winnebago force was lost in a storm on Lake Michigan or Lake Winnebago or Little Lake Butte des Mortes (scholars disagree on the location). After that came the Winnebagos' troubles with the Illinois, as learned later by Father Allouez:

> About thirty years ago, all the people of this Nation were killed or taken captive by the Iliniouek, with the exception of a single man who escaped, shot through the body with an arrow. When the Iliniouetz had sent back his captive countrymen to inhabit the country anew, he was made Captain of his Nation, as having never been a slave.

Perrot tells of some other tribes also turning against the Winnebagos, including the Ottawas after the Winnebagos "had the cruelty to eat" some Ottawa peace envoys. But following the destruction of the 500 Winnebago warriors, according to Perrot, other tribes felt compassion and the Illinois sent some 500 men with abundant provisions. The Winnebagos, however, pretended to welcome their benefactors and were hosts for a dance—during which they cut the Illinois' bow-strings, then massacred their guests "and made a general feast of their flesh." The surviving Illinois waited two years, then searched out the Winnebagos' settlement, located on an island. Pursuing the tribe on its hunt, they laid siege: "So vigorous was their attack that they killed, wounded, or made prisoners all the Puans [Winnebagos], except a few who escaped, and who reached the Malhominis' [Menominees'] village, but severely wounded by arrows." The Winnebagos were disorganized, dispirited, and ready to be overwhelmed by outside influences, Indian or European.

Warfare's pervasiveness even reached to sports and is believed to be entwined with one of the Great Lakes Indians' favorite games, lacrosse. Lacrosse was popular in many areas of the continent, especially among some southern tribes, and involved massive fields with large teams and games lasting for days. Nicholas Perrot saw a brief but still spectacular lacrosse contest, put on for his benefit, at a Miami village near Green Bay in 1667:

> More than two thousand persons assembled in a great plain, each with his racket; and a wooden ball, as large as a tennis-ball, was thrown into the air. Then all that could be seen was the flourishes and motion through the air of all those rackets, which made a noise like that of weapons which is heard in a battle. Half of all those savages endeavored to send the ball in the direction of the northwest, the length of the plain, and the others tried to make it go to the southeast; the strife, which lasted half an hour, was doubtful.

Perrot added that such games "are usually followed by broken heads, arms and legs; and often persons are killed therein without any other injury occurring to them." Zebulon Pike reported no injuries or deaths in the game between the Sioux and a Winnebago-Fox team, at Prairie du Chien in 1806, but he admitted, "It is an interesting sight to see two or three hundred naked savages contending on the plain who shall bear off the palm of victory."

Lacrosse, with many variations, was popular among all of Wisconsin's tribes, and when the Winnebagos moved from Green Bay at the end of the colonial era they carried the game with them to a site along the Mississippi. The French translated their name for the location to Prairie de la Crosse, and today it is known simply as La Crosse.

Indians Join the Fur Trade

The growing fur trade meshed neatly with age-old Indian practices. The name *Ottawa* comes from an Algonquian word meaning "trading people," and the eagerness with which the Ottawas and other tribes competed to participate in the French network indicates there was nothing new in the idea of exchanging surplus or easily obtainable goods for objects of more value. The fur trade with its requirements for seeking out animals over a broad area was especially suited to the lifestyles of the Chippewas and other hunter-gatherer tribes. Agricultural tribes of eastern and southern Wisconsin had more adjusting to do, but eventually all were brought within the trade networks. Many moved into multi-tribe settlements at least partly because these offered better access to French traders. The lure of European goods could be overwhelming: Perrot recounts that when the Sioux returned home with their hatchets, knives, and awls, people from other villages showed up and begged them to share "that iron, which they regarded as a divinity."

Soon a veritable cornucopia of European objects was pouring in on the Indians, making their day-to-day lives much easier while drawing them steadily, inexorably into another way of life. Guns were popular, their power so mysterious that musket shots first sent Indians running in fright but soon had them battling to obtain the weapons. Hatchets, awls, knives, iron kettles, and metal points quickly entered everyday Indian life in the Upper Lakes. La Potherie described Indians catching sturgeon with metal-tipped spears in 1668.

Recent archeological finds have also shown the importance of the Europeans' innovative devices for starting fires, using iron formed into easily gripped fire steels which produced sparks when struck against rock. Excavations at the site of Fort Michilimackinac turned up forty fire steel specimens, some oval, others with flat bottoms, dating from the French and British presence. Shipment records indicate these were often destined for use as gifts for Indians, with forty fire steels worth one trade gun; twenty gunflints equaled one of the fire starters. These would have made Indian life easier during extremely cold weather, when failure to start a fire could hold tragic consequences. But the iron kettle, another common item in the fur trade, was no less significant, for its portability brought greater freedom of movement to traveling clans; it also made possible extensive maple sugaring. Other European goods that became popular included cloth, earrings, looking glasses, burning glasses, wire, beads, and, especially, brandy.

Missionaries

Missionaries followed closely behind the traders at many sites. They were often controversial figures in the seventeenth and eighteenth centuries, and scholars still argue over their impact. Did they improve the lives of Indians or make them worse? Did they merely provide religious justification for European subjugation of the natives? Were they simply a fur trade auxiliary, or a moral counterbalance to the traders' power? Could they stand up to economic interests? —to French imperial interests?

The Society of Jesus, or Jesuits, became the dominant missionary order in New France, although members of the Recollet order such as Father Louis Hennepin were sometimes present also. Jesuits sought to convert the Indians without altering their customs. And so they became proficient in Indian languages, lived among the Indians in villages from the mouth of the St. Lawrence to the most distant posts in the west, and in the process left their mark on the development of the Wisconsin frontier. Taking over the Huron Mission which the Recollets had started in 1615, the Jesuits began to learn things about which most Frenchmen in the St. Lawrence settlements were ignorant: routes to the interior, locations of inland tribes, languages, peculiarities of different Indian groupings, tribal animosities and alliances.

A Jesuit established the first European settlement in Wisconsin when Father Claude Allouez began the La Pointe mission on Chequamegon Bay in 1665. Father Jacques Marquette succeeded

Allouez at La Pointe in 1669, staying until the mission was abandoned in 1671. But Allouez was not Wisconsin's first missionary: that was Father René Ménard, who was sent west in 1660 to work among the Indians along Lake Superior's southern shore and in the process became Wisconsin's first Christian martyr. Ménard disappeared in 1661 while trying to reach the starving Hurons, then living as refugees in northern Wisconsin. Ménard became separated from his traveling companion on their journey and was never found; a story heard long afterward claimed that some of his religious items were seen later in an Indian dwelling. Others left more tangible results: the first permanent mission house in Wisconsin was built on the lower Fox River in 1671–72 by Father Louis André and Father Allouez; the name of the city of De Pere (at the *Rapides des peres*, "rapids of the fathers") commemorates that institution.

Father Marquette is best known of the early Jesuits in the Northwest because of his journey with Louis Jolliet to the Mississippi in 1673. Frenchmen had been hearing of the great river for years before the decision was made to send Marquette and Jolliet westward to find it. The priest had been transferred from Chequamegon Bay to St. Ignace on the north edge of the Straits of Mackinac, and it was there that he and Jolliet began preparations in late 1672, leaving the following May 17 with five others in two canoes. They reached Green Bay and met with Menominees, who tried to get them to turn back by warning that the great river to the west "was full of horrible monsters, which devoured men and canoes together." The seven Frenchmen ignored their dissuasion and moved up the Fox, encountering Miamis, Mascoutins, and Kickapoos who welcomed them to their villages, the Miamis providing guides. At the portage where they crossed from the Fox to the Wisconsin rivers—a hike "of 2,700 paces," the priest dutifully reported—the guides turned back and the Frenchmen were on their own, soon floating down what Father Marquette called the "Meskousing" (he later wrote it as "Meskous," without explaining its meaning; this was evidently changed to "Mesconsin" by a writing error in his report; it was thereafter usually spelled "Ouisconsin" during the French period). He noted the significance of this geographic point in mid-Wisconsin: "Thus we left the waters flowing to Quebeq, four or five hundred leagues from here, to float on those that would thenceforward take us through strange lands."

The pair and their cohorts moved swiftly along the lower Wisconsin, and Marquette and Jolliet reached the Mississippi on June 17, 1673, becoming the first Europeans to enter the famous waterway from the north; the Spaniard Hernando de Soto had crossed the river near modern-day Memphis in 1541. The Frenchmen went as far south as the mouth of the Arkansas, at which point they concluded correctly that the Mississippi emptied into the Gulf of Mexico. Then they returned to Lake Michigan via the Illinois River and the Chicago portage. Father Marquette died in 1675 after making a return visit to the Illinois tribes.

Six missionaries served the *pays d'en haut* by that time, their westernmost outposts located at Indian villages on the upper Fox and Wolf rivers. But the Jesuits' hopes in the west were gradually fading, as attacks were launched against them by fur traders and government officials alike. The important mission at Sault Ste. Marie was closed in 1696 and the one at Michilimackinac by 1711; the latter reopened in 1715 but then served mainly French and mixed-bloods (*métis*), not Indians.

The missionaries reveal themselves through their writings to have been a complex lot. They often looked down upon the Indians, but just as frequently showed appreciation for tribal cultures and hospitality. Many apparently agreed with Father Hennepin's statement that "the Indian must be civilized before he can be Christianized." Hennepin had a long list of complaints about their uncivilized behavior—they "break wind before everyone regardless," they chewed lice, the women urinated in public, "they belch continually," they had no concept of washing plates or hands after contact with dogs or other unsanitary items, their wigwams were dirty.

Such behavior was not unknown among European peasants either, of course. And as unhappy as the missionaries were with Indian religious and sanitary practices, one of their major complaints centered not on something from Indian culture but a trade item which the French themselves had introduced: alcohol. A priest who lived for two years among the Illinois argued that alcohol "is among the Indians the greatest obstacle to Christianity, and the source of an infinite number of their most shocking crimes." One visitor told of an Indian woman who threw her baby into the fire while intoxicated; others described murder and various acts of violence by drunken Indians. It was the "horror of horrors" when natives became drunk.

And so the priests waged war against alcohol, receiving sporadic support from French authorities but unceasing opposition from the traders. French policies zigzagged, and after each tightening of restrictions on alcohol's use the traders rushed eastward to protest to the authorities. Without brandy, they successfully argued, the Indians would turn to the British to sell their furs and the French trade would fail. While French authorities made occasional threats against the use of alcohol in the fur trade, a consistent, effective policy was never developed—not by the French, nor the British, nor the Americans.

Coureurs de bois

Missionaries were preceded into every distant bay, every Indian village, by the independent traders known as *coureurs de bois*. They were later called *voyageurs*, but in the seventeenth century they were *coureurs de bois* and were held in disrepute by the authorities. New France required licenses to trade in the interior, but these independent traders went without them. They largely escaped capture, using the vastness of the Great Lakes country and the eagerness of Indians for European goods to become the new, very successful middlemen in the fur trade.

Coureurs de bois preceded Father Allouez at Chequamegon Bay in 1665, and when priests arrived at Sault Ste. Marie in 1670 they found twenty to twenty-five French traders already there. Two years later the deputy intendant for New France estimated they numbered 400 in the western regions; this rose to at least 800 by 1680 when the Crown offered them amnesty if they would return from the west and work in the St. Lawrence settlements. By 1701 it was estimated there were still 200 of them in the interior regions.

Opposition to the *coureurs de bois* grew. When the Montreal fur fairs began to decline because Indians no longer made the trip, merchants there complained that the illegal French traders were purchasing furs in the interior and circumventing the fairs. Missionaries objected to the Frenchmen taking Indian women with them to do their woodchopping and cooking and sharing their bed. Operating freely across the region, these traders escaped all regulations, whether proclaimed by the government, clergy, or monopoly companies.

The trading system, whether used by licensed or unlicensed traders, operated on credit. Leaving Montreal or some other central point (such as Michilimackinac) with French goods in ninety-pound bales, the traders headed west in canoes of five to eight men. Through the winter they lived with Indians or in French posts, and it was often two or three years before they returned to the St. Lawrence; some remained in the west for years. One report noted that each man received a daily allowance of one quart of corn, mashed and dried, with fat to cook it in as a sort of mush. Some accounts describe diets on canoe trips that also included wild rice, dried peas, and sun-dried meat strips called pemmican. Recent archeological excavations at Michilimackinac further reveal the overwhelming dependence of the French—in contrast to later British occupants—upon local plants and animals for their food.

New France's policies regarding these western traders underwent frequent changes. Officials soon realized that the *coureurs de bois* would detour to British trade centers any time they could earn more; the Indians shared this lack of allegiance to France. This fact was behind the French Crown's refusal to block the use of alcohol in the trade, realizing that Indians would seek out the British if necessary to obtain their brandy.

Green Bay became such a booming center for illegal *coureurs de bois* activity that in 1696 it was temporarily ordered closed by the Crown, along with posts at Michilimackinac and St. Joseph at the south end of Lake Michigan. All trading licenses for the west were canceled. Such efforts were doomed to failure, however, for the French needed the trade. Rankled by Crown orders, some of the illegal traders simply linked up with English or illegal French buyers. Soon the fur trade was spreading beyond the

Mississippi, up the Missouri River and west from Grand Portage on the north shore of Lake Superior. The law could not keep up with the *coureurs de bois* there.

Frenchmen and Canoes

More than other Europeans in North America during the seventeenth century, these French fur traders learned the ways of the frontier. For unlike most Spanish, Portuguese, Dutch, and British, the Frenchmen became like Indians, eating, traveling, fighting, even dressing in Indian fashion. They learned Indian languages and medicines, wore moccasins, gambled as did the Indians, discarded French customs and mores. And they adapted Indian devices for travel: snowshoes in the winter, canoes the rest of the year.

In traveling into Wisconsin and other areas of the *pays d'en haut* the French traders followed the routes of the Indians and relied on the birchbark canoe—a contrivance ideally suited to the waterways of the northern forest. Invented in the dim mists of prehistory, the canoe had evolved into such a state of perfection by the Europeans' arrival that its basic form has never been changed: sportsmen's aluminum canoes today follow the same principles as those of the Chippewas, Menominees, and other northern tribes.

The French learned very early that they would have to switch to the birchbark canoe. Jacques Cartier must have ruminated on this in 1534 when he saw Indians plying their easily maneuverable craft as they hunted seals at the mouth of the St. Lawrence. But a more dramatic lesson came sixty-five years later when Samuel de Champlain was able to compare the Indians' craft with his own and found French boats inadequate. While near Saguenay, Champlain saw some two hundred Indian canoes which went "extraordinarily well" and much faster than his own shallop. But the French leader became especially interested in their portability when he ascended the St. Lawrence near Montreal and confronted the rapids:

> We at once made ready our skiff, which had been constructed on purpose for passing the said rapid. . . . We had scarce gone three

hundred paces, when we were forced to get out, and some sailors had to get into the water to free our skiff. The savages' canoe passed easily.

Portaging impressed Champlain with the canoes' advantages again:

> But he who would pass [the rapids] must provide himself with the canoes of the savages, which a man can easily carry; for to transport a boat is a thing that cannot be done in the short time necessary to enable one to return to France to winter. . . . But with the canoes of the savages one may travel freely and quickly throughout the country, as well up the little rivers as up the large ones.

The enthusiasm for canoes shown by Champlain never waned among the French as they crossed North America. Everywhere in the north country they found waterways, and when they arrived in Wisconsin the rivers and lakes were numerous, mostly interlaced with short portages, and located perfectly to tap prime beaver areas. The canoeing French went everywhere—up narrow streams, through ponds created by beaver dams, down roaring chutes and even hugging the shores of Lakes Superior and Michigan, where they learned to protect themselves from the sudden squalls that could bring disaster.

As the French explored farther they realized that much of the northeastern quarter of Wisconsin drained into Lake Michigan and thence to the St. Lawrence and the Atlantic, while Lake Superior received waters from several small northern streams such as the Bois Brule, the Bad (Mauvais), and the Montreal. The rest of Wisconsin's waterways, however, flowed generally southward: the Namekagon and St. Croix moving through prime fur territory in the northwestern corner, the Chippewa cutting across north-central Wisconsin and its pinelands until its arrival at the foot of Lake Pepin, the Black likewise draining forest and savanna on its way to the Mississipi, and the Wisconsin rising in the northern highlands and twisting its way to the great river.

This was country made for the canoe. Because the canoe required the paper birch, it was a vessel used only by tribes living where large paper birch trees grew. The birch thrived within a broad ribbon of territory that wound across the North American continent, its leaves brilliantly displayed in autumn as a band of gold through the north country. For this reason the birchbark canoe was an integral part of everyday life among the Chippewas, Menominees, and Sacs; in fact, those studying the Sacs' pre-contact background have located it in northern areas because Sac tribesmen used canoes. Related tribes such as the Foxes, Miamis, and Kickapoo did not, and are presumed to have come from more southerly regions where the paper birch was unknown; they in turn did not adapt well to northern areas when forced to reside there, directing their hunting to the south and west and eventually moving south once again.

Indeed, Father Allouez noted the use or non-use of the canoe as a way to distinguish among the tribes gathered at Chequamegon Bay: the Foxes traveled by land, he wrote: "Canoes they do not use." They were similar to the Illinois who "are hunters and warriors, using bows and arrows, rarely muskets, and never canoes." When Father Marquette and Louis Jolliet journeyed out of the north country they encountered tribes farther down the Mississippi who were unfamiliar with their mode of transport, and at an Illinois camp the missionary wrote that they had embarked in view of the tribesmen, "who admire our little canoes, for they have never seen any like them." Similarly, when a British official later met a group of southern Potawatomis, he noted they were "totally ignorant of Bark canoes." Tribes from the south or west, originating in prairies, plains, or savannas, such as the Winnebagos, frequently made dugouts or used elm bark to cover their vessels. Father Hennepin noted a major advantage of the birchbark canoe when he was with the Santee Sioux on the Mississippi: "Their enemies had only pirogues or wooden canoes, which on account of their weight could not be paddled as fast as those of bark. Only the northern tribes have birch for making bark canoes."

Soon the French discovered that different types of canoes worked better in different conditions: the larger *canot de maître* or Montreal canoe might run thirty-three feet or more in length, with a four and one-half foot beam; but smaller types abounded, including the more maneuverable *canot du nord* or North canoe. ("What handicapped me was that I had no small canoe, and had to use my large canoe, which gave us a Great Deal of trouble," reported one trader.) The larger canoe worked best along the St.

Lawrence or on the Great Lakes; the smaller was the only kind that could safely ply most of Wisconsin's waters.

The Ottawas were an early source of canoes for the French, who purchased these as well as furs from the busy Indian middlemen. But soon the French established their own canoe factory, at Trois Rivières below Montreal, perhaps as early as 1700. Finding Indian sources unreliable, the French launched an enterprise that was producing twenty large canoes a year by 1751, each one thirty-six feet long, with a beam of five and one-half feet and a depth of thirty-three inches.

Few accounts of canoe construction remain from the colonial era. One of the best is that of visiting Swedish naturalist Peter Kalm, who watched construction of a canoe in 1749 at a time when they were becoming "daily more expensive":

> All the strips and ribs in them are made of white cedar . . .; the space between the latter varying in breadth between that of a palm and the width of three digits. The [length-wise] strips are placed so close to one another that one cannot see the birch-bark between them. All seams are held together by spruce roots or ropes made of the same material split. In all seams the birch-bark has been turned in double. The seams are made like a tailor's cross-stitch. In place of pitch they use melted resin on the outside seams. If there is a small hole in the birch-bark, resin is melted over it. The inner side of the bark or that nearest the tree always becomes the outer side of the boat. The whole canoe consists ordinarily of six pieces of birch-bark only, of which two are located underneath and two on either side. . . . [N]o one should set out in them without bringing resin and even birch-bark along.

These vessels were prone to leak. Father Hennepin was forced to bail furiously with a bark dish as the Sioux took him up the Mississippi; to repair this canoe and others the Indians had to travel four days downstream to obtain the proper birchbark. Indian women constructed frameworks for new canoes while the men searched for the bark.

Traveling from the St. Lawrence to the Upper Lakes required difficult paddling and portaging. Forty-five to forty-eight strokes to the minute was the usual paddling rate, although wind and river current obviously affected this considerably. Breaks from paddling were called "pipes" because smoking was the major activity during these respites, breaking up stretches that could range from thirty minutes to two hours. The larger Montreal canoes each transported sixty packs, or *pieces*, of European trade goods on the westward journey, which the eight canoemen hauled on their backs across portages in two ninety-pound packs apiece per carry. It took several trips back and forth to get all the packs and the canoe over a portage.

But portaging was not the only way to pass over a difficult rapids: going downstream, paddlers could partially unload their canoe and shoot through, or going upstream it could be unloaded and pulled over the rapids using ropes, without the need to transport it overland on the men's shoulders. Rest stops divided up the long portages, usually those over a half-mile long; these stops were called pauses or *posés*. The difficult uphill portage between the Bois Brule and St. Croix River in northwestern Wisconsin was done in two pauses; one easy portage was referred to as only "one-half pause" long. On the other hand, northern Wisconsin had one of the longest portages on record: the forty-five mile carry from Lac du Flambeau to reach the Montreal River flowing northward into Lake Superior. It had 122 *posés*; a trader reported that his crew did forty pauses the first day, but he stopped them at twenty the following day because "the men are complaining greatly of pains in their legs and it is necessary to spare them."

Noteworthy carries during the fur trade era, in addition to those at Portage between the Fox and Wisconsin, and those noted above, included the three-mile "Sioux Portage" between the Yellow and St. Croix (which saved thirteen miles of paddling on the latter), the *Portage de la Femme* ("woman's portage") on the upper St. Croix where the river was so shallow that women had to walk around it while men paddled through, and several along the Fox. An early nineteenth century traveler, Elizabeth Thérèse Baird, recalled the trip down the Fox after the men had reloaded their fur *piecés* at Portage:

> . . . then [they] returned for the boats, and reloading them would run down to the Big Chute, now Appleton. Here the boats again had to be unloaded, and the furs portaged around by the men. The boats,

however, made the journey down the swift water, which was called "jumping the rapids," and was an interesting sight if one had nerve enough to look on. The unloading was repeated at Grand Kaukauna; but at Rapides Croche and at Rapides des Peres, now DePere, the loads would be carried through, all of the men walking in the water to guide the boats and their valuable loads.

As the fur trade extended its reach and enlarged its volume, faster trips with bigger loads were attempted. Sails began to be used occasionally with the Montreal canoes on the Great Lakes. After winning his concession in 1678 to trade in buffalo robes, La Salle returned to New France and organized construction of the first sailing ship on the Great Lakes, the *Griffon*. Built at Cayuga Creek near Niagara Falls, the ship was launched on August 7, 1679, with La Salle and Father Hennepin on board. It reached Washington Island at the entrance to Green Bay on September 2. There the vessel was loaded with furs and ordered back to Niagara Falls while La Salle and Hennepin pursued other activities. The *Griffon* was never heard of again, the first sailing ship on the Great Lakes and the first lost on those waters.

As the seventeenth century ended, the French who had canoed halfway across North America to tap the wealth of furs in Wisconsin and other parts of the *pays d'en haut*, and the Indians with whom they traded, were changed peoples. They were learning to use each other's goods and adapting to each other's ways. But the French were also attempting to impress the native inhabitants with their own greatness and superiority. Father Allouez, in his grandiloquent exhortation at the 1671 pageant at the Sault, sought to awe the tribesmen by comparing the French king, his vast armada and the land he ruled, with the accomplishments of the tribes living about the Great Lakes:

> Your canoes hold only four or five men—or, at the very most, ten or twelve. Our ships in France hold four or five hundred, and even as many as a thousand. . . . You count yourselves rich when you have ten or twelve sacks of corn, some hatchets, glass beads, kettles, or other things of that sort. He has towns of his own, more in number than you have people in all these countries five hundred leagues around; while in each town there are warehouses containing enough

hatchets to cut down all your forests, kettles to cook all your moose, and glass beads to fill all your cabins.

The Indians gathered for the pageant were reportedly impressed.

But if the Indians of the Great Lakes marveled at these tales of French greatness, they might also have noted that the frontier French now dressed, ate, traveled, and even spoke in Indian ways. They might have pondered which way of life was more suited to the Upper Lakes. A ship holding 500 men, after all, was useless going along a stream in the northern fur trade, but a canoe manned by four or five worked wonderfully. And a handful of wild rice could sustain a man for a long time, without recourse to foodstuffs in those warehouses in France.

The pageant at the Sault in 1671 helped open the frontier era across Wisconsin and the region, but it was soon apparent that the two cultures were coming together in ways the French authorities may not have realized or welcomed. It was one thing to issue orders from Paris or Quebec; but there was apt symbolism in the fact that a proclamation might not be heard over the roar of the Sault's waters. France's claim of sovereignty could be effective, after all, only if it could be enforced—but enforcement would be difficult across the *pays d'en haut*. This was quickly grasped by the *coureurs de bois* as well as the Indians, who found increasing opportunities to investigate the trade goods of other Europeans. Soon Englishmen were crossing the Appalachians and entering that vast area of midcontinent which the St. Lawrence had opened much earlier to the men of New France. The resulting competition entwined the Wisconsin fur trade with the struggles of Europe's Great Powers.

4.

AN ARENA FOR INTERNATIONAL COMPETITION

The Frontier Transformed

If the seventeenth century left many Indians bewildered as the French penetrated the Great Lakes region, the eighteenth century drew Wisconsin and its fur trade into the international arena with such force that the French, English, Americans, and Indians often seemed unsure of which course to pursue. One of the British traders who witnessed the turmoil of competing national claims later admitted to a friend something of the human toll exacted by events in the Upper Lakes during that century. "I always lived in hopes but I am at last beginning to despair," John Lawe wrote from Michilimackinac in 1824. "[T]he old times is no more[,] that pleasant reign is over & never to return any more[.] I am a fraid and [un]certain in this Country any more." And Lawe lamented, in phrases of one who has seen his way of life passed by, "I am the only unfortunate fellow of those that came in this Country at the same time with me."

Lawe had witnessed the final stages of the transformation of the Upper Lakes into a frontier region no longer controlled by orders from Europe, but after 1783 theoretically—and only theoretically—under the domination of the new United States. This was the last of the governmental changes that occurred sporadically throughout the century, paralleled by shifts also in the fur trade—from an individualistic operation into a highly organized big business dominated by a few large firms, with thousands of employees spanning the continent, warring with competitors and governments. For the fur trade was being thrust into the crucible of international rivalry, and while traders often faced Indian challenges, they were now the targets more frequently of governmental regulation. In this way, the eighteenth century fur trade in Wisconsin followed what was to become a typical frontier pattern.

The British Appear

Britain was at the center of the upheavals. As early as 1686 reports were heard of occasional British fur traders reaching the Upper Lakes, some even entering the Green Bay district in an attempt to trade with the Foxes. The Indians quickly learned that the British gave more for their furs and usually had better trade goods. Unhampered by the rigid controls of the French, free as well from monopolies based on royal favor, Britain's independent traders who roved the North American interior also were unhampered by the stiff French tariff of one-fourth of all furs exported. Englishmen and Scotsmen began to thrive in this environment uncluttered by legal restrictions. To the north their nation's Hudson's Bay Company—founded back in 1670—now began to reach into prime fur-producing areas, using the advantages inherent in a heavily financed organization.

French policies were often wavering and inconsistent in the face of this growing challenge. The 1696 French ban on trading in the interior, and orders to *coureurs de bois* as well as to legal traders to evacuate the west, were incompetently enforced but nevertheless brought distress to many tribes and were rescinded in 1700. The abandonment of western fur posts was partially reversed the following year with creation of new French trading and military forts at Detroit as well as at Kaskaskia, a new settlement along the Mississippi in the Illinois country. These were at least partly aimed at blocking British expansion.

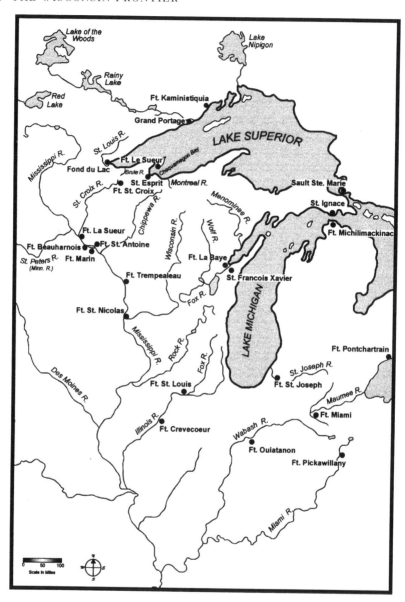

The French in the Great Lakes Country — The French penetrated the North American interior early, advancing in canoes up the St. Lawrence and using the Ottawa River as a cutoff to connect with Lake Huron, going from there into Lakes Michigan and Superior. French military posts were anchored on the region's rivers and at strategic points on the lakes. MAP ADAPTED BY JILL FREUND THOMAS AND MICHAEL MAST FROM ALICE E. SMITH, *The History of Wisconsin. Volume I: From Exploration to Statehood* (STATE HISTORICAL SOCIETY OF WISCONSIN, 1973).

After the 1713 Treaty of Utrecht gave both France and Britain equal rights of trade with the Indians, the French reopened Michilimackinac in 1715, Fort St. Francis at Green Bay in 1717, La Pointe near a Chippewa village on Chequamegon Bay in 1718, and Fort Beauharnois on the west side of Lake Pepin on the Mississippi in 1727, among other new posts. A fort was also built at Kaministiquia, on Lake Superior's north shore, for entry into the Canadian northwest trading regions. La Pointe was strategically located to watch over the Chippewas, the western end of Lake Superior, and connections to the St. Croix and other southward-flowing streams. The post on Lake Pepin—soon moved upriver on the Wisconsin side—became crucial to growing contacts between Green Bay and areas controlled by the Sioux. Licensed fur trading was underway by 1720 at these points as well as at Green Bay, which was rapidly strengthened into a formidable post: when a new commander arrived in 1721 he found a strongly fortified fort with pickets thirty feet high.

Other Changes

New France's attempt to remove fur traders from the interior, though ultimately reversed, occurred at a time when French missionaries were leaving also. They would never appear again in the numbers and activity seen in the famous seventeenth century campaigns of such priests as Allouez and Marquette. Allouez's 1671 mission at the Rapides des Peres burned in 1689 and was not rebuilt; nevertheless, a priest was present at the nearby Green Bay post from 1701 until at least 1734.

The missionaries left no permanent Christian population behind in Wisconsin, but they had served as real or potential checks on the excesses of French traders, particularly the *coureurs de bois.* The eighteenth century saw scattered attempts by governments to protect Indians from the traders, but government agents were even scarcer than missionaries at the backwoods trading sites. If the missionaries were largely ineffective, their efforts stand in stark contrast to the profit-driven activities of the Frenchmen, Britons, and Americans who arrived after them.

The French determined to launch vast changes in their mid-continent empire. The foundations for Louisiana were laid in

1699, with construction of a French fort at Biloxi on the Gulf Coast as part of a plan to dominate the Mississippi Valley. This would create a potential downriver outlet for furs from Wisconsin and the rest of New France's Upper Lakes region.

Despite the failures of its earlier attempts to restrict trade, France struggled sporadically to apply licenses and canoe limits, succeeding only in confusing its Indian cohorts and angering its traders. In 1742 the Crown again revoked the licensing system; monopoly rights for trading at different posts would now be auctioned off. But the monopoly system proved ineffective as well, for Indians were angered at the lack of competing buyers, and they turned again to illegal traders waiting in the woods. No one would bid for the Green Bay lease in 1746 because of the condition of the trade there. In 1749 New France went back to using individual licenses for traders and abandoned the system of monopolies at different posts, but some posts were still awarded to court favorites. The conclusion was inescapable: the French government's search for a workable policy had failed. In the process it had exasperated both Indians and traders and weakened its grip on the Upper Lakes.

A new burst of activity then appeared in the Wisconsin trade at mid-century, however. Pierre Paul Marin was named French commander at Green Bay, while his son Joseph became head of the Chequamegon post. Between them they stimulated trading activity, quickly raising the number of traders in the Green Bay district to 190 (the total stood at six in 1738). Paul Marin constructed another fort on the west side of Lake Pepin, named Fort La Jonquiere after New France's new governor-general; this was to funnel the growing Sioux trade through Green Bay. To bring in more furs, the largest trading outfit ever dispatched westward was brought to Green Bay; the pelts attracted by this outpouring of trade goods brought the French profits equal to half a million dollars annually for 1749–51.

Frenchmen and Indians Adapt

As they sought out furs in isolated backwoods camps, canoed and worked with the native inhabitants, Frenchmen in the interior continued to acquire skills of many sorts from the Indians. Increasingly they learned not only from being around Indian trappers, but from marrying into Indian families. This was partly a result of the early failure of French companies to obey government orders to emigrate several hundred colonists a year. Orphan girls were carried over from France by the Crown in the seventeenth century, but these *filles du Roi* were quickly married off to Frenchmen along the St. Lawrence and did not make it to the interior.

Lacking French women—only one is recorded in midcontinent during this period, Pierre LeSueur's wife, who came to the Illinois Country around 1695—the *coureurs de bois* turned for companionship and help to Indian women. In doing so they eventually created a new people, the *métis*, or "mixed" people of the Northwoods. Others would call them "mixed-bloods," or more commonly, "half-breeds," and their history took strange twists in Canada and the United States over the next three hundred years. The sharp rise in interracial marriages in the 1690s may in part have been an attempt by illegal traders to establish links to the tribes when French government trade restrictions were worsening. British and Americans would later choose Indian wives also, discovering as had the French that these liaisons were usually not opposed by the tribes: marriages were seen as contracts between groups, so an Indian marriage to a European could help the tribe in its trade dealings. It could also, of course, help the white trader.

From these unions came the *métis*, with feet in both Indian and French worlds, their lives centered on the fur trade which they soon came to dominate. Familiar with both Indian and European ways while enjoying the support of their nearby Indian relatives, knowledgeable about languages as well as intricacies of the trade, the *métis* had crucial advantages over outsiders. One historian estimates that half of all European-American traders had Indian wives; in 1970 an eminent Canadian biologist asserted that 40 percent of French-Canadians had Indian ancestors.

The influence went the other way also. The *métis* provided a human contact, an entry point for European goods and customs to gain acceptance by tribes of Wisconsin and the Great Lakes, and quickly European items were being used for more than trapping and hunting. Gift-giving, already a fixture of Indian life, became engrafted onto relations between the Indians and Europeans and, later, the Americans. Gifts were given to "cover the dead," as part of the mourning process, and came to be expected whenever Frenchmen showed up in a village. A Jesuit missionary realized this:

> Presents among these peoples despatch all the affairs of the country. They dry up tears; they appease anger; they open the doors of foreign countries; they deliver prisoners; they bring the dead back to life; one hardly ever speaks or answers except by presents!

The importance of gifts was revealed in the journal of Joseph Marin, named French commandant (succeeding his father) at Green Bay in 1753, most notably when he visited local tribes:

> Aug. 23 (with the "Folle Avoine," or Menominees): "After they paid me their compliments, I gave them the gifts for their village. . . ."
> Aug. 24–26 (at Fort LaBaye, with Menominees, Chippewas, and Ottawas): "I gave them a gift commensurate with their number. . . . I covered their dead and tended their father[s'] mourning as usual."
> Sept. 5 (at the Winnebago village): "After answering them on the fine reception they gave me, I gave them the usual presents and told them the news. . . . Then I sent for the war chief and spoke to him alone. I gave him some gifts for his young man and told him I didn't want him leaving to do bad business. . . ."
> Sept. 12 (at the Sac village on the lower Wisconsin River): "After smoking the peacepipes I went to camp across from their village in the usual place. I sent for the few remaining men and gave them gifts."

Marin's experiences pointed to potential trouble ahead: gift-giving was getting out of hand, troubling a distant Versailles regime that faced mounting deficits. The Indians now expected gifts regularly; these were one of the costs of loyalty—an expectation that would bedevil French and British officials alike. True, sometimes they merely craved excitement, as with fireworks dis-

plays put on by the French, or new devices: this was the case
when the Green Bay commander warned his French chief that
Indians were on their way east for a visit—"If you could find it
fitting to show the magic lantern to my Indians, I would be really
indebted to you, for I as much as promised them you would show
them that kindness." Such incidents make clear that a large pro-
portion of the French gifts had no connections to specific Indian
actions.

The other side of the gift process was that the tribes' dependence on European items was mounting throughout the eighteenth century. Indians generally acquired French goods not to
revolutionize their lives, however, but to make accustomed tasks
easier. Iron hoes were preferable to clamshells; iron kettles worked
better and were more transportable than those made of clay.
Recent archeological work at a Huron site at St. Ignace, Michigan, has found that the village's residents at the close of the seventeenth century used many French goods without becoming dependent on them, just as they incorporated Christian elements
such as Jesuit rings without becoming Christians. Both Indian
and French pipes were found, as well as European pots and some
tools; French tools were used to carve bone bracelets, and it was
clear that these Hurons still ate traditional foods prepared in
customary ways. Overall, evidence from such sites shows that
neither the Indians' technological nor their food patterns were
fundamentally altered. Further, status within a tribe did not adapt
easily to these impulses from Europe: the Indians simply did not
accept the Europeans' view that tangible wealth could raise status, and they berated the missionaries for the lack of sharing
among the French.

It is nevertheless clear that the use of European tools by Great
Lakes tribes was increasing dramatically, until by 1800 nearly
all tools and implements employed by Upper Great Lakes Indians came from Europe. New implements such as spring-operated animal traps, construction tools, corn mills, and burning
glasses, as well as personal ornaments, all became prominent in
tribal inventories. French words crept into Indian languages as
well, and "*boju!*" became an Algonquian greeting after the French

"bonjour"; similarly, the French word for English, "anglais," can be traced in the Chippewas' *shaganash*, while the Chippewas by 1778 were calling a coat *kapotewian* after the French *capote*.

Mixing was proceeding in many aspects of daily life. Archeologists have found that Indians often used their own materials to copy European goods, creating such items as shoulder yokes for carrying heavy burdens, lead bullet casts, and clothing. They also mixed European and native goods together, attaching their own frames to hand mirrors, and decorating imported clothing with Indian beads and dyed porcupine quills. These goods could be a mixed blessing, of course, for the arrival of European muskets presumably displaced skilled archers, who would have to develop new skills. Eventually a reaction appeared, and tribal conservatives began to preach a return to traditional ways. Seeds of this development, which affected many Wisconsin tribes, likely rose in part from the frustrations of those who saw the need for their skills being eliminated by European goods.

The eighteenth century also witnessed shifts in the locations of Wisconsin tribes. Some, such as the Kickapoos, Mascoutins, Potawatomis, and Miamis, left Wisconsin to move south and would return only for hunting or battles. The Sacs and Foxes left the Fox River Valley around 1734, and appeared later along the Wisconsin River until settling below Prairie du Chien on the Mississippi.

The decline of the beaver also drove tribes to seek new areas within Wisconsin. Hunting and trapping, now necessary for the Indians to continue purchasing European goods, went on as long as game was available; there appear to have been no deliberate conservation efforts. As game grew scarcer the Chippewas were finally drawn out of the northern forests, into the savannas and more open areas along the Chippewa, St. Croix, and Wisconsin rivers. The Menominees gave up their earlier dependence upon fisheries and sought pelts, urged on by traders who tried to push them and other tribes into the fur-rich areas of western Wisconsin.

As the fur trade moved westward up the St. Lawrence and into the Upper Lakes it brought an unwelcome visitor into the

Indian villages: disease. Europeans regularly carried diseases into a continent whose inhabitants had not developed immunities to them. On one French ship arriving in 1663, sixty of the 225 passengers had died during the crossing. Typhus and other outbreaks occurred on vessels landing in the St. Lawrence in 1659, 1663, 1665, and 1670. Smallpox proved to be the worst killer as it spread to Great Lakes tribes, but other diseases were also among the Europeans' imports: whooping cough, measles, influenza, typhoid, diphtheria, colds, chicken pox, scarlet fever, tuberculosis, and streptococcal infections.

The Green Bay region was hit by epidemics in 1666, 1676, and 1683. After their initial meeting with Allouez in 1634, the Winnebagos appeared less frequently on the stage of Wisconsin history for decades, their numbers finally so insignificant that the Jesuits did not bother to learn their language. La Potherie explains that after drawing together into one village with 4,000 to 5,000 men, the Winnebagos were leveled by disease, "and the exhalations from the rotting corpses caused great mortality. They could not bury the dead, and were soon reduced to fifteen hundred men." During the Montreal treaty sessions in 1701 that involved some 700 Indians, those arriving from Michilimackinac reported an epidemic raging at home, and *la maladie* swept Indian camps near Montreal as well. In the early 1750s the Upper Lakes country was hit again by smallpox, with Miami and Ottawa chiefs among the victims; when the French and their Indian allies attacked Fort William Henry on Lake George in New York in 1757, the unwitting Menominees and Potawatomis entered the British fort's smallpox ward and carried the disease home. When Menominees met the new British commander at Green Bay in 1762 they admitted having lost 300 warriors to the disease. Jean Baptiste Cadotte, who traded at La Pointe and other areas along the south shore of Lake Superior, wrote in 1783 to a British official and summed up the "news from Lake Superior" with one sentence: "All the Indians from fond du Lac,[1]

---

1. This "fond du lac" refers to the site of Duluth-Superior, known today as "head of the lakes"—not to the Wisconsin city of that name on Lake Winnebago.

rainy Lake, Sandy lake, and surrounding places are dead from smallpox."

Seemingly contradicting such reports, modern anthropologists have argued that most Wisconsin tribes did not decline precipitously despite these ravages. Only the Illinois and Miamis fell sharply in numbers among tribes in the Upper Lakes. Epidemics generally hit with less impact after the mid-eighteenth century; immunities may have developed among the tribes by then.

Indian Wars

Disease was not the only cause of large-scale Indian deaths, however, for wars between tribes continued to take a toll during the eighteenth century. Two long-running disputes stand out both for their ferocity and duration: Chippewa-Sioux warfare, which erupted repeatedly despite frantic French efforts to patch up a peace treaty, and the bitter battles of the Foxes against other tribes, which usually drew in the French and were sometimes instigated by them. Eventually the French sought total destruction of the Foxes.

Chippewa vs. Sioux

The Chippewas and the Sioux became competitors in the seventeenth century as Chippewa bands moved into northern Wisconsin, territory that had long been home to many of the Santee Sioux. Earlier, when the Chippewas were located farther to the east, beyond Sault Ste. Marie, clashes with the Sioux were apparently rare. The Sioux dominated large parts of western and central Wisconsin, and because of this frequently challenged eastern Wisconsin tribes seeking to extend their hunting grounds. Neither the Sioux nor the Chippewas were a unified tribe; each was linked across scattered villages by language and culture, joining mainly for warfare or treaties.

The arriving Chippewas battled the Sioux in their traditional Wisconsin hunting grounds, and when this strife imperiled the fur trade, the French brokered Sioux-Chippewa treaties in 1679 and 1695. But France's decision to open up posts along the Upper Mississippi—such as on Prairie Island, just below the St. Croix River's mouth—upset the underlying conditions by giving the Sioux direct contact with the French. This removed their need for Chippewa middlemen, and by eliminating a reason for cooperation the door was opened for warfare.

There were frequent quarrels, raids, and battles over the years despite the attempts at peacemaking. Major struggles began in the 1730s when the Sioux and Chippewas came into open territorial conflict that involved control of the fur trade, contacts with the French, and revenge for past wrongs. The spark that finally terminated the earlier French-brokered peace flared in 1736 when a Sioux war party near Lake of the Woods in northern Minnesota slaughtered twenty-one Frenchmen; Chippewas retaliated by attacking the Sioux at Lake Pepin. The new wave of warfare across Wisconsin and Minnesota would endure for more than a century. Chippewas became allied with two tribes northwest of Lake Superior, the Crees and Assiniboins, and turned broad regions of Wisconsin into a war zone, where anyone would hunt at his peril.

A large tract of western Wisconsin was virtually unoccupied in the latter half of the eighteenth century. Jonathan Carver, traveling up the Chippewa River in 1767, passed the Red Cedar branch and reported that "the track between the two branches of this river is termed the Road of War between the Chipéway and Naudowessie [Sioux] Indians." The contested areas generally ran along the ecological transition between the heavy northern forest of Wisconsin and Minnesota and the savanna–mixed deciduous districts lying to the south; game was abundant there because the overlapping conditions were favorable to many different animals.

Damage to the fur trade from this warfare was extensive. French officials in 1750 instructed the commander at Green Bay to bring about peace between the Green Bay region's tribes and the Sioux, a move "essential for the good of trade and the safety of the French." And when the British became dominant twenty years later, Montreal traders urged Britain to divide the area between the two tribes so outsiders could enter. A 1775 attempt at a treaty failed, and a 1787 session at Mackinac led only to exclusion from the zone of all tribes except the Menominees. Through these years of forays, raids, attacks, and reprisals, the Chippewas gradually expanded across Wisconsin and into Minnesota, while the Sioux moved west, vacating districts where they had once been dominant.

Augustin Grignon, a *métis* trader interviewed in 1857, recalled his family's tales of the viciousness of the Sioux-Chippewa struggle and how the French survived. Sometime before 1784, he said, two traders fought with Chippewas on the lower rapids of the Chippewa River, fending them off and getting away with the scalps of two warriors. They "hastened to the Sioux, and made the two Chippewa scalps serve as a recommendation to the favor and good graces of the Sioux. . . . The traders were very kindly received by the Sioux, who complimented them with presents, and patronized them liberally." Soon afterward one of the men fought with a Sioux, killed him and carried his scalp to the Chippewa, "which he made use of in securing the friendship, favor and patronage of his new friends."

The Fox Wars

As important as the Sioux-Chippewa struggle was in the colonial era, broader changes were set in motion by the ferocity of the Fox wars. More than other tribal antagonisms, the Fox challenge was aimed at the very heart of what New France was seeking to accomplish in the New World; this competition had to be met if the French empire was to expand. France based its abilities to control the Great Lakes region upon its skills in drawing Indian tribes together in alliances, using gifts, forts, missionaries, explorers, and government controls to mediate the rifts and jealousies that could upset operations. In the east, the threat to French activity came primarily from the Iroquois, but this was seemingly ended in 1700 and 1701 at Montreal treaty sessions joined also by the Chippewas, Potawatomis, Sacs, Winnebagos, Menominees, Kickapoos, Mascoutins, and Foxes. France seemed at the brink of a new era of peace for its traders in the *pays d'en haut.*

But the Foxes seemed reluctant at the Montreal meetings, refusing to bow fully to French controls. There was some reason for this. Foxes had been cool to the French from their earliest contacts, and Father Allouez found in the early 1670s that the Foxes still talked of maltreatment of their tribesmen on an earlier visit to Montreal—when they were so poorly dealt with that "now they were determined to advenge themselves for the bad treatment they had received in the French settlements." They also complained of some traders' actions. As a result, Foxes formed a military group whose main purpose, Father Allouez learned, was in "treating our Frenchmen who were in these regions in the same way as the Soldiers at our French settlements had treated them." After a Fox attack, a tribal spokesmen told some Frenchmen that "the Soldiers had not used the French so ill as they themselves had been used by the latter at our settlements."

From these beginnings, nurtured by insults and maltreatment whose severity can only be guessed at from surviving records, the French and the Foxes veered steadily toward a clash that held heavy risks for each. France's danger lay in upsetting its relations with the tribes as the British were becoming more active in the region. For the Foxes, the risk was in confronting an opponent armed with the latest weaponry, who could operate on a broad scale and could count on support from many allied tribes.

The British threat, though still in the distance, was real. As early as the 1680s, Iroquois contacts had convinced the Foxes that trade links through the Five Nations to the British might be beneficial. By that time the Foxes were restricting French fur traders in their areas, and they harried travelers along the Fox-Wisconsin route. French officials were furious. Father Jean de St. Cosme was forced to turn south on Lake Michigan to the Chicago portage in 1698, explaining that his detour was required because the Foxes "who live on that little river that one ascends on leaving the bay to reach the Ouiskonsin, will not allow any persons to pass lest they might go to the Sioux, with whom they are at war, and consequently have already pillaged several Frenchmen who tried to go that way."

A French plan aimed primarily at blocking British entry ito the region led to a major clash with the Foxes. Fort Ponchartrain was established at Detroit in 1699 to draw tribes to the area to undergo civilizing—and, in the process, to cement their loyalty to France and help bar the British from the Upper Lakes. The plan gained adherents slowly, but eventually the Hurons and Ottawas accepted the invitation, followed by a group of Chippewas, Potawatomis, and Miamis, among others. Finally, in 1710, some 1,000 Foxes from the Green Bay area also journeyed to Detroit, joined by small numbers of Kickapoos and Mascoutins.

The Foxes quickly angered the new French leader, Charles Regnault, Sieur DuBuisson, who charged they "brought nothing but disorder"—acting haughty, stealing livestock, talking openly of trading with the British. Feuds between the tribes escalated suddenly in 1712 when news came that a group of Ottawas had attacked a nearby Mascoutin village. The Foxes, closely allied with the Mascoutins, became agitated and seized several Ottawa women and set fire to the Ottawa village. The French soon joined with other tribes in May 1712 to slay about 1,000 men, women, and children, nearly all the Fox-Mascoutin group.

Official reports of the 1712 Detroit clash reveal French antagonism toward the Fox had deepened; the end result at Detroit was in line with French desires. In the Upper Lakes region the Foxes, like the beaver, had become fair game. A Jesuit missionary stated flatly at the time that the French had joined with the Ottawas to destroy the Foxes. Sieur DuBuisson's official report quoted Indians in council as stating "that they knew the desire of the governor to exterminate the Foxes"; adding elsewhere, "Just as soon as the siege was over, the allies set out for Quebec to get the reward which they say, Sir, that you promised them."

The Foxes who made it back to Wisconsin began attacking the French and their Indian allies over a broad area, extending as far south as the Illinois village near Lake Peoria. The fur trade was stifled. Expecting a French invasion, the Foxes drew together during the summer of 1715 into a large village overlooking the south shore of Little Lake Butte des Morts, on the Upper Fox River southwest of Green Bay. Their fortifications included "triple oak stakes" with an interior ditch; corn and dried meat were cached, arrows prepared, lead and gunpowder collected.

The attack came in 1716, led by Louis de La Porte de Louvigny. With more than 800 soldiers, *coureurs de bois* (given amnesty), merchants, and Indian allies, the main force traveled from

Montreal via Michilimackinac in late June or early July, in an armada that included two small brass cannons, a brass grenade mortar, and 100 grenades. After four days' siege, the Foxes proposed a peace settlement which was accepted: prisoners would be returned, the Foxes would again participate in the trade and through this make good the costs of the French military expedition. Further, the Foxes would make peace with all tribes allied to the French. Six Fox hostages were taken away to assure fulfillment.

As if nothing had happened, the Foxes quickly seized control of the routes to the west again, even winning domination over the Illinois River in 1722 with an attack that drove the Illinois from Starved Rock to their villages below Cahokia on the Mississippi. Years later, Augustin Grignon recalled his family's stories of Fox control over the rivers in those years:

> The Outagamies or Foxes . . . made it a point, whenever a trader's boat approached, to place a torch upon the bank, as a signal for the traders to come ashore, and pay the customary tribute which they exacted from all. To refuse this tribute, was sure to incur the displeasure of the Foxes, and robbery would be the mildest punishment inflicted. This haughty, imperious conduct of the Foxes, was a source of no little annoyance to the traders, who made their complaints to the Commandants of the Western posts, and in due time these grievances reached the ears of the Governor of Canada.

More than Quebec officialdom was angered, for opposition to the Foxes was also rising among other tribes. The Winnebagos joined the French for a 1729 attack, and after the Foxes tried a siege against the Winnebago in 1730 the Foxes were isolated: no French-allied tribes supported them, and they could no longer count on finding refuge among the Sioux or the Iowas to the west. Their former allies were now silent.

Believing they might still find a home among the Senecas in New York, some 900 Fox men, women, and children fled southward into Illinois in the summer of 1730 on the first stage of an eastward march; however, they were soon pushed even farther south onto the prairies by the Cahokia of the Illinois confederacy. They were surrounded in August 1730 by a combined force of French and warriors from many tribes across the region—Cahokia, Potawatomi, Kickapoo, Mascoutin, Sac, Miami, Piankashaw, and Wea. Trying to escape during a thunderstorm, some 300 Fox men and boys were caught and slaughtered; the attackers then turned on the women and children. Some Foxes were taken prisoner; several escaped through the tall prairie grass. The tribe was crushed.

French officials cheered. One of them argued, "This will give peace to the colony and will increase its commerce" because other Indians could now hunt in territories they had avoided "for fear of these fearsome enemies." He also foresaw trade opening to the Sioux, an end to warfare around Green Bay, even "a general peace" over the entire region.

The Foxes refused to disappear, however. Several tribes took pity and released Fox prisoners and slaves from earlier battles, allowing the tribe to begin rebuilding. In succeeding years the French made several more attempts to exterminate the tribe, including sending some of its leaders into slavery in South America. The reduced tribe then split, some joining Sacs moving into Iowa, others going to northwestern Illinois, the rest eventually settling in a village on the lower Wisconsin River. By 1750 most were living near Rock Island on the Mississippi, where their rebirth began as allies of the Sacs.

French actions in these years of turmoil did not bode well for the future. French ineffectiveness had been demonstrated repeatedly, and other tribes could clearly observe the way commercial desires drove French policies. The government's earlier approach of mediating between all Upper Great Lakes tribes had reversed: France's 1712 decision to side with anti-Fox groups—even goading them into their attacks on the Foxes at Detroit—marked a new direction. Certainly the French officials' desire to exterminate a single tribe, and their failure to accomplish this, left a record of weakness as well as a warning to other Indians. And because of the continuous warfare in Wisconsin, French traders began to turn south to the Ohio River, entering into direct competition with the stream of westward-moving British and Americans. The stage was being set in the North American interior for an international war.

International Competition

France vs. Great Britain

The French and Indian War, also known as the Seven Years' War, was an international conflict fought in Africa, India, the Caribbean, and Europe, as well as in North America. Regardless of international intrigue and settling European scores, the basic fact involving North America was that British colonists were pushing relentlessly into mid-continent in the first half of the eighteenth century, into regions with no accepted boundary between British and French claims. After New York's governor built Fort Oswego in 1725 on Lake Ontario, east of the French fort at Niagara, competition for furs in the Lower Lakes became intense. This worsened in 1748 when English and Virginia leaders created the Ohio Company and promptly obtained a royal grant of 500,000 acres in the Ohio Valley. Other British companies won large grants on land also claimed by France. To keep the record straight on its possessions, and to counter the flurry of British fort construction, the French sent a delegation down the Ohio in 1749, installing lead markers at river mouths to establish their claims. Lead plates did not deter Britain, which was awakening to its numerical advantage: France, which had emigrated fewer than 11,000 colonists into New France from its founding until 1763, could count a colonial population of only 70,000 by that year; the British colonies numbered 1.5 million.

But the Indians were overwhelmingly loyal to France in the interior and this helped counterbalance Britain's population advantage. A key figure in this developing struggle was a young *métis* from the Upper Lakes who was to become one of the key figures of Wisconsin life by the end of the eighteenth century: Charles de Langlade, born in Michilimackinac of a French father and an Ottawa mother, later France's Green Bay agent and progenitor of generations of fur trade and business leaders in Wisconsin. It was Langlade who convinced Detroit authorities in 1752 to let him lead an attack on the British trading post at Pickawillany in northwestern Ohio. Langlade collected some 240 Indian allies and routed the British and their Indian cohorts.

Langlade's bold move drew Indian tribes such as the Miami and Huron back into the French fold and expelled the British from the Ohio Valley for several years. The official start of the Seven Years' War would await further instigation by the two powers, however. In 1754 the French began to construct Fort Duquesne at the forks of the Ohio (eventually it would become Pittsburgh), and rebuffed a challenge from a British force led by a young Virginian, George Washington; a year later a larger British force under General Edward Braddock was slaughtered nine miles short of Duquesne. Langlade's 1,500 Indians—largely drawn from Wisconsin and Upper Michigan—were important in the follow-up attack that pinned down Braddock's army. The following year in Europe, Frederick the Great's army invaded Saxony and *La Guerre de Sept Ans* officially opened with the great powers maneuvering in different parts of the globe. In North America, the British strengthened their alliance by conferring upon the Iroquois the status of British subjects.

The Upper Lakes would play a small role in this clash of nations, although control of the distant frontier was one of many goals of the war. Wisconsin's posts were abandoned except for a small force kept at Green Bay, but in 1759 as the tide of war turned against France, Langlade was again ordered to raise the Wisconsin Indians and come to the defense of the Versailles regime. His force arrived at Quebec just as the climactic struggle between Montcalm and Wolfe was underway; a year later he was also present as the French were again defeated in the final battle at Montreal.

The French captain at Michilimackinac fled in October 1760, taking his 132 troops first to Green Bay and then into the Fox-Wisconsin link to the Mississippi, the first stage of a long journey to New Orleans. Freezing weather forced the troops to stop before reaching the great river, however, and they spent one more winter in the *pays d'en haut*, camped with Sacs and Foxes near the Rock River. This was Wisconsin's last contact with official France. Charles de Langlade, however, remained at Michilimackinac, where he was left in charge until the British arrived to take over the post in September 1761.

In the 1763 peace treaty France gave up Wisconsin along with virtually all of its claims in North America. The fur trade had again been a crucial factor behind a frontier conflict and Wiscon- sin's Indians were on the losing side. Spain, which had sided with France, was given Louisiana by France as compensation for its other losses in the war.

Early Years of British Rule

The British entered the Great Lakes region with some uncertainties. The Chippewa Chief Minavavana at Michilimackinac warned the incoming English trader Alexander Henry, "Englishman, although you have conquered the French, you have not yet conquered us! We are not your slaves. These lakes, these woods and mountains were left to us by our ancestors. They are our inheritance; and we will part with them to none." Faced with this Indian coolness, if not opposition, and fully aware that the interior regions were still home to numerous French fur traders, the British strained to enunciate policies that would help them gain full control.

Many British officials were unhappy with what they knew and discovered of French frontier policy, a system one official called not "worthy of our imitation." Accordingly, the new rulers ordered that trade was to be carried out at posts under military command, by traders holding British licenses or passports, rather than under the more recent French system of granting monopolies to royal favorites. Green Bay was among the five Western posts opened—the others were Michilimackinac, Detroit, Ouiatanon on the Wabash, and Kaministiquia on the north shore of Lake Superior.

Among the French policies condemned by the British was the long-standing practice of presenting numerous gifts to tribes. The British considered these bribes.

One of the first to confront this issue in the new British west was Lt. James Gorrell, who traveled to Green Bay in October 1761 with the unit that began British occupation of Wisconsin. Gorrell and his accompanying sergeant, corporal, and fifteen privates took up occupancy of a fort fallen into decay and disrepair and then turned to the question of relations with the Indians, most of whom were off hunting.

The new British lieutenant quickly learned from the local residents that the French "always gave [the Indians] belts, rum, and money, presents by which they renewed their peace annually." This was the same policy that British leaders had been criticizing so vigorously, but Gorrell soon realized the French were right: gifts were the key to winning over the Indians. In fact, when promised wampum belts did not arrive he was forced to purchase wampum from an English trader and local Indian women, and then to have this made into belts. The fact that French traders were still active, spreading tales of a coming attempt to reassert France's control, made solidifying a British-Indian alliance even more crucial.

In spring 1762, when the tribes returned from their winter hunt to the Green Bay post (now named Fort Edward Augustus), Gorrell presented belts to the Menominees, Winnebagos, Ottawas, Sacs, Foxes, and what he called the "Avoys" (probably Iowas); smaller presents were given to later arrivals, including a group of Chippewas and representatives of the combined tribes at the Milwaukee settlement. He explained the gifts in his speech to the Menominee and Winnebago chiefs:

> Brothers!—As you may have lost some of y'r brothers in the war in which you imprudently engaged with the French against your brothers, the English, and tho' by it you ought to have brought a just indignation upon you, yet we will condescend so far to forget whatever hath happened, that I am glad to take this opportunity to condole with you on the loss you have met with. At the same time, by these belts, I wipe away all the blood that was spilt, and bury all your brothers' bones that remain unburied on the face of the earth, that they may grieve you no more, as my intention is henceforward, not to grieve but to rejoice among you.

The Menominee spokesman thanked Gorrell for the speech and presents, said the tribe needed a gunsmith, and added pointedly that the French commandant "always gave them rum as a true token of friendship." Gorrell refused to go along with the latter, saying that their "great father, King George," had forbidden that rum be brought to the Indians.

Pontiac's Conspiracy

Gorrell's problems over gifts at Green Bay paralleled the situation elsewhere as the Crown sought to exert control over the regions won in battle. France had been increasing its presents to Indians as the eighteenth century progressed, and its annual appropriation of 20,000 livres for gifts during the early years of the century had grown to 65,000 by 1740: powder, balls, guns, vermilion, knives, cloth, fire steels, and similar items were most popular. But that flow of gifts for the tribes suddenly stopped with the British takeover. Anger spread rapidly across Indian America, especially after a 40-percent reduction in British appropriations brought an end to accustomed gifts for the 1762–63 winter.

Further, several high-ranking British officials revealed contempt for their new Indian charges, and Frenchmen trading among the tribes used this fact to spur anti-British feeling. With the French government no longer present, Indians were unable to play one side against the other any longer. In this worsening environment, Neolin, a prophet among the Delaware in Ohio, gained a wide following with his call for the destruction of white people; his words went out to many tribes in deerskin drawings showing whites blocking the pathway of Indians going from earth to happiness.

These factors were present to some extent in Wisconsin in the early 1760s, although one concern of eastern tribes had not yet reached the Upper Lakes. It was later summarized by an Onondaga chief, who blamed the fighting of 1763–64 on the land question: "we saw the English coming towards us from all Parts, and they have cheated us so often, that we could not think well of it. We were afraid, that in a little time, you would be at our very Castles."

The Senecas of the Iroquois confederation were most offended by the British refusal to demolish wartime posts built on Iroquois lands. They threw in their lot with Pontiac, an Ottawa leader who was putting together a broad alliance of tribes. This mammoth Indian force sought to overthrow the British in the west in a frontier struggle that ran through the summer and fall of 1763. Pontiac's effort, one of the most successful pan-Indian attempts in North American history, brought greatest results along the Ohio where British policies had hit tribes severely. Pontiac's forces had less success farther inland; at Green Bay, Gorrell's acts placated the Menominees, Sacs, Foxes, and Winnebagos, who generally remained loyal to the British.

The Chippewas, however, backed Pontiac. This strengthened the pro-British stance of the Menominees and Sacs, competitors of the Chippewas for hunting territory. Pontiac has been called "the virtual head of the Chippewas" at this time. Chippewas helped carry out the most famous fort attack during the rebellion, during a lacrosse game at Michilimackinac in June 1763: playing against the visiting Sac team, the Chippewa players artfully dropped the ball over the stockade wall several times and retrieved it peacefully, then lobbed it over again and rushed the unsuspecting sentry, quickly overwhelming the British within. The Chippewa attackers slew a trader, several officers, and about two-thirds of the soldiers. Other whites around the fort were taken prisoner; Charles de Langlade tried without success to block harsh actions against them. When news of the attack reached Green Bay, Gorrell's unit abandoned the fort. Gorrell left quickly for Michilimackinac, where he won release for the remaining prisoners, who then traveled on to Montreal.

Fort Edward Augustus at Green Bay was never reoccupied by the British after that 1763 evacuation, and Pontiac's rebellion did not spread to Wisconsin. The British also lost forts Sandusky, St. Joseph, Miami, Ouiatenon, Benango, Le Boeuf, and Presque Isle; Pitt (formerly France's Fort Duquesne) and Detroit were besieged but not overthrown before the rebellion collapsed in the closing months of 1763. The British sent several expeditions west late that year and in 1764 to drive off the Indians and force them to end hostilities. In the summer of 1764 the British held a huge peace conference at Niagara attended by more than 2,000 Indians from the Upper Lakes, including Chippewas, Sacs, Winnebagos, Foxes, and Menominees from Wisconsin. After that

Michilimackinac was garrisoned again, and the British finally succeeded in occupying the French posts along the Mississippi in Illinois.

British Policy after 1763

Even before the French-British peace accord settling the Seven Years' War was completed in fall 1763, British policies toward the Indians and the fur trade were changing. It had become obvious that a reversal was needed, for conditions on the frontier showed the necessity for friendly relations with the tribes, including showering them again with gifts and discouraging white settlement.

In recognition of these realities, Great Britain issued the Proclamation of 1763: it banned colonial officials from issuing warrants for possessing lands west of the Appalachians' crest, and forbade any "private person" from purchasing or taking possession of Indian lands. Theoretically, this would end growing land speculation in the west by American politicians and business leaders; now, only royal officials could deal with the Indians regarding their lands. The fur trade, however, would be open to anyone with a British license.

These attempts were almost totally ineffective. British traders were soon pouring into the Great Lakes region, elbowing out the French who often were reduced to becoming their employees, trading illegally, frequently clashing with British military officials in frontier posts.

In 1765, sixty-three Montreal fur merchants and traders protested to British officials about the new regulations. They argued that a rule limiting trade to the British posts had reduced "to penury" those who carried goods to the upper country, "and thereby the internal Trade of the Province is ruined." They noted that Indians at Green Bay, Chequamegon Bay, and St. Joseph's (at the south end of Lake Michigan) could simply carry their furs down the Mississippi to New Orleans—"and should that City pass into the Hands of the Spaniards their Allies the French will nevertheless supplie them with Suitable goods at a cheaper rate."

When the English and Canadians stop showing up in their villages, the Indians "will thereby grow Disgusted," the merchants argued, and this could "kindle afresh the flames of War." Canada's governor supported the Montrealers' argument, and in 1767 he called for restraints to be taken off the fur trade or "this Province [will] be nearly ruined, Great Britain [will] be a considerable Loser, and France the sole Gainer, as they must turn the greatest Part of the Furrs down the Mississippi."

Perhaps the Mississippi served some illegal traders as an escape route to the south, but it also became a route to profits for the Montreal-based British traders. One of the chroniclers of this change was Jonathan Carver, who came into Wisconsin just as the British were recovering from the Pontiac wars and beginning to discover the wealth they had won. Carver wrote the first English account of journeying in the region: *Travels Through the Interior Parts of North America, in the Years 1766, 1767, and 1768.*

Carver, a New Englander, traveled westward through Albany, Niagara, Detroit, and Michilimackinac, reaching Green Bay on Sept. 18, 1766 (where he found the old fort "much decayed" and "scarcely defensible against small arms"). His party arrived on October 8 at the Sac village on the lower Wisconsin, marveling at the Indians' corn, beans, melons, and other crops which made it the "best market for traders to furnish themselves with provisions" within eight hundred miles. Carver was well impressed with this "Great Town of the Saukies":

> This is the largest and best built Indian town I ever saw. It contains about ninety houses, each large enough for several families. These are built of hewn plank neatly jointed, and covered with bark so compactly as to keep out the most penetrating rains. Before the doors are placed comfortable sheds, in which the inhabitants sit, when the weather will permit, and smoak their pipes. The streets are regular and spacious; so that it appears more like a civilized town than the abode of savages.[2]

----

2. The "Great Town of the Saukies" was at the site of modern Prairie du Sac and Sauk City.

Arriving at the great river in mid-October, Carver visited the fur trade center of Prairie du Chien, then headed up the Mississippi with a French Canadian and a Mohawk as his employees. Below Lake Pepin they were almost plundered by a group of unidentified Indians, renegrades from various tribes. But near the mouth of the St. Croix they came upon three "River Bands" of Sioux, with some 400 warriors. Others suddenly arrived with reports of a large Chippewa force in pursuit, and Carver accepted the role of mediator. He met the attackers and convinced them to put off their warfare.

Carver spent the winter among the Sioux in Minnesota, then in the spring of 1767 he and his party canoed up the Chippewa River to the Chippewa village at Lac Court Oreilles, in an area which Indians called (with Carver's agreement) "mosquito country." With some forty houses and neat gardens, the village was home to around a hundred warriors but the inhabitants "seemed to be the nastiest people I had ever been among," Carver concluded. Carver then made his way to the Brule and on to Lake Superior, proceeding to Grand Portage on the north shore of Minnesota, before heading east and eventually home.

Carver's published journal brought information about a largely unknown region to a European public that was eager to receive it—a prerequisite to further development of this frontier. Carver wrote of Indian religious beliefs, their homes and methods of warfare, and described specific plants and animals; he detailed "The Manner in which they construct their Sweating Stoves" as well as presenting a "Descriptive Specimen of their Hieroglyphicks." And, looking to the future, Carver presented "The Probability of the interior Parts of North America becoming Commercial Colonies."

The American Revolution

At this point the Wisconsin Indians were still untouched by the westward surge of American settlement. Indians in the entire Great Lakes region perhaps numbered some 60,000 in 1768; within this total the estimates for tribes in the Wisconsin region are as follows: Chippewas (south and east of Lake Superior, but including northern Minnesota), 5,000; Sacs, 2,000; Winnebagos, 1,500; Foxes, 1,500; Kickapoos and Mascoutins, 2,000; Menominees, 800; and Potawatomis, 3,000; the Sioux River Bands totaled 6,000.

Because of their locations these tribes were far removed from rising tensions in the east as ties between Americans and Britons began to fray in the late 1760s and early 1770s. If no major Revolutionary War incidents occurred in Wisconsin, it is still apparent that the region was beginning to acquire a geographic and economic reality in eastern colonists' dreams; expectations for the west would be an issue in the looming conflict. On the seaboard, men had images of western lands and wealth awaiting the first-comers, but Britain had prohibited settlement beyond the Appalachians. George Washington criticized the 1763 Proclamation as a "temporary expedient to quiet the minds of the Indians," and increasing numbers of his peers agreed. Indians saw the issue differently, and early in 1777 the Chippewas joined with the Iroquois to send a warning to Virginians and Pennsylvanians who had "feloniously taken Possession of part of our Country on the branches of the Ohio, as well as the Susquehanna." The tribal message was blunt: "We now tell you in a peaceful manner to quit our Lands wherever you have possessed yourselves of them immediately, or blame yourselves for whatever may happen."

As fighting began in 1775, Britain placed its agents on the frontier on a war footing, giving new urgency to treating the Indians in a friendly manner. Soon Michilimackinac was transformed into a carefully designed military garrison, replacing the scattered buildings of the former French post. The contrast was noted by a recent archeological excavation, which found that the French houses at Michilimackinac "are architecturally fascinating. You never know what to expect when you start on a new one in that each is different." In contrast, British structures there revealed a conformity of styles, for the new regime built a "strict military post," eventually moving it from the south side of the Straits of Mackinac to Mackinac Island during the winter of 1780–81 when it became Fort Mackinac.

Wisconsin did not figure in Revolutionary War battles, but its tribes were courted by both sides as attempted earlier during Pontiac's Rebellion. There was extensive switching of allegiances as the war dragged on and advantages to different tribes appeared to lie with first one, then the other side. Most western Great Lakes tribes aligned themselves with the British because they saw the British as less threatening to their lands. However, support for the Americans was not insignificant, largely because of lingering distaste for British actions in replacing the French. Major Indian support for Americans in Wisconsin came from the mixed settlement at Milwaukee, where Siggenauk, a Chippewa/Potawatomi leader also known as Blackbird, rallied the community's disparate peoples—Chippewas, Illinois, Ottawas, Potawatomis, and Sacs. Siggenauk went to Kaskaskia on the Mississippi in the winter of 1778–79 to meet with the American military leader George Rogers Clark, and the Milwaukee warrior was a continuing worry to British policy-makers although not a serious problem to the British military.

Clark, whose force of 175 had seized Kaskaskia in 1778, made peace with some twelve Midwestern Indian tribes during a five-week treaty session. He later admitted in a letter to George Mason, "I always thought we took the wrong method of treating with Indians, and strove as soon as possible to make myself acquainted with the French and Spanish mode." He gave the tribes his interpretation of the war between Great Britain and the United States, arguing that the king had decided the Americans were so rich and numerous that he could force them to pay tribute. Eventually, Clark warned, the British leader "would then make the Indians pay likewise." Part of the king's plan was to get the Americans and Indians quarreling. But the Americans could take it no longer:

> We bore their Taxes for many Years, at last they were so hard that if we killed a Deer they would take the Skin away and leave us only the Meat, and made us buy Blankets with Corn to fead their Soldiers with. By such usage we got Poor and was obliged to go naked; And at last we complained.

Clark's Cahokia conference in 1778 drew Chippewas, Ottawas, Potawatomis, Missisaugas, Winnebagos, Sacs, Foxes, Osages,

Iowas, and Miamis, plus some unidentified others. Daniel Linctot of Prairie du Chien, one of the pro-American traders at that growing trade center, apparently led the Wisconsin tribes southward to the Cahokia meetings. Not all of these tribes came into the American tent, however, nor did all members of the pro-American tribes remain loyal. Clark would later report to Governor Patrick Henry of Virginia, who had dispatched him to seize the Illinois Country, that the tribes actively opposing the Americans included about half of the Chippewas, plus the Potawatomis, Iowas, Ottawas, and Miamis, as well as the Iroquois and Shawnees to the east. "Part of the Chessaweys [Chippewa] have also treated, and are peaceable," he added. "I continually keep agents among them, to watch their motions and keep them peaceably inclined."

The British at Michilimackinac and other western posts soon grew concerned over Clark's diplomacy. One report told of Clark's agents purchasing horses from the Sacs, and planning to attack Green Bay with 300 men (although the British commandant feared they would instead march on Detroit—known to be the key American target). A British official found an American belt among the Sacs and Foxes as he traveled along the lower Wisconsin in 1778; warnings came that the Americans could easily transport supplies down the Mississippi from northern Wisconsin.

Much of British activity involving Wisconsin centered on a downriver attack in 1780, aimed at establishing British sovereignty over the settlements on the Mississippi which Clark had seized. The campaign also targeted St. Louis, now controlled by Spain as part of its new dominion over Louisiana; Spain declared war on Great Britain in May 1779. Launched from Michilimackinac, the 1780 British force was put under control of Emanuel Hesse, a Prairie du Chien trader who had formerly served in Britain's Royal American regiment.

Many Indian allies joined this attack to overrun St. Louis, Cahokia, and Kaskaskia. Capt. Patrick Sinclair at Michilimackinac reported that these included "Winipigoes, Scioux, Ottawa, Ochipwa [Chippewa], Iowa & a few of the Outagamies [Fox], Sacks, Mascoutins, Kickapous, and Pottawatamies." The Sioux under Wabashaw and the Chippewas under Matchekewis were given major roles in the downriver operation, but some participants went reluctantly, notably the Sacs and Foxes who had been recruited with difficulty. They were, after all, recent allies of the Americans.

As the invasion force moved south, the Dubuque lead mines were first captured, and Menominee warriors seized a boat coming upstream from St. Louis with fur trade supplies. These acts sent strong alarms rippling southward, and because of these warnings both the Spanish at St. Louis and the Americans at Cahokia (joined by George Rogers Clark at the last minute) were able to drive off the 1,200 attackers. The invaders then retreated north, some along the Mississippi, others paddling up the Illinois to the Chicago portage where they escaped an attack from Siggenauk's Milwaukee coalition. The pursuing Americans, joined by Kaskaskia Indian allies, retaliated against the Sacs' Rock River villages while one detachment proceeded northwest to Prairie du Chien, where they narrowly missed catching a British force that had just evacuated some 300 packs of furs. This pursuit is believed to mark the first American expedition into Wisconsin.

General Washington's victory at Yorktown in 1781 and the final acts in the Revolutionary War dramatically threw open the trans-Appalachian country to American settlement. As fighting continued in some areas through 1782, diplomats meeting in Paris were approaching agreement on key questions in the final treaty: granting to the United States the territory reaching to the Mississippi, and tracing the northern boundary through the Great Lakes, to Lake of the Woods in northern Minnesota. The trans-Appalachian frontier would come within the domain of the new United States, and key fur trade centers would fall into American territory: Grand Portage, Green Bay, Michilimackinac, Detroit, Niagara, and Oswego.

News of the peace treaty reached the Upper Lakes in the spring of 1783. By then various British officials were trying to win reimbursment for their payments to the Indians during the war. White traders also needed to be paid for their help to the British cause. The Mackinac commander granted to Charles de Langlade the land that he was then occupying at Green Bay, as well as meadows and woods he used there, plus 3,000 acres in Canada;

eventually the British would further award him an annuity of $800, half-pay for as long as he lived, for his services to the British cause.

If the British scattered around the Upper Lakes were disbelieving and bitter at the defeat, their many Indian allies had good reason to be fearful and uncertain of the future. As the Fox chief Vimotolaque told a council at Prairie du Chien in May 1783, "truly our Head is bewildered." The Indians had once again backed the losing side in an international war. But American settlers were still far off, just beginning to enter the Ohio country. British and French fur traders were already on hand, however, and they looked with doubts on the new United States government and wondered how it would now confront frontier issues that had bedeviled the French and British.

5·

STRUGGLE OVER THE
UPPER LAKES

As the new United States of America became legal claimant to
Wisconsin and the rest of the trans-Appalachian frontier, the British in Canada were understandably nervous about their new competitors in the fur trade. But James McGill, a Montreal trader,
assured Great Britain's lieutenant-governor in 1785 that there
was little need to worry about the Americans: much of the region
so rich in furs could be reached only in birchbark canoes, "which
will require them a long time to become accustomed to," while
the experienced British traders could both carry European goods
to, and furs from, distant posts at less expense. The fur trade
south of Lake Superior was run from Montreal, McGill noted,
and it would not be "an easy matter for the Americans to get any
part of it, notwithstanding the Country is within their Line."

The line he referred to ran through each of the Great Lakes
and west to the headwaters of the Mississippi, dividing British
America (Canada) on the north from the United States on the
south. In the years since the French were overthrown in 1761,
British businessmen had seized control of the bulk of the fur
trade on both sides of this border, led by McGill and hundreds of
other Scots and Englishmen. Large Montreal firms were soon
swooping down on Michilimackinac, Green Bay, Prairie du Chien,

La Pointe, and dozens of other frontier posts; they were also pushing westward, past Grand Portage on the North Shore of Lake Superior, to Winnipeg and beyond into the Canadian West. This fact lay behind Britain's refusal to evacuate Wisconsin and other parts of the Upper Great Lakes region despite what was dictated by the treaty ending the Revolutionary War. The resulting struggles—between nations, companies, and traders—tore at Wisconsin in the years leading up to the War of 1812. Only then did the United States finally displace Great Britain as sovereign over a rich frontier that the Americans had already won during the Revolutionary War some thirty years earlier. The wealth of this frontier, which for almost 200 years had lured the European powers inland with eagerness for profits, was once again drawing Wisconsin and the Upper Lakes into international competition.

A Fur Trade Revolution

"What the Trade was in the time of the French, no two Persons can agree about," noted Sir William Johnson soon after the British government he represented had displaced France as landlords over the vast region beyond the Appalachians. Nevertheless, the British soon began attempting what the French had tried, including a licensing system for traders and showering Indians with gifts; they also ordered a ban on the westward movement of settlers.

Green Bay remained important in this new, British-dominated trade. During a single year near the end of French rule, in 1757, some 500 to 600 packs of furs had been shipped from the post, exceeded in the Great Lakes region only by Michilimackinac (600–700 packs) and Detroit (800–1,000). Boom times remained after the British became landlords: in 1767 nearly one-third of the canoes and trade goods going out of Michilimackinac went to Green Bay and its many dependencies. In the 1790s, when Green Bay remained under actual British control despite being legally part of the United States, the post's 300 outgoing packs ranked second only to the Illinois fur output (600) among subsidiary posts; Milwaukee had 120.

But the numbers of beaver were declining. Over-hunted, their pelts began to be supplanted by other furs. Pelts sent out from Green Bay in 1767 included 9,002 deer and 6,506 raccoon, but only 5,357 beaver; there were also 1,100 otter, 446 marten, 300 fisher, 286 muskrat, 267 bear, 103 mink, and smaller numbers of red fox, wolf, bobcat, bison, elk, and wolverine. Beaver had fallen to 24 percent of the post's annual production, even though Indians were extending their hunts.

Beaver remained abundant to the west, in the Upper Mississippi country and north and west of Lake Superior. This provided new challenges, as did changing European tastes in furs, but it also brought greater costs. The advantage soon shifted to large firms prepared to operate at greater distances from Montreal and to make plans beyond the current season.

The Prairie du Chien rendezvous experienced its best years in this period, enjoying a resurgence late in the century when it became a jumping-off point for traders leaving for areas under Spanish sovereignty west of the Mississippi. While independents were present, it was the major traders who took the lead in organizing the canoe brigade for transporting fur packs in late summer up the Wisconsin, down the Fox, to Green Bay and on to Mackinac, which remained the fur entrepôt for Prairie du Chien. One of those who had visited the post on the Mississippi in 1773–74, just before its late-century boom period, was a New Englander named Peter Pond; he later described (in his own inimitable style) what he witnessed that autumn at the "Planes of the Dogs,"

> the Grate Plase of Randavues for the traders and Indans Before thay Dispars for thare wintering Grounds Hear we Meat with a Larg Number of french & Indans Makeing out thare arangments for the InSewing winter and Sending of thare canues to Differant Parts Like wise Giveing Creadets to the Indans who ware all to Randavese thare in Spring.

Pond noted that boats paddled by thirty-six men arrived from New Orleans loaded with wine, ham, and cheese, among other trade goods, an indication that some of the region's furs were being siphoned off downriver rather than out through the St. Lawrence.

Many minor Wisconsin trade centers were small "jack-knife"

posts, run by a single trader with his employees, or in some cases by a few related families; often these were connected to the large Montreal firms. Records of these operations show the continuing importance of French and *métis* traders in Wisconsin. Jacques Vieau set up such a trade center at Milwaukee in 1795, the first post there; he also established jack-knife posts that year at Kewaunee, Sheboygan, and Manitowoc, run by resident agents. La-Pointe at Chequamegon Bay became a post again, and there were jack-knife posts also at Lac Vieux Desert on the Michigan border, Lac du Flambeau, Lac Court Oreilles, Kaukauna, and Butte des Morts, as well as the sites of Portage, Chippewa Falls, Hudson, and Chicago. Frequently these were located adjacent to the hunting territory of an Indian band connected through marriage to a trader. Eventually some traders settled in Green Bay, leaving others in charge of their jack-knife posts in the hinterland; examples of such traders were John Lawe, Jacques Porlier, and several of the Grignons.

Another family rising in importance in the Wisconsin fur trade in the closing decades of the eighteenth century was the Cadottes—Jean Baptiste, Sr., who was interpreter at Michilimackinac when the British replaced the French, and who became a partner of Alexander Henry in 1765 at LaPointe; and his sons Jean Baptiste, Jr., and Michel, both of whom also married Chippewa women. The senior Cadotte's wife, an influential member of the Awause clan of the Lake Superior Chippewa, played a crucial role in his success. She was related to several native leaders around Michilimackinac where the Cadottes lived for many years. It is apparent that the British soon learned of Cadotte's importance, for the post's commander wrote in 1765 that the Indians who arrived in eighty canoes from Lake Superior had "beged I would send some Trader to them, and asked for Mr. Caddot." He agreed: "I propose to let Mr. Caddot go to Lapoint in Lake Superior, . . . am Convinced that all the Indians will remain in our Interest." In 1784 his son Jean Baptiste, Jr., was given control of the newly opened post at Folle Avoine on the Yellow River in northwest Wisconsin, while the other son, Michel, developed an extensive trade in northern Wisconsin from his base in Chequamegon Bay on Michael's Island—later renamed Madeline Island in honor of his Chippewa wife.

The Northwest Company and Its Competitors

Both Cadotte sons eventually signed on with the first major firm to enter British fur operations since the Hudson's Bay Company: the Northwest Company, launched on a restricted basis in 1779 by leading merchants of Montreal and Michilimackinac, then reorganized in 1783. The new company was born of the new conditions of the trade, and was itself instigator of many radical departures.

The trade's enormous profits soon lured others. The Michilimackinac Company operated from 1785–88 along the Mississippi, followed by the General Company of Lake Superior and the South which then entered the Upper Mississippi. The X Y Company appeared in 1798, and clashed repeatedly with North West for control of northern Wisconsin before the two firms merged in 1804. Other minor enterprises operated out of Prairie du Chien and Michilmackinac.

Then came the first major U.S. entry into this growing competition, John Jacob Astor's American Fur Company. Astor immigrated from Germany in 1784 after a four-year stopover in England and quickly threw himself into American business activity. By 1788 he was selling furs in New York City and soon perceived American advantages in the trade. Beginning small, by 1808 Astor had accumulated enough wealth to challenge the North West Company, both in the Great Lakes and eventually in the Pacific Northwest. In 1811 Astor reached an agreement with Montreal firms that led to a division of territory and profits. Now there was a major American competitor in the booming fur business.

Advantages of these large operators were many, and some had been evident years earlier. La Salle's ship *Griffon* in 1679 had pointed the way for large vessels to haul trade goods and furs in larger quantities, and much more cheaply, than was possible with birchbark canoes. But it was not until 1730 that the next large ship was recorded in the western lakes: a forty-ton French trade sloop, described as the first vessel on Lake Superior "with sail larger than an Indian blanket." The expanding trade increasingly turned to such ships, and the North West Company had three vessels on Lake Superior by 1793, helping the firm win control of more than three-fourths of the fur trade of Canada by 1795. Three years later North West employed 50 clerks, 71 interpreters, 1,120 voyageurs, and 35 guides. Elbowing its way into the fur business, the X Y Company also built a schooner on Lake Superior in 1802.

Soon, new posts were being created by the Montreal firms. At Madeline Island, North West built a post on the island's southwest end; recent archeological investigations have unearthed British-style gunflints, ornaments made of trade silver, beads, awls, iron fishing spears, white clay pipes, and even English dishware.

Four Traders

Journals and memoirs of four fur traders active in northern Wisconsin in this period reveal how the fur trade was transforming this frontier and its inhabitants. These writings record the activities of Jean Baptiste Perrault, 1783–99; George Nelson, 1802–3; Michael Curot, 1803–4, and François Malhiot, 1804–5.

The four witnessed, and sometimes carried out, the worst excesses in the competition between the large Montreal-based companies, as gifts and alcohol became bribes that debauched both recipient and giver. By the closing decades of the eighteenth century it is clear that Indians were becoming heavily dependent upon European trade goods, and tribes that once held aloof now rushed to seek out the traders. This competition was played out amid the continuing Sioux-Chippewa warfare that erupted across northwestern Wisconsin and westward into northern Minnesota.

Jean Baptiste Perrault was born in Trois Rivières on the St. Lawrence in 1761, entered the fur trade in 1783, and did not return from the west for a visit to the lower lakes for twenty-two years. Perrault first went as a trader to Cahokia, in Illinois, then was on the Red Cedar near the site of Menomonie in 1785, came to Prairie du Chien at the time of the 1786–87 treaty sessions, clerked for Pierre Grignon at Green Bay immediately thereafter, ran a place on the Red Cedar in 1788–89, and traded at Lac Vieux Desert in 1792 when he began twelve years with the North West Company. In 1799 he was on the Red Cedar again. "I could not settle down in any place," he later admitted.

Perrault's operations in 1792 centered on what would become Wisconsin's northeastern border with Michigan, at Lac Vieux Desert, headwaters of the Wisconsin River. Perrault selected six men at Mackinac and gave them "good wages, for no one was obliged to enter here, Because of the Length of the portage." They indeed earned their pay, for low water in the Ontonagon River forced the crew to cache their canoes until spring and portage all their goods—40 packs—for thirty-three days. At one point Perrault stopped to separately cache five kegs of rum, one of gunpowder, and two of lead and balls. Another trader was already operating out of Lac Vieux Desert, and Perrault joined with him to cover the area from l'Anse at the foot of Keweenaw Bay to Lac du Flambeau. Their first Indian visitors, coming from the Wisconsin River headwaters, were given tobacco and a two-gallon keg of rum to distribute to other Indians to encourage their hunting activities. Perrault and his crew soon faced new difficulties: they had to make fishing nets, and also had to hollow out a log to use as a boat since they were unable to construct one of birchbark. Next spring an Indian was hired to make three canoes of moose skins for them to use in descending the river—demonstrating again the traders' dependence on Indians.

Meat from moose and other large game was plentiful at Lac Vieux Desert. Also, Perrault had the men carve out 450 wooden bowls to use in making maple sugar; seven kegs of sugar were ultimately produced. But in the end the meat, fish, and sugar at Lac Vieux Desert proved more abundant than furs: despite a good beginning, Perrault received only 200 *plus*[1] of peltries, and half a pack of beaver. He told the Indians he would not return—the district was simply unprofitable, the portage too difficult.

During Perrault's years in the fur trade in Wisconsin he wit-

---

1. A *plus* was the basic measurement of pelts, defined as enough furs to equal one beaver pelt. Perrault's trappers had therefore caught furs of many animals, worth 200 beaver skins.

nessed the extreme reliance of Indians upon trade goods: as one Chippewa told Perrault at the Red Cedar post, whites "are the support of the savages[;] we could not live without Them." But trapping conditions were changing, and the Indians could not always bring in enough furs to erase their extensive credit—at Lac Vieux Desert the Indians had been given 300 *plus* worth of credits, but supplied only 200 *plus* in furs.

Although Perrault labored for the North West Company for twelve years after 1793, he did not grow to love his employer. In 1810, while with another company, he had a run-in with North West and was threatened; he later explained, "It is necessary to remark that at that time the [North West] was Legislator and King; it killed, hanged, stole, and violated, etc. The enormity of their crimes led to Their Fall."

George Nelson knew some of the same country. Native of a small town near Montreal, he came to Wisconsin in 1802 as an apprentice clerk with one of the member firms of the X Y Company, which sent him into the Upper St. Croix country to a post on the Yellow River. In this period, he later recalled, the lackadaisical ways of French operations were giving way to a trade "so perfectly organized that large fortunes were rapidly made, and almost as rapidly wasted." He stands out from the others in this story because he alone of the four under review was not a French-Canadian.

Nelson was sent initially to the X Y post at Grand Portage, where a fight with some North West men at their joint loading point was only narrowly averted: "We at last embarked fully determined to defend ourselves, fight, & kill, if driven too it; & armed for the purpose." He and three others headed out by canoe into Lake Superior and ascended the Brule in mid-September, portaged into the St. Croix and paddled downriver to the region known as Folle Avoine to trade among the Chippewas in northwestern Wisconsin and eastern Minnesota. Arriving at the mouth of the Yellow River, near the site of Danbury, they found that the North West men had already gotten the local Indians drunk; "after a while, when they saw we had no rum, they gradually dispersed." Later the crew headed up the Yellow to a spot below Yellow Lake, where Nelson and his companions built a structure "sixteen or eighteen feet long," located just sixty yards away from the North West post despite a proposal from that firm to build even closer because of the Sioux threat. But Nelson realized that because of the North West's strength, "no indian could come to us that was not more or less indebted to them virtually or impliedly;" this forced X Y to build far enough away from the North West structures so that the opposition could not observe which Indians were trading with X Y.[2]

Nelson had mixed experiences with Indians. Upon arrival he met Chippewa tribesmen when they gathered around to inspect him—they "laughed with me & tapped me friendly on the shoulders and head. . . . I never felt the least fear." Later, however, one of his co-workers was so offended by Indian lack of sanitation that he could hardly bear to eat: the Indian cook's child had diarrhea, coming out in "yellow stuff like mustard." No matter—she "scolded & laying the bratt on her lap opened the *cheeks* & with the back of her knife Scraped off the Stuff, scolded him again for a dirty little dog, wiped her knife upon the brush, scooped water with her right hand out of the Kettle in which our meat was, to wash both, & finished cutting up, with the same knife, a piece of beautiful fat meat, as a relish to what she had put on before."

But Nelson—an introspective trader, as revealed in his journal—grew in his acceptance of the Indians, and his ethnocentrism softened over the winter. Seeing Chippewas painted black with charcoal and grease for mourning, he studied his Bible for guidance in understanding their behavior and later admitted that he "became quite reconciled," especially because the Indians "took great pity upon me," one of them even adopting him as a son. This reconciliation can be seen in his account of two local boys who covered their faces with charcoal and fasted as a way of mourning their dead fathers; the boys' mothers would also leave the post and weep and moan in the distance in "a voice not to be misunderstood even by me, young, thoughtless & boistrous as I

---

2. The Folle Avoine location of the North West and X Y posts has recently been restored as a historic site. It is west of Hwy. 35, between Danbury and Webster, Wis.

was." Nelson decided their actions did not represent barbarism, realizing that their mourning had a transforming influence, for the Indians returned in a cheerful state. He later admitted such scenes "have left an indelible impression, which, with my years increases & furnish subject for reflection."

Michael Curot followed Nelson the succeeding winter at the Yellow River post; in fact, he and Nelson met in August 1803 when Curot was passing through the Fond du Lac post (near the site of Duluth-Superior), heading for the Brule–St. Croix portage, and Nelson was en route westward to another X Y post. Curot's 1803–4 journal is filled with detailed accounts of trading activities at the "house" (his X Y post) and the "fort" (the North West post) on the Yellow. Wild rice was abundant in the district, and traders purchased it in great amounts for transport to their companies' outposts elsewhere. The rice accumulated to such an extent in the traders' storeroom that in January the post even sold rice to some Indians who had been reduced to eating "strips of wood" for three days.

Curot's reports make it clear that employees of the X Y and North West were well aware of what the other firm was doing, whether sixty yards apart in their posts, or traveling through the deep woods. Curot frequently referred to his competitors disparagingly, and it was not until New Year's Day that he went "For The first time to make a daylight call on Mr. Sayer alone." Later, in March, he spent more time there and observed that Sayer, the North West post's head, went to bed drunk every night. When the time came to press the furs into packs, however, Sayer permitted the X Y men to use his press if they would help him when he needed to press his own furs. At that time they pressed a total of twenty-one packs (six of them beaver) for North West; nine (three beaver) for the X Y. Ten seems to have been the X Y total when they finally departed in May, while North West's traders carried out thirty-seven packs, sixteen of them beaver and three of bear skins.

François Victor Malhiot worked for the North West Company at its post on Lac du Flambeau from 1804 to 1807, a time which included North West's merger with X Y after years of bitter competition. As he left Fort Kaministikwia, some sixty miles northeast of Grand Portage (later Fort William, Canada), in July 1804, Malhiot's beginning outfit of trade goods totaled eleven bales, including twenty kegs of double-strength rum, five bags of shot and bullets, half a bale of kettles, a case of guns, twelve traps, and four rolls of tobacco. For the sustenance of his crew of nine he also transported 400 pounds of flour, two and one-half barrels of pork, forty pounds of biscuit, a keg of rum, a keg of double-strength high wines, two kegs of sugar, four pounds of tea, a ham, and some bread, butter, and assorted other foods.

The final leg of the trip, beginning at the Montreal River east of Chequamegon Bay, must not have provided his canoemen with much optimism about the future, for they met three North West men coming back from the Flambeau post and, Malhiot observed, they were "thin and emaciated like real skeletons." The men reported that "half the time they had nothing to eat," while the North West agent had dined well. Malhiot gave each of them some rum, two double-handfuls of flour, and two pounds of pork.

Ascending the Montreal was difficult, made worse by Malhiot's severe toothache. They stopped on the first afternoon after only twenty "pauses;" his men complained of leg pains and he provided each "a drink of shrub"—rum. The Montreal River portage was figured at forty-five miles, with 120 pauses—sections between stops—which averaged up to a half mile in length. After five days they reached Lac du Flambeau.

North West's operations there were in turmoil. Malhiot's predecessor was incompetent, and the nearby Indians had often been provoked into a frenzy. Short weeks after arriving Malhiot presented a coat and flag to one Chippewa headman, a coat to another leader, and laced jackets to two others, as well as rum. His speech to the principal leader demonstrated both the diplomacy and wiles of traders in dealing with the egos of tribal leaders; it also showed that French-Canadians still dominated the fur trade in the interior:

> Kinsman—The coat I have put on thee is sent thee by the Great Trader [William McGillvray, head of North West]; by such coats he distinguishes the most highly considered persons of a tribe. The Flag is a true symbol of a Chief and thou must deem thyself honored by it, because we do not give them to the first comers among the Sav-

ages. One must do as thou dost to get one, that is: love the French as thou dost, watch over their preservation and enable them to make up packs of furs.

Malhiot explained that he had been ordered to make no such gifts until spring—"but, on account of all the good things I have heard of thee from the French, I did not hesitate a moment to make thee glorious, for I am convinced thou wilt always be the same for the Fort." As "first chief," the Indian was told that he must "make every effort so that all the Savages may come and trade here in the spring."

Competition between the North West and X Y was bitter. Malhiot warned the Indians to look at the opposition X Y fort at Lac du Flambeau "only from afar" if they wished to obtain their desires. He further sent word to LaPointe to tell Michel Cadotte to pursue the competition against the X Y's agent on the Chippewa River—"have him followed step by step and even have him accompanied thus until the spring."

After only a few weeks at Lac du Flambeau, Malhiot was lamenting the life of the trader. He worked himself and his men hard: in the course of the next ten months they constructed a house twenty feet square; chopped seventy cords of firewood; sawed pickets for the fort and covered a bastion on the wall, and cleared a field for planting eight kegs of potatoes. Everything was against them, he wrote in his journal: "Little to eat, much work to do; sometimes ill, uncertain of obtaining returns, with reproaches to be dreaded from the Partners, anxiety about the goods out of the fort, Savages to satisfy, and adversaries to watch. What a life!!" On May 2, 1805, however, the news arrived that North West and X Y had merged. The competition was over.

When he and his crew finally vacated the fort, on May 23, 1805, Malhiot could look back on a difficult but productive season. He had started his record-keeping the previous October—after a month at the post—when he reported having taken in 528 deer skins, 840 muskrat skins, 107 pounds of beaver, 44 otter skins, 16 bear skins, 7 marten skins, and one mink skin, making sixteen packs. Since that date his monthly reports told of

the arrivals of many more *plus*, which were probably transported
out periodically rather than awaiting Malhiot's departure in May.

Traders and Alcohol

These years of bitter struggle between North West, X Y, and smaller companies carried to extremes the worst aspects of the fur trade. One of these was the use of alcohol.

There was nothing new in the use of alcoholic beverages as a tool in the fur trade. The French had discovered very early that their brandy was sought avidly by the Indians, and its negative effects were soon noticed; repeated efforts were made by French government officials and missionaries over the years to cut off the westward movement of these supplies. In 1720 a French official argued that the Indians "no longer Think of hunting in order to Clothe Themselves but only to get drink. Brandy is making them poor and miserable."

Initially Great Britain banned alcohol from its posts in 1761, as part of tightening up what was believed to have been a lenient French policy. This did not go over well with the tribes. One of the first British subjects to arrive at Michilimackinac was Alexander Henry, and the Chippewas there immediately asked to taste his "English milk"—"they were very desirous to know whether or not there were any differences between the English milk and the French." Whether they found a difference is not recorded, but several years later a commander at the post pleaded for rum to be sent quickly to give to the Indians: "as you know it is their God." As competition worsened between the Montreal companies, rum importation into the Upper Lakes doubled between 1800 and 1803. This new frenzy for alcohol paid off in the companies' profits, but it was a disaster for the Indians. Debauchery weakened the native cultures just when strength and discipline were needed to confront the American influx in the nineteenth century.

The four Wisconsin fur traders—Perrault, Nelson, Curot, and Malhiot—provide ample evidence in their journals and memoirs of alcohol's central position in the business. (When Nelson arrived at the Yellow River, the Indians waiting there yelled, "Rum,

Rum, what are you come to do here without rum?") All four reported that vast amounts of alcohol were brought in with their outfits. Perrault carried eighteen kegs of whiskey on one journey, each holding eight gallons. They often transported "H.W."—high wine, nearly pure alcohol, which then was diluted for presentation to the Indians; as Perrault wrote, "That evening we made one keg of rum into two, and we began to trade." If one company could not supply it, the competitor would.

Its uses were varied, i.e., to buy pelts, stop a fight, win friends, curry favor. Curot and his men needed meat at the end of winter, but the Indians told them "they would not Bring it to him because he had no Rum to give them." Perrault once announced to some Indians that the price of rum was twenty fawn skins per keg: "A moment after[,] they brought out 60 fawnskins Of wild rice which they placed in three rows, demanding three kegs of rum. I Delivered it on the spot."

But it could also make Indians belligerent or threatening. Curot and his men were canoeing on the Eau Claire River, near the site of Gordon, "when Ouêza rejoined us in a canoe with his wife, and said that if I did not give him some Rum something bad would happen to someone." Ouêza got his rum.

Nelson and his fellow-workers had to contend with ten days of "drunken songs & noise," during which two young Indians "plotted to kill *us* all"; two Indian women alerted them and they blocked the murder attempt. Curot reported, "The savages are fighting over the Liquor. Le petit noir was stabbed twice with a knife on his thigh by the women." One of Malhiot's comrades arrived back from a visit to an Indian camp with news "that the Savages stabbed one another during the drinking bout, and that he would have been killed had it not been for 'l'Outarde.'" Malhiot witnessed numerous fights following drinking bouts. "We had a great deal of trouble last night owing to the liquor," he reported on Aug. 11, 1804. Previously he had found these Indians to be well-behaved and gentle, but in this row Malhiot "found them detestable." The next morning the Indians apologized, "saying that such a thing had never happened to them, that they were too drunk—the usual excuses of such black dogs!"

The experiences of these four traders have many parallels in reports of Indian-white dealings across North America. One interpretation of intoxicated Indians' violence is that Indians repressed violence against others within the group, but when violent acts were committed by an intoxicated member they were overlooked. Anthropologist Robert Ritzenthaler, one of Wisconsin's leading authorities on Indian life, once commented, "I have never seen any Wisconsin Indians fighting except when under the influence of alcohol. Except in war, their traditional release of aggression was an indirect one"—gossip or shamanism.

Women and Blacks

Indian women had crucial, though often unreported, roles in the fur trade. These were often buried in traders' reports, as when Michel Curot wrote that his co-worker Savoyard was asked to travel for the winter with a group of Indians; he "would have been glad to go There with his wife, if she had been here, he could not without Some one to dress skins; she has been with her mother since the 24 of last Month."

Accounts reveal some differences between tribes, but it is generally true that rigid spheres of action encircled women's lives. By 1800, women still controlled their traditional regulation of living space and campsite selection; they were in charge of raising children, growing crops, preparing food and clothing. They dried and smoked fish, made maple sugar, concocted medicines, and hauled baggage when camps were moved. It is likely that European goods might decrease women's importance in making clothes, while their pottery making was certainly undermined as the French and English brought metal cookware. But for some, trading created opportunities for independent action.

For the Indian woman had become a partner, often a crucial partner, in the fur trade. Changes in the trade would affect her also. Perrault makes fleeting reference to an Indian widow who was loaded with goods from the government "as by her trading." A British list of the "Outfit commonly given to Indians," apparently from the 1790s, includes a separate listing for a "Chiefs Lady," consisting of "5 Yards fine cloth for a Blanket, Petticoat and legings, 36 Yds Ribbon, 200 Broaches, 1 blanket 2½ points,

2½ Yds Linen or Callico, 1 Plain Hat, 2 Silk Handkfs." Any children were to be given a blanket and linen or "Embossed Sirge to make them shirts." For the wife of a "Common Indian," the list included "4½ Strouds for a blanket & Petticoat, 1 Yd Molton for Legings, 2½ Yds Linen or Callico, 1 plain Hat, 1 Blanket 2½ points."

The gift list for men is longer, but there is significance in the fact that women were not left out; in fact, their gifts were obviously prepared specifically for their day-to-day life, i.e., these were not only to enable them to do a better job at scraping furs. Women were important enough to warrant special treatment— no doubt because they were economically important. As such, they would have been in a position to urge their men to bring in more furs, so the flow of traders' goods could continue.

Explorers and traders frequently encountered Indian women. When Jonathan Carver met with the Winnebagos on the Fox River in 1766, he found that their leader was a woman, a "queen," as Carver termed her. The death of a husband could raise some women politically or affect them in the trade, as Augustin Grignon recalled in describing a Chippewa woman who lived on the Upper Fox at the end of the eighteenth century. O-cha-own had no children and lived alone, with wigwam and garden-patch, hunting through the winter with her dogs quite as successfully as did the men.

The trader Curot's food search sometimes took him to Indian women, from whom he purchased at one point a "Big birch bark basket Full of rice." Malhiot's detailed payment record for 1804–5 notes payments to several women at Lac du Flambeau: the wife of Petit Jour (for two dishes of wild rice); the mother-in-law of Bazinet (for a sack of wild rice); the mother of Le Canard (for half a sack of wild rice); several women (for husking five sacks of corn); an old woman (for dressing six deer skins, lacing four pairs of snowshoes, and cutting a doe skin into thongs); and the sister of L'Epaule de Canard (for half a sack of corn). The items purchased and the activities rewarded give some idea of tasks performed in the fur trade by Indian women.

Curot reported several incidents at the Yellow River post that reflected the freedom of Chippewa women to leave their husbands. Subagent Gardant Smith had trouble keeping a wife during the 1803–4 year: in October Curot wrote that Smith's wife left him, but he took another. In November, "Smith's wife went off with a savage of the fond du Lac who came last evening"; however, the following day Curot reported a fight between two Indians in which one was killed while the other had his nose cut off. Curot explained: "They were Jealous of one another Concerning Smith's wife, who wished, as Men have two wives, to have two husbands." But four days later he noted that "Smith's Wife came back from her promenade last evening." Smith's troubles were not over, for in December, his new wife went to spend the winter with other Indians, and in January Curot recorded the arrival of Le Sel, "who has Smith's wife For his own."

Another group usually passed over in discussing the fur trade were descendants of African slaves. Both free and enslaved Africans were present in the Upper Lakes fur trade. When the French gave up the trans-Appalachian country to the British, the French governor instructed his subjects that by the articles of capitulation, they "may keep their negro and Pawnee slaves," except those captured from the British. British records of 1779 mention blacks working on ships carrying goods on Lake Michigan to Michilimackinac. That year brought the most famous black fur trader to the Chicago portage: Jean Baptiste Point du Sable, who arrived about 1779, set up a trading post, and is recognized as the first settler in Chicago. Du Sable was arrested by the British and sent to Michilimackinac during the Revolution, but returned to trade at Chicago until moving with his Indian wife to Peoria in 1800.

The expansion of the trade in these years drew many men of diverse backgrounds, and not surprisingly fur trade records contain references to blacks. Perrault recounted a murder story from Mackinac in 1791, in which the Indian also stabbed "an old negro named Bongà" who was in his way as he fled. In 1794 the Mackinac parish register recorded the marriage of "jean bouga and of jeanne, the former a negro, the latter a negress, both free." They had formerly been slaves of the Mackinac commandant. This is probably the person referred to earlier by Perrault; it is also possibly a relative of "Pierre Bonza," listed as "a negro" who traded on the Red River with Alexander Henry, Jr., between 1800–6 and who was at Fort William in 1816. On the Yellow River in 1804, "The negro" arrived with voyageurs one day, according to Michel Curot's journal.

At about the time of the Mackinac incident in 1791, two black traders from there established a trading post at the mouth of the Menominee River (site of Marinette). Augustin Gringon would later recollect that they were good at sleight-of-hand performances, and "impressed the Indians with the belief that they were medicine-men, and held communications with the spirit world." However, when Indian children began to die, blame centered on the two blacks, and "one Menominee and several Chippewas attacked the negroes in their house, killed one, and shot the other as he was endeavoring to escape from the window." Three of the killers spent three years in prison in Montreal for the crime, Grignon recalled.

There were both black and Indian slaves at Green Bay. Grignon—born around 1780—remembered Indian slaves brought from the Plains, particularly Pawnees, who served Wisconsin Indians as well as whites. He also recalled seeing two black slaves at Green Bay, one of whom was later purchased by the first U.S. Indian agent at Prairie du Chien. Most white families had Indian slaves at Green Bay at the time of the American Revolution, and in the 1790s a Mackinac man was purchasing black slaves in Illinois and selling them in Prairie du Chien, Green Bay, and Mackinac. Free blacks and black slaves, free Indians and Indian slaves, *métis*, French, British, and Americans, would continue to co-exist in Wisconsin in the decades following the Revolution. In that sense the frontier was a coming-together of peoples.

Chippewa-Sioux Warfare

Fighting between Chippewas and Sioux continued unabated during the British era, despite repeated attempts by Montreal traders and the British government to bring about a peace. Americans were still too far removed from the scene to become involved.

Traders Perrault, Nelson, and Curot had to deal with the continuing Sioux-Chippewa warfare frequently. Perrault was at Prairie du Chien during the 1787 peace gathering, and learned only later that a group of Sioux from St. Peter's River (in Minnesota) went up the St. Croix at that time and attacked a clan of Chippewas, while the rest of the Chippewas were absent. "This mortified them very much on their return," he wrote.

Perrault's trading at the Red Cedar was repeatedly confounded by this strife, but his work was drastically upset in November 1788, at a time when he already had collected eight packs of beaver and was brimming with optimism over prospects for winter. Six Chippewas came to trade, but before they departed twenty-eight Sioux suddenly arrived with their headmen. "I would have preferred to Be a Long way off then," Perrault admitted. He brokered peace talks, each side seemed courteous, and things went well. The Sioux explained that they had just come to hunt deer in the thick woods during the winter and then would leave; the Chippewa graciously said they could remain until March. But when the Chippewas later departed they fell into a Sioux ambush, losing two of their warriors. One day several months later, in early spring, Perrault looked up and saw the Red Cedar "Covered with people"—it was the Chippewas, come to punish him for his alleged role in the ambush. Perrault was able to save himself by winning the support of La merde D'aigle, one of the intruders; he also softened the tribe's anger by "covering the dead" with cloth, overcoats, blankets, ammunition, two kegs of rum, and other gifts, and by allowing the Chippewas to eat fifteen deer carcasses stored at the post as well as carrying off "Many Trifles."

Nelson and Curot on the Yellow River similarly found themselves in tense situations because of the Sioux-Chippewa conflict. On one occasion Curot sent two of his men searching for others, but they returned early, traveling overnight, after hearing the hooting of an owl—"since the Sioux Imitate it The most freqently in their cries." Nelson and his men were once so terrified by an owl's "ooing in the woods," fearing it might be "a Scouter of the Scioux," that they sent two Indians to investigate; but it was only an owl and they drove it away. Nelson eventually moved his X Y shed within the North West fort for protection.

The reason for the switch within the North West's barricade was that Nelson's crew was finding increasing signs in the woods of Sioux presence. Chippewa scouts claimed that some 200 Sioux were nearby; "Other of our indians said they counted 410 Sticks, as it [was] customary with [the Sioux] that each man leaves a Small stick by his fire." The traders made a pact with each other: if one were captured, in order to save themselves the others would not let him into the fort even if he were being butchered alive.

During Curot's time on the Yellow the Sioux threat became progressively more serious, bits of evidence filtering in almost weekly. One day a trader arrived from across the St. Croix with news that the Sioux had discovered him; later Curot learned that local Indians had deserted their nearby hunting area after hearing gunshots, traveling away from the Sioux. Then word came of Sioux interfering with other traders along the St. Croix, and on March 5, 1804, Curot wrote: "This evening The Sioux Spies came to listen and prowl around the fort," and tracks were seen coming from Yellow Lake. Some six weeks later, in April, one of his workers said his dog had refused to run in the woods as it usually did; an Indian told of seeing "a Strange Savage that he thought was a Sioux." But despite these foreboding signs, they were spared any Sioux attacks on the post.

Although the Sioux in these years were sporadically moving westward, patronizing French traders in the lower Minnesota valley and joining western Sioux on the Plains, tribesmen made one more major thrust against the Chippewas in this period. Oral traditions report an attack in 1806 at Mole Lake, in northeastern Wisconsin, where the Chippewas thrashed the Sioux. The Sioux, in fact, never again returned to Wisconsin in large numbers.

The Final Struggle: Britain vs. the United States

Conflicts and Tensions

Americans were largely shut out of the Upper Great Lakes trade wars in the years immediately following the Revolution. However, traders from the Ohio Valley and Michigan had visited

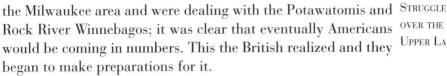
the Milwaukee area and were dealing with the Potawatomis and Rock River Winnebagos; it was clear that eventually Americans would be coming in numbers. This the British realized and they began to make preparations for it.

The United States was establishing a military presence also. The crucial American victory at the Battle of Fallen Timbers in Ohio in 1794 clarified not only that the United States was determined to secure its title to the Old Northwest, but that it was able to do so through force. Wisconsin Indians were part of the British alliance at Fallen Timbers, and were among those fleeing who were refused safe haven at Britain's nearby Fort Miami. U.S. General Anthony Wayne's followup Treaty of Greenville transferred almost all of Ohio and eastern Indiana to United States control, and specified that in remaining areas of the Northwest Territory, Indians could sell their lands only to the United States government.

Jay's Treaty, also in 1794, required the British to abandon all posts on American soil by June 1, 1796, although it left British traders still free to "navigate all the lakes, rivers and waters" in the two countries' territories, and Americans could also cross into Canada; Prairie du Chien on the Mississippi was to be open for use of citizens of both nations. As a result of Jay's Treaty, during 1796 Detroit was taken over by U.S. forces on July 11, and Mackinac on September 1.

But loyalty toward the British remained strong among the region's Indians, who heard frightening tales of the approaching Americans, the "Long Knives." The British continued to shower gifts and medals on the tribes and repeatedly sought through diplomacy to reopen the boundary question, leaving the Indians as occupants, British traders with full travel and business freedom, and—they hoped—American settlers excluded. All British proposals would have left Wisconsin as an Indian territory or buffer state. The British ambassador at one point urged the United States to reconstitute the Northwest Territory as an Indian hunting ground, with Mackinac and Detroit to be delivered to the Indians. Other British proposals would have stopped the Americans in their westward and northward push at various natural or artificial boundaries, even along the Fox-Wisconsin route, or—as a last resort if all other proposals were rejected—then along the south side of Lake Superior straight west to the Mississippi.

American Efforts

In truth, Wisconsin lay far from most Americans' concerns at the end of the eighteenth century, for the United States was developing an interest in the region only slowly and sporadically. In 1796, however, the new federal government launched a system for regulating the fur trade, then obviously out of control and dominated by British companies. By installing trading "factories" at crucial sites throughout the west, President George Washington sought to supply goods to the Indians at fair prices while protecting them from unscrupulous traders. The "principal object" of the factories was "to secure the Friendship of the Indians in our country in a way the most beneficial to them and the most effectual and economical to the United States;" the factors who ran the posts were to inspire "full confidence" in the nation's honor, integrity, and good faith. Alcohol was banned; as restated in an 1802 memo to all Indian agents, "no trader should be allowed to vend any Goods, to the Indians, who shall carry ardent Spirits into their Country for sale or other purposes."

Beginning among tribes in the south, the system was expanded northward in 1802 with factories at Detroit and Fort Wayne; in 1805 the Detroit factory was transferred to Chicago, where Fort Dearborn became a U.S. military post. This meant that British traders were now facing American regulation as well as competition (Prairie du Chien had its first licensed U.S. trader in 1801). The challenge became more serious in 1807 when U.S. Indian agents were named for Prairie du Chien and Fort Madison (Iowa), and in 1809 when a new U.S. factory opened at Mackinac.

U.S. agents arriving at these new outposts quickly saw the seriousness of the situation. Nicolas Boilvin, agent at Prairie du Chien, wrote to President Madison in 1809 that British subjects working for the Michilimackinac Company were jealous of the factories and U.S. agents and were trying to sow discord. Boilvin saw three things as "absolutely necessary" for the Sioux, Menominee, Winnebago, Fox, and Sac tribes he dealt with:

to know that there are small presents for them every year; or a company of brave soldiers to control the [Michilimackinac] Company . . . as well as the Indians; or to prohibit the Company from trading with them. Just as soon as one of these three measures goes into effect, I do not doubt at all that perfect harmony will reign among the different tribes and beween the tribes and our government.

The factories faced other difficulties beyond the British challenge. Most important of these was their inability to issue credit and their failure to block traders from bringing in alcohol. Perhaps most self-defeating of all, the American factors were not supplied with gifts to distribute among the tribes. Early mistakes of the British were being repeated by the frontier's new rulers.

The first U.S. flag to fly officially in Wisconsin arrived with Lt. Zebulon M. Pike, sent from St. Louis in 1805–6 to explore the Upper Mississippi country. Like Lewis and Clark, making their journey up the Missouri at the same time, Pike traveled with a long list of official goals, including: to bring about peace between the Sioux and Chippewas, to seek alliances with Indian tribes, to locate sites for government posts, and to learn the numbers and locations of British traders on U.S. territory.

Leaving St. Louis on August 5, 1805, Pike and the twenty men under his command alternately sailed, rowed, poled, and towed the seventy-foot keelboat up the Mississippi. They made two stops at Prairie du Chien: going upstream, a four-day visit starting September 4, 1805; going downstream, a five-day stay beginning April 18, 1806.

During the return stopover, Winnebagos handed over their British medals and flags to Pike, something he frequently demanded of tribes but seldom received. Athletic events took a more prominent position in the schedule this time, however, probably because of the hundreds of Indians present. In an enormous game of lacrosse, the Sioux took on a combined Winnebago and Fox team. Bets up to $1,000 in value were made, then the ball was thrown out for the game to begin on the half-mile field. Victory went to the Sioux because (Pike concluded) of their superior ball-handling skills, although the Winnebago and Fox were better runners.

Historians have argued over the importance of Pike's Mississippi expedition. He did not find the true source of the Mississippi; his warnings to British traders to fly only the U.S. flag had no effect; his attempts to bring about an Indian peace were thwarted. The purchase of a site for Fort Snelling, near modern St. Paul, Minnesota, emerged as one of the expedition's few long-lasting accomplishments. ("You will perceive that we have obtained about 100,000 acres for a song," Pike wrote triumphantly to his commander in St. Louis.) However, it should be added that Pike carried the American flag into regions where it was unknown; he added greatly to American knowledge of the Upper Mississippi, and drew attention to the Great Valley while establishing an American presence.

Other U.S. government actions in the period revealed American determination to expand into the Upper Mississippi. In late 1804 five lower-ranking leaders of the combined Sac-Fox tribes were in St. Louis at the same time as visiting Governor William Henry Harrison. The Indians had come to retrieve a tribesman jailed there on a murder charge; Harrison was present because Indiana Territory temporarily had jurisdiction over the area beyond the Mississippi recently acquired in the Louisiana Purchase. For an annuity of $1,000, the Sacs and Foxes gave up their claims to lands between the Illinois and the lower Wisconsin rivers, covering much of the Rock River watershed, extending as far east as the Fox River which runs north from the Illinois near Chicago. It included a significant section of southern Wisconsin although not the Lake Michigan shore.

The War of 1812

Americans and British were moving cumberously toward another conflict in these years, with the Upper Lakes frontier and its furs as one major bone of contention. The highly competitive fur trade was now attracting more Americans who sought a share of its fabulous profits; Indians were being wooed by both sides— but most successfully by the British—throughout the Old Northwest (eventually the states of Ohio, Indiana, Illinois, Michigan, Wisconsin, and Minnesota east of the Mississippi). With the new American factory system in place, Indian agencies, and military forts, the U.S. government demonstrated its determination to control the region. British diplomats, meanwhile, made it abundantly clear they did not regard the Upper Lakes as permanently American.

When war finally erupted in 1812 it quickly drew in Wisconsin. From early stirrings of Indian revolt under the Shawnee leader Tecumseh and his brother Lalawethika, Wisconsin tribes were actively recruited by the British and fought for them. Some blood was shed in Wisconsin, mainly around the Prairie du Chien post. And when the last British soldier left Prairie du Chien in 1815, an era ended both for Wisconsin and the young nation.

Lalawethika had a religious experience in 1805 that changed him from a drunken, unpopular Shawnee misfit into a religious mystic who took the name Tenskwatawa, the Prophet. The Prophet would no longer drink the "white man's poison"—whiskey—nor would he wear American clothes; he called for a return to traditional ways, including caring for the elderly, ending sexual promiscuity, and rejecting the accumulation of property. Revitalization in this manner has been a recurring theme throughout Native American history as overwhelmed Indians turned inward for strength to carry on; the pattern would appear again, within Wisconsin and elsewhere, long after the Shawnee Prophet had passed from the scene.

The Prophet's teachings spread rapidly through the trans-Appalachian frontier. The Chippewas south of Lake Superior were drawn to the movement and eventually also the Menominees around Green Bay, the Winnebagos, and the Sacs and Foxes (now virtually merged into one tribe). The storekeeper at a British post near Mackinac wrote to his father in 1807 that "all the Ottawas from L'arbe au Croche adhere strictly to the Shawney Prophet's advice they do not wear Hats, Drink or Conjure, they intend all to visit him this Autumn, which will occasion a great scarcity of corn at this post & Makina." These Indians did not buy a gallon a month of whiskey or rum, he noted. Similarly, Augustin Grignon recalled that part of the Prophet's call warned Indians against furnishing meat any longer to whites, and during the 1810–11 winter was only able to obtain it from Menominee and Winnebago hunters in the Pine River area by refusing them ammunition unless they provided him the meat.

Tensions on the high seas between the two nations were

matched on the frontier as traders and government agents contested for control repeatedly, Americans charging that the British were encouraging Indian warfare. The British carefully cultivated Tecumseh, who had been angered by the large southern Indiana land cession won by the Americans from tribes in 1809. The Prophet by then had moved his settlement to northwestern Indiana, which became the site of the Battle of Tippecanoe in November 1811, where Americans not only pummeled the Indians but largely discredited the Prophet. Leadership then passed to Tecumseh as the United States declared war on Britain on June 18, 1812.

The British moved quickly to seize key points on the Great Lakes. In July the British commander at St. Joseph Island received instructions to seize the American fort on Mackinac Island, forty miles away. His force was considerably strengthened by some 120 Sioux, Menominees, and Winnebagos just arrived from Prairie du Chien with Robert Dickson, a British trader and one of the most influential British partisans in the Upper Lakes. Mackinac capitulated on July 17, 1812, its U.S. defenders not even aware their country was at war. Chicago and Detroit also fell quickly. Tribes from the Upper Lakes, conditioned by decades of British gifts, their anti-Americanism further whetted by the Prophet's teachings and Tecumseh's organizing, went over totally to the British.

The Americans still had one outpost on the Upper Mississippi, however, at Prairie du Chien. But upon receiving news of British successes the Americans there fled, as did the lone American at Green Bay. Since both communities were now cleared of anyone either officially or openly sympathizing with the Americans, Dickson turned both sites into rallying points for collecting warriors for expeditions against United States targets.

The movement for a pan-Indian confederacy was finally stopped in 1813, however, when U.S. forces overwhelmed British defenders at the Battle of the Thames, north of Lake Erie in Canada; Tecumseh was slain there. British hopes in the west were set back severely.

Realizing that control of Prairie du Chien might be crucial, Governor William Clark of St. Louis launched a drive up the

Mississippi in May 1814, with five barges carrying himself and some 200 U.S. soldiers and volunteers. The small British force at Prairie du Chien fled at their approach, but Clark's men killed seven Winnebagos when they tried to escape imprisonment. Fort Shelby was built on a mound at the rear of the village, and Clark soon returned to St. Louis. Villagers at first planned to contest the American occupation; finding they were undisturbed, however, they soon returned to their usual activities.

Plotting regional strategy from his position at Mackinac, the British commander quickly saw the significance of Clark's move. Col. Robert McDouall wrote to his superiors that the Americans had to be dislodged, and in the process he revealed the fur trade links that were entwined with British policies: if Prairie du Chien were not restored to the British, McDouall said, "our connexion with the Indians" would end, "for if allowed to settle themselves by dint of threats, bribes, & sowing divisions among them, tribe after tribe would be gained over [to the Americans] or subdued, & thus would be destroyed the only barrier which protects the great trading establishments of the North West and the Hudson's Bay Companies."

Prairie du Chien fell quickly to a 650-man British and Indian invading force after three days of siege on July 20, 1814. Augustin Grignon later recalled his role with the British expedition, going forward at night with two Indians and another *méti* to sneak into the post and return with a Prairie du Chien resident, who provided details on the Americans' positions. After the attack was launched, the crew of a protecting U.S. gunboat eventually gave up the fight and floated downstream to safety. The small American force in the fort surrendered, and American reinforcements coming up the Mississippi in barges were driven back at the mouth of the Rock River. The British had retaken Wisconsin and the Upper Mississippi.

Meanwhile, negotiators for the two warring powers were meeting in Ghent, Belgium, holding talks that initially stalled because of the Americans' rejection of a British demand: Great Britain sought to retain its western posts and create a neutral Indian state west of the Great Lakes, which would have taken in Wisconsin. Failing in their aim for an Indian territory, the British next demanded that each side simply hold on to territory it then held: the Americans would keep part of Upper Canada, east of Detroit, but the British would retain Wisconsin and the Upper Peninsula which they had won in battle. Eventually, however, the *status ante bellum* became the basis for the accord, and sovereignty for each side remained what it had legally held when the war began in 1812. Wisconsin was still part of the United States.

Receiving early reports that the peace talks had failed, Britain's Capt. Alfred Bulger at Prairie du Chien continued to keep the Indians in southern Wisconsin and along the Mississippi poised for further action against the Americans. He instructed his agent with the Sacs on Rock River to impress upon the Indians why the British were fighting:

> . . . that it is *solely on their* account that the war is now carried on. That the King their Great Father always true to his promises is resolved not to lay down the Casse-tété till the Indians are restored to their rights, and their future independence secured.

The British did abandon the Indians, however. News of the abandonment, carried out in the Ghent treaty of Dec. 24, 1814, was a long time traveling to the frontier, and when it reached Mackinac the British commander complained, "Our negociators as usual, have been egregiously duped: as usual, they have shown themselves profoundly ignorant of the concerns of this part of the Empire." He urged, however, that care be given to avoid giving the Americans an excuse for more fighting, "until our Fleet on Lake Erie is restored, & until we have the supremacy *of this*"— meaning Lake Michigan. In the end Mackinac was evacuated, also Prairie du Chien, and the British left the region south of the lakes they had largely controlled since 1761.

The leave-taking was difficult for all, but it is likely that no British commander had the excruciating embarrassment of Captain Bulger on the Mississippi. Weeks earlier, in April, he had gathered some 1,200 warriors at Prairie du Chien to announce that peace talks had failed because of American refusal to yield on the Indians' retaining possession of their own lands. He then revealed plans to carry the war to the St. Louis area, and preparations were well underway when the news of the treaty arrived. The downriver attack died before it could be born. "Upon no other occasion in the course of the war had so choice a body of Indians been arrayed under the British flag," Bulger later recalled wistfully. But now he had to break the news to these same tribesmen—whose desire to defend their homelands had been stirred to a high pitch—that the war was indeed over and the British had abandoned them. For although the treaty stated that Indians were being restored to their lands, it also gave the Americans retention of Prairie du Chien. Captain Bulger called his position "most mortifying."

Losing no time, Bulger and his assistants began meeting with the tribes. Because they feared retaliation from angry Indians, his men remained at the ready, under arms, within the fort for two weeks, while Bulger and his aides struggled to convince the chiefs to accept the diplomats' decree. Gradually, most tribal leaders began to come around to the view that it was acceptable, or, perhaps, unavoidable. But Bulger took no chances, and when the treaty ceremony began May 22 in the Indian council house (with some seventy leaders and other tribal members jammed inside), British soldiers in the nearby fort stood with guns ready.

The Indians did not revolt. Instead, the five-hour ceremony gave the British their final opportunity to unloose all their symbols, arguments, and cajolery for dealing with the Indians. Captain Bulger presented the great war belt which had originally called the tribes to war: it featured a drawing of the castle of St. Louis, with Indians standing hand-in-hand with their English father. But the belt's original coloration of red, for war, had now been changed to blue, for peace. As the king's order was brought forth to be read, the British flag was dramatically raised above the council house and a royal salute of twenty-guns fired from within the fort. At this point "a deathlike silence prevailed throughout the whole assembly." The treaty was explained and translated. All tribal leaders then stood up and spoke in turn, only the Sac war-chief—undoubtedly Black Hawk—expressing reservations but finally agreeing to go along with the "good counsel" of the British.

Two days later Bulger and his troops left Prairie du Chien.

They headed up the Wisconsin River with all their weaponry, including previously seized guns which were supposed to be turned over to the incoming Americans at an official ceremony. But tensions with the Indians were too high: to await the Americans' arrival "would have proved fatal to the British garrison," Bulger admitted in a letter to his commander.

Wisconsin's future now lay with the young republic whose expansion westward was gaining momentum, moving along on the feet of settlers rather than in birchbark canoes. These were men and women who cared more for farmland than furs, who looked upon forests as sources of lumber more than peltry. Many of the issues that the British and French had confronted in the Upper Lakes would now be faced by newcomers who had different uses for their frontier. They would find new challenges as they entered the land of oak openings, prairie, lakes, and dark forest that beckoned beyond Lake Michigan.

6.

MINERS, INDIAN WARS, AND A FRONTIER TRANSFORMED

Americans wasted little time in bringing enormous changes to the Wisconsin they regained in 1815, for this time the legal control authorized by diplomats was quickly followed by actual occupation. Men and women from Illinois and Missouri, New York and Massachusetts, arrived to compete for commercial and political power with Indians and French-speakers whose ties still stretched to the Mackinac country or settlements along the St. Lawrence.

Contrasts and conflicts appeared that were greater than Wisconsin would ever—probably—know again. The lead mining districts of southwestern Wisconsin were overrun by men seeking instant wealth, and in the process welcomed such European nobles as Vincent Dziewanowski, who fled the Polish revolution of 1832 and wound up working at a smelter in Muscoda, and Adéle Maria Antoinette Gratiot, whose mother had been lady-in-waiting to Queen Marie Antoinette at the time of the French Revolution. European nobility and genteel Easterners rubbed elbows with rough types who cussed and fought; in 1842 one of the miners' representatives in the Territorial Legislature shot and killed a colleague at the close of a heated debate in the Council Chambers.

The fur trade settlements brought old and new together in dramatic fashion. A visitor to Prairie du Chien saw a small girl who "was going minus her scalp," victim of an Indian uprising. She "was shown to us as one of the curiosities of the place," he reported. But slightly earlier in the same village, a young military doctor named William Beaumont performed medical experiments upon a fur trader who had been accidentally shot in the stomach—experiments which provided the scientific world with its first accurate look at gastric juices and the digestibility of different foods. The research had begun at Fort Mackinac, where Beaumont as an Army surgeon became interested in the condition of Alexis St. Martin, a French trader whose stomach wound would not heal. Both men were at Prairie du Chien from 1829–31, where the experiments continued, with food inserted through the stomach hole, then checked for the progress of digestion at different times. Beaumont's notes were published as *Experiments and Observations on the Gastric Juice and the Physiology of Digestion*, and received extensive notice in the east and in Europe.

At the other old trading settlement, Green Bay, a new resident found in the late 1820s that each family not directly engaged in the fur trade hired an Indian on a permanent basis; they "had to keep such a hunter" to provide them with meat. Steamboats were then entering the Upper Lakes, but the old ways remained: Juliette Kinzie encountered this reality in 1830 when she accompanied her husband to the Portage and his new post at Fort Winnebago, traveling up the Fox River in a thirty-foot Mackinaw boat propelled by singing French-Canadian voyageurs: "a more exhilarating mode of travel can hardly be imagined than a voyage over these waters," Mrs. Kinzie wrote in her memoir *Wau-Bun*, "amid all the wild magnificence of nature, with the measured strokes of the oar keeping time to the strains of 'Le Rosier Blanc,' 'En roulant ma Boule,' or 'Lève ton pied, ma jolie Bergere.'"

It was a land still dependent upon the outside world. Just as lonely fur traders two centuries earlier had counted on European preferences for beaver hats to provide them with a living, now distant needs and sources still dominated frontier life. This dependence even extended to the lumber needed to house a burgeoning population, and an 1837 visitor was surprised to encounter

129

MINERS,
INDIAN WARS,
AND A
FRONTIER
TRANSFORMED

Juliet Magill Kinzie came with her husband to Fort Winnebago in 1830, two years after the fort was built to control the Fox-Wisconsin portage. A New Englander, she approached the frontier with keen perception and appreciation for differences in peoples—whether Indians around the post, lead miners, or *métis* traders. Her *Wau-Bun: The Early Day in the Northwest*, is considered a classic of Wisconsin literature. COURTESY STATE HISTORICAL SOCIETY OF WISCONSIN, WHI (X3) 30186.

pine boards that had originated in the upper reaches of the Allegheny River in New York State, were cut in Pittsburgh sawmills, then carried down the Ohio and up the Mississippi to be used to build a house in Wisconsin.

But with foodstuffs it was even more serious on this changing frontier, for fur traders and miners did not produce edibles, and farmers were not yet numerous amid the oak openings and along the riverbottoms. A traveler trying to obtain a meal in Mineral Point in 1837 found that its citizens "were as dependent upon others as if they were on board a ship." Each autumn in the 1820s, 1830s, and 1840s Wisconsin's growing population looked anxiously into its cellars, crocks, and barrels and contemplated the frigid months ahead when nothing would arrive from "outside." The winter of 1838–39 was especially hard on communities accustomed to surviving on imported foods. Green Bay's shipping season in 1838 began on April 15 and had apparently ended November 22, but when another vessel made it through before freezeup the local newspaper cheered that its docking "has put an end to all fear of want." However, the southwestern mining districts that winter faced "utter destitution" when Mississippi River navigation closed for the season before adequate food supplies could be stockpiled. A fur agent reported in late November "there is not a pound of Pork, Sugar, Tea, Coffee, Lard, Butter for sale in this place—all the merchants are entirely destitute of groceries & have all been caught with their supplies on the way up." A local editor used the occasion to condemn the mining region's dependence on "foreign produce."

Residents of these fast-growing but still frontier communities could only await warmer weather, and desperation mingled with springtime excitement in the Mississippi and Lake Michigan communities when shouts announced arrival of the first ship. The *Wisconsin Democrat* caught this spirit when the first steamboat of 1839 was sighted coming up Green Bay one day in late April:

> No person who has not lived in a section of country like this, where the people are for the space of four or five months, during the close of the season of navigation, literally imprisoned, shut *in* or *out* from the rest of the world, can imagine the sensation which is created by the first cry of "Steam-boat Ahoy!"

The transportation revolution then transforming America heavily affected Wisconsin and channeled its frontier development into specific pathways. Detroit first saw a steamboat in 1818, and in 1838 eleven steamboats were operating on the Upper Lakes; by 1845 there were sixty. Steam power quickly reached the Upper Mississippi, also, the first steamboat arriving in Prairie du Chien in 1823. A traveler reported that three steamboats had ascended as far as the falls of the St. Croix River in 1838. This revolution meant that a New Yorker using the Erie Canal could reach Green Bay in eight days by the mid–1830s, instead of three weeks as was the case before the Erie Canal and steamboating. Nothing changed the frontier as quickly as steam transportation.

The rapid acceleration into a new age lifted to importance men who had little interest in the fur trade or swapping goods with the Indians. When politicians created the first Great Seal of Wisconsin Territory in 1836 it revealed the power of these new

🐚 131

MINERS,
INDIAN WARS,
AND A
FRONTIER
TRANSFORMED

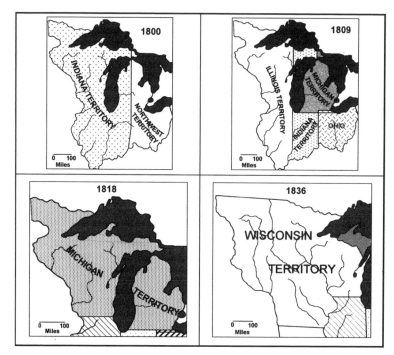

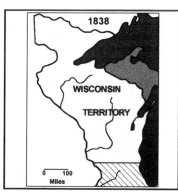

Wisconsin was initially part of the Territory Northwest of the Ohio— the "Old Northwest"—and then was included in Indiana (1800), Illinois (1809), and Michigan (1818) Territories before achieving separate territorial status in 1836; statehood came in 1848. MAP ADAPTED BY JILL FREUND THOMAS AND MICHAEL MAST, FROM ALICE E. SMITH, *The History of Wisconsin. Volume I: From Exploration to Statehood* (STATE HISTORICAL SOCIETY OF WISCONSIN, 1973).

interests, for the emblem depicted neither Indian nor fur trader: it showed only a miner's arm, clutching a pick, aiming at a pile of rocks that presumably contained lead ore.

Such were the contrasts as Wisconsin's population continued to climb: in 1820 all of Michigan Territory—which then included Wisconsin—counted fewer than 9,000 inhabitants; by 1830 that territory's counties west of Lake Michigan still had only some 3,000. But when Wisconsin gained territorial status in 1836 a special census found 11,683. And only four years later in the 1840 census the territory's total had climbed—amazingly—to 30,945.

The Fur Trade Settlements

Only two permanent settlements existed when the British evacuated Wisconsin in 1815. Green Bay and Prairie du Chien were both basically French-Canadian, Indian, *métis* villages, their town lots extending back from the Fox or Mississippi in the system adapted from French communities along the St. Lawrence. Running at right angles to the river, these long-lots varied in width, and were usually of indeterminate length; Green Bay residents told U.S. Land Commissioners their claims covered eighty arpents, approximately three miles in depth. At Prairie du Chien, more involved in agriculture with its Mississippi River bottomland, town lots ran back from the river in St. Lawrence style, while outside the settlement the residents created a French-style common grazing ground and an area of several thousand acres for open-field agriculture.

U.S. soldiers arriving at Green Bay in 1816 erected Fort Howard, forming a central focus for the community spread loosely along the shoreline of the bay and the Fox River. Six miles up that river lay the De Pere rapids, and soon other communities would spring up—Navarino, Astor, Menomoneeville (or "Shantytown"), all known collectively as Green Bay. When Henry Schoolcraft visited in 1820 he found sixty houses and a population of some 500 people outside the fort. He was on an expedition to explore the vast region encompassed by Michigan Territory, led by Territorial Governor Lewis Cass; Schoolcraft commented that Green Bay's inhabitants were "with few exceptions, French, who have intermarried with Indian women, and are said generally, to be indolent, gay, intemperate, and illiterate."

In 1824 the government Indian agent reported there were no more than 130 white men, seven white women, and twenty-two white children in the Green Bay vicinity; a later study put the percentage of *métis* or part-Indian households at just under 60

133

MINERS,
INDIAN WARS,
AND A
FRONTIER
TRANSFORMED

Built in 1816, Fort Howard on the west bank of the
Fox River established an American military presence
in the Upper Lakes; it was paired with Fort Crawford
at Prairie du Chien, built the same year. LITHOGRAPH BY
LIGNY ET CIE., FROM *Vues et Souvenirs de l'Amerique du Nord*,
BY FRANCIS (COMTE) DE CASTELNAU (PARIS, 1842). COURTESY STATE
HISTORICAL SOCIETY OF WISCONSIN, WHI (X3) 32689.

percent of the total. French was their language. A visitor in 1830
observed that "it is common in this region for the business men
to marry those half Blood Ladies."

This world of French-speakers and mixed-breeds was strange
to many newly arriving Americans. Maj. Stephen Long called
Prairie du Chien's French-Indian population "degenerating . . .
instead of improving." Some years later Caleb Atwater agreed
with this assessment, calling the village's people "as motley a
group of creatures, (I can scarcely call them human beings) as
the world ever beheld. . . . each one consisting of Negro, Indian,
French, English, American, Scotch, Irish and Spanish blood."
New Yorker James Lockwood came to Green Bay with a military
supply operation but soon wound up with the fur trade in Prairie

du Chien, where he found a "singular state of society": in addition to the crude culinary situation, Lockwood mentioned the problem of "gentlemen selecting wives of the nut-brown natives, and raising children of mixed blood." He later looked back on the era and concluded that the old fur trading posts were unchanged for years, "until the Americans emigrated to them, and took hold of them with their enterprise, when they at once improved, and most of them became places of business and importance."

With American domination came a new system of law, and these changes began to grate on those used to the old ways. The first grand jury called to session after the American takeover of Green Bay showed how far the challenge to tradition could go. Judge James Duane Doty, a New Yorker and the first circuit judge sent in by Michigan Territory, directed the jury in 1824 to take up the question of persons living together who had not been legally wed. It was a typical frontier situation, common in Wisconsin's early settlements, where whites were nominally Catholics but where no clergymen had been present for years and so "marriages" took place in Indian camps located far from a justice of the peace. In this the French frontiersmen had again adapted to the ways of the Indians. But the Green Bay grand jury, acting under Judge Doty's instructions, wound up indicting thirty-six persons—Green Bay's principal male citizens—for fornication; two others were charged with adultery. All were informed that if they married within ten days no fines would be issued; all except two did this.

Fur Traders

The fur trade chafed under the new regime also. Earlier attempts by the French and British to control the trade had failed while provoking the wrath of both Indians and traders; now their criticism was directed at U.S. government regulations which were imposed on a system of declining peltry in operations requiring extensive granting of credit over long periods of time. Robert Dickson, the prominent British trader at Prairie du Chien who had earlier been the nemesis of Americans, admitted in 1820 that "the Indian trade in this country is not in my opinion worth following, it is like walking in the Mud untill you get soussed over head & Ears."

The governmental factory system entered a bleak season, despite erection of forts Crawford at Prairie du Chien and Howard at Green Bay, which might have been expected to provide adequate enforcement of U.S. fur trade regulations. These included the 1816 prohibition of foreigners participating in the American trade, and the 1820 embargo on Canadian (British) goods being used. Finally, yielding to pressure from John Jacob Astor's American Fur Company and other traders, the government abolished the factory system in 1822. The company used government rules to establish a nearly complete fur trade monopoly over Wisconsin and most of the Upper Lakes.

The American Fur Company's problems were paralleled—indeed, had some of their origins—in troubles on the local level. Most established traders ran into debt as the value of fur returns declined. A chorus of lament comes from the fur trade records of Wisconsin from the 1820s on, as seen in John Lawe's report from Green Bay that year:

> You see the famous returns we have made. oh! what a shame it is for us to Carry on Indian Trade as we do under so many disadvantages & what a heavy loss we meet with again this Year much more then last and what is to be done I do not know.

Four years later Lawe was again complaining, arguing that every year since the War of 1812 "I have been loosing Money & not a little in that cursed Indian Trade that I have allways persisted and do Still persist to continue which will soon put me a beggar."

Lead Miners Arrive

While fur traders were struggling to adapt to the new regime, events were taking place in southwestern Wisconsin that would soon dominate both the new era and the new territory aborning. Unlike the fur trade, however, the new economic enterprises in the southwest did not depend on cooperating with the Indians.

Lead mines were the magnet that transformed a little-known,

distant corner of Michigan Territory into the population center of Wisconsin Territory, created by Congress in 1836. While the lead district also extended into adjacent areas of Illinois and Iowa, some 90 percent of the lead deposits were in Wisconsin, covering modern Iowa, Grant, and Lafayette counties.

Indians had discovered galena, the grey mineral that contained lead, in several areas of Wisconsin in the distant past. Archeologists have uncovered evidence of lead smelting at the Bell site near Lake Winnebago, a Fox village of the late seventeenth and early eighteenth centuries, and at Crabapple Point by Lake Koshkonong, a Winnebago camp from the late eighteenth or early nineteenth century. Archeological work at many Midwestern Indian sites reveals the presence of lead obtained through elaborate trade networks.

The French learned of the Upper Mississippi lead deposits early, possibly from seeing Illiniwek Indians painted with ocher containing galena. Initial French sites in Illinois reveal a wealth of pieces of melted lead, in addition to lead musket balls, baling seals, and crosses; soon word of this abundance spread to others. During the American Revolution a group of Menominee Indians, part of the British expedition to Prairie du Chien, captured seventeen Spaniards and Americans in the lead mines along with fifty tons of lead ore and "a good supply of provisions."

Roads built by the Spanish for transporting ore were encountered by a French Canadian, Julien Dubuque, when he entered the district in the early 1780s. Dubuque, born on the lower St. Lawrence, married a Fox woman, then won approval from her tribe in 1788 to develop the mines. He made two trips yearly to St. Louis, shipping the lead downriver in pirogues and enjoying the high life of the city during his visits. He told Captain Zebulon Pike in 1805 that he produced 20,000 to 40,000 pounds of lead a year; that this was a deliberate understatement can be inferred from a report for 1818 by the U.S. factors at Prairie du Chien, who received almost 200,000 pounds of lead in trade from Indians in the area.

Visits by Americans soon became more than sporadic fly-by-night events. So much lead was shipped to St. Louis that word spread about the wealth of the "Fever River mines," as the district was known. Indians generally blocked Americans from en-

137

MINERS,
INDIAN WARS,
AND A
FRONTIER
TRANSFORMED

tering the area, but one American who succeeded in the fall of 1815 took out seventy tons of the metal.

Indian Agent Thomas Forsyth, who knew the Rock River country well from his work with the Sacs and Foxes, reported to the Secretary of War in 1822 that Winnebagos on the Pecatonica River had been working lead mines "for many years," and the country around "Coshconong" was "full of lead ore." That year brought Col. James Johnson of Kentucky to the Fever River country, in an expedition that included Moses Meeker, a Cincinnati manufacturer of white lead who had read of the district in St. Louis newspapers. The federal government exended its Missouri lead mine leasing system to Fever River, allowing miners to lease claims with a payment of ten percent of all lead smelted. With federal interest officially proclaimed, Johnson's group—which included several black slaves—obtained military protection and the troops awed the Foxes and Sacs to at least temporarily acquiesce in the miners' presence.

The rush began in earnest in the spring of 1823. The Fever River mines had exploded into one of the brief moments of unusual opportunity seen from time to time on the American frontier: a chance to become rich by being among the first into an area abundant with nature's windfalls. One incoming miner in 1825 met a common laborer who had worked for two months and sold his discovery mine for $1,300. With such stories spreading rapidly, veteran miners pouring in from Missouri jostled on the roads with men and women from Kentucky, Tennessee, southern Illinois, and states to the east. About 100 of them were mining in the Fever River diggings by mid–1825, over 400 by mid–1826.

The true stampede began in the spring of 1827, when the St. Louis wharf thronged with men waiting for the next steamboat north to the mines. Several thousand headed up to Fever River over the next several months, and by 1829 there were 10,000 miners in the district, producing 13.3 million pounds of lead. The Fever River District had passed the Missouri mines to become America's major source of lead at a time when the need for house paint, pipes, sheeting, printers' type, and bullets brought new demands for the metal. By 1840 the district produced half of America's lead. Meanwhile, the federal government's unpopular leasing system had been reduced in 1830 to levying miners only six percent of their lead, instead of the previous ten percent; the system was dropped in 1846.

The nature of the district's strata favored individual miners and small groups—men without much capital, equipment, or technical knowledge. Most galena was near the surface, in sheets filling vertical fissures or in crevices that occasionally bulged with chunks of loose lead ore. The miners soon went below surface scratchings, sinking shafts and then following veins. Windlasses lowered them into mines they could not enter through tunnels. Shovels, picks, gads, crowbars, hand drills, and blasting powder were the miners' tools and accessories, and if the early workers were not all skilled miners many soon became skilled.

John Reynolds commented on the "medley of people" who seemed to be "literally crazy" in their rush for wealth; he also noted that "many indulged in habits not recognized in any part of the decalogue." This latter point bothered Juliette Kinzie, traveling through the "diggings" en route from Portage to Chicago. She found the miners distinctly "the roughest-looking set of men I ever beheld, and their language was as uncouth as their persons." Each had a large hunting-knife stuck in his belt; she talked with one who was obviously an Army deserter. But the democracy of the mining camp, later to win high praise in the California gold rush, was present also that winter at Hamilton's Diggings, as the miners chatted uncowed with their distinguished guests, and called their employer "Uncle Billy." He was Col. William Stephen Hamilton, a West Point graduate and son of Alexander Hamilton, one of America's Founding Fathers.

Two other newcomers, Adéle Gratiot and Strange Palmer, would not forget their first look at the miners either. Mrs. Gratiot's introduction came on the Fourth of July in 1826, when she saw miners "with uncut hair, red flannel shirts, and heavy boots drawn over their pants . . . all eager to dance and enjoy themselves to the worth of their money." Palmer also met the "lawless adventurers," who spent their free time gambling, dancing, singing, and drinking at the numerous "groceries" where alcoholic beverages were sold. But Mrs. Gratiot noted that the miners "all behaved like gentlemen," and she commented on the presence of

139

MINERS,
INDIAN WARS,
AND A
FRONTIER
TRANSFORMED

"several very polished persons." Palmer told of "upright, intelligent citizens" who were generous and courteous, some of whom later nursed him back to health from a near-fatal illness.

Their early styles of housing provided Wisconsin with its state nickname, "Badgers," after the burrowing animal common across the district. Reasons for the analogy can be seen in the report of an 1827 migrant at New Diggings, in Lafayette County:

> Instead of houses, they usually lived in dens or caves; a large hole or excavation being made in the side of a hill or bluff, the top being covered over with poles, grass and sods. A level way from the edge of the hole at the bottom was dug out, some ten or twelve feet; and this gang-way being closed upon either side, was covered over on top thus, forming a sheltered entrance to the "*dug-out*," as such places were usually called. In these holes or dug-outs, families lived in apparent comfort and the most perfect satisfaction for years, buoyed up by the constant expectation of soon striking a *big lead*.

Similarly, because the miners from southern Illinois usually arrived in the spring and returned home in the fall, they were called "Suckers," after the migratory fish, and their diggings were known as "sucker-holes." Until recent times Illinois' symbol from the natural world was as the "Sucker state," making it the second state to obtain its natural species motif from the mining district.

Swiss immigrant Theodore Rodolf witnessed another aspect of frontier life at a public hanging that drew an immense crowd to Mineral Point. The convicted murderer, William Caffee, had stabbed a man to death at a housewarming in Berry's Grove, at White Oak Springs in Lafayette County. Rodolf described "the crowd of morbid sight-seers that poured into the village," everyone from old men to babies arriving from as far as forty miles away, traveling by wagon, horse, and on foot "in a continuous stream." Mineral Point's shops boomed on what was from then on referred to as "hanging day." But Rodolf did not consider it as happy occasion; rather, he said the public's "eagerness and morbidity" in watching the hanging was "not calculated to elevate public morals."

Many settlements formed as mining boomed in the 1820s and 1830s. Mineral Point continued to be the district's major town north of the border, followed by Platteville, Dodgeville, Schulls-berg, Hardscrabble (later Hazel Green), New Diggings, Mus-coda (also called English Prairie), Gratiot's Grove, Blue Mounds, and Helena. A shot-tower was constructed in the early 1830s at Helena, on a bluff overlooking the Wisconsin River.[1]

Skilled Cornish miners began showing up in the district and gave a new impetus to mining, smelting, and community life. They came from a "land of bondage," where Cornwall's declin-ing copper- and tin-mining industry was dominated by a rigid economic system above ground and strenuous working condi-tions below. When the mining boom began in southern Wiscon-sin they were attracted to it immediately, the first miner from Cornwall arriving in 1827. Cornishmen came increasingly dur-ing the 1830s, then by boatloads during the "Hungry Forties."

The Cornish made a difference in Wisconsin. Abandoned sur-face diggings now yielded to the Cornishmen's knowledge of hard-rock mining; crude smelting that had changed little from the In-dians' methods—piling galena atop burning logs on a slanting hearth—modernized quickly under the experienced hands of the "Cousin Jacks." With their "pasties" (meat pies) and their Meth-odist church, they soon fastened their identity on the district, until they made up an estimated fifty percent of the population by 1850. Large numbers went on the California gold rush, but some three-fourths of them returned and took up farming in Wisconsin, keeping the Cornish heritage alive in names, customs, and institutions. "Shake-Rag" became Mineral Point's nickname, drawn from the custom of Cornish housewives calling their men to lunch, down from their mines on the hillside across the gulch, by shaking a white rag at noontime.[2]

Henry Dodge, an early resident of the mining district, pro-vided a major contrast with the Cornish. Dodge was scarcely an average person, of course: eventually governor of Wisconsin Ter-ritory and U.S. senator, over the years he was repeatedly chosen by the citizenry to lead local governmental and military activi-

---

1. The shot-tower has been restored and is part of Tower Hill State Park, near Spring Green.
2. Several Cornish homes, such as Pendarvis, have been rebuilt at Mineral Point.

141

MINERS,
INDIAN WARS,
AND A
FRONTIER
TRANSFORMED

ties. It is clear that for most of his life Dodge represented what had become the American pioneer ideal; his attitudes toward the land and its Indian occupants, as well as his enthusiasm for democracy and self-government, were closely entwined with those of frontier America. He was born in 1782 at Vincennes, Indiana, into a family that for generations had been moving westward, fighting Indians or British as required by the situation. As a boy he lived in Kentucky, then traveled to Missouri's lead mining region west of Ste. Genevieve, and eventually succeeded his father as sheriff there in 1805. He later served in the 1820 Missouri constitutional convention.

At manhood Henry Dodge was strong, straight, and six feet tall. He used his strength to fight and defeat nine of the grand jury members in Missouri who had indicted him for treason after he tried to join the ill-fated Aaron Burr expedition to overwhelm Mexico. Dodge also gained a reputation as an Indian fighter, but could protect Indians when he felt this was called for: during service in the War of 1812 he once forced angry American soldiers to back down from their threat to murder a group of Miami Indians who had just surrendered; later in Wisconsin he would similarly prevent the murder of an Indian.

Despite several such incidents, most activities in Dodge's life make it clear that through his blood ran the popular belief that Indians were blocking the onward rush of civilization. His grandparents had been besieged by Indians in a Kentucky stockade for a lengthy period; his mother gained fame as a teenager by rushing out during an Indian raid to bring in a newborn calf while arrows fell around her. Such an inheritance was common among the vanguard of families pushing west. James Hall's 1835 book, *Sketches of History, Life, and Manners, in the West,* emphasized the cumulative impact of this "violent animosity . . . between the people of our frontier and the Indians," when early clashes during the colonial era entered into family lore:

> Every child thus reared, learns to hate an Indian because he always hears him spoken of as an enemy. From the cradle, he listens continually to horrid tales of savage violence, and becomes familiar with narratives of aboriginal cunning and ferocity. Every family can number some of its members or relatives among the victims of a

midnight massacre. . . . With persons thus reared, hatred towards an Indian becomes a part of their nature, and revenge an instinctive principle.

Backwoodsmen often remained in contact with new groups moving into an area, Hall added, giving the "tone" to public opinion although they may have been a small minority. The newcomers perhaps had no personal contact with hostile Indians, but they quickly learned to fear and hate them: "They have only heard one side, and that with all the exaggerations of fear, sorrow, indignation and resentment."

What Hall neglected to mention was that the same process was operating among Indians. Stories of whites cheating them of their lands were common, and were similarly passed down from generation to generation. At the close of a Wisconsin treaty session in 1848, one of the Menominee leaders protested government pressure to give up their lands. He recalled hearing that Pontiac in 1763 told the western tribes that whites were rapidly crowding them off the long bench, although the whites had initially asked only for a resting corner. "The American never comes unless he wants something! Without a want, he never takes us by the hand," the Menominee proclaimed. This speech was followed by "a wild burst of enthusiasm" from the rest of his tribesmen, according to a Green Bay trader who was present.

Into this land where suspicions and fears were welded onto folk beliefs, conflicting tribal claims, and rising white expectations of sudden wealth, came Dodge and his family in 1827. They were accompanied by a family of black slaves. Dodge had winning ways: plain-spoken, affable, outspoken at times yet reserved at others, and "scrupulously honest." He was always well-armed; one critic complained that "he pursues the barbarous practice of daily wearing arms or offensive weapons." But Dodge had military experience and it was called for quickly, for short days after his arrival there erupted the first Indian hostilities in Wisconsin since the British evacuation.

The Red Bird War

The Winnebago War, also called the Red Bird War, erupted from the volatile mix of rising Winnebago anger at miners' intrusions as well as specific incidents. Indian agent Joseph Street, at Prairie du Chien, criticized the miners' "great contempt for 'naked Indians'" as they pushed past treaty boundaries onto Indian lands and "behaved like blackguards amongst them." Ill will spread rapidly on both sides, and Governor Lewis Cass of Michigan Territory learned that the Winnebagos "had assumed an attitude of hostility toward the whites." As Cass passed through the region that summer of 1827 he visited a Winnebago camp and found its people sullen, "particularly the young men." Pushing farther down the Wisconsin, Cass went to Prairie du Chien where he found the white residents "in the greatest state of alarm."

But wars seldom have just one cause, and the Red Bird War was no exception. Whites had been complaining that the Winnebagos were hostile, and in March a family from Prairie du Chien was slain at their maple sugar camp, a crime to which a Winnebago reportedly confessed. The focus of the summer hostilities, however, was on a well-liked Winnebago warrior named Red Bird. Most sources agree that the Winnebagos were angered when they heard an allegation that two from their tribe had been executed at Fort Snelling, after U.S. officials turned them over to their Chippewa enemies. The report was later proven to be false, but it stirred the tribe into revenge and Red Bird was delegated to carry out retaliation. He and two companions attacked the Registre Gagnier home near Prairie du Chien in late June, 1827, killing two men and scalping a daughter and leaving her for dead; Madame Gagnier and her eldest son escaped.[3]

At almost the same time a short distance up the Mississippi, two keelboats were returning from Fort Snelling when a Winnebago party attacked. By the time the incident ended late that night, four of the crew were dead and two wounded, while seven Winnebagos were killed and fourteen wounded.

Henry Dodge had just arrived in Galena when news came of the Winnebago hostilities. Panic spread through the mining district, as families fled their outlying diggings and rushed to larger settlements; one report claimed some 3,000 persons converged

---

3. The scalped child survived; she was the girl referred to some years later as "one of the curiosities of the place," as noted at the beginning of this chapter.

at the head of Apple River during the first night. A hundred miners quickly formed a militia company with veteran Indian-fight-
er Dodge as commander. From St. Louis a force of 600 infantry
and 150 mounted men made its way to Galena; a unit from Fort
Snelling arrived at Prairie du Chien, while other troops came
from Fort Howard at Green Bay and the Governor of Illinois
called up troops also. Soon this mixed force, made up of both
regulars and militia, swarmed up the Wisconsin River after Red
Bird.

This concentration of military power quickly convinced the
Winnebago warriors to surrender. Red Bird and his accomplice
We-kau arrived at the Portage at noon on Sept. 3, 1827, carrying a white flag. His face was painted red on one side, the other
side intermixed green and white. A collar of blue and white wampum hung around his neck, its rim encircled with panther or
wildcat claws. Col. Thomas McKenney, who attended in his capacity as head of the U.S. Bureau of Indian Affairs, was moved
by the scene:

> In height, he is about six feet; straight, but without restraint. . . .
> He was clothed in a Yankton dress—new and beautiful. The material
> is of dressed elk, or deer-skin, almost a pure white. . . . [The fringe]
> ran down the seams of the leggins, these being made of the same
> material. Blue beads were employed to vary and enrich the fringe of
> the leggins. On his feet he wore moccasins.
>
> A piece of scarlet cloth of about a quarter of a yard deep, and
> double that width, a slit being cut in its middle, so as to admit the
> passing through of his head, rested, one half on his breast . . . and
> the other on his back. On one shoulder, and near his breast, was a
> beautifully ornamented feather, nearly white; and about opposite,
> on the other shoulder, was another feather, nearly black, near which
> were two pieces of thinly shaven wood in the form of compasses, a
> little open, each about six inches long, richly wrapped around with
> porcupine's quills, dyed yellow, red, and blue. On the tip of one
> shoulder was a tuft of horse-hair, dyed red, and a little curled, mixed
> up with ornaments. Across the breast, in a diagonal position, and
> bound tight to it, was his war-pipe, at least three feet long. . . . In
> one of his hands he held the white flag, and in the other the calumet,
> or pipe of peace.

145

MINERS,
INDIAN WARS,
AND A
FRONTIER
TRANSFORMED

McKenney asked himself, "Can this man be a murderer? Is he the same who shot, scalped and cut the throat of Gagnier?"

The Indians sought to bargain, offering twenty horses in exchange for the two men. The U.S. officials told them that the two would be tried by the same laws that applied to whites; they would not be put in irons, they would have food to eat and tobacco to smoke. They were warned to tell their tribesmen not to kill whites, and were reminded of the extent of U.S. military power and the weakness of the Indians. Then Red Bird rose and spoke to Major Whistler, as recorded by Colonel McKenney:

> "I am ready." Then advancing a step or two, he paused, saying, "I do not wish to be put in irons. Let me be free. I have given away my life—it is gone"—(stooping and taking some dust between his finger and thumb, and blowing it away)—like that—eyeing the dust as it fell and vanished from his sight, then adding: "I would not take it back. It is gone."

Red Bird was imprisoned in Prairie du Chien, where he soon died. Winnebago leaders disclaimed any role in his acts. Two accomplices were convicted in U.S. court and sentenced to be hanged, but President John Quincy Adams pardoned them in return for a Winnebago promise to cede land in the mining district. In 1828 the U.S. government reached a temporary agreement with tribes claiming parts of the mining region, paying the Winnebagos $20,000 for intrusions until a permanent treaty could be signed. That treaty came a year later, in 1829, when Chippewas, Ottawas, Potawatomis, and Winnebagos gave up their claims to the mining region east of the Mississippi.

The Black Hawk War

The miners' pressure on the Indians did not stop with the government's crushing of the Winnebago outbreak. Several U.S. officials showed concern for the Indians' position, however, especially Indian Agent Joseph Street. Within months Street heard rumors that Henry Dodge, with a large number of others, was mining well inside Winnebago territory (near the site of Dodgeville). It was reported that Dodge was raising 2,000 pounds of galena and smelting fifty bars each day. A traveler reported that Dodge lived inside a "formidable stockade" whose cabin walls were covered with guns, and that Dodge "said that he had a man for every gun, and would not leave the country unless the Indians were stronger than he." But Dodge rebuffed efforts to evict him and his 130 armed miners, and the commander of Fort Crawford at Prairie du Chien refused to send in troops. The miners had won again.

But soon whites moving into the lead region and Illinois areas along the Rock River to the south faced a new challenge, one that could not be ignored as easily as complaints by a government official. It involved the dissident Sac leader Black Hawk and a series of events that erupted as the Black Hawk War of 1832. The outbreak was created from many strands, including white pressure on lands, and Indian resistance; tribal divisions, and strife between tribes. But the major cause of the Black Hawk War was the long-term buildup of fear and hatred between Indians and whites along the Mississippi.

As far as specific events go, the buildup to war began in 1804. In that year Governor William Henry Harrison visited St. Louis, briefly included within his Indiana Territory, and ran into a local controversy over some young Sac warriors who had killed trespassing whites on the Cuivre River. Harrison seized the opportunity to provide the Sacs with a chance to escape American punishment for the killings: they could do so by ceding a vast extent of land which included the Fever River mining district south of the Wisconsin River, a large portion of northwestern Illinois above the Illinois River, and a portion of Missouri north of the St. Louis area. Immediate payment would be in goods valued at $2,234.50, with an annuity of $1,000 worth of goods. Five Sac and Fox leaders signed the 1804 treaty, evidence of the close alliance between the two tribes. Included was a promise to guarantee the Sacs and Foxes the secure possession of their lands, with this proviso: "As long as the lands which are now ceded to the United States remain their property, the Indians belonging to the said tribes, shall enjoy the privilege of living and hunting upon them."

The treaty angered many in the tribes, who charged that the delegation had no authority to make a land cession. A Sac spokes-

147

MINERS,
INDIAN WARS,
AND A
FRONTIER
TRANSFORMED

man argued further that they were inexperienced in land sales: "we have given away a great Country to Governor Harrison for a little thing." But since few whites were moving into the areas involved, and the War of 1812 intervened, the Sac and Fox did not suffer for years over their misunderstood negotiations of 1804.

The incident served to deepen some of the splits within the tribes, however. One prominent Sac warrior linked with the pro-British grouping was Black Hawk. He was born in 1767 in Sauk-enuk, a Sac village at the mouth of the Rock River where the tribe's women annually planted some 800 acres to corn, pump-kins, squash, and beans. Black Hawk was at Tecumseh's side at the Battle of the Thames in 1813, and according to his later ac-count he was goaded into further action against the Americans by a fatal attack made by some whites upon an aged friend back in Saukenuk. In the latter months of the War of 1812 Black Hawk participated in attacks on American forces coming up the Missis-sippi to Prairie du Chien, then saw all he had fought for dashed to pieces in the Treaty of Ghent. At the end of the war a frus-trated Black Hawk vowed to the British commander at Prairie du Chien, "I have fought the Big Knives, and will continue to fight them till they are off of our lands." But the close of that conflict not only opened the way for Americans to enter Sac and Fox lands, it also produced a rival Sac leader: Keokuk, a shrewd politician able to win concessions from the newly powerful Am-ericans.

Black Hawk drew together many Sacs, some Foxes, and even Kickapoos and Winnebagos into his "British band," largely Indi-ans who were angry at the Americans. Also, traditionalists op-posed to challenges to custom, along with those harboring specific grievances against American settlers, were included in the group, which by the late 1820s numbered some 400 men and older boys, with approximately as many women and children. They were still receiving gifts from the British.

New pressures on the Indians began to energize Black Hawk's band. The mining rush was paralleled short miles to the south by arrivals of white farmers seeking the rich lands tilled for genera-tions by Indian women in the Saukenuk area. As game declined, the Sacs and Foxes were forced to extend their hunts farther westward into Sioux territories, leading to renewed clashes there. An 1825 peace treaty between the Sac and Sioux was broken by fighting in 1828 and again in 1830 (when Elizabeth Thérèse Baird witnessed the victorious Sioux parading through Prairie du Chien, "displaying on poles the scalps and dismembered human fragments taken from the bodies of their victims").

Returning from their winter hunt in spring 1829, the Sacs found their Saukenuk lodges destroyed, fences damaged, and white settlers' livestock wandering their fields. Although the government agent sympathized with the Indians, the War Department ordered the Sacs across the Mississippi; early in October 1829, their lands at Saukenuk were put up for sale. Once the land was sold, by stipulations of the Treaty of 1804, it could no longer be used by the Indians.

The Illinois governor sent 1,400 militiamen to march on the Sac villages in 1831, forcing the Indians to sign another treaty promising they would move across the river, never return without permission, and abandon all further contact with the British. The tribes obeyed and crossed the Mississippi into Iowa.

These events increased the popularity of Black Hawk with some groups within the Sac-Fox tribe. Dissidents from a raid on a Menominee camp flocked to his side; his aide Neapope brought a report (later refuted by other sources) that the British promised help if war with the Americans broke out. Meanwhile, White Cloud (Wabokieshiek), already revered by many as a Winnebago Prophet at his village up the Rock valley, claimed that a large number of Illinois, Wisconsin, and even Plains tribes would rally to Black Hawk in the event of fighting.

This was the situation as 1832 opened. The Black Hawk and Keokuk factions were both camped west of the Mississippi, facing shortages of food after being forced from their Saukenuk lands. American officials were determined to apprehend those Indians who had raided the Menominees, as a necessary first step in preventing even broader intertribal warfare. On April 8 the Army sent 220 troops upriver from St. Louis in a show of force. But when they arrived at the Des Moines rapids on April 11, 1832, General Henry Atkinson learned that Black Hawk's followers—numbering perhaps 2,000, including warriors and family members—had recently crossed over into Illinois south of Saukenuk and were making their way north.

This set off alarms, even panic, across the Upper Mississippi. Governor Reynolds again called up Illinois militiamen and told federal authorities that these citizen-soldiers would move the Indians "dead or alive" back across the Mississippi. Black Hawk's band of men, women, and children trekked up the Rock River as American officials sent messengers to dissuade him. Soon he learned that what the Americans were claiming was true: the main body of Winnebagos would not help him, nor would the Potawatomis; neither tribe wanted his band to move in with them. Further, there had been no British promise of assistance.

At this point Black Hawk decided to surrender. As he explained later in his *Autobiography*, "I concluded to tell my people, that if the White Beaver [General Atkinson] came after us, we would go back—as it was useless to think of stopping or going on without provisions." A deserter reported this to the military at Rock Island on May 4. But soon news came up the Rock to the Indians that soldiers were approaching. Black Hawk sent three emissaries downstream, their white flag aloft, to make contact with these troops and prepare for the surrender. Five other members of his band were ordered to follow behind to observe.

The soldiers they encountered were not U.S. Army regulars, however. They were instead part of the Illinois militia, 275 citizen soldiers under Maj. Isaiah Stillman—untrained, undisciplined, frustrated at the slow-moving nature of the campaign thus far, eager for Indian blood. (Governor Reynolds argued that regular soldiers were ineffective against Indians—they "could not move with celerity so as to strike terror into the hearts of the Indians. Moreover, the Indians dreaded the backwoods white men. They knew the volunteers were their natural enemies and would destroy them on all occasions.")

The militia had stopped for the night, and was setting up camp just three miles down the Rock River from Black Hawk. To ease their unhappiness and frustration, the volunteers had started drinking. When the three Indians appeared they were rushed and brought into camp; then someone spotted the observers and these were chased and two of them slain. One of the Indian flag-bearers was also killed. Stimulated by these successes, the disorganized "Sucker Militia" set off on a frenzied chase to catch Black Hawk.

Black Hawk was with some forty of his council when word came of the attack on the flag-bearers. Fearing extermination, he harangued the group to avenge what had been done to their fellows. The forty then hid behind bushes while the militia stormed into them: at the first fusillade and war-whoops from the Indians, the soldiers panicked and fled, pursued by some twenty-five Sacs until nightfall. Although the Indians turned back, Stillman's troopers kept running, crashing through swamps and creeks until they reached Dixon's Ferry, twenty-five miles away. The first arrivals claimed they had been crushed by an Indian force of 1,000 warriors, leaving few survivors, but over the next twenty hours, as more and more of the militiamen dragged in, the death toll subsided to eleven whites killed, and perhaps eight Indians. Rather than fight on to regain their reputation, Stillman's militia deserted and returned to their Illinois homes.

There were several outcomes to this "Battle of Stillman's Run." Most important was the realization that Black Hawk's surrender would not be a simple matter of negotiation and removal. Events now would have to be carried to their tragic end. Indian anger over the death of their comrades was paralleled by white indignity at Indian acts: bodies of the eleven white victims were found mutilated, and arms, legs, heads, hearts, and genitals removed. Reynolds quickly called up another 2,000 militia. Five companies of militia were organized at Galena, joined by Col. Henry Dodge and his Wisconsin miners. Black Hawk, meanwhile, moved his women and children northeastward up the Kishwaukee River into Wisconsin toward the swamps near Lake Koshkonong, while several of his band raided farms across northern Illinois, further spreading panic.

Settlers rushed to "fort up." In the mining district stockades were quickly erected at Mineral Point, Dodge's Diggins, Blue Mounds, Hamilton's (Wiota), Gratiot's, White Oak Springs, Elk Grove, Diamond Grove, and other spots. Dodge's anger boiled anew when he got word of derogatory comments about white men uttered by White Crow, a Winnebago leader who brought some ransomed whites to Blue Mounds. Dodge warned the Winnebagos that they would be treated as enemies unless they could give solid evidence that they supported the American side. The Winnebagos assured the Americans they were with them; only some of their young men had gone with the British band.

But Black Hawk's band was still undefeated and the whites were chasing shadows—until the "Battle of Pecatonica" on June 14 near Wiota, when Dodge led a group of volunteers against some Indians who had just slain six persons. Before attacking, however, Dodge's twenty-nine militiamen were reminded of the inglorious drubbing given Stillman's undisciplined horde: they waited for Dodge's orders, then overran and killed the thirteen Sac warriors, losing three of their own.

Over the next four weeks the British band, now fewer than 1,000 men, women, and children, kept eluding its pursuers, shaking the 4,000 Americans soldiers again and again as they moved northward toward Koshkonong. On July 15, however, Dodge and General James Henry were returning from Fort Winnebago at Portage with supplies when their 600 militiamen came across a suspected Black Hawk camp at the Rock River rapids, south of Sinissipi Lake. Three days later they found a fresh trail and by July 20 the final pursuit of Black Hawk was underway.

The new chase wound through the Four Lakes (Madison), then angled northwestward toward the Wisconsin River as soldiers began to find evidence that the Indians' lack of food and rest was pushing them to disaster: bodies of elderly tribesmen were found along the wayside, and the advance force came upon an Indian sitting passively on the grave of his wife. The grieving husband bared his naked breast to his attackers, and the editor of the Galena *Galenian*, Dr. Addison Philleo, shot and scalped him. (This act drew editorial comment from the Cincinnati *Chronicle:* "We trust that the Galenian is the only paper in the Union that could boast of such a feat, and that its editor is the only one of the fraternity capable of perpetrating so disgusting and cruel an act.")

As they fled toward the Wisconsin River, Black Hawk's men used feints, brief attacks, and other moves to deflect their pursuers. On the south shore of the river some twenty miles below Portage, across from the site of Sauk City, the Battle of Wiscon-

sin Heights took place on the afternoon of July 23. Sixty-eight of
Black Hawk's band were killed as the Americans drove them down
from the bluffs into the swampy river bottom during a rainstorm.
When the battle was stopped that evening, the militia's interpreter and several of its Winnebago scouts left to return to Fort
Winnebago. Under cover of darkness, Black Hawk sent many of
the band's women, children, and elderly on hurriedly built rafts
and canoes down the Wisconsin.

The second surrender attempt by the British band occurred
that night. Shortly before first light, the Americans were suddenly awakened by a sharp voice calling from a nearby hill. One
soldier described it as "loud distinct and strange ejaculations,
which echoed through the camp and woods. . . . The effect was
almost electric." Many participants commented on the Indian's
earnest speech, which no one could understand because the interpreters had left. Some feared it was the beginning of a night
attack, and General James Henry warned his Illinois militia that
this was their chance to "vindicate the valor of the Suckers and
the Sucker State." When several Indians were captured in later
days, the Americans learned the truth: the speech had offered
surrender and promised no more harm if the band could be permitted to cross the Mississippi in peace.

The eager American units took on new life as provisions and
rested troops arrived from Blue Mounds. The newly organized
force of 1,300 soldiers—made up of 400 regulars and the militia
units under Dodge and others—crossed the Wisconsin at Helena
on rafts made from the wood of abandoned cabins. Troops were
also stationed downriver near the Mississippi, where they shot at
canoes and rafts passing through at night.

All was tense at Prairie du Chien. Winnebagos and Sioux in
the area were alerted to block the British band from escaping
across the Mississippi; the Indian agent sent a representative with
a white flag to search out fleeing Indians and urge their surrender. Some were brought in "almost dying with starvation, and
are mere shadows."

Black Hawk and his exhausted band, now down to some 500
members because of death and desertion, arrived at the Mississippi on August 1, near the mouth of the Bad Axe River some

153

MINERS,
INDIAN WARS,
AND A
FRONTIER
TRANSFORMED

forty miles north of Prairie du Chien. Some members fashioned rafts and made it to the other side, where sixty-eight were later killed by the Sioux.

Then the steamboat *Warrior* came into view, returning from an upstream trip to alert the Sioux. Black Hawk made his third surrender attempt at this point. As one of the women later told those examining the prisoners, "Black Hawk said to the women, 'run and get me the white flag. I will go on board that boat.' He told the men to put down their guns, and the women got behind trees." Another testified that he called out, "I am Black Hawk— and I wish to come and shake hands with you." But he shouted in Winnebago which was mistranslated by the ship's interpreter, who reported they were Winnebagos. The captain ordered the Indians to come on board, but no canoes were available. In the confused situation the captain feared a trap, and shooting began and continued for two hours before the *Warrior* was forced to turn downstream to obtain more wood. Faulty translation had again blocked a peaceful ending.

Black Hawk could persuade only a few of his followers to flee to the north with him that night, the remainder hoping to cross the river before the soldiers found them. But the next morning— August 2—the pursuing troops arrived, shooting from the river bluffs, charging down the steep hills, crowding the Indians along the shoreline. Just then the *Warrior* returned from Prairie du Chien, its captain exclaiming to the soldiers and Menominees aboard as they hove into view, "Dodge is giving them h—l!" John Fonda, a soldier on the *Warrior*, recalled that one group of Indians held out a white flag—then shot at the ship as it drew near. The Indians were in a vise: they were being fired on from the bluffs, "while we kept steaming back and forth on the river, running down those who attempted to cross, and shooting at the Indians on shore." Fonda watched the Indians being scalped by the volunteers, who pulled out their knives "and cutting two parallel gashes down their backs, would strip the skin from the quivering flesh, to make razor straps of."

The Battle of Bad Axe was a massacre. Soldiers fired at women swimming with children on their backs; sands on the shores were soon stained with Indian blood. The fighting lasted some eight

Black Hawk and his band of Sac and Fox Indians attempted in 1832 to retake tribal lands along the Rock and Mississippi Rivers, ceded in earlier treaties that were questionable from an ethical if not legal standpoint. Their attempt to surrender frustrated, the band then fled up the Rock, through the Lake Koshkonong and Four Lakes (Madison) areas, then west to the Mississippi where they were slaughtered in the Battle of Bad Axe. This painting by Robert Sully was done in 1833 when Black Hawk was a prisoner at Fortress Monroe in Virginia. Courtesy State Historical Society of Wisconsin, WHi (X32) 38600.

🏺 **155**

MINERS,
INDIAN WARS,
AND A
FRONTIER
TRANSFORMED

hours, and the situation was so confused that only a rough esti-mate can be given of the Indian losses—150, as opposed to eleven killed among the white attackers. But many Indians were killed on the Mississippi and their bodies were carried downstream by the current; others were caught by the Sioux. Some undoubtedly escaped.

Black Hawk, the Prophet, and several others were apprehended three days later near the site of Wisconsin Dells by Winnebagos who sought the reward of $100 in cash and twenty ponies. Brought to the Indian agency in Prairie du Chien, Black Hawk was even-tually taken on to Washington where he met President Andrew Jackson, toured Eastern cities, then was returned to Rock Island, near his beloved Saukenuk. Almost one year after the Battle of Bad Axe, Black Hawk was released to the care of Keokuk, his old rival. He lived until October 3, 1838, largely ignored by tribal leaders but venerated by his people. But peace would remain a stranger even in death, for after he died Black Hawk's bones were dug up by grave robbers; later they were housed in a Bur-lington, Iowa, museum but were destroyed when the museum burned in 1855.

The campaign bolstered the reputation of Henry Dodge, who had been present at all the government force's victories. But not one of the other participants who became national figures, such as Army officers Jefferson Davis and Zachary Taylor, and militia member Abraham Lincoln, ever pointed with pride to his role in the Black Hawk War. And for all the recognition that Black Hawk received for fighting for his homeland, his own record was not without blemishes, for he refused to accept unwanted news, was naive about the realities of the government's power, and his stub-bornness got in the way of careful thought that might have saved his band. Faulty planning combined with bad luck to assure his defeat. Keokuk, in contrast, knew when to be stern, when to bend, and when to be accommodating; he and his group sur-vived. And more than translation problems were involved, for the whites' attitude of contempt, starting long before the miners' encroachments, stirred bitter resentment among the Indians—resentment that festered for years before erupting. This problem did not begin or end with the Black Hawk War.

In the sweep of Wisconsin history, the Black Hawk War emerges as an expected, almost predictable event; the time as well as the issues can be seen in retrospect to be without surprise. When the fur trade, based on barter and cooperation between white and Indian, gave way to the new society of land-seeking miners, the Indian was in the way, an impediment to progress. Farmers, too, would find Indians blocking their routes as the Wisconsin frontier underwent further transformation in the decades leading up to mid-century.

7.

RUSH TO THE LAND

The seven-year-old Vermont boy peered at the atlas laid before him and his brothers, following his father's forefinger as it moved along the map to the area west of Lake Michigan, stopping at the Milwaukee River's mouth. "Boys," the father announced, "there's where we want to go; that country offers splendid inducements for settlers. There must be water powers and timber."

It was a story repeated often in New England, New York, and other eastern areas during the 1830s and 1840s and 1850s, as southeastern Wisconsin succeeded the mining district as the magnet for thousands. Now they could board a steamboat in Buffalo on a Sunday evening and arrive at Racine the following Friday, or head west in an ox-drawn wagon to Chicago and then proceed north on new but rough-hewn roads. This new "Western fever" was the latest eruption in a euphoria that swept through settled regions to the east and south and eventually infected Europe. Changes came rapidly throughout much of the Mississippi Valley but were especially dramatic in largely unsettled Wisconsin; by early 1836 it was claimed there was *not a foot of vacant land, from the Illinois line to the Koshkonong!*"

This rush to the land was breathtaking for many who witnessed it. In 1832, a Green Bay editor later recalled, "there was but one house, on the whole route from this place to Chicago; & the Journey required the preparation of a month." And when three men traveled south from Green Bay the following year, heading to the trading post at Milwaukee, they found only Indian villages there as well as at Sheboygan, Manitowoc, Waukesha, and Fond du Lac. But a road was already pushing north from Chicago along the lakeshore toward that Milwaukee settlement, and in the resulting excitement Solomon Juneau, Milwaukee's leading fur trader, laid out one town east of the river, while surveyor Byron Kilbourn planned another west of the river. In the spring of 1835 Milwaukee already had "20 or 30 houses," and by August 1836 the sheriff there counted a population of 2,893. Prices on town lots rose 100 percent in thirty days, some lots bringing $5,000. The same story was repeated in Racine and Southport (Kenosha) to the south, and again in Sheboygan and Manitowoc to the north as the road extended northward. Madison, meanwhile, boomed when it became the site of the new territorial capital in 1838.

Rising land values stoked the fires of migration, renewing in Wisconsin a well-worn frontier slogan: Go west and grow up with the country. The Green Bay editor proclaimed that this was "the time for enterprise" in Wisconsin:

> A vast extent of beautiful country is just opened, and those who enter EARLY have opportunity of acquiring fortunes by choice selections. Many important points are yet without an inhabitant, which in five years will be flourishing towns. The first to enter those places, will of course grow with their growth, and may in a short period become men of wealth by the inhancement of their lands.

As it had migrated westward with previous generations of settlers, this belief continued its course across Wisconsin, enunciated most enthusiastically by community promoters. Some three decades later a Chippewa Falls editor reported one major reason to move to the town: "The value of real property is increasing so fast that any one purchasing or locating now will be sure to become rich at no distant day by the mere rise of property."

But more than rising land values were behind the population

increases in southeastern Wisconsin, as the district's numbers climbed from a negligible total in 1836 to 7,163 by the 1840 census, while Wisconsin Territory's overall population rose phenomenally from 30,749 in 1840, to 155,277 by 1846, to 304,756 by 1850.

One man who was lured by other things than property values was Omar Morse, slaving away for a New York farmer who treated his workers "like brutes." Morse announced to his employer one day that he was a free man, "had never been sold into bondage and no white man less than sixteen feet between the eyes could ever make a slave of me!" Five minutes after this announcement Morse made up his mind to head for Wisconsin, reaching Sheboygan within eight days. Ebenezer Childs had a different sort of problem: the Town Collector in Barre, Mass., called upon him for payment of the $1.75 minister tax which Childs, a 19-year-old laboring for 50 cents a day, was unable to pay. Rather than go to jail, one morning Childs rode away on his horse—violating another Massachusetts law, forbidding travel on Sundays. He crossed into New York State and began working his way west, eventually signing on as a Mackinac trader and traveling to Green Bay. Childs, Morse, and many others like them provided the surge of settlers into Wisconsin with a considerable segment whose motivation was not mainly economic.

One result was that Wisconsin from the 1830s to the Civil War represented a mingling of diverse migrant streams, the earlier southern thrust to the mining district now joined by a larger flow from New England, New York, and states south of Lake Ontario and Lake Erie. Soon Europeans were coming as well—farmers, religious dissidents, artisans—and a new phase of the frontier began.

Treaties to 1855

Pressure on Indian lands, growing since the British exodus of 1815, now mounted rapidly. Land hunger infected even French Canadians, and a report told of Indians near Green Bay who asked their government agent "if there is no way of stopping *Peter Chalison* & *Isaac Jacques* two frenchmen that is taking possession of their sugar camps. . . . These Indians have had these sugar camps all their lifetimes & have been born there." Their letter stated that the two Frenchmen said "they dont care for any person & they will do as they please."

It was an attitude toward Indian occupancy common across the frontier. The government was pressured to clear the territory of Indians, but each new land cession only added to the publicity which brought in more settlers seeking land, demanding more and more of the Indians' claims. The Winnebagos had been forced to clear the lead region following the Red Bird War of 1827; in 1829 (and in a smaller treaty in 1832) the government obtained all Winnebago claims south of the Wisconsin and Fox rivers. For this cession the Winnebagos were promised a $10,000 annuity for twenty-seven years, as well as land west of the Mississippi, plus funds for oxen, plows, a blacksmith, a school, and demonstration farmers. The tribe in turn promised that no Winnebago would reside, plant, fish, or hunt in any part of the ceded lands. Then the focus shifted to the southeast, where the Menominee tribe claimed several million acres. The 1831 treaty, completed after talks in Washington, turned over to the government the eastern portions of the Menominee domain, from the Fox-Wisconsin route as far south as the Milwaukee River; the Menominees were still permitted to hunt in their western claims which ran to the Chippewa River. The Menominees' claims were further complicated by the presence of the so-called "New York Indians," discussed below.

With these cessions the lakeshore between Green Bay and Chicago began exciting special interest among potential settlers and speculators. Its transfer to government control came in an 1833 treaty session in Chicago, mainly involving the Potawatomis and their claims around lower Lake Michigan. The sessions drew 5,000 to 8,000 Potawatomis, Ottawas, and southern Chippewas to Chicago, and closed with a massive procession as the Potawatomis headed west. In exchange for some five million acres around Lake Michigan, the tribe was given annuities; funds for mills, farm implements, and similar items; and five million acres west of the Mississippi to serve as their new home.

Another round of treaty-making with the Menominees followed.

With Territorial Governor Henry Dodge handling the talks, the Cedar Point treaty of 1836 turned over to the government some four million acres of Menominee lands lying west of Green Bay as far as the Wolf River—removing from the tribe a "civilizing center" set up earlier beside Lake Winnebago—along with some strips of land along the Wisconsin. A twenty-year $20,000 annuity, with $80,000 for the *métis*, was provided as payment.

The year 1836 brought other changes, as Congress yielded to a flood of petitions and created a sprawling Wisconsin Territory, taking in modern Iowa, Minnesota, and the Dakotas east of the Missouri River. This was reduced in size two years later when the western border was set at the Mississippi River to its source, then north to the international boundary. Criticized over the years for treating the frontier like a colony, Congress took a step toward permitting more self-rule in the territories when it allowed Wisconsin Territory voters to choose all township and county officials except judges, sheriffs, and militia officers. Congress also permitted all free adult white males to vote in the first Wisconsin territorial elections and made them all eligible for any office.

The following year, 1837, proved to be the most costly for Wisconsin's tribes in terms of lands lost. The Winnebago treaty that year also dropped the government's treaty-making ethics to a low point: the tribe's negotiators were kept in Washington all winter and were finally assured they could remain another eight years on the ceded Wisconsin lands. With that promise, the Winnebagos gave up all their remaining lands east of the Mississippi. When they returned home, however, they were informed they could stay only eight months.

During 1837 the Sioux and the Chippewas, perennial enemies, were also brought to treaty sessions, the Sioux ceding a wedge of land in western Wisconsin between the Black and the Mississippi. The Chippewas of northern Wisconsin gave up their claims south of the divide between the rivers flowing north into Lake Superior and those flowing southward into the Mississippi; however—in a legal statement that would have importance a century and a half later—they retained hunting, fishing, and wild rice gathering rights there. It was reported that fifteen hours after the Chippewa treaty was signed at St. Peters (in southern Minne-

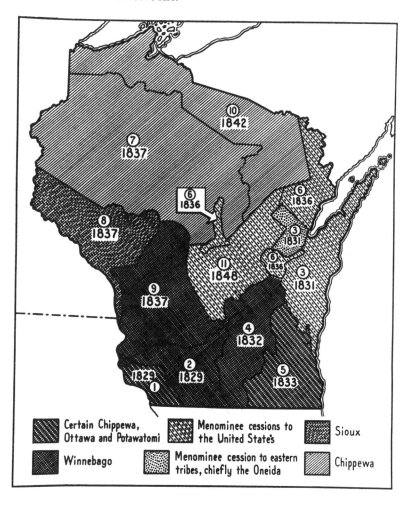

Once the United States fastened its hold on Wisconsin after the War of 1812, pressures on Indian lands mounted. A series of treaty sessions, from 1829 to 1848, both defined tribal boundaries and restricted Indian claims. COURTESY STATE HISTORICAL SOCIETY OF WISCONSIN, WHi (X3) 30336. ORIGINALLY APPEARED IN WILLIAM F. RANEY, *Wisconsin: A Story of Progress* (NEW YORK, 1940).

sota), an agent for a sawmill company arrived at the falls of the St. Croix, ready to claim the millsite.

Only small areas remained unceded after the treaties of 1837, but the tribes gave up most of these before long. The 1842 La Pointe treaty ceded the remaining Chippewa lands in Wisconsin and Michigan to the United States, and this was followed by another cession at La Pointe in 1854 in which the Chippewas of Lake Superior and the Chippewas of the Mississippi sold all their lands in the Lake Superior vicinity. In 1848 the Menominees gave up the rest of their claims.[1]

Treaty sessions were complicated with misunderstandings, as weeks and sometimes months were devoted to determining competing claims, as well as tribal memberships and relationships, both sides in the meantime fending off traders waiting to collect Indian debts. One Menominee leader pleaded, "We are ignorant of the way you measure land. We do not know what you mean by the *Acres* you speak of—What is it?" Even the system of currency proved confusing, for in determining traders' debts the government was forced to use the fur trade's system of *plus*, equating goods to peltry, leading to further disputes over relative values.

The New York Indians

Many other factors confused the treaty sessions, not the least of which in the Menominees' case was the presence on their land of the "New York Indians"—groups of several hundred Indians moved to Wisconsin starting in 1823. Their transfer resulted from growing concern in the east over the plight of the Indians: what to do when white settlement overwhelmed and corrupted the tribes? One solution was simply to move the Indians to open lands in the west, and the west of the early nineteenth century included Wisconsin and the forests that many Easterners considered impossible areas for white settlement. The transfer idea enjoyed considerable popularity, and as late as 1834 the Indian Agency head at Green Bay asked "whether the Government now intends to establish an Indian colony east of the Mississippi, and west of the lakes, or has it abandoned the idea?" The New York Indians' removal reflected the continuing popularity of the plan.

The Oneidas of southern New York were prepared for the gov-

---

1. Removal attempts, and creation of Indian reservations, will be discussed in chapter 9.

ernment's offer (pushed vigorously by the Holland Land Company, which sough Oneida lands) through the efforts of two clerics, Presbyterian Jedediah Morse and Eleazer Williams, an Episcopal missionary who grew up among his father's band of St. Regis Indians. Williams pushed hard for his concept of a massive Indian exodus to form an Indian colony near Green Bay. In 1821 he received government permission to send a delegation to look over the area.

The Menominees and the Winnebagos eventually yielded these groups a small piece of land along the Fox River. An initial party of Oneidas and Stockbridges traveled west in 1823 and settled at Little Kakalin (Kaukauna), moving later to Duck Creek, where several years later the Indian Agent pronounced them "good thriving farmers and independent livers." More made the trek west over the next several years. They were joined by the Munsees and some remnant bands of New England Christian tribes, known as the Brothertown Indians.

Eventually a compromise treaty provided the New York Indians with 500,000 acres from Menominee lands. The Oneidas gave up much of this in 1838, reducing their own claims to eight by twelve miles in size—some 60,000 acres—on Duck Creek near Green Bay.

Church leaders hoped that the influence of these Christian tribes would improve the Menominees. The extent of the New York tribes' assimilation can be seen in a newspaper advertisement seeking the whereabouts of Patience Fowler, a lost 12-year-old from the Brothertown tribe: she "had black hair, black eyes and a fair complexion; spoke no language but the English when she left home." The 200 adult male Brothertowns at Deansburg, on the east side of Lake Winnebago, sought to separate themselves further from the Menominees when they petitioned for U.S. citizenship in 1839 and asked for the right to own lands individually rather than as a tribe:

> We have long lived in the State of New York and in the New England states, where we have acquired most all of the arts and sciences of the citizens of the United States, which renders us incompetent to pursue the manners and customs and way of living of the native Indians.

Métis and the Treaties

The New York Indians were an issue mainly in the Green Bay area; the *métis*, however, had become an issue wherever Indians resided, and their presence complicated treaty-making. Especially numerous around fur trade centers, whether large or small, they showed up in large numbers at treaty sessions and from 1817 onward they were usually included in the final agreements—obtaining small reserves of land at first, after 1833 given money.

Tribes often fought to obtain payments for their *métis*, for they were usually close relatives, but to government officials it was seen as part of a game. Preparing for the enormous Chicago sessions with the Potawatomis, Ottawas, and Chippewas in 1833, Secretary of War Lewis Cass complained that "the whites and half-breeds press upon the Indians, and induce them to ask for these gratuities, to which they have no just pretensions." Cass's negotiators nevertheless set aside $100,000 "to satisfy sundry individuals," most of them mixed bloods, and a supplemental article gave another $10,000 for thirty more. Similarly, in the Menominee talks concerning the New York Indians' requests for more lands, a Menominee spokesman interjected, "One thing that we would like to have done— There are some of these half breeds who have been brought up among us—and live among us, and we wish them to have some of our land." The Green Bay Indian Agent warned in 1840 that "all *Indians*, (and none in a greater degree than the Menomonees) are unfortunately under the entire control and management of a few designing and unprincipled men, the Traders and half-blood relatives." But he noted the possible benefits of this: in treaty-making, "it is only necessary to conciliate some *dozen of Traders and half-breeds.*"

Rather than accepting assignment to a tribe, many *métis* fought to be included in the white world. When the government withheld $100,000 promised to Chippewa mixed-bloods over a controversy stemming from a murder, the "Council of Half-Breeds" at La Pointe protested: "We are regarded as Indians or white men, to suit the Exigencies of the Case," and they argued that various courts had given them the rights of free white citizens. A letter that month from the Indian Agent at La Pointe defined the *métis* as "a proud, sensitive people who are anxious to be recognized by the Government as citizens of the United States and to receive protection from its laws."

The mixed-bloods had a staunch defender in the person of Alfred Brunson, sometime Methodist missionary who was briefly sub-agent at La Pointe. After the 1842 land cession had omitted payments to *métis*, Brunson saw omens of a "threatening storm": he told of reports that they planned to march 500 strong to the next annuity payment "and sieze the money & goods & appropriate them to their own use, or prevent the treaty from going into operation till their claims are regarded."

In a letter to Territorial Governor James Doty, Brunson defended the *métis*, arguing that many were "educated, intelligent, & highly cultivated," and the tribe would make no moves without their advice. More important, they were pioneers in civilizing the Indians, providing a public service in carrying out governmental policy: "They were born & reared upon the soil, & having by degrees introduced habits of civilization, they have greatly changed the savage character of their relatives of deeper blood. . . . Every half breed who lives in habits of civilization, is half an Indian civilized." Brunson was soon fired for his zealous defense of the *métis*.

Problems of Payments

Clashing interests of *métis* and traders sometimes turned annuity sessions into disasters. Such results challenged expectations of government officials, one of whom had confidently predicted in Prairie du Chien in 1830 that funds for blacksmiths, farming implements, and similar items would lead the tribes "to turn their attention more and more towards agriculture." But it was not to be, at least that soon, for while $18,000 was paid to the Indians at that session, within thirty-six hours, $16,000 of it was in the hands of traders. Indian Agent Joseph Street looked back on several years of such activity and concluded, "The traders look on the Indian annuities as belonging to them."

One of the underlying problems was that after two centuries of contact with European traders, Indians in the Upper Lakes were heavily reliant upon manufactured items. Now they used spring-operated traps; they built with iron nails and handsaws; they ground their corn not in a stone pestle but in corn mills, and they hunted with trade guns improved with enlarged trigger guards. Even ornamentation was changing, for Europeans manufactured an array of "trade silver" items solely for the North American Indian market. The Indians bought these from the traders; the traders had to be paid.

Their degree of dependence can be seen in the Indian accounts of Green Bay merchant Francis Desnoyers from 1844 through 1849. Desnoyers kept a separate page for each member of the Menominee tribe who purchased goods from him on credit; they paid primarily with pelts. Some were probably *métis*, such as the customer identified as "Babtiste or Pa Gish," who bought calico, ribbon, sugar, salt, cotton, pork, a blue coat, (musk)rat traps, a (musk)rat spear, a blanket, a rifle, a bar of lead, powder, silk, flints, a Dutch pipe, needles and thread. And—showing how far the Menominees had changed—Babtiste also purchased a pair of "mockisons" from Desnoyers. His credits revealed one aspect of the problems of overdependence: a buck skin only brought Babtiste a credit of 75 cents; 19 "rats" (muskrats), $1.90; a coon skin, 38 cents. But the blue coat had cost him $10 and the six traps, $4.50. His basic problem was that he was providing raw materials but was purchasing manufactured goods. At the end of the long list of credits and debits, Babtiste still owed $15.77.

Sometimes the debts were never collected. When Wa Ka Che Na Pa got to the fall of 1845 he owed Desnoyers $4.76—but the page ended with a brief notation: "Stabbed May & died in the fall 1845." Similarly, there was $1.50 owed by Glaude when "found dead Thursday night on the ice near Wright (Jany '46)."

Many items were for women, as shown in Babtiste's list of purchases. In this way Indian women may have kept pressure on their husbands to pursue the hunt, with its immediate financial rewards, permitting purchases at the store, rather than turning to agriculture with its delayed benefits. Cloth, combs, socks, ribbons, needles, shawls, and soap appeared frequently on the merchant's lists.

The records of Cut Nose (Misquanene), a well-known Menominee leader, ran the gamut of men's and women's items and also revealed the new importance of other pelts than beaver. Cut Nose's purchases included a pair of boots, two pairs of moccasins, two buck skins, even a fur cape. One day he brought in twenty-five buck skins for $5.00 credit; 18 "rats" (muskrats) for $1.44; a fox for $1.00; a marten for $1.00; and a fisher for $2.25. Then he bought blue cloths for $5 and a shawl for 75 cents, before coming in again with fourteen deer skins for $2.94, two fishers for $6, another fisher for $2, and four martens for $6. He later purchased flints, pork, sugar, tea, a keg of whiskey, a gun, a plug of tobacco, peppermint, an otter trap, powder and shot, an axe, a calico shirt, a knife, and fire steels; during spring planting he obtained on credit two bushels of corn, a half bushel of oats, and a bushel of peas. Springtime also brought a chance to reduce his debt, for Cut Nose brought in 54 pounds of maple sugar, good for $3.24 credit. He also brought in the skins of martens, bears, otters, muskrats, raccoons, and fishers. But at the end of the report Cut Nose, like almost all of his fellow Menominees, remained in debt to Desnoyers.

The Indians' penchant for running up bills at the store led to a desperate reliance upon the annual government payments. Local merchants depended entirely on Indian annuities being paid. When Green Bay Agent George Boyd went to Winnecone Lake to pay the Menominees, he found that "Traders & Whiskey Sellers (Synonymous terms) had their Shantees, permanently erected for the coming payment."

It took the eyes and pen of an outsider, Gustave de Neveu, a newcomer from France, to capture the degree of debauchery that typified annuity day. De Neveu canoed up the Fox from Green Bay to watch payment to the Menominees at Winneconne in October, 1838.

The traders were active long before Agent Boyd and his force arrived with thirty boxes, each holding $1,000. Already, de Neveu discovered, "the rapacious traffickers had sold whiskey to the savages, taking in pledge their guns, blankets, and other possessions, in order to make sure of their pay as soon as the Indians received their money." The opening session had to be delayed a day because "the larger portion of them were already drunk." Agent Boyd then ordered his fifty accompanying soldiers to go through the Indian camp and destroy all the alcohol, and placed sentinels along the river bank to block any Indians from crossing over to the drinking booths set up on the opposite shore.

Sobriety returned, and talks began the next morning, each chief enumerating families and family members in his band. Food provisions were distributed in the afternoon—"fat beeves," flour, salt, salt pork, corn, tobacco—and next morning the head of each family was called forward to receive $10 for himself, $10 for his wife, and $10 for each of his unmarried children. Some got up to $100. Half-breeds were included and some were able to sign the document indicating they had been paid; others simply touched the end of the pen with their fingers.

While this was proceeding, traders had worked their way to the exit door of the building. The Indians "had hardly drawn their money with one hand, when they were obliged with the other to give the greater part of it to these rapacious and insatible men—veritable vampires that attach to them like leeches," de Neveu wrote. Some of the Indians rushed past, their creditors chasing them briefly until realizing that to do so would keep them from collecting other payments. The traders had another opportunity to separate the Indian from his money, however, for at nearby booths the Indians "bought guns, kettles, knives, cloth, parti-colored bead collars, powder and lead, blankets, calicoes, rings and earrings, and other objects for which they paid partly in peltries but chiefly in money." Most Menominees kept back part of their funds, however, and the Frenchman saw their purpose the following morning: there was "profound silence" as Boyd and his military escort rowed away, but as soon as they were gone, shouts rang out and heavily loaded boats were rowed swiftly from the liquor-sellers' camp on the opposite shore.

> [Soon] there was then nothing but a fearful tumult of hoarse cries, savage howls—in fact, an infernal uproar, such as can only be produced by an entire tribe plunged into drunkenness. . . . Let the reader picture to himself the men of an entire nation, with almost no exception, indulging in a profound orgy, staggering, singing, shouting, fighting one another, smoking, or lying in the dust; the women following, or at the most presenting the same spectacle; the maidens, running through the camp and inviting the whites, by gestures and

speech, to partake of their favors. You can even then have only a very feeble idea of what passed under my eyes.

Two Indians were killed during the debauch—one a baby who was smothered by his parents, the other a woman whose husband bit off her nose. De Neveu did not blame the government, which he saw had carefully tried to keep the traders at bay and whiskey removed from the scene—but admitted he almost wept "at the state of degradation to which the white man had reduced the poor Indians, whose nature is so noble and so generous, when it has not been polluted by his pernicious whiskey." It was an event whose horror would long remain in his memory.

Removal

Some whites continued to hope that the Indians could be led away from the hunting path into the independence of farm life. This was the basic philosophy of the U.S. government. But many began to question this, especially in frontier districts. Scenes such as de Neveu witnessed at Winneconne were reported by many, including the Superintendent of Indian Affairs—a former champion of assimilation who changed course in 1830 and admitted that the Indians had not improved. Others argued that God's plan was for land to be farmed, not to be squandered upon those who sauntered around hunting, i.e., Indians. Increasingly as the nineteenth century wore on, Christian leaders in the East came to believe that tribes needed to be physically separated from frontier debauchery. The concept of removal gained strength in part because it drew Indian-haters and Indian-lovers into brief alliance: both decided that the Indians east of the Mississippi had to be moved to open lands in the West. Some whites wanted Indian lands; others saw it as the only way to save the tribes from annihilation. By the 1830s the focus was shifting away from protecting settlers from the Indians, to protecting Indians from the settlers.

The first Indians removed under the government's new policy were such southeastern and southern tribes as the Cherokees, Creeks, and Chickasaws, during the 1830s. They were taken to the "Great American Desert," an area of the southern Plains where, early explorers predicted, whites would never be able to live.

Juliette Kinzie, an Indian sympathizer during her years at Fort Winnebago and other frontier posts, typified the changes coming over many Wisconsin whites. There was "no alternative" to removal, Mrs. Kinzie concluded: if they stayed, "and become surrounded and hemmed in by the white settlers, their situation is more deplorable than if they surrender their homes altogether." Moving to distant lands might save them from destruction.

The aftermath of the Black Hawk War had seen the Sacs and Foxes forced across the Mississippi to Iowa, and the 1833 Chicago treaty dispatched the Potawatomis westward also. Like the Sacs and Foxes, the Winnebagos had confronted whites in the lead region and hard feelings remained. When early attempts to move them westward appeared ineffectual, the *Miners Free Press* at Mineral Point called for quick military action: "The Winnebagoes are a cringing, fawning, cowardly, treacherous set of dogs, and if they determine not to go peaceably, they must be gathered together and kicked away." The 1837 Winnebago treaty, revised in 1846, obligated that nation to move west of the Mississippi to 800,000 acres reserved for them north of the Minnesota River; after government policy shifts in the early 1850s they moved again in 1855 to the Blue Earth River, south of the Minnesota. Large numbers eventually trailed back to Wisconsin.[2]

Wisconsin was different from most of the Old Northwest on the removal issue, however, for within its borders was a different type of "Great American Desert," the northern forests that many in the east regarded as non-agricultural. During the opening national debate over where to move the Indians, Rev. Jedediah Morse argued in 1822 that Wisconsin itself might serve as an Indian enclave, and Secretary of War Calhoun picked up on this idea in 1825 when he urged that Indians from Ohio, Michigan, and Illinois should be put in the region west of Lake Michigan. In truth, the northwoods had an attraction to eastern Indians who disliked the thought of heading out on the Great Plains, and in the mid–1830s Indians were observed heading to those northern ar-

---

2. Winnebago removal will be discussed in chapter 9.

eas, even to Canada, rather than to obey the dictates of the 1833 Chicago removal treaty. A Green Bay editor watched them passing through, trading their horses for canoes to continue northward. "We learn that a considerable portion of them who were parties to the [Chicago] treaty . . . are averse to passing beyond the Mississippi."

Decline of the Fur Trade

The fur trade was buffeted by crosswinds also. Indian trappers and hunters were shifted or removed, settlers began moving onto prime game habitat, as beavers and other animals declined in numbers rapidly.

Despite these changes, John Jacob Astor's American Fur Company, now dominant across the region, paid little attention to long-term needs, such as maintaining adequate numbers of fur-bearing animals for future endeavors. Smaller operators were no different, and the environmental results were predictable as the nineteenth century wore on. Beavers became extinct in southern Wisconsin by 1825, although they remained abundant in some northern areas. Marten, fisher, and otter were scarce. In 1832 two Sioux Indians killed a bison on the Trempealeau River, believed to be the finale for that species in Wisconsin. Caribou were seen in small numbers near Chequamegon Bay in 1845, and apparently disappeared soon after. Wild turkeys disappeared from eastern Wisconsin by 1846. Occasional elk hides were listed in early nineteenth century fur trade reports from Green Bay, and while large herds were later spotted in the Chippewa River Valley, the declining fur totals showed that elk too were vanishing from Wisconsin. The return of many of these animals would await wildlife management efforts of the twentieth century.

These declines did not signal the end of the fur trade. Instead, they drove traders to new intensity in seeking other species, pushing the Indians to wider searches even while the government was forcing tribes to give up more and more territory. In the 1830s the replacement for beaver became muskrat, and it soon made up 95 percent of the furs shipped from the region; deer skins ranked a distant second. One study found that the total number of furs and skins shipped from the Upper Mississippi country actually tripled between 1836 and 1870—but rather than high-priced beaver or marten, the bulk of the increase was low-priced "rats" (muskrat), deer, and raccoon. Meanwhile, demand was shifting as Europeans began to prefer silk to beaver hats. Amid these changes the American Fur Company tried to expand operations with larger vessels on the Great Lakes and even a fishing operation on Lake Superior, but the firm finally collapsed in 1842.

Further, the traders were facing a different Indian in some respects—more dependent upon whites for food, but now able to obtain money from government annuities. Traders frequently had to provide food to the Indians, reversing earlier conditions; Chippewas were given flour and wheat at the start of fall hunting, and traders even introduced potato cultivation in their villages. But the use of alcohol in the trade did not let up, and efforts by the U.S. government to block its entry were as ineffective as those of the French and British during earlier times.

The Land Rush

The French Claims

Residents of the old fur trade communities became apprehensive when the U.S. government announced it would require good titles to secure landholdings. As more and more newcomers began to seek out unclaimed properties, French-Canadians at Prairie du Chien and Green Bay suddenly had qualms about whether the new rulers would recognize their long-lot holdings anchored on the shores of the Mississippi or Fox, an old colonial system at odds with American practice and law.

In the early 1820s federal officials began to receive pleas from French Canadians nervous about their landholdings. An 1821 Green Bay petition argued that the signers in that "remote situation, having little intercourse with any part of the American territory in which the laws of the country were known & enforced and generally ignorant of the language" of the laws, had continued to occupy lands given them by the Indians "without being aware that they were infringing the laws of the American government." One reason for their uncertainty was that the first Congressional attempt to deal with these claims, in 1820, had required that claimants prove occupancy back to 1796. Many lacked any sort of documentary evidence, or were afraid that the Americans would find their evidence too flimsy. Congress eventually advanced the cutoff date for proving occupancy to 1812, but worries remained.

The government sent Col. Isaac Lee, a French speaker, to Prairie du Chien and Green Bay in 1820 and 1821 to collect statements from those claiming land. As late as 1843 the situation was still not completely settled, however, and both French land divisions and the French language were entangled in the process. Typical of the complications was the Prairie du Chien suit involving trader Hercules Dousman. It originated with his wife, Jane F. Rolette Dousman, and centered on two tracts in "the old French settlement" there. The land had been owned by John Cardinal "before deeds of conveyance were used among the French settlers at Prairie du Chien." Cardinal sold the plots to Jane's father, who in turn sold them to her after she married Joseph Rolette. Confusion grew when the U.S. Commissioner confirmed these to Jane but mistakenly entered her name as *Jean*, "which mistake probably arose from the supposition of the person who made the said entries that *Jean* was the French mode of spelling *Jane* instead of *John*, the name of a man, which it really is." A daughter by her previous marriage also claimed the land, but justices of the Supreme Court of the new State of Wisconsin backed Jane F. Rolette Dousman's claim.

Surveys and Sales

French-Canadian claims as well as the vast territories being ceded by Wisconsin's Indian tribes now had to be placed under the American land system. That system originated as a body of law in 1785, when Congress under the Articles of Confederation drew on Jefferson's genius and the experiences of the colonial era. The result was a rectangular system of townships six miles by six miles, subdivided into one-mile square sections of 640 acres each, with larger aggregations of these extending east and west of meridian lines in ranges.

As soon as the Black Hawk War was over and cessions were authorized the surveyors began their labors in Wisconsin, starting in what was then the area of heaviest population, the mining region. By the close of 1833 most of southwestern Wisconsin as far east as the Rock River had been surveyed; in 1834 surveyors moved to the lower Fox Valley but had to abandon the square grid system when working along the riverbanks and adapt to the French long-lots. In the rest of Wisconsin the deputies hired by the General Land Office stretched their chains and struggled uphill and down to mark parallel lines one mile apart, blazing trees, battling insects and snakes, while taking notes on plants, topography, soil, and the condition of the land.

Over the winter months these surveyors' notes were transformed by government clerks into land plats, maps indicating boundaries, subdivisions, and other information needed by potential buyers. One copy was sent to the district land office, where notices were prepared specifying which tracts were to be sold and when. On sale days, people thronged the register and clerks, who sat on a platform, calling off the first section of the first township. The clerk waited at least 30 seconds for a bid, then moved on. This was the "land office business," a time fraught with consequences, as families took steps that might affect them and their descendants for generations.

Sales moved slowly at first, for settlers were not yet converging on most of Wisconsin's lands by the mid–1830s. Mineral Point's land office sold 14,336 acres of land in 1834, its first year; Green Bay's sales were also slight then, and in 1835 the two offices together sold only 217,000 acres, considerably below Illinois' 2 million and Michigan's 1.8 million acres. The government's continued refusal to sell mineral lands helped dampen interest in southwestern Wisconsin. In 1839, however, when Milwaukee's land office opened and southeastern lands were finally offered, sales in Wisconsin Territory topped 650,000 acres, four times Michigan's total for the year and almost double that of Illinois. By 1845 almost three million acres had been sold in Wisconsin, bringing the government $3,768,106.51. The Mineral Point office received a boost in sales in 1846 when the government finally permitted mineral lands to be sold. Other land offices were opened at St. Croix Falls in 1848 (moved to Stillwater, Minnesota, the following year); Willow River (Hudson) in 1849; Stevens Point in 1852; La Crosse in 1853, Superior and Eau Claire in 1857, and others followed at Menasha, Wausau, and Bayfield, as surveys were completed. The state's last land office, at Wausau, closed in 1928.

Squatters were often on the ground long before surveyors and land offices arrived. The term *squatter* originally had a negative connotation in the east, where unscrupulous persons sometimes settled on lands already claimed in hopes of profiting through defects in the title or somehow wresting control. But in the Old Northwest the surveyors' inability to keep ahead of the surge of settlement opened the way for vast numbers of squatters occupying unclaimed land who sometimes held their acreage simply by planting a turnip patch. Though attacked in Congress as "lawless rabble," the numbers of squatters continued to grow, and western politicians soon included defense of the squatter as part of their basic stump speeches.

Claim associations became the squatter's vehicle to protect his claim. The aim was to protect a squatter on land he had settled on and "improved"—that is, had made a cabin or other structure and had started farming—but also to keep the price at $1.25 without seeing it raised through competitive bidding. To accomplish this, so-called "Squatters' Protective Societies" simply blocked others from bidding on members' claims. More than a thousand settlers converged on Milwaukee's first claims association meeting in 1837; their rules included a requirement that within six months of registering a claim with the group the member had to improve and cultivate at least three acres, the improved total increasing as more land was claimed. At the public sale, the group's agent would make bids on members' claims "and no person shall in any case be countenanced in bidding in opposition to said agent on behalf of the settlers."

At Sun Prairie in 1845 the association set a 160-acre limit and warned that if anyone purchased land claimed by members "they shall be disregarded as neighbors, and that no dealings of any kind be had with them. That we will neither lend to them, nor visit them, nor act with them in any capacity whatsoever, nor upon any occasion." Anyone violating the organization's rules would be rebuked "with such severity as has been common in the settlement of this western country." Similarly, Waukesha County's "shark committees" had such a well-developed system that it was said "disobedience to claim laws was almost wholly unknown." At sales, the sharks' agent "took his stand near the register, and when any claimed section or quarter was offered, would bid ten shillings [i.e., $1.25 per acre] for it. . . . The real claimant made no bid; but if any speculator began bidding to run the land up above the lowest Government price, the 'shark committee' would grab him and start for the river. He generally would withdraw his bid before going; but if not, he was 'doused' until he did."

The target of most of this pre-sale maneuvering was the specu-lator—a feared, often detested, but frequently essential person on the American frontier. The speculator bought up land, then sold it when prices had risen. It was an old American confronta-tion—perhaps as old as American settlement itself. Sometimes the speculator served as a source of credit; he could divide large parcels into plots that the settler could afford. Frontier schizo-phrenia was exhibited when officials urged the immigration of men of wealth—while settlers attacked the large purchases these men often made as sheer speculation, a type of gambling.

Nationally, it was estimated that 8 million of the 13 million acres of public lands sold in 1835—much of it in the Old North-west—went to speculators rather than settlers. That this could occur, in the midst of claim associations and crowds of farmers scowling at outsiders at the land sales, suggests that many of the speculators were themselves settlers, claiming more land than they expected to farm, planning to sell it later at a high price. Profits from such sales enabled the settler-speculator to buy live-stock or farm implements; such funds were not drained to the east.

The truth of this was discovered by a surveyor working in the Milwaukee district in 1835, who encountered Indiana and Michi-gan squatters. Their "general mode," he reported, "was to lay up a square pen of poles—about 4 high—throw together a few brush—and put their name on a tree or two with red chalk. . . . They do not all stop at one claim—I learnt from one that he had made six pitches—should hold on to one, and sell out the others to other emigrants—His usual price $250—a claim."

Passage of the federal Pre-Emption Law in 1841 allowed settlers to have first chance to purchase lands they had already
settled, and at the minimum price of $1.25 an acre. This law was
later succeeded by the 1862 Homestead Act—a free quarter-section to the settler who would farm it for five years.

Statemaking

And so Wisconsin was thrown open, the army of surveyors
eventually followed by land sales agents and settlers. The 1825
inauguration of the Erie Canal opened a waterway from the popu-
lous east to Wisconsin's eastern shores, enabling thousands of
New Englanders and New Yorkers—called York Staters—to travel
with speed and some ease to the Mississippi Valley. In Wisconsin
these groups concentrated in the southeastern regions along Lake
Michigan; southerners, with the addition of miners from Illinois,
remained numerous in the southeastern lead districts.

With settlement increasing so rapidly, Wisconsin lumbered
steadily from territorial status to statehood. New territorial delegate Henry Dodge, elected in 1841, fought for the rights of squatters to be first purchasers of lands they had improved; he also
worked to end the system of leasing mineral lands and pushed
for federal aid for roads and harbors.

But the statehood question began to loom over all, agitated
most noisily by a chorus of politicians eager for the spoils of an
enlarged field of operations. Others eventually joined the campaign, and supported the call for statehood by voting in favor by
a six to one ratio in 1846. The Northwest Ordinance's requirement for 60,000 as the minimum population for statehood was
reduced by Congress to 40,000, but it was a moot point, for Wisconsin had counted 155,000 during a mid-decade census. The
first constitutional convention of 1846 has been termed a gathering of "young Yankee farmers;" the average delegate had lived
in three states (U.S. or foreign), and four had moved at least
eight times. Their convention was marked by shouting and bom-
bast, and the delegates produced a controversial document noted
mainly for its attack on banking; voters rejected it in 1847.

But a new convention was called and began meeting in late

1847 with fewer and more serious delegates. This document avoided getting caught up in controversial issues such as banking, Negro suffrage, and married women's property rights. However, it included a clause giving an Indian male the right to vote if he had been declared a U.S. citizen or was not a member of a tribe. Voters approved it 16,759 to 6,384 on March 13, 1848, and Congress added its assent in May. Wisconsin was a state.

The 1850 census showed Wisconsin's population at 304,756, grown tenfold from the 30,749 of ten years earlier. Residents born in New England or New York numbered 95,624, almost one-third of the new state's population. One Dodge County township in 1860 had 81 American families—78 of them headed by New Englanders or New Yorkers. This was far from unusual in the southeast. In Waukesha County, the New England influx was seen in the presence of a Congregational Church in virtually every town, and in the New England birthplaces of large numbers of the prominent figures featured in the 1880 county history. European immigrants were present in increasing numbers.[3]

Farming the Frontier

As the first era of large-scale settlement closed, many more settlers were arriving in family groups than was true when fur trading and mining were Wisconsin's principal occupations. Women had creativity forced upon them in these early frontier farms. Traditional roles of farm wives remained but were usually much more difficult to carry out in frontier conditions and involved additional responsibilities. Initial structures built to hold a claim were often little more than lean-tos, or half-shelters; one Rock County family lived in a haystack for three months.

Frontier openness to visitors placed extra duties upon the housewife in these claim shanties; no one could be turned away. Mrs. John Weaver, who came with her husband from Oneida County, N.Y., to start a farm 18 miles west of Milwaukee in 1836, found that when they finally built their cabin—her husband sawing boards by hand from logs—two other families joined them

---

3. The European influx is discussed in chapter 8.

for four weeks while they built their own cabins. Often men look-ing for land would stop by to spend the night in the one-room cabin; they were always welcomed even though "our floor was strewn with men." Mrs. Weaver stressed that "we were only too glad to divide our small room, and accommodate, as well as it was possible in our poor way, for we wanted neighbors as well as they wanted homes." And when no visitors were on hand for a night, she recalled, "we felt rather lonely." A year later the Weavers reaped some reward for frontier friendliness: sick oxen having ruined their chances for a first summer's crop, they were forced to borrow food from their neighbors, who gave it willingly.

Frontier illnesses required a farm woman to be a medicine-dispenser and, on occasion, the one to amputate frozen toes; preg-nancies required her to serve as midwife regardless of training or experience. But it was in providing food for the family that most creativity was required. Lacking flour, the frontier woman had to grind up corn: "Some grated it on an instrument made by punching small holes through a piece of tin or sheet-iron, and fastening it upon a board in concave shape, with the rough side out. Upon this the ear was rubbed to produce the meal." Others used a coffee-mill, while some tried "pestling" by pounding the kernels in a bowl-shaped cavity in a piece of wood, much as Indian women had done for centuries (but were now abandoning in favor of specially built "corn mills"). When wheat or buck-wheat were grown the early methods of thrashing were so rough—usually driving cattle over the sheaves until the heads were re-moved—that the resulting flour was filled with smut, dirt, and weed seeds. After such an operation, Mrs. Weaver recalled, "we made something we *called* buckwheat cakes."

The onrush of work and the demand for answers to sudden crises kept the frontier woman busy in a way that may have been a godsend if it enabled her to forget her loneliness. Far from neighbors, beset by wolves' howling at night (a Pewaukee family returned from a brief absence to find a she-wolf and her whelps had taken over their cabin), she was frequently alone while her husband took logging or other distant jobs to bring in needed cash. It was different from the French-Canadian settlements which collected families in villages, from which members walked out to work their surrounding farm plots, as at Prairie du Chien. The American system featured separate, isolated farms, the dwelling standing alone on the acreage. This isolation and work regimen were particularly difficult for many women from New England or Europe who had grown up in cozy neighborhoods with relatives and neighbors close at hand. Such American and European women faced the isolation of frontier living with some trepidation. "My wife was often sorry she came to the wilderness of Wisconsin for her father had a fine farm and servants," a Norwegian admitted.

More than men, women, and children were needed to settle a frontier, however. One Waukesha County farmer who had walked west from Genesee County, N.Y., in 1836 recalled the importance of "the faithful ox. We may all thank God for the ox." Horses needed grain for feed, but none had been planted before the settler arrived and what was available for sale was expensive. The ox, however, could be worked all day, "then turned loose to pick his own food at night." Marsh hay provided the first winter's food for oxen. And the ox could frequently be hired out: the fee for breaking a half acre of virgin land was generally $10.

In addition to bringing oxen and other farm animals, the arriving settlers also carried names, blanketing the territory and state with a nomenclature that frequently reflected distant homes and homelands. And so Dane County soon had a town called Roxbury, given its name by a settler from the small town of Roxbury, N.Y., which itself had been settled a century earlier by newcomers moving west from Roxbury, Mass. Such continuities on the frontier were numerous.

Prairie awaited these newcomers in many areas of southeastern Wisconsin, but it was intermixed with groves, swamps, lakes, and the much-touted "oak openings"—the savannas of occasional oak trees and open areas, where prairie fires had blocked the growth of forest. Writers of travel books hailed the rolling prairie as "one of nature's fairest works," but prospective settlers revealed both their backgrounds and their practicality in generally choosing either the oak openings or the forested lands. Prairie land could be broken more easily—often up to one and a half to two acres a day—but growing a crop on such an expanse would require plenty of timber for fencing. One settler who crossed Dane County's twenty-mile-long prairie with ox team was asked whether the vast open area would ever be settled: "Yes, but not in your day or mine." Instead, oak openings were generally the first selected for settlement, for not only could they be plowed easily, but they held abundant wood for fencing, cabins, and fuel. Although the "Yankees" eventually turned to prairie lands, in Dane County at least no group of newcomers initially settled on the prairie.

Roads were nonexistent or dismal in the opening years of the settlement boom, forcing settlers to pay close attention to transportation routes in making their claims. From interior areas to Milwaukee, Racine, and Southport (Kenosha), transport was entirely by team and wagon. From Walworth County, the journey to the shoreline forty-one miles away required one and one-half days.

The Military Road, hacked out of the wilderness by the Army in 1835 from Prairie du Chien to Green Bay via Portage, did not tap the territory's new farming regions and added little to the fledgling agricultural transport network. By 1840 the major settlements were connected by rough trails which were hopeless in wet weather, difficult the rest of the time. Plank roads, which charged tolls for riding over pathways covered by heavy boards, were an early response, and a large portion of the southern oak forest was sacrificed for building plank roads inland from Milwaukee from the early 1840s on. Some 150 plank road companies were chartered from 1845 to 1870.

It was the railroad, however, that made the crucial links that would both open new areas to exploitation and settlement, and would inexorably bring the end of the Wisconsin frontier. As early as 1836 Milwaukeeans began petitioning the Legislature to charter a route connecting their city and the Mississippi by rail, through Mineral Point. No rails were laid in Wisconsin until 1851, however, and the first train traveled the twenty miles between Milwaukee and Waukesha later that year. This Milwaukee and Mississippi line reached Madison in 1854 and Prairie du Chien in 1857; the Milwaukee and Watertown Railroad reached Watertown in 1855, Columbus in 1857, and Sun Prairie in 1859. The

Milwaukee and Horicon ran to Horicon by 1855 and reached Berlin two years later; its southern branch made it to La Crosse by 1858. Chicago was spreading its rail network in the same period, and Janesville was tapped by the Chicago and Northwestern in 1855. Congress was an active participant in these projects, and it dispensed public lands freely: by 1872 almost three million acres—8 percent of Wisconsin's surface—had been given to railroad companies to finance construction.

The railroads' success meant that a frequent frontier stage, the wheat frontier, could now proceed. Cheap lands and the growth of rail lines—both fostered by Congress—worked to stimulate wheat as the frontier farmers' best cash crop during a time of rising U.S. and European demand. Wheat became identified with certain frontier areas because its requirements were minor for labor, skill, and capital. A profit on his first crop could normally be expected by the pioneer farmer, and as a cash crop wheat made possible purchases of animals, farm implements, and building supplies. Many of the farmers from western New York, Pennsylvania, and Ohio had wheat raising backgrounds.

Lumber mills were frequently erected first in the new communities, but flour and corn mills followed quickly; the gristmill has been called the first institution, except the school, in which all the early settlers had an interest. The first public meeting of Whitewater's settlers occurred when they realized the man who had claimed the only possible millsite was not going to build a gristmill. He was told to proceed or sell out, and chose the latter. When a new owner was found, "the whole countryside" turned out to help erect the new mill.

Eventually, however, the wheat boom rolled on, becoming established in the new territories of Minnesota and Dakota where cheap, dry lands and the spreading railroad network made wheat a logical crop. By then, farming was transforming Wisconsin's physical and natural landscape in many ways—fenced fields and the spread of apple orchards and dairying through southern and central regions were paralleled by the appearance of imported weeds that thrived where native plants were plowed or crowded out. As plows and cattle became common, they encouraged the spread of Canada thistle, quack grass, dandelions, and mustard, among others. In the process, rust, smut, and the chinch bug caught up with wheat and helped speed its departure as the major Wisconsin crop after 1879.

The stages of Wisconsin's frontier until now had included the fur trade, mining, Indian removal, and early farm settlement, and now the wheat era was rolling on. With steamboats plying the lakes and rivers, and railroads crossing the prairies and savannas, new influxes of outsiders were now poised to migrate.

8.

AN ETHNIC AND
RELIGIOUS JUMBLE

The Immigrants

Winds suddenly shifted off Gävle, Sweden, one June day in 1841, filling the sails of the *Minnet* and starting it on its long journey to America. Among its passengers was 30-year-old Gustaf Unonius of nearby Uppsala, a minor government official, traveling to America with his wife and three friends.

Gustaf and Margareta Unonius were caught up in the "America Fever," a contagion that spread across the continent and swept up millions of Europeans who by any objective reckoning ought to have stayed home. But few humans can take a purely objective look at their own situations, and certainly not Gustaf Unonius, who saw himself hemmed in without a future in Uppsala, while across the Atlantic waited a new land of liberty, opportunity, and prosperity. The newlyweds left Sweden possessing only vague plans of settling somewhere in America, but later while traveling across New York State on the Erie Canal they began to pick up stories—of the fertility of Wisconsin, of Milwaukee as the great entry point, of speculators already controlling most land in Illinois. After transferring to a Great Lakes steamer the Swedish couple heard more tales, eagerly bandied about by fellow passengers, and when the vessel approached Milwaukee they made

Gustaf Unonius called himself Sweden's "first emigrant," since he was first to take advantage of a new law permitting Swedes to leave without permission of the Crown. He and his wife came to Wisconsin in 1841, settling at Pine Lake near the eventual site of Oconomoc. Unonius praised American democracy and opportunity, but nevertheless returned to his homeland in 1858. COURTESY STATE HISTORICAL SOCIETY OF WISCONSIN, WHi (X3) 14482.

their decision: Gustaf and Margareta Unonius informed the captain they would disembark in Wisconsin.

In the hotel a waitress exclaimed in Norwegian, "De ere da saa Gud svenske folk!" (Well, I declare, if you are not Swedes!) She directed them to another Swede, who led them to the land office. Hiking inland to examine the possibilities, Unonius saw only one cabin in the first ten miles tramping west from Milwaukee. He eventually found suitable land thirty miles into the interior on a lake near the site of Oconomowoc, made his claim, built a cabin, and named the fledgling settlement "New Uppsala."

Gustaf and Margareta Unonius were part of the early trickle of European immigration into the American Midwest, a trickle that rapidly became a flood in the 1840s. Thousands left their homes and headed for a region which was seemingly too good for description, which drew such comments as this (by French visitor Alexis de Toqueville): "All things considered, the valley of the Mississippi is the most magnificent habitation ever prepared by God for man." New Yorkers now shared passage across the Great Lakes with Irishmen; Vermonters came down the plank in Milwaukee with Prussians; Massachusetts families found their new Wisconsin neighbors to be Norwegians.

And these diverse origins left their marks on the Wisconsin landscape. Today, many generations later, the names on the land hark back to distant homelands, and one can wander Wisconsin's main roads and backroads and encounter on the signposts many reminders of Europe: there are Denmark and Poland, Belgium and Holland, Norway and Sweden, Luxembourg and Erin, as well as other town names from provinces and states such as Holland's Friesland, or from the Schleswig, Hanover, and Rhine that went into the new Germany after 1870. Ancient names such as Helvetia live on in the Wisconsin landscape, carried by immigrants. If one turns to European city names the list is even more extensive—Wisconsin has Berlin, Hamburg, Wien, Stettin, Casimir, Freistadt, Brussels, Stockholm, Oulu, Cambridge, Bangor (for the Welsh hometown of its founder); it once had an Amsterdam. Or consider adjectives: Erin Prairie east of New Richmond, Russian Coulee near La Crosse, Norway Grove in Dane County, Dutch Hollow in Sauk County, English Ridge in Richland County, and Swiss Lake northeast of Merrill. And there are many, many others.

There is more from that era, of course—many barns across Wisconsin still show influences of European architecture, as do numerous dwellings that date back to the early nineteenth century. Court records reveal judges and juries grappling with translations and interpretations, whether someone who slandered a woman in German could be sued by presenting an English translation, whether an Irishman could sue if his opponent said he had murdered someone back in Ireland. Wisconsin quickly became a heterogeneous conglomeration of names, churches, architecture, foods, and stories carried from distant homelands.

The Lures

They came for many specific reasons as well as general dreams or complaints. Virgin soil and the availability of land were magnets to people used to rocky landscapes and tiny plots. En route, Unonius heard Wisconsin called "one of the most attractive and fertile districts in the great West." To a Devonshire farmer near Mineral Point writing home to England in 1851, it was noteworthy that "a person may keep as many cattle as he pleases and turn them out and feed where they like." No fences or gates were needed: "They may go over thousands of acres." For a Welshman at Ixonia, life was comfortable with taxes tiny "and everyone living on their own land." Compared to Europe with its large military establishments and hordes of officials, Wisconsin had little of either; Unonius's comment on the government was, "we hardly noticed that we had any." George Hopfengaertner in Waukesha County wrote back to his father in Germany:

> One is under little expense here. There are no dues, no tithes here, no taxes (there is taxation, of course, but compared to yours they amount to almost nothing), no community dues, no dog license, no—etc. etc., no (mounted) police, no beggars, no skinners. . . . What a man raises is his.

Wisconsin and the entire Midwest enjoyed a good press overseas, especially when newspapers published emigrant letters. There was also a growing number of emigrant advice books, providing useful information and U.S. statistics seeking to prove the likelihood of success.

The chance for advancement, always a frontier characteristic in the popular mind, now loomed ever larger as success stories multiplied. When a Wisconsin Dane returned home he lectured to his countrymen about what had happened to him in Dodge County: he bought a farm for $200 and five years later sold the improved property for $5,000. Colonies were organized by persons dreaming of having their own communal settlement in the Wisconsin wilds, such as Pottersville, launched by unemployed potters from Staffordshire, England, who sent 134 members to Columbia County in 1846. Another British group began a temperance colony in Iowa and Dane counties, and Owenite and Fourier communes appeared in Waukesha County and at Ceresco, near Ripon. All ultimately failed.

Wisconsin vigorously recruited these Europeans. In addition

to efforts by railroad and land companies to bring in customers, the territory in 1846 allowed immigrants to vote for delegates to the constitutional convention, and repeated this two years later in the new state constitution: male immigrants with at least one year's residence were legal voters, the first such action by an American state. Wisconsin was also first to send an agent to meet immigrant ships in New York, a step taken in 1852 when the legislature authorized appointment of a commissioner of immigration. The agent distributed pamphlets, met with shipping officers, even ran advertisements in European newspapers.

By that time reports were growing about Wisconsin's mix of peoples. Across the new state in 1850 the census-takers found that fully one-third of the 305,391 population was foreign-born, topped by 38,054 Germans, 21,043 Irish, and 18,952 English. Norwegians totaled 8,651, French-Canadians 8,277, while Welsh numbered 4,319 and Scotch 3,527. There were also 1,244 Swiss, 1,157 Dutch, 146 Swedes, and 88 Danes. Short years later Belgians began arriving in the lakeshore districts, Icelanders came to Washington Island, and Finns reached the Gogebic mining region in northeastern Wisconsin during the Civil War. Other groups flooded into the north as well, and by 1876 the Wisconsin exhibit at the Philadelphia Centennial Exposition could note that Burnett County had 1,136 Norwegians and only 298 native-born (white) Americans. As with the earlier arrivals who headed for the mining region or the lakeshore districts, these newer groups were generally bound for sparsely settled areas where land was available and cheap.

The Census Bureau's frontier line—setting off the area with less than two inhabitants per square mile—moved northward rapidly under the new rush of settlers. The Lake Michigan shoreline attracted larger numbers, but away from that the 1840 line ran east-west approximately at the level of Milwaukee, dipping below Madison; by 1850 the line slanted toward the southwest from Green Bay, encompassing Fond du Lac and Portage. Ten years later the frontier line was more nearly east-west again, anchored on the east at the Menominee River's entrance into Green Bay, and shearing north only as it neared the Minnesota border. (See map in chapter 10.)

From the British Isles

Immigrants from Cornwall led a substantial movement from Great Britain into Wisconsin, entering the lead region in 1830 in an influx that would not let up for twenty years. One estimate puts 7,000 Cornish in the lead region by 1850, most in mining, although the Civil War's stimulus to farm prices encouraged many to switch to agriculture. They were therefore early participants in the Wisconsin frontier and soon had neighbors from Devon and other nearby areas of England.

Irish miners also appeared in the lead region, even becoming dominant in the Schullsburg area. But they soon scattered throughout the territory and state, and Gustaf Unonius encountered two Irishmen in Delafield in 1841 who were the only persons marking Christmas there. Although it has become a commonplace in American history books that the Irish gathered in cities, in fact large numbers were drawn to settle on midwestern farmland, often after earning their initial American dollars working on canals; many were brought in to construct the Fox-Wisconsin waterway's dams and locks in the late 1830s.

John Solon, who arrived with his family in 1847 at the height of the Irish potato famine, recalled the land hunger that pulled them to Wisconsin and an 80-acre farm in Dodge County, in the Town of Shields. The Solons finally had their land, as well as Irish neighbors. Similarly, William Lalor gloried in his crops and his holdings in the Town of Dunn near Madison as he penned a letter to his brother in Ireland in 1868. Despite some problems there was one saving grace, Lalor noted: "We own the land." That was the crucial difference on the frontier of mid-America.

Frontier soil also served as a magnet for the Welsh, entering the territory in 1840 and concentrating in the southeast, especially Waukesha County, and in Columbia County, although some headed first into the Racine area or the mining region. "The land generally is exceptionally good," John and Margred Owen in Baraboo wrote to their brother back in Wales in 1847, "and although thousands are coming here, the country is so immense that there is still plenty of government land. There are miles of it near me not yet taken up." But Americans, they added, were "keen on claiming (as they call it) the land before the Welsh."

Scots came also, perhaps drawn more than most other groups to the towns springing up rapidly to serve the new farming folk. The Scots' encounter with the Wisconsin frontier is better known than that of some other groups because of the chronicles of John Muir, who later became America's most famous advocate of wilderness from his outpost in the California Sierras. Muir's candid memoir, *The Story of My Boyhood and Youth,* gives insight into the exhilaration as well as the crushing drudgery of farm life— the excitement over passenger pigeons blocking the sky, the roaring of a frozen lake making ice on a winter's night, as well as the endless round of caring for livestock, and plowing, and building fence.

Part of the family, including eleven-year-old John, arrived from Dunbar, Scotland, in 1849, making the last leg of the trip inland from Milwaukee on a wheat wagon. Eventually settling near what is now Ennis Lake, a dozen miles north of Portage (a county park marks the site today), the nine Muirs struggled on a farm that in retrospect was simply too far north of the rich oak openings and prairies of southern Wisconsin; this was only marginal farmland.

Chores such as feeding animals and chopping wood took the early hours of daylight, and then mowing and cradling hay, or harvesting, ran until darkness—"then supper, and still more chores, family worship, and to bed, making altogether a hard, sweaty day of about sixteen or seventeen hours." The year after arriving, when he was twelve, John Muir was assigned the task of plowing the stump-filled fields, doing the man's work his father expected of him. The youth was also called upon to chip down ninety feet through sandstone for the family's well, lowered each day in a bucket. At the eighty-foot level carbonic acid gas almost killed him but he was finally dragged out, barely alive.

Life was difficult, but "no other wild country I have ever known extended a kinder welcome to poor immigrants," John Muir would write of that frontier. Gardens and farm animals produced enough food for survival, but in Muir's opinion the Scots, English, and Irish who settled in the neighborhood never achieved enough to fully satisfy their land hunger, driving themselves relentlessly to develop attractive, well-kept farms. "To accomplish this without the means for hiring help was impossible," Muir concluded.

The Germans

Early German settlement largely coincided with southeastern Wisconsin's maple forests, and German farms soon stretched like a marching army northward toward the pine areas near Green Bay. Eventually the heavily German region reached over to central Wisconsin, then jumped to Grant, La Crosse, and Buffalo counties along the Mississippi. This was a movement pushed from across the Atlantic by conditions within the fragmented German states, where revolution was brewing in a storm that would finally hit in 1848; in the meantime, many sought to flee the coming upheaval and Wisconsin became one of their major destinations.

Because Germans soon became Wisconsin's largest immigrant group—forming a higher percentage in Wisconsin by 1880 than in any other state in the union—their history has become well known. Some hoped to form a separate German state in Wisconsin; immigrants arriving in Milwaukee as early as 1852 found that "all English speaking suddenly ended, and we heard nothing but German."

Probably no other immigrant group revealed such deep internal divisions as the Germans; in fact, these cleavages decreed that despite a massive exodus to different frontiers, the German states would leave almost no mark as colonizing powers. Early settlement in the 1840s was heavily from the Rhine provinces, aiming primarily at Wisconsin's eastern areas but also at Dane and Sauk counties. Soon, however, the flow of north German Lutherans increased, especially from Pomerania, Prussia, and Hanover. Religious persecution and Lutheran doctrinal differences had forced many from the north starting in 1839; chief among these was the group known as "Old Lutherans" who fled while resisting Prussia's efforts to form a single Lutheran church.

Their numbers in Wisconsin became so great—38,064 by 1850, leaping to 123,879 in 1860 and 265,756 by 1885—that Germans were present in every major economic and political endeavor. They generally did not seek the isolation of a subsistence farm far from neighbors or transportation, but paid keen attention to marketing possibilities and the availability of timber. "I would not recommend land farther than 10 miles from the lake [Michigan]," immigrant John Kerler wrote home in 1850, because rains made roads impassable "and when living inland one is obliged to take produce a great distance to the market, whereby most of the profit is lost, and animals and wagons ruined." It was a lesson followed by many of his countrymen.

Swiss

The availability of farmland frequently attracted organized group emigration, and Wisconsin's most famous case was that of the Swiss who founded New Glarus in 1845. As in many other European areas, rising population in the canton of Glarus in the early decades of the century began to place extreme pressures on landholdings. Group emigration under governmental control was finally decided upon. The Emigration Society provided $5,600, and a site was eventually selected on the Little Sugar River in Green County, Wisconsin.

In April 1845, 193 persons left Glarus and finally arrived at the southern Wisconsin site by mid-August. Land was soon divided by lot, twenty acres per family. Thus began the years of trial for the small Swiss settlement, when the dozen pans and kettles carried from Switzerland served for all, a large portion of the food came from fish caught in the creek, and divisions and antagonisms of the homeland sometimes reasserted themselves: twenty-five members from an isolated valley back in Glarus briefly withdrew from New Glarus and constructed their own shelter, away from the main group once again.

But the story of this experiment on the Wisconsin frontier is, in the main, one of the success of group endeavor—of money shared in a common fund, tasks divided within the group, four yoke of oxen purchased jointly and then used in turn by the colonists. By 1847, 109 acres had been broken by the plow, expanding to 280 acres by 1849, and within five more years another influx of Swiss began, drawn from other Swiss cantons. A young immigrant of those years later wrote that "at the close of the year 1854 it could be safely announced that the colony was a success."

Scandinavians

Another major Wisconsin immigrant group receiving extensive study is the Norwegians, whose initial foray into the United States came in 1825. Early settlement in northeastern Illinois drew others to the Midwest, and Muskego—twenty miles west of Milwaukee—was launched as Wisconsin's first Norwegian center in 1839 by a group from Norway's Telemark and Stavanger districts. As with other settlements, these tended to be filled with immigrants from the same neighborhoods at home, in a process called "chain migration." Although Norway had its religious disputes, early settlers were primarily driven by land hunger—seeking soil they could prosper upon, a farm they could leave to their children, land with timber as well as prairie. That these immigrants did not wish to cut ties with their past can be seen in their architecture, which despite rapid assimilation of local styles still has left many examples in the Coon Valley, Stoughton, and Luther Valley areas of loft cottages, *sval* enclosed passageways, and other Norwegian building patterns. Their woodworking skills were put to extensive use in Wisconsin.

Similarly, their frontier farming was initially dominated by crops known in Norway, principally barley and oats, but Norwegians learned from the Americans that corn did extremely well, and that with better transportation wheat would become a moneymaker. Until these boom times came many Norwegians faced difficult struggles, severe enough to unleash a flow of anti-immigration letters back to Norway.

Gustaf Unonius saw hard work pay off for some fifty Norwegian families who settled in the Pine Lake area without money, initially working for other farmers. Their wives obtained laundry work and other occasional jobs, daughters found employment in Milwaukee. "In this way they soon improved their condition, so that in a couple of years their plowed fields and the cows and oxen grazing in their pastures testified to the fact that America can offer great opportunities to the poor immigrant." But, the Swede added, there were two requirements: "he must be a workman, and he must work." Those from well-off backgrounds—such as some of Unonius' fellow Swedes at Pine Lake— should stay home.

Other European Groups

Others were arriving from Europe in numbers, including a large contingent of Danes who initially concentrated in Racine. Hollanders began showing up in Sheboygan County in the 1840s, forming Amsterdam and Oostburg, while a Dutch Catholic group arrived in the Fox River valley. More came after 1848, the year of European revolutions which stimulated an exodus from most countries on the continent.

Ten Belgian families arrived in Green Bay in 1853, having picked Wisconsin from a pamphlet read on shipboard; they were the first of a wave of some 15,000 Belgians who settled in Brown, Kewaunee, and Door counties over the next three years. A new arrival in 1857 found them felling trees, making shingles by hand to sell in Green Bay, harvesting, threshing with flails, making beer, and "nearly all the men were smoking tobacco which they had raised on their own land." Lacking a tradition of log construction, they were forced by their situation to build houses of local hardwoods, which they often covered with a red brick veneer more akin to what they remembered—often including a "bulls-eye" window under the gable, a decorative feature tied to loving memory for many Belgians. Roadside chapels of wood or stone soon appeared as well; many remain in Belgian communities in Door County.

During that pre–Civil War decade another group, the Poles, immigrated into Portage County and areas immediately to the north, forming a major enclave around Stevens Point; they were drawn at least in part by their earlier contacts with Prussians who were traveling there in large numbers. This mix of ethnic groups itself became an encouragement to the Poles, for their homeland included Germans, Kashubians, Lithuanians, Poznanians, Silesians, Galicians, Ukrainians, and Russians, among others. Poland in that era has been called an "ethnic jumble." This term applies equally to Wisconsin.

Immigrant Struggles

It was a new world for the immigrants in many ways. Not only were customs and language different, but the conditions of life were often so crude, so trying that there was always an ebb tide, a reverse migration heading back to Europe. A touring Norwegian Consul met many who confessed they would never have left home "if they had known that they would have to endure all the hardships which they have suffered in America." It was even more difficult trying to farm in the north, in heavily forested districts. Some forty German families walked in to the central townships of Marathon County by 1858, then faced the enormity of the forest and lack of roads: harvests were impossible there for at least three years, and it took the group ten years to break forty acres; grain had to be carried sixty miles to be ground. To the east around Green Bay in this period, Belgians suffered from a similar inability to plant and harvest crops until they had cleared adequate areas; many lacked bread for weeks at a time and lived off fish, wild roots, and wild onions. They were then attacked by a form of cholera which cost some families as many as five members within one week. News of this put a check on Belgian immigration for several years.

Gender roles were frequently changed in frontier labor, and not just among the wealthy. Along with others in the family, women were thrown in the early years into a dawn-to-dusk battle with nature where victories were only won at heavy cost. Traditions in many European countries dictated that women would care for the livestock, but in these new settlements in early years they often had to labor in the fields as well, man's work back in Europe. As years went by changes began to appear, however, and visiting Frederika Bremer found at Pine Lake that "It is the men in this country who milk the cows, as well as attend to all kinds of out-of-door business." Large families—a bane in many congested areas of Europe—became an asset in Wisconsin, because of the crying need for farm labor and the inability to hire help; households with numerous progeny had future money in the bank although more children added to the wife's responsibilities.

Changes came slowly. Weather was frequently an opponent, predators thrived on farm animals, and visitations by influenza and cholera were frequent. Bremer encountered a Swedish woman who had "endured incredible hardships": even while suckling her children, Mrs. Petterson had had to labor hard, sometimes bent double with rheumatism. But although worn out and "finished before her time," the Swedish frontierwoman told Bremer she did not regret her family's immigration because of the new world it opened for their children. Such were the trade-offs in frontier life.

Immigrants and the Native-born

Ethnic strife could be predicted in a community as mixed as Wisconsin had become by the mid-nineteenth century. The historian of early Belgian settlements around Green Bay noted that despite the extreme poverty of the first three years, the people "had not attracted that sympathy and help which is generally accorded to new settlers under the same conditions and circumstances." Nearby were Scandinavian, German, and Irish settlements, but no help had come from these. Church exclusiveness often added to the isolation of ethnic groups. Clannishness by one group was criticized by another, and Americans often took advantage of the newcomers' desire to cluster by grabbing land within ethnic settlements and then selling it for profit to latecomers eager to live among their own countrymen.

Another group present in this ethnic mix was Indians, usually a wonder to the Europeans—strange, almost mystical, sometimes regarded as part of nature and at other times as mere humans like themselves, and sometimes as subhumans. Indians frequently camped near the immigrants' cabins, ignoring them; or at times they would appear silently, suddenly, fully painted, mysterious. Gustaf Unonius noted the tribes' displacement and decline, and argued that just as certain species had disappeared, "it seems that Providence has destined this race for extinction." John Muir's father and a Scottish neighbor argued over the Indians' right to the land, the neighbor holding that whites had no right to drive off the original occupants. But Daniel Muir had picked up the centuries-old claim of the American settler and adapted it to the new ethnic situation in Wisconsin, arguing that "it could never have been the intention of God to allow Indians to rove and hunt over so fertile a country and hold it forever in unproductive wildness, while Scotch and Irish and English farmers could put it to so much better use."

Assimilation of this diverse population, breaking immigrants out of an isolation that was frequently self-imposed, proceeded unevenly. Such was the case in Trempealeau County along the Mississippi, populated heavily by Norwegians along with Scots, English, Irish, Prussians, Polish (one township was almost entirely Polish), and Bohemians, as well as Americans. There was little intermarriage before 1880, and non-English speakers lagged in school attendance; still, immigrants began rising both in property holdings and political activity, the latter prodded by the need for town meetings, road and school authorization, and similar steps to accomplish basic community tasks. In this sense democracy was imposed on frontier residents.

Gustaf Unonius encountered the need for joint action on several occasions, most notably when a wealthy American purchased land which a poor immigrant had already occupied. A settlers' meeting was called, an American was elected chairman, and Unonius was nominated for secretary but declined. The main speech of the evening was given by an American frontiersman—dressed in a mixture of Indian and white clothing, with deerskin moccasins—who argued vociferously for "the duty of every citizen to guard the sacred freedom for which our fathers bled and died, and to protect each other in our enjoyment thereof." An Irishman then proposed that the group tar and feather the wealthy claim jumper and burn his house; a Swede offered a less violent plan, to simply shun the interloper, excommunicating him from all contacts in the community, until he would agree to deed the land to the actual settler. The Swede's idea was accepted, carried out, and quickly brought success, demonstrating to immigrants and native-born alike how crucial was cooperation in a frontier still beyond the ready reach of the law.

House-raisings also showed what people of diverse backgrounds could accomplish by working together. An Englishman helped

Wisconsin's forests provided housing for incoming
settlers, replacing the wigwams and tents of the
Indians and fur traders. Although some Americans
arriving in the early nineteenth century disassembled
their houses in the East and brought the lumber with
them, others soon recognized that the trees already on
hand could be used to build homes, as was done with
this Chippewa Valley cabin in the 1880s. COURTESY
STATE HISTORICAL SOCIETY OF WISCONSIN, WHi (W6) 19726.

Unonius organize his house-raising, and on the appointed day
the neighbors arrived, mainly Swedes and Americans, totaling
twenty-three. Unonius had found in spreading word of the event
that most "not only were perfectly willing but even showed real
eagerness to give the newcomers help, which everybody seemed
to consider it a point of honor not to refuse."

By 11 A.M. on a clear but chilly day in late autumn the men
began arriving and went to work on the readied materials: logs,
handspikes (the slender, smooth trees to lean against walls for
sliding up the top logs), and forked branches for lifting and rolling the logs. This process, so familiar to frontier families, was
new to the immigrants and Unonius described it in detail:

> The first two logs on the longer side were laid right on the ground,
> here and there supported with stones and pieces of wood to make
> them lie in an approximately horizontal position. On these, four or
> five feet apart, the cross-timbers, or floor sills, were laid, their upper

side having been peeled and leveled off. A man now posted himself at every corner to notch and fit the logs into each other. . . . Between each round of logs there is . . . left, depending on the supply of logs, openings up to five or six inches, to be closed after the logs have been put in place . . . . Those who do not work with their axes and at the corners help to roll the logs, which, since they are of oak and freshly cut, are very heavy, and that is the main reason why the assistance of the neighbors is called for. . . .

When we had come to the height necessary for the main room, a few peeled cross-timbers were fitted to support the ceiling, and on them were laid a few more layers of logs still so as to provide for an attic room in addition to the main room on the first floor.

When the project was finished later in the afternoon—after openings were sawed for a door and two windows—Unonius looked with awe and pride on this log skeleton, twelve feet high, twenty-two feet long, and eighteen feet wide. Despite its crudeness it was "the beginning of *our* home, built from logs we had cut ourselves, and so in a special sense the work of our own hands." He doubted any rich man could have taken more satisfaction from his mansion. After sharing a final drink and some sandwiches and cookies, the gathering broke up and, Unonius concluded, "we took leave of one another like good friends and faithful neighbors."

The Unonius house-raising at Pine Lake in 1841 was a get-together typical of frontier America, joining peoples of disparate backgrounds and beliefs in a common cause. The foundations for the frontier log cabin became in a very real sense the foundations for a society where cooperation had become more important than competition.

Religion Enters the Great Valley

Saving the Frontier

The fledgling settlements taking root as the tide of population entered the Great Valley of the Mississippi were followed with growing concern in the East and Europe. Settled regions had always frowned as their sons and daughters headed westward, but in this case the frowns deepened as New Englanders in particular watched the western states gaining population and influence—such as the twelve western representatives added to the U.S. House of Representatives after the 1840 census.

This raised the moral as well as the political stakes. Rev. Lyman Beecher, one of the nation's most prominent preachers in the antebellum period, was vehement on this point in his 1835 volume *Plea for the West.* The West represented the nation's religious and political destiny, he argued, and the growing confrontation in the Great Valley was to be "a conflict of institutions for the education of her sons, for purposes of superstition, or evangelical light; of despotism, or liberty."

A recurring argument was that a new society was in the process of being created on this frontier, and the growing army of missionaries used metaphors of planting and "seed time" repeatedly when discussing Wisconsin and the region: "The character, Sir, of this Ter. is now in a forming state," Rev. Cutting Marsh wrote from Stockbridge near Green Bay in 1837. A touring Catholic priest urged a speedy presence for his church, arguing "It is now the time to plant." Religion was crucial during that brief moment when new settlers and new communities were open to influence. As one prominent clergymen put it, the West could be speedily gained or just as speedily lost, and "if *once* lost, will be lost *but once.*" There would be no second chance.

The "irreligion" which clergy warned against lay mainly in the possibility that another church would arrive first. "If the Protestant sects are beforehand with us, it will be difficult to destroy their influence," a frontier Catholic bishop warned in 1830. A New England Protestant added from his perspective, "If we do not furnish preachers of the truth to the new settlements, the ENEMY OF SOULS will send them preachers of Infidelity, Romanism, and other dangerous errors." Norwegians at Muskego called an early meeting to seek an ordained Lutheran minister from Norway, to serve a people who "have lived like sheep without a shepherd," their children "constantly exposed to the danger of either lapsing entirely into worldly mindedness" or being "ensnared by the well-nigh countless heretical teachers" circling about.

The reality of this became apparent in Watertown as that community was emerging from its frontier beginnings in 1857 and its population reached 8,000, half foreigners: Watertown's churches by then included one Irish Catholic, one German Catholic, three German Lutheran, one German Moravian, and one German Methodist; the Americans were served by one Congregational, one Methodist, one Episcopalian, and one Baptist church. Wisconsin was a religious jumble as well as an ethnic jumble.

Missionaries

Missionaries flocked to Wisconsin, arriving with the tide of settlement let loose by the opening of the Erie Canal and the mining boom. Apparently the first organized congregation in what would become Wisconsin—after the efforts of French Jesuits in earlier times—appeared in Prairie du Chien in 1817, when Father Marie Joseph Dunand arrived from St. Louis and launched a Catholic Church among the French-Canadians there. The monk baptized 135 adults and children, performed fourteen weddings, and blessed a cemetery during a month spent among the inhabitants. Green Bay saw several visiting priests over the years, including Father Gabriel Richard who arrived in 1821 for a brief stay and began construction of a church, an edifice completed in 1825 under Father Vincent Badin for the group of sixty Catholic families. In the spring of 1831 one of Wisconsin's most famous missionaries, the Italian Father Samuel Mazzuchelli, arrived at Green Bay and began service to Indians and whites that would last until his death in 1864.

Protestants rushed in also. The first Protestant religious service of record was held in Green Bay in 1820, conducted by a government Indian agent. Sporadic services were being conducted at the military posts by 1826. The first organized Protestant church began that year, when a Protestant Episcopal Church was formally launched in Green Bay. In 1829 the New England religious impulse arrived in the lead region as Rev. Aratus Kent responded to a request sent by the joint Presbyterian-Congregational American Home Missionary Society (AHMS). The following year a Congregational minister, Rev. Cutting Marsh, was sent to work with the Stockbridge tribe at Kaukauna by his church's American Board of Commissioners for Foreign Missions. Marsh frequently preached to whites in nearby Green Bay, who in 1835 organized a Presbyterian Church; in 1837 he helped Milwaukee Presbyterians organize a church, demonstrating the close frontier cooperation of Congregationalists and Presbyterians.

Methodists began to direct their missionary activities toward Wisconsin in the same period, as a circuit rider rode north over the border from Galena during 1828 and 1829. In 1832 a plea for frontier missions was made at a Philadelphia Methodist conference, and John Clark responded and soon headed west to serve the New York Indians around Kaukauna, up the Fox River from Green Bay. The following year, in 1833, a Methodist society was organized at Platteville, the first of that denomination within the borders of the eventual state of Wisconsin, and in 1834 Methodists at Mineral Point erected the first Protestant church building in Wisconsin. Methodists had a solid foothold by then among the Cornish in the lead region.

Baptists also entered Wisconsin through the lead region, when Samuel T. Smith, a New Yorker, left mining in 1831 to organize a Sunday School in an unnamed mining district. Smith soon left the state, but returned in 1852 and started a Baptist Church in La Crosse. By that time there were twenty-one Baptist missionaries in Wisconsin. Theologically close to the Baptists were the Disciples of Christ (Campbellites), who also gained ground across the frontier. Mormons made several forays into Wisconsin during this period, the most famous being the brief kingdom established at Voree, Walworth County, by James Jesse Strang. Strang claimed to be the successor to recently slain Mormon leader Joseph Smith.

Surrounded by evangelizing Americans, watching many of their members being lured away or simply turning their backs on church life, immigrant churches began to call for help from across the ocean. The bishop of Charleston, S.C., set the tone by arguing that the Catholic Church ought to have a U.S. membership of 5 million, instead of the 1.25 million recorded in 1836; the remainder were simply lost. The Prince-Archbishop of Vienna responded by creating the Leopoldinen-Stiftung to aid American Catholics, King Louis I of Bavaria formed the Ludwig-

Missionsverein, and the French Society for the Propagation of the Faith also sent aid to the west. In Ireland, All Hallows Seminary was launched to provide priests for America; during the first century after its founding in 1842 more than 1,000 priests were sent abroad. Lutheran groups sent missionaries also, such as the Evangelische Gesellschaft für die Protestantischen Deutschen in Nordamerika. They could not stand by while their members were being lost to the faith overseas.

New Conditions, New Methods

Conditions on America's frontiers forced change upon these incoming clergymen, for—as a Wisconsin priest wrote—"All the resolutions made in Europe dissolve as soon as one feels the breezes of the American coastline," so every tie had to be retied "before it can be said that it is secure."

Such a setting required creative adaptation. This was faced by Father Mazzuchelli, who began using interpreters to stand by and hear confessions by Menominee Indians, whose language he could not understand. This marked so fundamental a change that Mazzuchelli felt obliged to explain it at length in his *Memoirs.* The Menominees had more *métis* than other tribes and consequently many potential interpreters, he explained, but the individual selected for such a break with tradition "must always be a devout person of proved maturity."

With no clergy present, gatherings of believers often turned to laymen for leadership. Methodists in Wisconsin as elsewhere on the frontier quickly extended rights to laymen to participate in church conferences, and used untrained local preachers and exhorters extensively. The denomination also formed separate Wisconsin churches for immigrants—Welsh, Norwegians, Germans, Danes, Swedes—and created a Welsh Circuit and Norwegian District; the Congregational-Presbyterian leaders also employed six missionaries in Wisconsin who preached in Welsh, two in German, and two in Norwegian. By 1860 the Methodists had 229 missionaries working among Germans across the nation, and thirty others among Scandinavians. Requirements for these positions were mainly spiritual, not academic: Gustaf Unonius encountered a fellow Swede who had been a rag collector at home; now he was a Methodist exhorter. He was also a walking, talking example (despite Unonius's derision) of the openness of frontier denominations to new leadership.

Frontier conditions similarly created an opening for women to participate in church services, and Methodists not only used women as preachers but allowed them to vote in church meetings. Women began praying out loud in Congregational and Prebyterian church meetings, too, although AHMS missionary Stephen Peet went to lengths to explain that some clergy "have only tolerated it as seemingly necessary under the circumstances," while others had discouraged it. Peet admitted that female praying in Green Bay had occurred in private meetings in homes when there was a lack of male attendance; he explained, however, in a somewhat defensive report to AHMS officials in the East, that female praying in Wisconsin "never was practiced in a church meeting or any, properly speaking, *public* meeting. . . . I think the practice will gradually decrease as our churches are enlarged and [will be] ultimately done away." His report provided blunt testimony to the democratizing nature of the frontier, even in the face of strong, imported religious traditions.

The circuit rider system was another example of new approaches on the frontier. All groups, including the Catholics, used it to some extent, but it was the Methodists who developed circuit riding extensively in Wisconsin and employed it with greatest effect. It was, after all, the system which had initially carried that new church into the West after it broke with the Church of England following the American Revolution. Spreading with the moving frontier, Methodist circuit riders would hold services at "appointments" several times a day, week in and week out, at widely scattered points. And as these far-flung itinerants searched out settlers they lifted Methodism from a membership total not far above zero at the time of the American Revolution, to become the nation's largest Protestant denomination by 1840 with more than a million members and almost 4,000 circuit riders.

The life of the circuit rider can be followed through a report by Rev. Salmon Stebbins, sent west in 1837 to serve seven mission circuits of the new Milwaukee Methodist District. On his first tour that fall he rode into Wisconsin from northeastern Illinois, visited the Southport (Racine) church, went to Oak Creek, spent several days in Milwaukee, and forded Cherry Creek and the Milwaukee River en route to Washington City; then he rode north along the lakeshore, sometimes in water up to the side of his horse, or alternately through thick forest. He swam the horse across the Sheboygan River, held a prayer meeting in Sheboygan, then pushed north across the "Manatoowoc" river on to Green Bay. After visiting the Oneida Indians' church he rode to Stockbridge and then to Fond du Lac, preaching next at Fort Winnebago at the Portage before proceeding to Madison, where the new capitol building was being constructed. From there he rode by the ancient ruins of Aztalan, through Fort Covington (Fort Atkinson), past Heart Prairie to Cornish Prairie (LaGrange), Meacham's Prairie (Troy), Spring Prairie, and eventually again to Southport. In seven weeks he had traveled 535 miles, most of it through a Wisconsin November.

One Methodist circuit rider got lost in the Kickapoo Woods of southwestern Wisconsin and wandered about for three days in midwinter, without food; as a result he lost one foot and never regained his full hearing. Another permanently ruined his health serving his flock amid the angular topography around La Crosse while following his 200-mile circuit.

Revival meetings also brought settlers into the church. Emotionalism ran high at these gatherings, and attendance was frequently enormous as people flocked from miles around, often sleeping in wagons during the days-long event. It was a rare occasion for many to listen to a real clergyman. An 1838 revival in Racine has been termed the first such event in Wisconsin, with attendance estimated at one thousand. A Methodist elder wrote in his diary afterward that on the final evening, half of those still unconverted "were at the altar for prayer, while Angels and Saints rejoiced over the repenting sinners." One participant said that a teen-aged boy in attendance "was the happiest soul I ever saw in my life, shouting and praising God." Some years later a preacher hailed the enthusiasm he met at a meeting in the Turner settlement in Sigel, near Chippewa Falls; the warmth of the community's welcome was understandable, for (a newspaper reported) "they had not listened to preaching or had religious services held in their neighborhood in nine years, and hence were very eager hearers."

At the core of these revivals was the Arminian doctrine of free-will—that an individual could by his own actions affect his redemption and eventual place in heaven. Freewill beliefs found fertile ground on the Midwestern frontier, where opportunity bred an optimism about the future that encouraged self-reliance. The new frontier sects, in particular the Methodists and Baptists, gave voice to these philosophies.

European missionaries frowned at the revivals and the beliefs proclaimed there. Father Mazzuchelli lashed out at the Protestant preachers whose eloquence "consists in much loud speaking, in quoting the Bible in every sense that may suit them, in pronouncing the name of Jesus innumerable times, in violently censuring sinners, inviting them to conversion through simple faith in the Savior." These itinerants could "weep at will," accompanying their preaching with "loud cries, prayers, exclamations, sobs, frenzies, trembling, sweats, contortions," and similar excesses. And all the while they heaped ridicule and insult upon the Catholic Church.

Many Protestants from European religious traditions also had trouble with what they saw on the frontier. A German living in New Berlin wrote home to his family in Bavaria in 1848 about what had bothered him at a German Methodist service:

> At the conclusion of the hymn, we are asked to pray and all fall on their knees, but not forward, for they turn around on the backless bench and then throw themselves down or lie on it. And the preacher (Hubmann substituting. Anybody can be a preacher, for they had no clergymen educated at a seminary) says a prayer. But not out of a prayerbook, for they don't consider that worth anything. (I with all my books am doomed to hell.) The prayer must come spontaneously from the heart, and they say that as soon as one has prayed fervidly and become penitent, he is saved.

Catholics felt themselves further burdened by their extra requirements as they pursued settlers into the wilderness. Father Mazzuchelli's complaints about Protestants noted that his free-wheeling competitors did not need to transport sacred vessels and altars to conduct their services. Father T. J. Van den Broek, a Dutch priest who came to the Green Bay area in 1834, pleaded with his European superior for a proper chalice, to replace his own of tin; he also called for a ciborium—the covered container holding the bread of the Eucharist—but added that his "greatest need" was "proper priestly attire." These were not problems faced by Protestant circuit riders.

Denominational competition also upset European Protestants. Leaders of the Old Lutheran movement—born out of controversies surrounding Prussia's attempts to force a Protestant Church Union—found the challenge to be enormous simply to maintain an identity amid the swirl of revivalistic, evangelistic sects. "The cultural situation was different from anything the Lutherans had met before," their historian has concluded. Accordingly, the Wisconsin Synod emphasized use of the German language and rejected any joint religious activity with persons not in doctrinal agreement; lay preaching was firmly outlawed.

Struggles were not only between Catholics and Protestants or Europeans and Americans, however, for many immigrants carried with them longstanding battles against the state churches at home. In Norway the Haugean movement, drawn from the campaigns led by Hans Nielsen Hauge (1771–1824), fought the "dead orthodoxy and nerveless rationalism" of the Norwegian State Church. This fight was transferred to America by Elling Eielsen, who went to Muskego in 1839 and seven years later at Jefferson Prairie helped create the Evangelical Lutheran Church in America, the first Norwegian church denomination in the United States. Swedes had their *Laesare* (readers) movement, also challenging the rigid hierarchy of the state church. Even the Augustana Synod, which eventually drew in most regular Lutherans from Sweden, was critical of the state church back home; many other Swedes split off into the Swedish Mission Covenant or Swedish Baptist churches. That the dissidents' arguments echoed so fervently around Wisconsin probably reveals that they reflected a new, basic philosophy running through frontier religion: here were settlers seeking a more personal voice in their relationship with their God, the widely held freewill doctrines clashing with the predestination preached by established churches, and laymen forced by circumstances to lead religious services.

Debates over these issues ran through various groups. Eielsen's preaching came under attack from the Lutheran minister at Koshkonong, Rev. J. W. C. Dietrichson, who described a Haugean service:

> After he has been preaching, [Eielsen] proceeds to ask one then another, in the audience, "How do you feel now? Did you feel the spirit working in you?" In this respect he sounds like the Methodists, who regard conversion as something that can come about in the twinkling of an eye. He accuses the old Lutheran church as we have it in our fatherland of being papistic and false. . . . Thus he destroys the unity of the Lutheran church.

In Trempealeau County the splintering eventually created six Norwegian Lutheran churches where there had been two.

Reformers and Immigrants

European immigrants and churches also confronted the reform campaigns led by American Protestants around the nation in those antebellum decades. These labeled drinking, dancing, tobacco use, Sabbath visiting, and many other practices as sinful. Antislavery would eventually become the focus of reformers by the mid–1850s, but before that time the attacks centered on personal activities common to most communities, activities which seemed to many incoming Europeans to be beyond criticism.

Congregational, Presbyterian, and Methodist proselytizers carried these movements into Wisconsin and all jousted repeatedly with immigrants. The AHMS missionary in Beloit argued that Germans—"most numerous and influential" of the Europeans pouring into the west—had struggled in their homeland against an oppressive government and church but in America were degenerating into hostility "to the Church, the Sabbath, the Bible, the cause of Temperance and the institution of marriage." What this could mean in a specific locality was soon demonstrated in West Bend, where the AHMS missionary reported that "infidel or Roman Catholic" Germans went so far as to block his church's use of the district school house for meetings; he added that "I myself have several times been *stoned* while passing the street."

The reformers' struggle in Wisconsin quickly focused on two

intertwined topics: immigrant drinking and immigrant violation of Sabbath peace. Immigrants carried with them a long tradition of widespread use of alcoholic beverages, as Gustaf Unonius was reminded when he officiated at a Norwegian funeral and saw a whiskey bottle making the rounds, the guests holding a hymnal in one hand and a glass of whiskey in the other; their drinking continued all the way to the graveyard. Father Mazzuchelli admitted that "the greater number of immigrants from Ireland" became "slaves to the sin of intemperance," a fact used by Protestant zealots to attack the church.

Immigrants, whose "Continental Sabbath" meant visiting friends or gathering at a beer garden or saloon, quickly challenged the reformers' attempts to make Sunday a day of quiet religiosity across the Mississippi Valley. It was the *"foreign population"* who hunted on Sundays and broke Sabbath peace in Menasha, one missionary reported; a Methodist conference complained that foreigners, "mostly Germans," were turning the Sabbath "into a holiday for all kinds of sports and wickedness." Similarly, it was the Germans in Barton (south of West Bend) who disrupted the Fourth of July, which fell on a Sunday in 1858. On that fateful Sabbath—which sabbatarians claimed should have been left peaceful, and Independence festivities postponed until Monday—the Germans

> made it a day of mirth, gambling, beer drinking, and parade. Even while [we were] engaged in our services, they were busy in marching with their music past our church; and frequently the hills echoed to the discharge—for the want of a better implement of demonstration— of an unseemly anvil, purloined from a blacksmith shop. At other times, the rest of the Sabbath was disturbed by the rattling of firecrackers, or the hurrahing of a motley group of boys and men, who never had a single drop of the blood of our forefathers in their veins.

For immigrants worried about fitting into American life, the reformers' attacks posed dilemmas: enjoy their rights in this land of freedom, or yield to the patriotically phrased demands of temperance and sabbatarian advocates? Norwegians in Madison discovered the perils of this on a warm Sunday in 1857 when, after church, they rowed across the lake for a boisterous picnic. They were perhaps not surprised when local newspapers criticized their revelry; what was not expected was an attack from their own pastor. In Madison's Norwegian newspaper the debate waxed hot: hilarity on Sunday was permitted in Norway—why not here? The pastor's reasoning left no alternative: if you do not stop, you will bring the church into disrepute.

Such behavior has been called "immigrant puritanism," the acceptance by immigrant leaders of strict American behavioral codes that contradicted their own traditions. Examples of it abound on the Wisconsin frontier. *Emigranten*, a central Wisconsin Norwegian newspaper, began to attack "night courting," a practice common in Norway which featured visits by young males to the rooms of young female servants. "This abominable social abuse unfortunately has been transferred here to the strange land," the newspaper complained. Trempealeau County Norwegian pastors similarly worried about their communities' high illegitimacy rates, and began condemning night courting and similar practices long accepted in Norway. Now the outside world was looking on. When Pastor J. W. C. Dietrichson asked his Koshkonong Norwegian congregation to expel a drunk, he confided to his diary that if the church refused, Methodists and other Americans "would now truly have reason to criticize us Lutherans—which they are generally so ready to do anyway—for receiving and retaining all kinds of ungodly people."

Summing Up: The Frontier Church

This frontier church provided much to pioneers: a place to encounter their God again in a new home; a setting where widely dispersed people could come together; a structure for holding school classes; a means to continue ties with the past amid a culture devoted to the new; a location for the exchange of stories, ideas, and even goods, and a socially acceptable setting in which young people could meet. But this institution also played a major role in controlling the actions of those beyond the reach of the law. As such it was a counter-argument to the claim that the Midwestern frontier was "over-churched."

The preachers' attacks on drunkenness, divorce, tobacco use,

Sabbath hilarity, frivolous recreations such as croquet and cards, and refusing to pray for President Lincoln must be viewed within a frontier environment often lacking in social controls. The clergy in nineteenth century America remained men of respect and influence in their communities, and in the newly settled areas of Wisconsin they did not hold back from exercising that influence amid scenes that sometimes bordered on chaos. More than half of the people of the territory were "on the side of Satan, utterly disregarding the Sabbath and every other Christian institution," according to a visiting Presbyterian preacher in Racine in 1836; he said he had never seen "such abominable wickedness" elsewhere. The campaign for Sabbath rest had added importance in new areas where the community had difficulty bringing pressure on an employer. A Norwegian laboring on the railroad as it pushed into Wisconsin's northwoods wrote in his diary on a Sunday evening: "Today too we worked. Oh forgiving God, forgive us for working on Sunday. We should have the 7th day for rest after the week's hard work. But if we don't work . . ."

Settlers from diverse backgrounds faced challenges in coming together as a community. A missionary in Willow Springs claimed the local citizenry was drawn from fourteen church denominations and seventeen different states and foreign countries. A parallel situation was reported by a missionary in another (unnamed) Wisconsin community:

> On the south, is a settlement of Scotch emigrants. Next succeeds a neighborhood of settlers from the island of Guernsey, some of whom cannot speak English. Among their number is a Methodist clergyman, who sometimes preaches to his countrymen in their own language. A society of Free-will Baptists comes next; and immediately contiguous is a colony from Wales, composed of Baptists and Whitfield Methodists, who are each supplied with preaching in their own tongue.

And so the missionaries set out after their flocks and attempted to mold their communities. A missionary in western Wisconsin reported proudly back to the AHMS that clerks of surrounding school districts "all expect me to furnish teachers for their schools," and he had obliged by giving employment to eleven that season, "most of whom are pious." Temperance was pushed in the schools and the pupils carried its ideals back to their homes. The Methodists' Alfred Brunson launched a "Literary Association for Mutual Improvement" in Prairie du Chien. But the impact of churches on moral life can best be seen through the week-by-week records of the local churches themselves.

At Green Bay, the First Presbyterian Church was less than sixteen months old when, in January 1837, it brought John Y. Smith and William J. Wood to trial in their dispute over a land sale: "Is it or is it not a fact that brother Wood has neglected to walk with this Church as a Christian ought to walk[?]" Wood was excommunicated. That first year also the church restored Charles Bull to membership, after he had been charged with dueling and keeping bad company; he eventually appeared before the board, deplored his conduct, and resolved "to lead a Christian life and desired the watch and prayers of his brethren." Other members were charged with intoxication, associating with wicked company, "indulging in vain amusements," and violating the Sabbath.

This was perhaps the most important role of the church on the Wisconsin frontier: helping a people find peace among themselves in situations that often brought on disputes—cattle wandering beyond boundaries, land claims and fencing arguments, problems stemming from faulty translation, in addition to the many ills common among those who depended heavily on such uncertainties as weather, insects, markets. As Wisconsin's frontier of settlement pushed farther north after mid-century, Swedes in the Wood River Baptist Church in Burnett County turned to their church to help solve the feud between F. O. Olson and Anders Ahlstrom, which apparently arose over "some gossip behind their backs." The two were brought forward, argued and answered questions, and then, as recorded in the church minutes, "Ahlstrom and Olson led in prayer, each asking God's forgiveness for faults and shortcomings. Then they grasped one another's hand as a token of reconciliation, desiring from now on to live in brotherly unity, forgetting the old misunderstanding and taking on a new attitude."

It was an ending that would have pleased Swedish immigrant

Gustaf Unonius, who worked to establish churches among his fellow men and women on the southeastern Wisconsin frontier. Around Pine Lake he witnessed his share of disagreements involving both immigrants and the native-born. And he ran up against the reform spirit frequently, including on one of his first trips when the thirsty immigrant was denied purchase of a glass of milk, because it was a Sunday. But the frontier was too broad to be controlled everywhere by such rules, and later on Unonius reached a spring; at the end of the day he and his companions came to another cabin whose occupants welcomed them to stay overnight. It was a good introduction to the Wisconsin frontier, which brought together saints and sinners and a vast array of folk somewhere in between, arriving with their hopes, dreams, and customs to create a new territory and a new state in the Great Valley.

9.

RESTRICTING THE INDIAN DOMAIN

Winnebago Removal

It was already past mid-December in 1873 when the troops under Capt. Charles A. Hunt began moving on the Winnebagos. The Indians had been ordered to show up in Sparta for their removal to a reservation in Nebraska, but had refused to appear. The Army was called and began to hunt the Winnebagos down. They soon found a group led by Big Hawk camping on the Baraboo River near Portage but the Indians, surprised in the midst of a feast, refused to turn over their rifles and were overpowered. Their leader was placed in handcuffs and the band was forced to march to the train in Portage.

That winter of 1873–74 was highly productive for troops rounding up the Winnebagos. The soldiers apprehended some 860, including several other late-December captures: seventy-three seized at Leroy in Juneau County, fifty-six in Trempeleau County, thirty-eight near Reedsburg. Sometimes the Army found only women and children in the winter camps, and these were taken away under the expectation—quickly fulfilled—that the men would eventually follow when they returned from hunting.

The soldiers acted at the enthusiastic urging of many nearby white settlers. A Black River Falls editor called the Winnebagos "a nuisance to the whites in this part of the country;" his counterpart on the Portage *Register* said of the tribe that "the great mass of whites" in the area were "sick of being annoyed by their everlasting begging and filthy presence." Only three years earlier the Wisconsin Legislature had asked Congress to shift the tribe to the north, and the previous summer the governor bluntly informed a Winnebago council they would have to leave Wisconsin.

Both the government's actions and the journalistic attacks were influenced by a new development in Winnebago removal, part of the government's policy shifts affecting tribes east of the Mississippi. As a result of government efforts, the western branch of the tribe—which had made six different moves since agreeing to cross the Mississippi in the 1830s—now had another new home, a reservation carved out of the Omaha reserve in Nebraska in 1865. A Black River Falls man who inspected the site characterized it as "better than any unoccupied lands in Wisconsin," praising its soil ("not hard to plow or cultivate") and noting that additional timberland for the reserve was being purchased from the Omahas.

But other changes were occurring also, their impact deeper than government policies or the lures of a reservation in Nebraska. These changes helped decree that the 1873–74 roundup of Winnebagos was the last attempt to force that tribe or any other group of Indians to leave the state. It was the last attempt partly because the Wisconsin frontier was moving into a new phase, no longer confronting only basic questions of settlement or primary disposal of the soil. Now the remaining Wisconsin Indians—the Winnebagos, the so-called New York tribes, the Potawatomis, the Menominees, and the Chippewas—were playing other roles than simply providing pelts for the fur trade, or occupying lands desired by settlers.

The Winnebagos' reactions to removal in 1873–74 reflected the new setting. Increasingly over the years many Winnebagos had simply refused to stay put after being moved. This occurred after an 1862 attempt to transfer them to Dakota Territory: just as the government escorts got back to St. Paul they saw the Winnebagos, who were returning also. Charles Round Low Cloud, born in 1872, grew up hearing stories of his tribe's removal ex-

ploits and suffering, and years later when he was "Indian report" newspaper columnist in Black River Falls he recounted
some of those memories in his unusual style:

> Some Indians has been discussing about old time, seventy-one
> years ago. A man, or William A. Hunter has been try to make difficult
> these Winnebago Indians. Move to Nebraska. This was 1873. . . . All
> he get so much "a head," or every person for $15, a head, and one
> winter stay up there came back 1874 in summer. Some are came
> back by a train half way and rest by foot.

Another Winnebago who grew up in the aftermath of the removal carried similar tales into her old age. Mountain Wolf
Woman recounted her mother's stories of the forced move to Nebraska, where they had relatives from earlier removals:

> But, mother said, some of the Wisconsin Winnebago did not like
> the removal. Some even cried because they were taken there. . . .
> Then spring came and mother said that the Winnebago died in great
> numbers. . . . In the spring they moved to the Missouri River where
> they cut down some big willow trees and made dugout canoes big
> enough for two, mother said. . . . Thus she returned home with some
> of her relatives.

As they came up the Mississippi, Mountain Wolf Woman said,
the group sent a little boy to ask the white people on shore where
they were. He reported back, "Prarsheen." They had arrived at
Prairie du Chien and were soon back in their Wisconsin home.

The Winnebagos' return in 1874 initially angered many whites.
"Nine-tenths of the people in northwestern Wisconsin favor their
removal," the Black River Falls editor proclaimed in February.
But they kept coming in scattered groups, until a majority had
returned by September, when they faced difficult preparations
for winter; armed guards were called out in Tomah area cran-
berry marshes to stop the Indians from stealing berries. A public
meeting in Necedah denounced the Indians' presence as "prejudicial in the highest degree to the welfare of the settlers." It attacked those who encouraged the "roving vagabonds" to return,
charging these men had a "selfish desire" for profit from selling
the Indians whiskey and buying their furs.

But during this debate something else appeared, something

that pointed to a transformation taking place within Wisconsin. Many white persons—and not just clergymen or fur traders— were beginning to defend the Indians, speaking out for their right to remain in the state, urging that citizenship be granted; these critics even challenged the government's authority to force removal.

It was part of a national development, for defenders of the Indians were becoming numerous and outspoken in many areas, sometimes revealing a belief in the "noble Indian," at other times seeking to bring Indians within the guarantees of American liberty. Poet Walt Whitman was among this growing number of Indian defenders in the East: while employed as a clerk by the U.S. Bureau of Indian Affairs after the Civil War he frequently met with visiting tribal groups, including Wisconsin Chippewas. One day Whitman saw Hole-in-the-Day, a Chippewa leader, "a handsome Indian, mild and calm, dress'd in drab buckskin leggings, dark gray surtout, and a soft black hat." The poet argued there was something remote and lofty in these Indians, "something that our literature, portrait painting, etc., have never caught, and that will almost certainly never be transmitted to the future, even as a reminiscence. No biographer, no historian, no artist, has grasp'd it—perhaps could not grasp it."

Reasons for Wisconsin whites' growing defense of the Indians are not entirely clear today, and may well have included (as was charged) an interest in tapping into tribal annuity payments. But it seems likely that less mercenary reasons were involved as well in the Winnebago controversy, when some 1,000 citizens of Jackson, Clark, and Columbia counties petitioned the Legislature opposing removal and calling for the return of Winnebagos who had been snared by the Army.

Jacob Spaulding of Black River Falls took the lead in these moves. A prominent local citizen—he was an early settler and businessman, having come from New York State in the 1830s and obtained key water power sites on the Black River—he was described by a later writer as "a man of wonderful force of character and indomitable will." Spaulding used both as he traveled to Washington in late 1873 seeking reversal of the government's removal order, arguing for Winnebago citizenship and for 80-

Jacob Spaulding, a prominent Black River Falls leader, helped win reversal of an 1873 removal order for the Winnebagos. After his death the following year, forty Winnebagos marched in his funeral procession. The local newspaper reported then that Spaulding had spurned a government agent's offer of money to convince the tribe to move: "I am poor, and need money badly," Spaulding said; "but, captain, you never saw money enough to induce me to be false to my Indian friends." COURTESY JACKSON COUNTY HISTORICAL SOCIETY.

acre allotments to be given each Winnebago family in Wisconsin. Spaulding must have been working to convince the local editor and townspeople as well, for by the end of 1874 the Black River Falls editor (who had earlier argued, "You might as well try to civilize the pine trees as these same Winnebagos") vowed that the new plans for citizenship and allotment of land would meet "no objections . . . by the citizens of this region." And when the Sparta *Republican* ripped into Spaulding for his defense of the Indians, the Black River Falls editor shot back that such criticism was "uncalled for upon a worthy citizen of Wisconsin"; whether the Sparta attack was withdrawn or not, however, "Uncle Jake will continue to do all he can to make the Winnebagos citizens of the State in which they were born, and which they inhabited long before the editor of that paper emigrated to this region."

A reservation for the Winnebagos was never created in Wisconsin. Starting in 1875, however, members of the tribe were allowed by Congress to take up forty- and eighty-acre home-steads, which were scattered from Jackson and Monroe counties northeastward to the Wisconsin Rapids and Wittenberg areas. In 1881 Congress agreed to split the Winnebago annuities, paying Indians who remained in Wisconsin under a separate roll, rather than insisting that all payments be made to those choosing to stay in Nebraska. In 1887 a newspaper reported that 400 Winnebagos received $8,000 at Tomah, 300 received $6,000 at Wausau, and 700 were given $13,000 at Black River Falls, averaging $19.25 apiece.

Removal Pressures

Potawatomis

The Winnebago experience had parallels elsewhere in Wisconsin, as calls for removing all Indians multiplied. The campaigns included the Potawatomis, left without a Wisconsin home as a result of treaties in the 1820s and 1830s which carved up their extensive Midwestern land claims. Many ended up in Kansas, where they became known as the Prairie Potawatomi.

But like the Winnebagos, many Wisconsin Potawatomis refused to move to the new reserves on the Plains. Large numbers fled into Canada, while others were mentioned in succeeding years as "strolling" or "roaming" about Wisconsin in "stray bands," drawing the ire of settlers. In 1848 troops were called out to force numbers of these Potawatomis across the river into Iowa, and an 1851 removal drive took more than 600 Potawatomis to their Kansas reservation.

They kept returning to their old homes, however, and by 1856 the Commissioner of Indian Affairs reported that "about 600 Potawatomis, strolling through Wisconsin, belong to Kansas Territory." Large numbers came back each year to the Muskego area, their *Mus-kee-Guac* or "fishing place." They also returned to Waukesha, where their former campsite became Carroll College; over the years their numbers dwindled, however, and by the 1880s only "gray and decrepit" members of the tribe continued to visit.

Powers Bluff near Arpin, in Wood County, became a Potawatomi center in central Wisconsin and site of annual homecom-
ings which drew Indians from other counties and states, many
arriving by train.

Called "probably the most fragmented tribal people" in the
Great Lakes region, the Potawatomis' numbers in Wisconsin were
variously reported in the Indian Commissioner's annual reports
of the 1870s and 1880s as 175, 180, 240, 280.

Menominees and New York Indians

The Menominees had survived intact through the waves of
early nineteenth century settlement in Wisconsin by their good
fortune in being located mainly north of areas where agriculture
flourished. Some of their initial problems came, in fact, not from
whites but from other tribes—because their area near Green Bay
was made the home of the Stockbridges, Munsees, Brothertowns,
and Oneidas who were moved into Wisconsin from New York
State in the 1820s. These tribes were placed on small reserves
purchased from the reluctant Menominees and Winnebagos.

After several 1830s cessions, in 1848 a treaty of removal was
forced on the tribe, under which the Menominees were to be given
$350,000 in annuities, in exchange for moving to 600,000 acres
in northwestern Minnesota. Tribal leaders delayed investigating
the site, however, perhaps influenced by the Winnebagos' troubles
in the same general district of Minnesota. When they finally inspected the Crow Wing area in 1850, the Menominees' representatives complained of the lack of game and wild rice, and the
war dangers from the presence of Chippewas and Sioux nearby.
Chief Oshkosh then led a delegation to Washington, where they
convinced the new President, Millard Fillmore, to permit the
Menominees to remain in Wisconsin. Petitions of support from
white settlers were rolling in by then—early ones came from
ninety-one citizens of Little Chute and from ninety-two residents
of northern Wisconsin; others arrived at the White House in en-
suing months, including one bearing 400 signatures. The President ultimately ordered a search for suitable land in Wisconsin,

Oshkosh, head of the Menominees' Bear clan, led the successful effort in 1848 to block the tribe's forced removal across the Mississippi, winning a reservation on the Wolf River in 1854. This photo is from a daguerrotype circa 1850 in the Oshkosh Public Museum. COURTESY STATE HISTORICAL SOCIETY OF WISCONSIN, WHI (X3) 29318.

taking the step because of the Menominees' "manifestation of great unwillingness . . . to remove to the country west of the Mississippi River," as well as their "desire to remain in the State of Wisconsin."

Chiefs LaMotte, Wau-ke-cheon, and Osh-ke-he-na-niew then guided two government officials on an expedition up the Wolf River. The officials found the land satisfactory, and reported, "The chiefs are highly pleased with the country." This area between the upper Wolf and Oconto rivers was designated a temporary home for the tribe, and the Menominees moved up the Wolf in 1852 to settle on their new reservation. In May 1854, a new treaty authorized the Menominee Tribe to occupy the 276,480 acres, in twelve townships, as a permanent reservation. The Legislature and Congress approved the pact and the Menominees had won their right to remain in Wisconsin. The tribe's challenges had not ended, however, for the Stockbridge and Munsee tribes successfully petitioned in 1856 to obtain two of the Menominees' twelve townships as a reserve.

Chippewas

The Chippewas of northern Wisconsin lost legal control over their Wisconsin lands under treaties of 1837 and 1842, but those documents had not included removal: the 1837 treaty confirmed hunting, fishing, and wild rice gathering "during the pleasure of the President of the United States," and the 1842 agreement provided for occupation of the homeland "until required to remove by the President of the United States." At the 1842 session at La Pointe the latter clause prompted repeated queries: how long would that be? The Indians were assured, according to witnesses, that this meant a long time, as long as they were "well behaved."

This was the legal situation when the government suddenly moved in the early 1850s to evict the Chippewas, scattered in bands across northern Wisconsin. Origins of the plan lay not in the demands of local whites, however. It was instead a product of political maneuvering and intrigue; looming in the background was the developing hunger of business interests for the north's mineral and logging resources. After the 1848 national election swept the Whigs to power the plotting began, apparently masterminded by two new Whig appointees, U.S. Indian Commissioner Orlando Brown and Minnesota Territorial Governor Alexander Ramsey. Existing records indicate they envisioned opportunities to make more appointments and exert more control if the Chippewas were moved.

Subagent John S. Watrous, appointed in April 1850, was dispatched to Chequamegon Bay to transfer the La Pointe subagency to Minnesota; it is clear that he also carried plans for bringing about removal of the Wisconsin Chippewas to Minnesota. When word of the subagency move spread it sparked controversy, but Watrous calmed the Chippewas with reassurances that paying their annuities over in Minnesota—at Sandy Lake, a Chippewa agency—did not mean they would have to move away from their Wisconsin homes.

At least that was what the Chippewas believed. And so when news came that payment day at Sandy Lake would be October 25, 1850, some 3,000 members of the tribe from northern Wisconsin and Michigan began the trip, a journey of almost 500 miles for some. Their arrival so late in the fall—forcing many to miss part of the wild rice harvest—would not likely have been a problem if the annuities had been given out as scheduled.

What the Indians did not know was that they were targets of a plot hatched by Brown and Ramsey to keep them in Minnesota. By distributing goods and making payments after the freezeup, it was predicted, the Chippewas would be unable to return to their homes and would have to remain in Minnesota.

But the Indians foiled one of the expectations of the plan when they traveled west not as family groups but largely as individuals, as adult men. Because they believed that payment would be on schedule, they came unequipped for a lengthy stay, many without rifles. Upon arrival in the closing weeks of October the Chippewas found not only that Watrous was absent, but that there were not enough government rations on hand; further, the spoiled food they were given led to an outbreak of dysentery, followed by a scourge of measles. They waited, without shelter, while the death toll reached as many as eight or nine daily, nearly exhausting the capabilities of survivors to handle the burials.

Watrous finally arrived November 24, a month late; many Indians had been waiting longer than that. He carried none of the expected funds because Congressional wrangling over the slavery issue and the Compromise of 1850 had delayed passage of the necessary authorization. Watrous quickly saw that the Indians had to be sent home, and he wangled some food and ammunition for them on credit from local traders (at terms up to six times what would have been paid in St. Paul). The camp finally broke up on December 3.

An estimated 400 Chippewas died as a result of the debacle at Sandy Lake, 12 percent of the tribal roll, drawn heavily from the tribe's active adult males. This included some 170 (Watrous admitted to 150) at Sandy Lake itself, and another 230 who perished on the return trip.

This disaster did not force the Lake Superior Chippewas to move. It had the opposite effect: the Sandy Lake debacle of 1850 fueled their anger and suspicion and made them determined to remain in their Wisconsin homeland.

Watrous tried again in 1851, informing Ramsey that it was his intention to conduct the transaction again in Minnesota but to delay payments to the Lake Superior Chippewas "until after navigation ceases, which is done to throw every obstacle in the way of their returning to their old homes." Payments were made this time as announced, but the Chippewas again went back to their Wisconsin homes as they had in 1850.

Voices opposed to this chicanery began to be heard, mainly among white residents along Lake Superior's shores. Missionary Leonard H. Wheeler, resident at Chequamegon Bay since 1841, attacked the removal project, arguing that it would be better to shoot the Indians than to send them into the midst of their traditional enemies, the Sioux. Whites in the area launched a letter-writing campaign against the government plan, and Michigan Agent Henry C. Gilbert argued that the Chippewas "will sooner submit to extermination than comply" with removal. Editors from Sault Ste. Marie and Detroit blasted the attempts, while mining entrepreneur (and Methodist lay leader) Cyrus Mendenhall circulated a petition claiming removal was "uncalled for by any interest of the Government or people of the United States, and . . . in a high degree prejudicial to the welfare of the Indians." The *New York Times* labeled Watrous' project an "iniquitous scheme" to force the Indians to move against the wishes of "the entire population of the Lake Superior country." Chief Buffalo, a young leader named Oshoga, and interpreter Benjamin Armstrong went east in June 1852 to meet with President Fillmore, where they laid out the list of Chippewa grievances and broken American promises, including reports of Agent Watrous' perfidy and the events at Sandy Lake in 1850. "Is it not the obligation of white men to fulfill their contracts?" Buffalo asked.

Fillmore was won over completely to the Chippewas' arguments: he rescinded the removal order, demanded an end to efforts to move the Chippewas, and specified that annuities were to be paid at La Pointe. The President was probably influenced as well by reports reaching Washington of the worsening situation west of the Mississippi, where resettlement of eastern tribes amid growing Plains warfare was creating new troubles rather than ending old ones.

Two years later the Treaty of 1854 gave the Chippewas reser-

vations at Bad River, with a fishing ground on Madeline Island;
Red Cliff; Lac Courte Oreilles, and Lac du Flambeau. This left
out several Chippewa groups scattered across northern Wisconsin, including the St. Croix and Sakaogan (Mole Lake) bands,
who were to remain landless until 1934 when they received title
to small acreages in Burnett, Polk, and Forest counties. The 1854
agreement also created Chippewa reservations in Michigan and
Minnesota.

The Reservation Era

With the addition of the Stockbridge and Munsee tribes to the
Menominee Reservation area in 1856, Wisconsin's Indian reservations were basically in place and major controversies were
settled regarding land claims—although not over how the land
would be used. The Bureau of Indian Affairs' Northern Superin-
tendency reported in 1856 that there were 2,930 Menominees,
978 Oneidas, 407 Stockbridges and Munsees, 2,546 Winnebagoes,
and 4,268 Chippewas of Lake Superior "of Minnesota, and Wisconsin"; in addition, he listed some 600 "strolling" Potawatomis
within Wisconsin.

Agents ran the reservations, but they were caught in a pecu-
liar vise, pressed on one side by the Indians and local whites, on
the other by politicians and a distant—and frequently bumbling—
government bureaucracy. When the horseless Chippewas were
presented by the government with saddles (some tried to attach
them to their birchbark canoes), it was the agent who had to
deal with the error and reassure the Indians they would eventually receive usable replacements. Agents frequently faced problems maintaining contact with all bands, especially in the early
years when no roads or railroads linked Chequamegon Bay with
the Chippewa reservations in the interior. As late as 1871 the
agent lamented that the interior bands were "so remote" that he
had not been able to visit them. Even after the first railroads
pushed north such a journey remained a disjointed expedition,
as seen in the Chippewa agent's connections to Lac Courte Oreilles,
less than eighty air miles distant: from La Pointe to Duluth by
water, then to St. Paul on the St. Paul and Duluth Railroad,

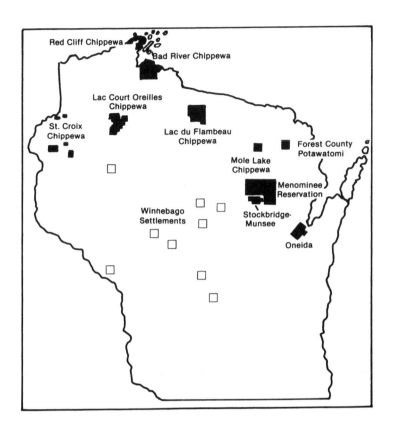

The year 1854 was a time of decision for Chippewas and Menominees, when both tribes won federal approval for reservations that let them remain in Wisconsin in traditional locations. Earlier the Oneidas from New York were authorized a reservation, in 1838; two other New York tribes, the Stockbridges and Munsees, later won part of the Menominee reserve. Congress recognized the plight of several families of Potawatomis in 1913 and purchased 14,439 acres for them in 80-acre family plots scattered through Forest County. Winnebagos did not get a reservation in the state. The St. Croix and Mole Lake bands of the Chippewas later received additional plots under New Deal legislation in 1934. MAP BY NANCY LURIE AND STATE HISTORICAL SOCIETY OF WISCONSIN.

then to Hudson to connect with the North Wisconsin Railroad route northward to Chandler, and finally by horse team to the reservation.

Persuading the Indians to change from hunting to agriculture proved a major challenge to the agents. The Green Bay agent worked diligently on the Menominees, spending $500 one year on seed potatoes, beans, and oats—only to see them eat the potatoes and beans and feed the oats to their animals. The new agent assigned to Red Cliff worked exceptionally hard to establish farming on the steep hillsides of his reservation, and happily reported that contrary to expectations, the Indians had planted "about four times the usual amount." Despite a dry summer with infestation of potato bugs and cutworms, he added, "the estimated crop for this year will be 4,000 bushels of potatoes, 50 bushels of turnips, 50 bushels of beans, 25 bushels of pease, 10 bushels of onions, 10 tons of hay cut, and 25 tons of sugar made."

In a system self-consciously paternalistic, the agent frequently acted as parent for his charges, depositing their off-reservation earnings in a bank and doling out weekly allowances, helping them through tough times by allowing them to work for food and clothing, having land cleared to enable them to farm, all the while cheering them on or condemning their laziness.

The agents were often men of religious zeal. Some reservations were centered at existing mission stations, as at Bad River and in the New York Indians' communities. Many agents were appointed as part of President Ulysses S. Grant's so-called peace policy, under which it became the government's goal to turn to religious groups and religious leaders to carry out Indian policy. Congregationalists were assigned the Chippewa agencies in Wisconsin during Grant's administration, and a newspaper noted in 1873 that the assistant agent at Chequamegon Bay received his salary from both the federal government and the American Missionary Association. The evangelical spirit was present in the person of the Menominees' agent, who banned Sabbath day trading at the reservation store so Indians could gain "some knowledge of the proper observance of this day."

Agents often worked in tandem with missionaries, who were present on all Wisconsin reservations though with less power than the government appointees. The colonial era's Roman Catholic missionary impulse was revived in the 1820s and 1830s with Fathers Samuel Mazzuchelli, Frederick Baraga, and others. Episcopalians had a long history with the Oneidas, dating back to the early colonial era when the Church of England—their predecessor body—established missions to serve the tribe in New York State. In 1881 the Green Bay agent reported that an Episcopalian and a Methodist worked with the Oneidas, while three Roman Catholic priests and two Franciscan lay brothers labored among the Menominees.

Both Protestants and Catholics converged on Chequamegon Bay's Chippewa bands in the 1830s, as Frederick Ayer came to La Pointe for the Congregational-Presbyterian American Board of Foreign Missions, and Frederick Baraga for the Roman Catholics. When reservations were created there in 1854, Bad River was set up for Protestants and the Catholics were assigned to Red Cliff.

Schools were in existence among all Wisconsin tribes well before the reservation era, supported both by the government and by religious denominations, and this system continued with day schools, boarding schools, and adult and manual training classes. In 1874, for example, the La Pointe agent reported that the government was paying the Presbyterians $587.50 each school quarter to run the Bad River boarding school, which had 26 Chippewa boys and girls.

But there were problems—problems for the Indians, attempting to cope with a rigid school setting directed not by tribal elders but by whites; and problems also for the white teachers. Missionary teachers soon learned that the Indians had different feelings about certain chastisements: beatings were acceptable, but pulling or cutting hair bordered on sacred violation. Further, going to school was not always top priority for Indian families; among the Oneidas, average daily attendance was sixty pupils during one year, out of 400 eligible. Despite being officially placed on reservations, Indians continued to travel widely. The Chippewas' mobility was said to permit their offspring only two months of classes, and then "parents and children emigrate to the sugar-camp or rice-field, or to a distant fishing-ground," for several months where the child would forget everything "amid his savage surroundings as readily as he acquired." One proposal called for the teacher to follow the pupils; another was to hold school in the summer when pupils might be corralled for some weeks before the rice harvest began. Eventually free lunches were offered, a solution which met with considerable success. Boarding schools also proved workable, and new ones were launched among the Oneidas and Winnebagos in the early 1890s.

Civilizing the Indian

The Processes of Civilization

It was all part of civilizing the Indian. The paternalistic policy of the United States government laid out a route to follow, under which Indians would be gradually improved through changing their way of life. The Commissioner of Indian Affairs put the issue starkly in 1881: since "savage and civilized life cannot live and prosper on the same ground," one system or the other must die. For the Indian, the choice was "civilization or extermination." Others felt, however, that Indians would simply fade from the scene, and Indians sometimes came to the same conclusion as they looked at the human wreckage about them. Chief Na-naw-ong-ga-be of the Chippewas admitted in 1855 that "sickness and hunger, whiskey and war are killing us fast. We are dying and fading away; we drop to the ground like the trees before the axe of the white man. . . . A few short winters, my people will be no more."

Wisconsin's territorial seal in 1836 had proclaimed "Civilitas successit barbarum"—Civilization succeeds barbarism—but many whites claimed that Indians could not achieve civilization. Even the Stockbridge agent was moved to comment that the tribe was "as far advanced in civilization as they can well be while remaining Indians." The *Ashland Press* suggested that if some of New England's "magnanimous Christians" could live beside a "lodge of dirty Indians," their love for the native peoples would soon be sharply reduced.

Such widely held beliefs reflected the traditional frontier prejudice against Indians and their *métis* brothers and sisters. Numerous incidents—some large, some so tiny and brief as to appear almost inconsequential—kept alive the long-held patterns of that prejudice. At an Ashland hotel a chambermaid nonchalantly commented one morning that all were down to breakfast "excepting the *big half-breed* in room—." This set off such an uproar that the local newspaper reported it in full, in the process revealing contemporary feelings about the proper place for each race:

> The landlady was terribly indignant upon hearing that such was the case, immediately repaired to the office to see about the matter, but finding no one there to give her the information, started for the apartment and was about to knock on the door, when to her great surprise, it opened and she was confronted by the manly form of Miles Carroll, who stands over six feet and is considerably tanned. She burst into a hearty laugh and informed Mr. C. what the girl had said.

Carroll tried to find the maid to convince her that he was not a half-breed, but she had fled.

But negative reports were increasingly being answered by more positive ones, and after the Menominees carried off the Shawano County fair's agricultural produce prizes, the Shawano *Journal* asked, "Why have the Menominees twice made a finer exhibit than has ever been made in Shawano?" Similarly, Chippewas put on a Fourth of July show in Bayfield in 1871 that drew high praise from local residents: canoe and boat races between Red Cliff and Bad River teams, including four-oared boats raced by women from the two reservations who sought the bolt of calico offered as first prize. (The editor commented, "if we were never before in favor of woman's rights, we are now since that race." Many a "dainty white lady" would give her poodle "if she could be blessed with the muscle displayed by these dusky daughters of the forest.") The celebration continued with foot races, wheelbarrow races, a sack race, an "Indian game of ball," and finally Indian dances and fireworks. The editor heaped praise on "our Chippewa friends," who "conducted themselves handsomely, keeping good order in their ranks throughout the day."

While more than county fair exhibits and canoe races were needed to convince skeptical whites that Indians could indeed be "civilized," other evidence was not long in appearing. Language, clothing, and housing were the prime criteria used for this evaluation.

Education became a prime means of assimilating Indians into white culture. Learning English, wearing "citizen clothing," and pursuing farming rather than hunting were the prime changes urged by agents on the reservations. These young Oneida Indians studied in the reservation schoolhouse circa 1900. COURTESY MILWAUKEE PUBLIC MUSEUM, A–621–2–J.

The U.S. Commissioner of Indian Affairs stressed language in his 1887 report. No Indian student supported by the government, he asserted, "is permitted to study any other language than our own vernacular—the language of the greatest, most powerful, and enterprising nationalities beneath the sun." There was evidence in Wisconsin that the commissioner's language rules were being followed. The agent for the Stockbridges and Munsees noted that the Indians were "all civilized, read and write the English language, and are fully capable of becoming citizens." (Another agent observed earlier that the Stockbridges "are so nearly civilized that a report of their condition must be similar to that of any community.") Progress among the Chippewa children at Bad River had gone so far that "they can speak, read, and write very intelligently," the resident missionary reported, and if their boarding school continued for twelve to fifteen more years, their own language would "soon lose its hold upon the hearts of the people." Among the Oneidas, however, it was discovered that despite reported gains in English they were still speaking their own language at home and among themselves. Not surprisingly, several years later the Oneida school superintendent found English understood by only twenty-one of the eighty entering boarding students.

Housing and clothing were mentioned almost as often as English when the Indians' progress was discussed. The Green Bay agent proudly reported in 1873 that a few Menominees, most Oneidas, "and all of the Stockbridges and Munsees speak English, and all, except a small portion of the Menominees, wear citizens' clothing and live in houses." Agents proudly reported statistics of houses being built, and often mentioned the Indians' style of clothing. Many of his charges spoke "some English," the La Pointe agent noted in 1892, and "They all dress like their white neighbors, and a blanket Indian is a rare spectacle among them." Attending a Winnebago dance in the same period, Mountain Wolf Woman wore what she called "citizens clothing": the literal translation of the Winnebago phrase is "I made myself into a white person." Statistics of the Bureau of Indian Affairs for 1894 claimed all of Wisconsin's reservation Indians wore "citizens' dress."

Citizenship

As they interacted more with their white neighbors, Indians were sometimes drawn into the political system. In the process, they raised fundamental challenges to assumptions about American citizenship.

Participation in the Civil War undoubtedly helped advance the Indians' acceptance into the body politic, as occurred also with large numbers of the state's European immigrants. Many Wisconsin Indians signed up with the Union Army, including 279 from the Menominee, Oneida, and Stockbridge reservations. Their Indianness was not disguised: when fourteen Chippewas arrived at the operations ground of the Wisconsin Seventh, they performed a war dance for their curious comrades-in-arms. That the decision to enlist may not always have resulted from careful deliberation was hinted in several incidents on the Menominee Reservation late in the war, when white men were caught trying to bribe Indians to serve as substitutes for whites who had been drafted. The "flesh brokers" returned in mid-March 1865, "and by spending a few dollars in money and making promises for more and plenty of whisky, induced two Indians to go with them as substitutes"—but these whites were waylaid by other Indians who chased them off. One Menominee who served as a substitute was Joseph Davis, a mixed-blood said to be the offspring of Jefferson Davis, President of the Confederacy, and an Indian woman whom the future Confederate leader had met while serving in Wisconsin during the Black Hawk War. Years after Appomattox, perhaps in response to new attempts to seize their lands, Menominee Indian veterans of the conflict formed their own Grand Army of the Republic Post, with twenty-three charter members.

Requirements for voting, laid out in the Wisconsin Constitution, specified that qualified voters included "persons of Indian blood and citizens of the United States" as well as "civilized Indians not members of any tribe." But who would decide who was "civilized"—was it enough to be English-speaking, house-dwelling, and pants-wearing? Were Indians who lived off-reservation considered free of tribal connections?

The 14th Amendment to the U.S. Constitution in 1868 conferred citizenship on all persons born or naturalized within the nation and subject to its jurisdiction, though it also noted that Indians not taxed could not be counted in determining a state's representation in Congress. Two years later, the 15th Amendment in 1870 gave voting rights to all males who were citizens.

Citizenship suddenly became a topic of discussion on the reservations. At Lac Courte Oreilles two Chippewas, John Squirrel and Frank Ozhoga, asked that their names be stricken from tribal rolls as they began steps to obtain citizenship. Other Indians' moves toward citizenship were revealed in 1874 by the Ashland *Press*:

The Chippewa Indians of Lake Superior are civilized and accustomed to the habits of the white race—they dress as white people—live in houses, labor in all the ordinary branches of industry, and have forsaken their pagan and superstitious religion for the Christian faith. The greater portion of them vote at our elections; are admitted upon juries and hold office. It is true they are not all fitted for these responsibilities, neither are all white people.

Later that year a controversy erupted when a newspaper charged that "hundreds of votes were cast by tribal Indians," including eighty-five ballots in La Pointe where there were "just eight legal voters." The Republican editor at Portage defended the balloting by arguing that the so-called Indian votes were really by "half-breeds, maintaining no tribal relations whatever"; some of these, he noted, had even held offices such as register of deeds and county clerk, or sat as members of the legislature.

Menominees in 1874–75 made numerous requests to become citizens; one poll found that 166 wished U.S. citizenship, only eighteen preferred to "remain as Indians," and eight others were undecided. At the same time in Black River Falls some 100 Winnebagos asked to become citizens; when their requests were rejected, many began drinking and got into a fight, causing the local newspaper to lecture that "if these Indians expect to become citizens very soon, they will have to quit such work."

It seems likely that the sensitivities of Wisconsin Indians on the issue were stirred by the national debate over black rights and the 14th and 15th Amendments. The Bayfield Lyceum debated the question, "Resolved, That all Indians residing in the State of Wisconsin are citizens and entitled to the elective franchise." In similar fashion at Shawano, the debating club took up citizenship and related issues when it addressed the question, "Resolved, That the general course of Government towards the Indians, has been equitable and just."

Finally the U.S. Supreme Court entered the fray, and in its 1884 ruling in Elk *v.* Wilkins the majority held that treaties' and various government documents' references to "Indians not taxed" over the years meant that special action by Congress was required for citizenship. John Elk as a result was legally barred from voting in Omaha even though he had abandoned tribal life and was living among white citizens. The confusion did not end until 1924, when Congress made citizens of all Indians who were not already classed as such.

Landowning

Reformers began to attack the very existence of tribes in the years following the Civil War. Asserting that they were acting in the best interests of the Indians, these whites contended that tribal connections held back Indians in their progress as individuals. These arguments gradually made headway as Americans turned away from debates of the Civil War era and began to confront the new situation regarding reservation Indians. In 1871 Congress formally ended recognition of tribes as separate nations with treaty-making powers, but reformers asserted that each Indian still needed his own land, to free him from tribal control and from the need to roam far and wide on the hunt.

This movement spread to Wisconsin. The Indian Commissioner charged at one point that advances among Wisconsin's Oneidas were "retarded by the fact of the tribal lands being held in common, by which the incentive to individual exertion is greatly impaired, and habits of industry and frugality discouraged." Such attacks on the very existence of the tribe became the new drumbeat of reform, part of the campaign to "emancipate the individual" by freeing him from control by the chief.

In fact, many Wisconsin Indians were already farming their own plots by the time the national allotment movement—a program to place each Indian family on a farm—was rolling to success in the late 1880s. The 1854 Chippewa Treaty had provided for eighty-acre allotments for family heads or single persons over age twenty-one, and agents used this power to set up many families with their own plots on the reservations. Allotment progress went furthest among the Red Cliff band, although Chippewas on other reservations from time to time were also allotted lands, and in 1883 the agent proudly reported approval of 122 80-acre allotments at Bad River and 188 at Lac Court Oreilles. The Oneida reservation was divided among individual Indians in 1881, and this was later done as well with the Stockbridges and Munsees. Many Winnebagos had homesteads by then.

Passage of the Dawes Act in 1887 therefore did not come as a sudden blow to Wisconsin's Indians, given these earlier steps toward individual landholding. Nationally, this allotment act meant that almost 90 percent of reservation land eventually passed into the hands of non-Indians. In Wisconsin, almost half of total reservation lands were allotted, with the Menominees alone retaining undivided possession of their reservation under the argument that its forests provided poor soil for farming.

The Dream Dance

Standing by helplessly as their reservations were carved up, warned to forget their native tongues, craving alcohol in dismal repetition of the disasters of previous generations—these and similar other developments began to weave a bewildering web around many Wisconsin Indians. In reality, they were being dispossessed of more than land, for they were also losing important parts of their cultures and many had good reason to look back sadly to happier times. The moment was ripe for a new religious movement for Indian renewal.

It had happened before in North America. And just as in the French and British eras, large numbers of Wisconsin Indians never quite gave up their religious traditions, despite the missionaries' urgings. As with continued use of Indian languages, there were always secret times and secret places to continue the old ways. When a reporter visited the Bad River reservation in 1874 he mused at first how it reminded him of "quiet New England towns"—but suddenly he was "rudely shaken" when he came upon a "Bad Spirit pole," with clothes of a sick child attached, "placed there to appease the Bad Spirit and to avert impending punishments." Such practices continued among the conservative groups present within all tribes; on the Menominee reservation it was the "pagan party" which eventually gathered at Zoar and made contact with like-minded traditionalists among other tribes.

Rituals and dances continued. The Midewiwin or Medicine Society brought both self-identification and renewal; its activities were witnessed by a visiting German on Chequamegon Bay in 1855 as an "unending succession of ceremonies" in a huge wigwam, and they were still being reported near Green Bay in

1893. Potawatomis were performing the medicine dance at Powers Bluff in Wood County well into the twentieth century. The Menominees with their sturgeon feast and dog dance, the Winnebagos' war or scalp dances, all showed the continuance of traditional practices.

Then a new dance, and a new movement, appeared among Wisconsin Indians in the 1870s. Its origins are somewhat obscure, for the Plains Indians were caught up in the Ghost Dance during the same years and white onlookers often assumed a close kinship. Modern experts link the "Dream Dance" or "Drum Dance" of the Wisconsin tribes to the Omaha Grass Dance which had spread among the Teton and Santee Sioux, among others, led by an institutionalized group with drummers and singers, featuring male dancers, serving dog or other meat, connected to an origin myth.

The generally accepted date for appearance of the Dream Dance in the state is 1878, when a Sioux girl visited the Chippewas and instructed them on its doctrines and forms. Interviewed by two white men near Ashland, she told of events in the spring of 1876 when she had hidden while her band was being massacred by Custer's army, several weeks before the Battle of Little Big Horn. During the twenty hours she lay in a pond, spirits told her "she must teach a new dance and to teach it to all the Indian tribes." The message: tribes must put away their small drum and make a larger one, ending their war and pipe dances and performing only the new dance. Interviews of Chippewas and Menominees in later years added details of the girl's rise into the sky where the Great Spirit told her the songs and ceremonies to teach her people. Back on earth, Sioux leaders regarded the girl's story as a direct revelation and, as one anthropologist concluded, "from that time on the dream dance cult spread from tribe to tribe and has superseded almost completely the older ceremonies of a somewhat similar nature."

The "moral character" of the Dream Dance was stressed by practitioners. Like the Ghost Dance, it preached the equality of all peoples, and pointed to a future reign of peace, good will, and justice. Two Chippewa chiefs from Lac Court Oreilles defended their dance when challenged in 1878:

We wish to tell you that this dance is not for war purposes, but for peace. We talk to the Great Spirit, and want him to help us to become all as one. We want to be friends with everybody, have no enemies and do what is right all the time. . . . if we can find that there is anything bad about the dance we will never dance it again, and will induce our men to stop also.

Among the Potawatomis, however, an early belief was that if the Indians beat the Dream Drum for four days and nights, all whites and Catholic Indians would fall to earth, paralyzed, where they would be tomahawked by believers. However, a Menominee told a census taker that the dance stressed peace, abstinence from liquor, truthfulness, and turning the other cheek to a blow.

The dance's spread was not always west-to-east. Wisconsin Indians frequently visited their removed brethren on the Plains, and in 1884 the agent for the Potawatomis in Kansas noted that the Dream Dance was embraced enthusiastically by his charges, "introduced by the Chippewas of Wisconsin." The dance came to the Menominee Reservation through Chippewa and Potawatomi representatives who arrived with their drum in 1881, and it was reported among the heavily Catholic Menominees that "a good many Catholics dropped their religion and went dancing." Consequently, fierce attacks were launched upon the dance by the tribe's agent as well as resident Franciscan missionaries, and finally a group of Catholic Indians broke up the drum sessions and U.S. soldiers arrived to occupy parts of the reservation. The incidents left an even wider division between Menominee traditionalists, who followed the new dance, and the modernists who opposed it.

These attacks by missionaries and the government grew out of the continued deep fears and suspicions of Indians still held by many whites who lived nearby. The major eruption, however, came not in the Menominee Reservation but in the forests of northwestern Wisconsin, beyond reservation boundaries, where Indian enthusiasm for the new dance combined with gunshots in the woods to panic a Swedish immigrant and set off a wild exodus of settlers.

The starting point was the news that Chippewas were "in a commotion over in Wisconsin," as the *Rush City* (Minn.) *Post* described it in June 1878. Members of the Sioux tribe were in council with Chippewas near Bayfield, the *Post* reported, "and they have resolved upon some movement which the white settlers have been unable to find out."

Rumors spread quickly, and inflated the Burnett County area's few hundred Chippewas to almost 2,000. Without doubt the Indians were excited and enthused; one white who witnessed their dances commented that the Chippewas "have suddenly taken a passion for this amusement. They practice it for hours at a time, and when they get warmed up they become wild and frantic and sometimes go into spasms of excitement and ecstacy." In the Chequamegon Bay area, an editor noted that in the previous year's dance activity "the only injury done is to half starve those who follow it up, instead of hunting for their living."

Reports of the new dance and its fervent following quickly heightened the anxieties of recently arrived immigrants, whose worries had already been agitated by reports in dime novels and such events as the 1862 Sioux Uprising in Minnesota, where many Scandinavian settlers were slain. This formed the emotional backdrop when a Swedish immigrant named Christian Olson heard gunshots one morning in June 1878, and concluded that the Indians were finally launching their attack in Burnett County. Olson hitched up his team and raced with his family westward for Rush City, spreading word to everyone along the way. Soon large numbers of settlers from Polk and Burnett Counties fled to the west; the *Burnett County Sentinel* claimed some 300 had left from the Trade Lake and Logging Creek settlements alone.

But the newspaper refused to be goaded into accepting the Indian attack as reality. "GREATEST FARCE ON RECORD," the *Sentinel* jibed. It called the Swede the "idiot Olson" and said he was "the direct cause of this whole last scare." The Bayfield *Press* agreed, terming the wild exodus "a most ridiculous Indian scare." Indians who were interviewed seemed nonplussed, and told investigating officials that "the dance was a new one they were learning, and they were devoting their whole time to it; that they did not want to fight; had no cause to, and were not foolish enough to do it." When told of the whites' panic they "were almost as much frightened as the settlers had been," the *Sentinel* added.

And so the Indian war of 1878 ended before it began. It had been a near thing—the Governors Guard was preparing to travel to Burnett County and the President's Cabinet in Washington, D.C., had been informed. Col. G. A. Forsyth, who investigated as representative of U.S. Army General Phil Sheridan's staff in Chicago, reported that he had "found a big scare without the least foundation for it." The Indians not only did not plunder the farms left vacant—"they did not even leave their dance." Forsyth told a reporter he would rather trust his family "today in those pine woods with a band of Chippewas than with three or four tramps." The Dream Dance scare of 1878 was over, testimony to continuing white fears of Indians, especially among recently arrived immigrants.

Joining the White Economy

By 1870 Wisconsin listed 1,206 "Indians taxed," the off-reservation Indians who presumably were making their way in farming and related activities or as wage earners. There were still 10,315 "not taxed" Indians maintaining tribal connections. The figures were probably low; counting the "roaming" Winnebagos and Potawatomis would have been difficult.

Indians throughout the state gave evidence of moving bit by bit into the white economy, building on skills they had acquired much earlier. Thus fishing, berry-picking, and maple sugar making were expanded as new markets appeared with the advance of settlement. The Bad River band's output by September 1873 included potatoes, oats, and corn—encouraged by the government farmer—but also some two tons of wild rice and 1,000 bushels of cranberries; that spring maple sugar production hit 95,000 pounds, worth $8,000. Mountain Wolf Woman's family continued to follow the traditional Winnebago route among the seasons, going from Black River Falls to the Mississippi, trapping muskrats, picking blueberries, cranberries, and other fruits. "Thus the Indians came through history," she observed. Black River Falls residents had tangible reasons to be satisfied with the Winnebagos' return: the Indians were bringing fifty to one hundred bushels of blueberries to town daily in the summer, most shipped immediately to Chicago and Milwaukee. The Indians

Indians began to participate in the economy in more than the fur trade as the nineteenth century progressed and towns and cities developed. In the Black River Falls area, Winnebago Indians picked cranberries and blueberries, often selling to brokers who shipped them to Milwaukee and Chicago. COURTESY JACKSON COUNTY HISTORICAL SOCIETY.

received a total of over $400 each day, "and now they have plenty of money," the local editor reported. Local residents also had plenty of berries.

Indian women adjusted well to this stage of market capitalism. The agent at Lac Court Oreilles noted that Indian women and children did "a large share of the work" there in sugar-making and gathering wild rice.

Indian men, in fact, sometimes rejected farming as "squaw work," and it was noticed that the men's agricultural failures were often saved by their spouses. Men could be shiftless in farm work, the La Pointe agent observed, but "the women can always be relied on to cultivate and harvest the crop." The Ashland *Press* headlined "INDIAN WOMEN WILL WORK," when its correspondent on the Bad River Reservation reported a project to transform birchbark into fans, tags, and lighters, which was saved by the efforts of Indian women: "The last day of the week there were twenty-five women, old and young, all talking, laughing and working away as cheery as possible." Birchbark was well known to Chippewa women, who traditionally used it to make a variety of containers; producing other items of birchbark would have used familiar skills.

But the government generally aimed its assistance, and its encouragement, at Indian men. This bothered the Green Bay agent, who told the Indian Bureau in 1888 that while men were given agricultural implements and articles and taught their use, "the women have been allowed to get along the best they could" without information and materials for "domestic arts." It was time to do more for women, he argued, for "they have as great influence on the rising generation, as well as the civilization of the tribe."

As the century entered its closing decades, however, changes in the economy would shift the focus further toward Indian men. The arrival of railroads provided employment opportunities and stimulated new demands for forest and other products that Indians could provide. Ginseng destined for far-off China was such a product, sent east by rail from Indian camps, including the one visited by a *Chippewa Herald* reporter who saw a purchaser paying up to 25 cents per pound in 1878: "While at Long Lake . . . recently, we noticed a considerable lot of it at an Indian encampment. They seem to devote considerable time towards gathering it, and must derive a fair return."

Soon Indian men were providing thousands of cords of wood for railroad ties and construction, as well as supplying hemlock bark for tanneries. They began to sign on at lumber and mining camps, sawmills, logging drives, railroad construction crews, and as day laborers; some were employed on Great Lakes freighters. The Chequamegon Bay Chippewas had an advantage with the growing economy of nearby Ashland, where men from the Red Cliff and Bad River reservations found work in sash-and-door factories, cooperages, and blacksmith and carpentry shops. It served to make the family or the individual into the basic economic unit, in place of the tribe.

Working directly under others for wages threw Indians into a new situation. Like other employees, they resented poor treatment and low pay, and as early as 1871 Indian and *métis* workers walked off a wagon road construction job and successfully shut down the railroad company project. Indians could rebel in berry-picking as well: forest fires in the Black River Falls area were blamed on Winnebagos who became indignant over being paid just five or six cents per quart of huckleberries.

Logging expanded on the reservations. Initially Indians were allowed to cut only dead trees, but this was enlarged sporadically, and outside companies were sometimes permitted entrance if they hired local Indians. In 1874 the Lac Courte Oreilles band signed a logging contract bringing yearly sums of $10,000 for the first five years and $5,000 for the next fifteen years. Red Cliff made early progress in employing its own members on reservation logging, but by 1903 the reservation's pine was gone and its hemlock and hardwood promised only another year's harvest.

But the major logging prize—and the biggest conflicts—centered on the Menominee Reservation and its white pine.In 1872 the Menominee tribe was allowed to cut its own timber and to sell the logs off the reservation; this brought $60,000 from 12 million feet of timber in its first year, and more than $3,000 in wages to the Menominees. But the "Pine Ring," a group of white businessmen, won a government order canceling tribal cutting; they also tried to force the Menominees to sell their reservation. The initial Pine Ring victory led Neopit, the Menominees' principal leader, to charge that the project would wipe out most tribal lands, "leaving us for homes and farms four townships of barren sand plains." The tribe was willing to sell timber for a fair price, Neopit continued. "But we will not consent to the sale of any more land. We want it for our children and grandchildren. We accepted our present reservation when it was considered of no value by our white friends. And all we ask is to be permitted to keep it as a home."

The tribe's magnificent stand of white pine appeared ever more vivid, almost stark, surrounded as it was by the denuded landscape of northeastern Wisconsin. A visitor noted how the Menominees' thick, abundant pinelands were "a perpetual eyesore to the lumbermen of this region." The tribe's forests "form an oasis in a desert of stumps, all the valuable timber for many miles on every side having been logged and driven to the mills on the lower river." With markets for the forest waiting, lumbermen "are eagerly watching it, each determined to get as much of it as possible, and for the smallest possible sum."

But the Menominees won. They blocked the Pine Ring's machinations, and again staved off Congress when it sought to impose the 1887 Dawes Act on them; the Menominees were one of only three tribes east of the Mississippi avoiding allotment. Led by traditionalists within the tribe, the Menominees convinced the government that individual farming plots would not succeed in most areas of their forested, sandy reservation.

Only three years later, in 1890, the tribe won passage of a law permitting it to log green timber as well as downed timber, with yearly limits of twenty million board feet. This act, in force until 1961, has been called "the first legislation conducive to a systematic control of the lumbering enterprise of the Menominees." It made possible further successes, for sustained, planned logging became the hallmark of the Menominee Reservation and produced a stable tribal economy. In 1908, with the energetic backing of Wisconsin Senator (and former governor) Robert M. La Follette, the Menominees won the right to take their logs to their own sawmill, and to control their forest with supervision by the U.S. Forest Service. The Menominee Reservation has ever since been a prime example of forest conservation through carefully planned, sustained logging.

As the frontier era was drawing to a close, the Wisconsin Indians who had fought off removal were now struggling to find their way in a new world. No longer linked to whites through the fur trade, the Chippewas, Menominees, Winnebagos, Potawatomis, and New York tribes now faced the challenges of life in a wage-earning or farming economy. Almost all national experiments in federal Indian policy had been tried on them, yet despite predictions of decline they were growing in numbers by century's end. White support for their continued residence in Wisconsin had been important in the Indians' resistance to removal. The sudden popularity of the Dream Dance demonstrated, however, that many of them felt adrift, seeking a new anchor, a reassurance of their identity as Indians.

10.

Logging the Pineries

The Chippewa River was boiling with spring runoff, filled with logs that forced the oncoming canoe to "hug first one side shore and then the other" as the men struggled upriver. One of the paddlers on that perilous journey in spring 1868, C. H. Cooke, admitted that "to do our best we had many collisions, resulting in scars and holes in our brave little craft." And still the logs came on, floating their rambunctious way to the booms and sawmills below.

Paddling upriver was a challenge at any time on the Chippewa, powerful main trunk of the second largest watershed in Wisconsin. Its major branch, the Flambeau, draws from streams rising near Lake Superior in the Upper Peninsula of Michigan; by the time the main Chippewa collides with the Mississippi at the bottom of Lake Pepin it has fallen nearly 900 feet in 267 miles, draining with its tributaries almost 10,000 square miles, 34 percent of northern Wisconsin's "pineries."

The section of the river over which Cooke and his cohorts struggled was called the "Wild Chippewa" because of the torrent of falls, chutes, and rapids through which it plummeted in dropping 211 feet in 43 miles. Rough traveling in any conditions, it was especially perilous during the annual spring log drive. "Several times we had to land and pull our canoe up on land to escape the rush of logs," Cooke wrote in his diary. And then came Brunet Falls, which the log drivers had warned was already choked. After portaging around the falls the canoeists faced new dangers:

> . . . the sudden on-coming of a mass of logs threatened to wreck us and caused us to halt. We walked back to the falls to see them in their mad rush go thundering and plunging through the boiling cataract. They ended over, piled up and hurled about exactly as a lot of corn cobs in a June threshet [*sic*].

Much of the drama that was the logging frontier was present in Cooke's travel upstream in that spring drive of 1868: the thundering rush of white pine, cut over the preceding winter by loggers scattered in camps along the Chippewa and its tributaries—the Flambeau, Red Cedar, Jump, Yellow, Court Oreilles, and the Eau Claire which joined the river downstream at the city of Eau Claire. Cooke watched the log drivers, brash daredevils armed only with pike poles or peavies who shouted to him for whiskey "and to show their scorn for danger performed a lot of antics whirling logs."

But the drive also revealed where the logging industry itself was headed as it drew together two major aspects of frontier development: harvesting nature's bounty—an activity that attracted many small operators seeking wealth—and growing control by large enterprises that thrived in the unfettered conditions. It had happened before in the fur trade; now it was happening in lumbering. Cooke and his friends met this combination in the person of Daniel Shaw, head of an Eau Claire logging firm, who was studying the passage of his logs from a perch beside the river. Cooke delivered him a letter, which Shaw quickly confirmed dealt with the worsening struggle between two large groups of lumbermen over the right to send their logs downriver without interference. This was the Beef Slough War, soon to reverberate through Wisconsin lumbering and ultimately to sharply restrict the independent lumbermen's work in the northwoods. The struggle over Beef Slough led to reorganization of the industry and eventual domination of much of the region's lumbering by a group of large operators. When Cooke told some of the passing drivers on the

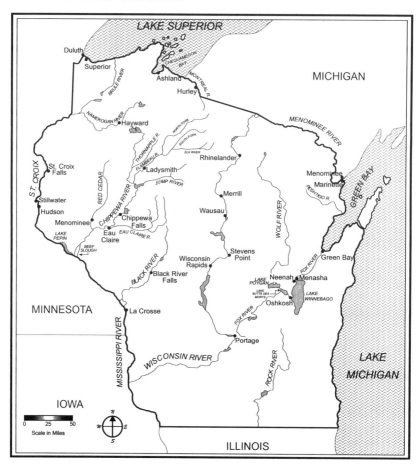

Several major rivers and many smaller ones drained the Northwoods and provided transportation routes from the pineries. The St. Croix, Chippewa, Black, Wisconsin, Wolf, and Menominee and their branches carried millions of board feet of logs during the heyday of Wisconsin lumbering. Logging also produced boomtowns, based on sawmill employment and their service as centers for logging camp provisions and the loggers' leisure-time activities. Most of the cities noted gained their initial growth from logging. MAP BY JILL FREUND THOMAS AND MICHAEL MAST.

Chippewa that he favored the Beef Slough lumbermen, a shouting match erupted—"The replies we got from those log drivers would not have made good reading for a Sunday School class."

Cooke concluded, after his encounters on the drive, "It looks as if there was a real war on between the Chippewa and Beef Slough crowd."

It *was* a real war, with fights and injuries and strategic attacks and withdrawals, and it marked the beginning of the end of one stage of the Wisconsin logging frontier. The battles centered on the towering white pine, but they also involved control of the rivers that carried the logs and lumber rafts and powered the sawmills—forty-seven mills along the Wisconsin River alone by 1849. For nature provided Wisconsin not only with abundant forests, but also with numerous watercourses to float logs to the waiting mills. The Chippewa was the largest of all pine-bearing tributaries of the Mississippi, holding in its watershed one-sixth of all pine timber west of the Appalachians. Lake Michigan with its watershed, which included the Menominee River and Green Bay, drained much of the forestland of northeastern Wisconsin and the Upper Peninsula and provided a direct route to the massive Chicago lumber market. The other major watersheds were the Wolf, Wisconsin, Black, Red Cedar, and St. Croix rivers.

Settlers moving westward provided a growing market for this lumber, and they soon were calling desperately for boards and planks to build homes, stores, and churches as they settled the Mississippi Valley and poured onto the treeless Great Plains beyond. But there was something else these humans carried with them: a lingering belief in the inexhaustible abundance of America's natural bounty. They carried it into Wisconsin, knowing it would never end, this forest—there was enough to supply America's wants "for all time to come," Rep. Ben Eastman of Wisconsin assured Congress in 1852. A year later the editor of the *Wisconsin Pinery* in Stevens Point responded to muted warnings of destruction of the forests by confiding that if lumbermen and surveyors were asked, "we shall be told that 50 years prosecution of the business will scarcely make an impression on these boundless forests." Similarly, a writer in 1880 described "many owners of pine timber lands who laugh at the prospect of exhausting their timber, within their lifetime."

Their lifetimes must have been short, for soon large portions of the northwoods were cut over—95 percent of Douglas County, according to a 1911 study, and from 60 to 70 percent of most other counties across the forested regions. By then the frontier of the lumberjacks and "river pigs," shantyboys and "road monkeys" was gone, and with it the last, unfettered rush at nature's windfalls amid the frontier of Wisconsin and the Great Lakes. The logging frontier held within it all the excesses of the frontier experience.

Beginnings

Lumbering began early in the nineteenth century when log cabins gave way in southern Wisconsin settlements to homes of sawed boards, cut in local sawmills from oak, walnut, basswood, elm, and maple. But the pine along much of Lake Michigan's shoreline, especially in Sheboygan and Manitowoc counties, led to a burst of sawmill construction beginning near De Pere in 1809 and at Kaukauna in 1816. Across the territory, an attempt by several Prairie du Chien men to supply their village with lumber led to construction of the first sawmill at the falls of the Black River in 1819; Indians soon destroyed it, however. Some Frenchmen were floating logs down the Chippewa to Prairie du Chien in 1821.

Starting in 1826 at Green Bay, the government authorized sawmill construction on Indian lands, as long as the Indians gave consent. The first lumber shipped to markets outside the Green Bay area did not leave the district until 1834 and soon Lake Michigan ports to the south were being supplied.

Despite these early sawmill beginnings, some settlers heading for Wisconsin still elected to bring their own lumber, as they tore down houses in the East and carried the boards with them on steamboats down the Ohio and up the Mississippi. This was the case in 1836 for lumber delivered to construct the first Wisconsin Territorial Capitol in Belmont; it had been purchased in Pittsburgh, Pennsylvania.

Sawmills kept multiplying along rivers, pushing northward with settlement and encouraged by the 1837 Chippewa treaty which ceded most of the Chippewa and St. Croix Valleys. Men seeking millsites arrived at the falls of the St. Croix immediately after the treaty's signing, and had the first sawmill operating there by 1840; the St. Croix Valley had several other mills by then, on both sides of the river. The Wisconsin and its tributaries were logged starting in the 1840s, sending pine downriver in rafts to Prairie du Chien and Iowa's river towns and even to St. Louis. Black River Falls launched a successful sawmill in 1839, and in 1843 Mormons rented the mill and ran lumber downstream to build their temple in Nauvoo, along the Mississippi in western Illinois.

By that time the Chippewa also was beginning to sprout sawmills along its banks, and from 1843 to 1855 the Chippewa Valley's annual output of lumber shot up from 5.5 million to 75 million board feet.[1] John H. Knapp and William Wilson acquired James Lockwood's Red Cedar mill at Menomonie, which formed the basis for the Knapp, Stout & Company operations. Two decades later this firm had grown to become the greatest lumber corporation in the world, drawing its logs and its reputation entirely from the Chippewa Valley. Eau Claire's first sawmill began operating in 1845–46, aided by natural reservoirs at Half Moon Lake and Blue Mill pond.

Across the state, the Wolf and the Menominee were busy logging streams by the 1850s. Oshkosh, Fond du Lac, Neenah, Winneconne, and Menasha turned to the Wolf for their logs, most of which were sorted in Lake Poygan before being hauled by steam tugs to the mills, which numbered twenty-two in Oshkosh alone by 1867. Marinette-Menominee became the milling center for logs from the Menominee River and its watershed that encompassed pinelands on both sides of the Wisconsin-Upper Peninsula border. Unlike watersheds to the west, the Wolf and Menominee had Chicago as major destination for their lumber. Chequamegon Bay lumbering began in the 1850s as well, and Bayfield's first mill in 1856 was quickly joined by others fed by logs from the Apostle Islands as well as pinelands around the bay.

Early operators maneuvered amid a land- and timber-buying system that was a hodgepodge of law and tradition. After the

---

1. A board foot is equal to a piece of wood one foot by one foot by one inch thick.

treaties were signed, there was little trouble with the previous tribal owners. Indians, in fact, frequently worked on logging crews, and reservation timber was occasionally logged. Lumbermen could buy "stumpage"—standing timber without the land it was on—from people who already owned the acreage, they could purchase land through public land sales, they could use the pre-emption law, and they could buy quarter-sections or more from speculators holding military scrip; some turned to Cornell University, which obtained 500,000 acres of Wisconsin forestland under the 1862 Morrill Act. Other firms simply trespassed, especially in the early years, and in 1853 the federal timber agent on the Black River estimated that more than 200 million board feet of logs had been stolen there in prior years. The temptation was always great to cut beyond the 40-acre boundaries left by surveyors, venturing into the edges of a neighboring quarter-section owned by someone else. These were the famous "round forties" of the lumbering era; as one participant later admitted, "The forties were much larger in those days than they are now."

This was a system filled with opportunities for those ready to grab them, made to order for men who had fled eastern lumbering when log scarcities and rising capital requirements made life difficult. But in the Lake States at mid-century, a small amount of capital, combined with hard work, basic lumbering skills, and luck, could lift a hard-driving lumberman to leadership. At the outset, each stage of lumbering was usually run by different men or companies—purchasing land, cutting trees, milling logs, transporting logs and/or lumber, and selling to wholesalers. At each step there was opportunity, and many grabbed it—such as Philetus Sawyer who sought out Wolf River pinelands, constructed mills, and in the process rose from Oshkosh mill hand to lumberman to U.S. Senator. (Sawyer once purchased a tract of pineland for $1,500, which he later sold for $63,000; his biographer estimates that his wealth was doubling almost every five years in the 1870s and 1880s.)

The Camps

It all rested on the camps. Late in the fall the crews headed upstream for their winter of labor in the pineries. In the early

Louis Blanchard was typical of those who manned the front lines of the logging frontier's advance through the Northwoods. Born in 1872 in Jim Falls, son of a French-Canadian father and a Belgian mother, "Louie" began cutting trees for a living while still the teen-ager pictured here, and spent much of his life logging on the "Chippeway" and its tributaries. In later years he achieved local fame as a spinner of lumberjack yarns in the Chippewa Valley community of Cornell, his home until his death in 1959. COURTESY WALKER D. WYMAN AND THE UNIVERSITY OF WISCONSIN–RIVER FALLS PRESS.

years operations were limited, the men cutting trees near the streams and dragging or rolling logs onto the ice. James Holden arrived from Michigan in 1862 and hired on that fall with Cogswell & Blaine, joining a dozen men at their camp on a forty located halfway between Brunet Falls and Little Falls:

> The camp was of the old "State of Maine" type, about 24 by 36 feet in size, with side walls about three logs high. As I recall it there was a space of about fifteen feet from the entrance door to the fireplace, which was an elevated platform of earth, about six feet long and perhaps four or five feet wide, and was for both cooking and heating purposes. An opening in the roof over the fireplace allowed the smoke to escape. . . . The men slept in a field bed on one side of the men's part, with their heads against the outside wall. They lay on a thick layer of hemlock boughs, a single very heavy quilt or comforter covered the entire bed. At their feet was a long bench, always called the "Deacon Seat." On the opposite side of the room was the water barrel, wash sink, grindstone, etc.

As operations expanded, the camps changed—logging farther from streams, hiring more men, erecting larger buildings, installing bunk beds along the walls. One lumberjack who experienced this transition was Louis Blanchard, born in Jim Falls in 1872 to a French-Canadian father and a Belgian mother. "Louie," as he was known, saw the lumbering world from the ground up and in later years gained local fame as a raconteur who described the winters without a bath, the smell of wet socks drying on the rafters, ethnic feuds, visits by peddlers and preachers. He devoted considerable attention to the meals, eaten on tin plates and cooked in large iron kettles and skillets. In the morning the cook yelled "Daylight in the swamp!" and the men wolfed down pancakes, called "sweat pads," with blackstrap molasses, sausage, and prunes. At midday the cooks often brought food out to the men in the woods on a sleigh—"baked beans and beef and bread and things like that." But at the end of the day they returned to the evening meal, for "Good grub was about all we had to look forward to all winter long." It was certainly filling:

> We had salt pork and beef, and plenty of potatoes, and baked beans to dress it up. Sometimes we had big barrels of sauerkraut, dried prunes, dried apples, dried currants, and always plenty of flour. The cook baked pies by the hundreds, maybe thousands, and we used to wolf 'em down like it was the last food left in the world. . . . The cook had a big bean hole outside the shack, and he'd bury a big pot filled with beans in it, cover the whole shebang with coals, and what came out of that hole was about as larapin-good as any food could ever be. We never had coffee in the early days, only tea.

Thus fortified, the loggers took on the pineries. There were "choppers," who in early times used axes to fell the large white pines, the only trees taken until scarcity forced the lumbermen to consider hemlock and eventually oak, maple, and other hardwoods. "Barkers" trimmed branches, and also the top bark when the downed tree was to be dragged by oxen to the shore or tote road through paths cleared by the "swampers." Scalers estimated the size—generally it took approximately four large logs to scale 1,000 board feet—and teamsters guided the ox or horse teams to the loading areas where logs would be hoisted on a sleigh under

Once the trees were dropped, sawyers sawed them into
lengths of twelve to sixteen feet; these were skidded to
tote roads and loaded on sleighs for transport to the
river banks. Date and location unknown; probably late
nineteenth century in the Chippewa Valley. COURTESY
CHIPPEWA VALLEY MUSEUM, EAU CLAIRE, WIS., 553200–0049–001.

direction of the "top-loader," highest paid employee in the camp.
Then the logs were hauled to the river for "banking," the broad
sleighs moving along roadways whose ruts had been iced by the
"road monkey." If it had not been done earlier, sawyers at the
shore bucked the logs into lengths of twelve, fourteen, or sixteen
feet, and these were then moved with pike poles, canthooks (a
lever with a moveable hook for rolling logs) or peaveys (a canthook
with a sharp point at the end) onto the ice or bank to await
spring runoff. Each log was struck on the end with a heavy marking hammer to leave a logmark, identifying its owner; bark marking was also used.

Although only white pine moved downstream in early decades—nothing else was even mentioned by early timber cruis-
ers—loggers often cut down everything, to demonstrate that their

contract had been completed. This meant unwanted logs were left on the ground with the slash. As Louie Blanchard put it, "when the cruiser come up in the spring, he'd walk along the main logging roads and when he couldn't see any trees standing, he'd say, 'You done a good job,' and then go on to the next camp."

It was a massive undertaking, involving men in a wide variety of jobs, with oxen and horses, in all kinds of weather. In early 1868 the Chippewa logging district above Jim Falls had 87 camps employing 1,103 men, using 339 teams of horses or oxen. As the shift to ever-larger operations continued, the Eau Claire Lumber Company in 1873 used 400 men, 150 horses, and eighty oxen in its fifteen camps to log 30,000,000 feet. Individual records abounded and were proudly noted: on the Black River, two sawyers in 1868 sawed 175 logs in two during the course of one day—which an editor claimed should entitle them to "run in opposition to a saw mill." That winter on the Trapper River, a tributary of the Wisconsin, the crew in Pearce's camp dealt with huge logs that during the final week averaged over 1,000 feet to a log; these included eleven logs with diameters of more than 47 inches apiece. A Pole, "Big Bill" Gliszinski, went to a church festival one day and missed work at his Portage County camp, but then worked hard to make up for it: he and partner Martin Rustad chopped down twenty huge white pines the following day, scaling 80,000 board feet. It was enough to keep a sawmill going for a week, and more than made up for his absence. Soon the axe was replaced by the cross-cut saw, enabling more of each tree to be saved and allowing two men to drop trees which previously required the efforts of four men.

Moving such monsters of the forest was difficult and dangerous. O'Brien's Hill just east of Hayward caused nightmares for teamsters who had to haul loads from the Round Lake flats over the hill and down the steep incline to the mills below. John O'Brien, the contractor, found it was not enough to use "drags"—chains looped around the sleigh runners—to stop the sleigh from overrunning the four horses and scattering the load. After several men and horses were injured or killed, O'Brien tried sending the load down without horses, but with a rider who frantically pushed out wads of hay when needed to slow it down. Finally O'Brien

Loading logs on a sleigh was an art as well as a
science, aided by an A-frame loader with block-and-
tackle but relying most heavily upon human skill and
both human and horse power. Teams competed to
create the largest loads, which were then pulled by
horses or oxen to the river banks. Circa 1905; location
unknown, probably Chippewa Valley. COURTESY CHIPPEWA
VALLEY MUSEUM, EAU CLAIRE, WIS., 553230–0049–001.

took a long rope, tied one end to the back of the sleigh, and
coiled the other end around a stump so that braking could be
applied when necessary. Descending O'Brien's Hill remained a
nightmare of Hayward area logging.

Injuries and deaths were frequent in such settings. "The principal items from the woods this week, have been in the shape of
crippled persons coming in," the *Shawano County Journal* lamented one day in the winter of 1879–80. It chronicled the past
week's toll along the Wolf and its tributaries: one man killed when
the chain broke on the load of logs he was driving; a Menomonie
Indian logger badly injured when a falling limb hit him on the
head; a man bruised when he fell off a load of logs going down-
hill, another bruised when he was pinned between two logs. It

was a bad week also on the Chippewa's tributaries in early January, 1881: in one camp Gilbert Ericson had chopped a large pine, which hit a leaning hemlock that then crushed Ericson's skull; elsewhere, a tree fell on a yoke of oxen and killed both instantly—"They were literally cut in two." But usually the victims were men and the camps sent hundreds of employees back to the sawmill towns as corpses.

Monthly wages ranged from $15 to $25 for common labor, with board, on up to $50 for highly skilled workers. Pay was given out at season's end, when the men were issued a "due bill"—this meant they would be paid when the logs were sold, usually at the end of the summer. Many cashed these checks earlier at discounts. Some companies were known for docking wages if an employee did not work the full season. The Wisconsin Factory Inspector noted how far this could be carried: "Peter Larson got killed in the woods while in the Company's employ. His wages were docked 20 percent for not working his time out. His widow returned to Norway. I don't blame her."

It was an industry characterized by here-today, gone-tomorrow crews. Fleas and lice could discourage lengthy residence, as men who scratched all day in the woods returned to their beds to scratch all night. When one bunkhouse burned down, the manager proclaimed the results: "Well, we got all the men and horses out anyway; only two million lives lost!" Louie Blanchard tried to best the "livestock" in his bedding and clothes with tobacco scattered about his blankets, by substituting fresh balsam boughs for his mattress, and by even more vigorous and creative methods:

> Every now and then we'd have a big Sunday boil, and several of us would throw our clothes in the big kettle and in that way cut down the louse population a bit. One of the best ways to fool the lice was to turn your underwear inside out when you went to bed at night. The lice then spent most of the night finding their way from the outside to the inside and didn't have much time left to do any biting before the cook yelled, "Daylight in the Swamp!"

The men sat on the "Deacon Seat" and smoked their pipes after a day in the woods. Comic lecturer Bill Nye visited a logging camp and reported that the reason the men called tobacco

"Scandihoovian" was because when it was smoked in Wisconsin, "folks could smell it in Scandihoovia." On Saturday nights the men found release from an exhausting week in the woods by playing bunkhouse games. Musical instruments were usually on hand, and a variety of activities filled the evening. James Holden arrived at the Cogswell & Blaine camp on the Chippewa about 8 P.M. on a Saturday evening as a tag dance was in progress, "and from the noise they made I thought that H-ll had broken loose." Then they danced a quadrille: "Each 'lady' had a handkerchief tied to his arm, to distinguish him from a mere man." At other times each logger had to sing a song, tell a story, or whistle, and if not he had to put a pound of tobacco in the "poor box." "Hot-ass" was another popular game, the man who was "it" covering his face with his hat and bending over while someone else whacked him on the backside. If he guessed who had hit him then that man had to take his place.

Driving the Logs

When winter's snows began to melt across the northland and March yielded grudgingly to April, turning the river ice to slush and finally exploding with the roar of spring runoff, it was time to launch the annual river drive. Several thousand men—carefully selected, the cream of Great Lakes logging crews—were given the task of moving the banked logs down the creeks and rivers, through the falls, around snags and sandbars and protruding rocks. At the end the company booms awaited, where logs were floated together in masses in wet storage until they passed into the maw of the sawmill. Only then could the "river pigs" finally blow off steam accumulated through the long months in camp.

The Wisconsin was the most difficult of the major rivers to drive, famed as "the longest and most crooked river in the state." Its twisting course with numerous rapids made it extremely hazardous, but the start of the season still excited residents of the valley when "the labor product of a whole year, is about moving; the ice is just gone, and all hands are on the alert. . . . Hope, expectation, confidence is written on every brow."

To sum up the process as "driving logs on a river" is over-simplifying something that was intricate, complicated, and dif-

The log drive was a springtime highlight of life along
the Black River, viewed here from the railroad bridge
in Black River Falls. The Black was one of the earliest
of Wisconsin's logging rivers, and became a major
provider of logs for La Crosse's mills. River drivers
who accompanied the drives worked to prevent jams,
while retrieving logs from swamps and inlets along the
way. Courtesy Jackson County Historical Society.

ficult in the extreme. As the Wisconsin Supreme Court stated in
1878, "In rivers like the Wisconsin it may not be always easy to
determine which is the main channel and which is the slough."
One writer compared it to moving haystacks of logs downriver;
stray logs were caught in underbrush and gullies, left far up on
shore when water levels suddenly dropped, engulfed in the quag-
mire of a swamp. The drivers had to rescue all of these, wading
waist deep in the icy water, jumping from log to log, pushing and
carrying with their pike poles or peavies or lifting with their arms.

The men started before dawn, rousted from their sleep by the
cook and given the first of their four or five meals of the day,
usually at the floating wannigan, which transported their packs
as well as providing meals. Out on the river, their red flannel
shirts now the proud uniform of the north country, climbing onto

a log moving downstream, digging their boot calks into the bark, jabbing their pike poles, the men challenged the vagaries of the river and early spring weather to maneuver a mass of logs through waters boiling with runoff. One group of men formed the vanguard, preceding in a bateau, a narrow-bottomed boat with upswept bow and stern, specially made to survive the swirling waters of a log drive and "next to impossible" to swamp. Bateau men and the river pigs who rode the first logs were charged with preventing jams from forming while the mass passed over dams and rapids. Other drivers coming farther behind had to deal with logs that refused to stay in the river, caught on land or rocks or deflected up some tributary creek. Many logs became "deadheads," stuck in the mud or brush; this "shrinkage"—sometimes put at 10 percent, higher in dry years—provided logs for settlers' cabins and barns along the way.

Water level was crucial. When winter had brought abundant snow, or early spring rains were heavy, the logs rode high and the drive was often only a ten-day effort. "The 'Wisconse' is 'up big' now," the *Wisconsin Pinery* announced happily in May 1853. But often the rivers were not "up big," as in 1874 when the spring runoff on the Black was so slight "that logs nearly stopped running," the *Badger State Banner* reported: "From loggers just returned from the upper waters of the river we learn that less than one fourth of the logs cut on the streams emptying into Black River have been driven into the main river." The newspaper added that "it will require heavy rains to make a raise sufficient to carry out the remainder of the logs this spring." In 1879 things were desperate in many areas: while the Wolf's crews had some success, "the Black, Chippewa, and Menominee drives are considered as hopelessly hung up." In 1900 the Ashland *Daily Press* reported the spring drought made log driving impossible.

Dropping water levels increased the chance for logjams, curse of the river pigs' existence. These added another element of danger to an occupation already among the most dangerous on the planet. The men attacked the jams with their peavies, fighting to keep the logs moving, finding key logs and muscling them out, breaking sections apart. When logs kept piling up, however, more drastic methods were employed: sometimes oxen with cables were brought to pull out crucial portions, and often dynamite was used. There were many famous jams, so gargantuan that they lived on in logging folklore for generations. The Jump River jam of 1879 ran thirteen miles, piled up to fifteen logs high; another on the Wisconsin at Wausau ran nearly four miles. Two steamboats were called in to help more than 200 men break a massive six-week jam above St. Croix Falls in 1886. Such jams could hold up operations for weeks; the 1869 jam at the big eddy just above Chippewa Falls took all summer to break.

River pigs hunted for the key log to bust up the jam, inching ahead cautiously as they picked their way through the intricate mass. Then one man moved forward for the final attack, as described by an Oshkosh reporter:

> A strong rope was placed under his arms, and a gang of smart young fellows held the end. The man shook hands with his comrades, and quietly walked out on the logs, ax in hand. . . . At any moment the jam might break of its own accord, and also, if he cut the log, unless he instantly got out of the way, he would be crushed by the falling timber.
>
> There was a dead silence while the keen ax was dropped with force and skill on the pine log. Now the notch was near half through the log; one or two more blows and a crack was heard. The men got in all the slack of the rope that held the axman; one more blow and there was a crash like thunder and down came the wall, to all appearances on the axman.

The reporter rushed forward but soon saw the logger "safe on the bank, certainly sadly bruised and bleeding from sundry wounds, but safe."

At long last these acrobats of the river delivered the logs to the booms in Wisconsin's sawmill towns, while masses of onlookers lined the banks. When Anton Kawleski, a Pole, piloted the logs through the Wisconsin River rapids above Stevens Point "he would lead the drive into the sorting boom, then gracefully step off onto the landing, dry as if he had come downriver on a yacht." It was a supreme moment.

They had arrived—men who had spent the previous three or four months eating beans and scratching fleas in camps along the Totagatic, Clam, Embarrass, and Peshtigo, eager now to paint the town red. "The boys coming down out of the woods seem not unwilling to again greet civilization," the *Shawano County Journal* hailed in March 1879. And greet it they did, with exuberance. After Louie Blanchard completed a drive, he often wound up in Chippewa Falls, where lumberjacks could cash their "due bill" checks for a 10-percent discount:

> At least half of the men spent their wages when they come down out of the woods in the spring. The single men would head for the saloons and the girls, and in a few days their winter's wages had stepped up business a lot in Chippeway. Saloonkeepers would bed them down until they was sober and send them along if they was broke. The married men might have a drink or two and then head for home. They had to pay off the storekeeper for grub and maybe pay some on the mortage. But the old saloons sure drawed more customers than the churches in the old days.

It was this picture—of drunken loggers making the streets of sawmill towns "unsafe for ladies"—that stayed with the logging frontier and gave birth to the saying that there were "three H's in northern Wisconsin": Hayward, Hurley, and Hell. A Norwegian pastor in Stevens Point watched the river pigs float by and condemned them as "the scum of humanity, the dregs both of Europe and America"—with their drinking, gambling, swearing and cursing, and "occasional murder."

The Infrastructure of Lumbering

Whether they ran mammoth operations or only contracted with local farmers for stumpage, employers had to contend with several basic issues: obtaining logs, hiring loggers, running camps, moving logs to the mills, sawing them into lumber, and transporting the lumber to market. After the early years many firms began combining these steps, some moving into vertical integration through which the log was controlled from the moment it was chopped to the moment it was sold as a board to a customer. Several went far afield into supporting activities, such as Daniel Shaw's development of a 900-acre farm near the mouth of the Flambeau, and Knapp, Stout's 6,000 acres in six farms, all supplying camp food for men, horses, and oxen.

Improving the water courses so logs could travel freely was a crucial activity for lumbering companies. Without improvement, the spring drives might amount to endless logjams, delays, lost lumber. As early as 1853, a "lumbermen's meeting" in Stevens Point called the improvement of the Wisconsin River rapids, from Point Bas to Jenny Bull Falls, "of utmost importance" to the prosperity of Marathon and Portage counties. The Black River Improvement Company, formed by cooperating sawmills, was typical of such efforts: it sent crews ahead on that "capricious river" to clear sand bars, build dams, and remove brush and snags. Philetus Sawyer's men once deepened key parts of the Wolf and, by constructing dams and booms, opened up a large stand of previously inaccessible timber at its headwaters.

A cooperative Chippewa Valley effort ultimately maintained 148 dams, the major one at Little Falls (Holcombe), where the Jump and Main Creek joined the Chippewa some fifty miles above Eau Claire. Built in 1878, its worth was shown repeatedly in dry years, notably in 1881 when the *Chippewa Herald* announced late in the summer that the flood coming out of the Little Falls Dam "will carry a quantity of lumber and logs down as far as the Mississippi." A later report claimed that releasing a sixteen-foot head of water at the dam would, in twenty-four hours, raise the water level by three feet at Beef Slough, 100 miles below.

Constructing booms was another crucial project for any up-and-coming lumber company, for without adequate storage reservoirs, the sawmills were limited to dealing with whatever floated down the river at the right moment. While there were several types of booms, two dominated in this era, jam booms and sheer booms. Jam booms were made of a string of logs linked together to form a barrier across the river channel, strengthened at crucial points with piles or stone-filled cribs; this was created to stop logs as they came downriver until the sawmills wanted them. If a logmark indicated a log was destined for some other mill farther below, the men working at the sorting works with their pike poles could steer it through. "Scrabble" were unmarked logs, usually fair game for anyone. The sheer boom was devised to shunt logs into a storage pond at the side, but it could be removed quickly if boats came through.

Transportation in Wisconsin lumbering relied heavily
on rivers, even after the arrival of railroads in the
1870s and 1880s. In sawmill ponds, rafts of sawed
lumber were made up and sent downriver in cribs,
each usually twelve feet wide by sixteen feet long, up
to twenty boards thick. These went in long, narrow
strings through a twisting route such as the Wisconsin
River, or they could be attached side-by-side as seen
with this lumber raft on the Mississippi near La
Crosse, circa 1905, with steamboats fore and aft for
power and control. Courtesy Murphy Library, University
of Wisconsin–La Crosse, Neg. 339.

The journey for many logs did not end at the boom, however.
Increasing numbers of logs were made up into rafts and sent on
to other sawmills below. Mills along the Mississippi gained in
importance as the oncoming parade of Wisconsin (and later, Minnesota) log rafts grew longer each year. On the St. Croix, the
number of logs cut in local mills exceeded the total sent downstream during only four years from 1878–1901.

Many mills, especially those along Lake Michigan's shoreline,
received their logs in rafts, and rafting became another colorful
aspect of Wisconsin lumbering. Rafts were composed either of
logs assembled at a boom, or of sawed lumber stacked in cribs
that were usually twelve feet wide by sixteen feet long, carefully
locked together in layers twelve to twenty boards deep. Rafts of
sawed lumber moved down Wisconsin's rivers and on Lake Michigan in strings that were often regrouped into broader floating

conglomerations, complete with tents erected on board; sometimes the raft drivers' families came along for the trip. These rafting operations often reached enormous size, sometimes with 150 cribs linked together; one sent from Eau Claire in 1872 had 284 cribs and was 576 feet long, 432 feet wide, and worth over $40,000.

Log rafts, in contrast, were composed of several "brails" of logs, up to 600 feet long and forty-five feet wide, held together by a rim of logs linked by chain. Steamboats came into early use for towing these floating behemoths on Lake Michigan, and also by 1848 on the St. Croix, on Lake Winnebago by the 1860s, on Chequamegon Bay by the 1870s (where a boom broke in 1874 and "badly scattered" 900 logs), and increasingly upon the Upper Mississippi until by 1893 it was reported that there were seventy-five steamboats exclusively involved in lumber and log rafting there.

When they reached their ultimate destination the logs were swallowed by the sawmills. On every major river and many smaller ones, and in such lakeshore towns as Manitowoc and Racine, sawmills began cutting up the logs, first with crude "undershot" waterwheels powering upright sash and muley saws with an up-and-down motion; then with overshot wheels in the 1850s and soon using steam engines, powering circular gang saws that turned out up to eight boards at a time. Band saws—endless bands running one direction—came in the 1880s. Technology moved rapidly in late nineteenth century lumbering, as logs entered the mill in an endless chain, were flipped by machine after cuts on the sawing table, the sawdust removed automatically, all part of the relentless drive for speed and efficiency.

Mississippi Millmen Arrive

In early years, raft pilots on the Mississippi headed downriver unsure of their final destination, sometimes sending an employee ahead in a boat to scout up sales at sawmills or lumberyards, at other times guiding their raft shoreward in response to waved signals. It was often impractical and, if signals were misunderstood, not economical, for this system occasionally resulted in the entire raft going on to St. Louis—where the raft owner had to accept whatever price was offered.

By the 1860s millmen from Davenport, Quincy, Hannibal, and other river towns began to poke their way northward, seeking to purchase logs upriver or even to buy stumpage, rather than waiting to see what was rafted down to them. At the same time, Wisconsin millmen began to venture southward to open up their own yards at key points along the Mississippi, with access to railroads. Knapp, Stout of Menomonie established wholesale yards at Fort Madison and Dubuque, Iowa, and St. Louis; Eau Claire's Ingram and Kennedy—eventually Empire Lumber—opened yards in St. Louis, Dubuque, Hannibal, and Winona. Others followed suit. This developing competition between Wisconsin and Mississippi mill owners brought to the fore a man who soon came to dominate American lumbering: Frederick Weyerhaeuser.

Weyerhaeuser arrived in the United States in 1852 at age 18, leaving his Upper Rhine village of Niedersaulheim, near Mainz, and following a chain of emigrants leaving the community following the failed 1848 Revolution. After a three-year stay among relatives in Pennsylvania, he headed to the Midwest and wound up in Rock Island, Illinois, where he found employment at a sawmill. He married a German girl, ran a branch lumberyard briefly, and in 1860 linked up with his wife's brother-in-law to purchase a Rock Island sawmill which became his first major business, Weyerhaeuser & Denkmann. Before long, this new company run by two German immigrants became one of the earliest Mississippi mills to seek its own logs to the north, selecting the Chippewa as its main field of operations.

Intramural feuding among the Mississippi men was an occasional problem, but it was minor compared to the anger of Chippewa Valley lumbermen when these "invaders" from the south began to enter what they considered their private domain. Wisconsin logs were not to be "stolen" by "aliens," to be milled at "foreign points."

The two sides slipped effortlessly into competition; the competitors drifted inexorably into war. It began when the Mississippi River men began to float their logs past the hungry sawmills of Chippewa Falls and Eau Claire, to temporary storage downriver in a magnificent boom fashioned by nature at Beef Slough. The slough was formed by the river's division forty-five miles below Eau Claire, with the more southeasterly branch spreading out and flowing sluggishly another twelve miles to the Mississippi above the town of Alma. It made a perfect log pond, and this was where the Illinois, Iowa, and Missouri men began to store their logs.

But upstream lumbermen, organized as the Chippewa River Improvement Company, fought back immediately, first through legal means but ultimately dispatching 300 men to build a dam blocking the slough's entrance. A sheriff's posse removed this obstruction after a fight, however.

The spring drive of 1868 produced more fireworks, when a battle erupted upstream at Jim Falls between drivers employed by the two groups; men working for the Mississippi companies cut the booms of French & Giddings, to allow their own logs to head down river; in the process they scattered logs of the Chippewa mills. Eau Claire police arrested the two masterminds of the escapade as they passed through town, and the sheriff stationed 150 armed men to guard booms at the city's mills. C. H. Cooke, returning from his upstream canoe trip, passed through Eau Claire at the height of the confrontation and reported, "Revolvers could be seen in the pockets of the lumberjacks and pikepoles and canthooks were carried about much as soldiers would carry guns, for attack and defense." As Cooke continued down the Chippewa to his home at Alma, he passed by Beef Slough where he saw an Irish boom operator who "wore a deep scar on his face, given him by a log driver of the Ingram & Kennedy crew at Eau Claire."

The following year the Mississippi group attempted to drive the Red Cedar, but abandoned this after learning that Knapp, Stout had an armed force prepared; the latter company's rifles were quickly transferred to Chippewa Falls when warnings came of an attempt there.

In 1870 Weyerhaeuser united the Mississippi men with a plan to lease Beef Slough and form the Mississippi River Logging Company. By then the Chippewa Valley firms were cooperating on their own log drives, usually letting the dominant firm on a stream handle the drive there. Similarly, in rafting, one firm would often take on lumber from a nearby cooperating mill to complete a raft. But the expansion of the Mississippi firms soon meant the outsiders owned two out of every three logs cut in the Valley, and one historian contends that at the end of the decade the Chippewa Valley "was divided by a feud so bitter that the entire history of lumbering could hardly show its like." At that point, Weyerhaeuser's goal of joining the two groups "seemed as far from realization as ever."

Then the transformation began, and in the process the logging frontier took giant steps away from its traditional position as a magnet for individual operators. Facing high water problems in the 1879 drive, Weyerhaeuser encouraged cooperation between his group and the Valley men by regulating the flow from his dam at Little Falls. The following year brought torrential rains in June, which suddenly raised the Chippewa twenty-three feet, and some 200 million board feet of logs swarmed away, wrecking booms and sorting works, hanging up on bushes three miles from the river, destroying piers and bridges, finally swooping away one entire Eau Claire sawmill. It also scattered downriver most of the logs owned by the Eau Claire and Chippewa Falls lumbermen. At this point Weyerhaeuser stepped in and proposed that in view of their common problem the northern and Mississippi lumbermen should work together: Chippewa millmen's logs that got as far as Beef Slough would be given to the Mississippi firms, being replaced at the Eau Claire and Chippewa Falls mills by logs of the Mississippi group that still remained in streams to the north. This log exchange opened an era of cooperation, and the following year in Chicago the two sides created the joint Chippewa River Logging Company (called the "Chippewa Pool"), with 35 percent ownership held by the Chippewa Valley sawmills and 65 percent by the Mississippi firms.

Individual companies kept operating, and the Chippewa firms continued to thrive, but Frederick Weyerhaeuser became the pool's dominant force—buying land, negotiating, lobbying the legislature. Bitter competition was over in Lake States lumbering. There were profits enough for all. The lumber industry had taken its first big step toward rationalization and could now move quickly when conditions changed—as it did in 1889 when Beef Slough

Beef Slough was a perfect storage area for logs coming down the Chippewa, and sawmill owners from down-river towns such as Rock Island, Ill., and Davenport, Iowa, took advantage of this. Their logs—bearing log-marks or bark marks—were guided into special chutes for each company, then formed into rafts for the remainder of the trip to the mills. Upstream millowners opposed the Beef Slough operation, leading to the "Beef Slough War" in the 1870s. New Jersey photographer J. P. Doremus took this picture during his 1874–76 Mississippi Valley expedition. COURTESY MURPHY LIBRARY, UNIVERSITY OF WISCONSIN–LA CROSSE, NEG. 32055.

silted up and the Slough's boom and sorting operations were simply moved six miles down the Mississippi to the West Newton Slough in Minnesota.

By the mid–1890s almost all Chippewa Valley merchantable timber, except the Knapp, Stout holdings, was owned by individuals or firms associated with Weyerhaeuser. He was president or the leading member of ten companies connected with northwoods lumbering.

The Railroads

Dominance by a few large operators was not the only new factor in Wisconsin lumbering by the 1870s and 1880s: the era also saw the railroad pushing into northern Wisconsin, making it possible for hardwoods to be cut and carried to sawmills, which now were usually powered by steam. Small towns, especially those far removed from navigable rivers, hungered for the railroad. "Every man in this region is ready to exclaim at a moment's notice, 'My country for a railroad,'" the Ashland *Press* announced in mid–1874, and community after community did its all to attract the Iron Horse. Eau Claire County's voters approved $50,000 in bonds for the West Wisconsin Railroad, completed to the city in 1870; in Ashland County the following year the vote was 83–1 to grant $200,000 in county bonds to the Wisconsin Central; when Burnett County in 1878 faced the issue of providing $20,000 in bonds for the North Wisconsin line, its five precincts voted in favor by 163–1, 49–1, 36–0, 26–0, and 15–1. And communities showed their support in other ways: when railroad construction was stalled a half-mile short of New Richmond, the Monday deadline just a weekend away, the entire population marched out with pick and shovel and finished laying the rails in time.

Railroads propelled logging into untouched regions, expanding that frontier while at the same time speeding its demise. The Wisconsin Central's carefully plotted route passed methodically between the Wisconsin and Chippewa river systems where timber had earlier been too far from navigable streams to be worth cutting. "This road has opened up an heretofore inaccessible pine forest," the *Wisconsin Pinery* proclaimed in 1874, and logging camps were soon established near Auburndale, Marshfield, and Waltham, not to float logs downstream but to send them via the new railway to existing mills. Rivers were still the cheapest route for delivering logs, but at tiny railroad stops along the Wisconsin Central the steam-powered sawmills now began to appear: Westboro, Chelsea, Medford, Stetsonville, Dorchester, Colby, Unity, Spencer, Manville, Auburndale, Waupaca, Weyauwega. It was called "the Wisconsin Central Railroad lumbering district." Other lines tapped the northwoods also.

Workers and Employers

By 1889 a quarter of all non-farm wage earners in the state were employed by the lumber industry, in its camps, in its sawmills, along the rivers. Like the businessmen who paid their wages, many of these workers had rushed into the Wisconsin frontier eager to make an "independence," which for most meant owning a farm free of debt. They were all present at that geographical and cultural point, at that elbow of history, where Wisconsin's fur trade and logging eras came together—a situation providing many opportunities for disagreement. When C. H. Cooke canoed up the Chippewa in 1868 during the spring log drive, he visited the camp of Jean Brunet, a veteran French-Canadian trader, and his Indian wife. A short distance away the coarse shouts of log drivers going over Brunet Falls provided a contrast with the steady Indian-*métis* fur trading world symbolized by Brunet. "The old Frenchman had been on the Chippewa for nearly half a century," Cooke wrote in his diary; "He said he was sorry to see the coming of the whites, who he said were spoiling the Indians and wronging their women."

Some of the newly arriving get-ahead Yankees looked askance at people like Brunet, considering them relics of earlier times. Progress required the leadership of a new race, they argued, for the fur traders were unable or unwilling to seize the economic opportunities offered by northern Wisconsin. Dewitt C. Clark, a New Englander who came to a logging camp above Chippewa Falls in 1856, wrote home that while the place was better than expected, changes were needed: "We want the French half breeds ousted out, root and branch and a class of active, free men to take their places. There are some white folks around here and a large immigration is expected next summer." A reporter from Winona ventured up the Chippewa Valley in 1868 as the lumber harvest was beginning to turn enormous profits, and while he saw "many French and Canadians" he seemed relieved to find "there is still enough of the Yankee element there to control and improve the great natural advantages of the situation."

Ethnic and job divisions among the logging and sawmill crews appeared quickly, as Scandinavians, Germans, Irish, and Poles were thrown together with French-Canadians and Yankees. But the same forces that led to integration of the activities of Weyerhaeuser, Sawyer, Shaw, Ingram, Norton, and dozens of other Wisconsin lumbermen were also pushing their employees toward joint action. Evidence began to mount that the individualism promoted by the early frontier's opportunities could yield quickly to cooperation when necessary.

And so the men who worked in the woods and on the rivers and in the sawmills began to join together to oppose employers, erupting only sporadically at first, often over such issues as better food in the camps. Log drivers on the Black River organized in 1869, scaring employers enough to form their own organization. Loggers walked out in wage disputes at the Little Falls Dam in 1883, and in the Wisconsin River camps in December, 1884. Eagle River log drivers struck and won a pay increase to $2.50 per day in April 1886, and on the South Fork of the Flambeau in 1889 the drivers fought unsuccessfully to obtain a 50-cent daily increase.

Most of the industrial confrontations in Wisconsin in the 1850–1900 period centered on the sawmills, where the frontier's bounty of huge pine logs met modern industrial processes in a fast-paced cacophony of whirring blades, sawdust, and steam that killed or injured many workers. Eau Claire and Oshkosh were dubbed "sawdust cities" for the large numbers of mills along their waterways, and both saw massive millworker strikes—the 1881 stoppage in Eau Claire launched by 2,000 workers seeking a reduction in their workdays from twelve to eleven hours; the 1898 wage-and-hours fight in Oshkosh eventually ended after fourteen weeks. Troops were called out in both disputes; workers won some gains in each.

A New Image for the Lumberman

It all marked a challenge to the total power of the lumber capitalists, a lessening of the universal praise in which they had basked for years. Once, the lumbermen had epitomized frontier opportunity; they also signified jobs and payrolls and business expansion, putting into effect the state motto of "Forward" by converting nature's bounty into human well-being. But times were changing. By the 1890s, lawsuits against the lumber giants multiplied—for destroying a dam, for not paying local taxes, for being a monopoly. They were now the "robber barons." And when a farmer named John Dietz fought the Weyerhaeuser syndicate at Cameron Dam he won enthusiastic support across the state and nation, a little man challenging the mighty.

The Dietz confrontation with Weyerhaeuser developed over several years, after Dietz agreed in 1901 to watch over Weyerhaeuser's Brunet River "splash dam," created to provide a sudden rise in water level when needed to lift logs and move them downstream. The Dietz family then moved to land along the nearby Thornapple River, on 160 acres that included Cameron Dam. Because the company had never paid Dietz the $1,700 he claimed for watching the Brunet splash dam, he eventually added to his bill another $8,000 in royalties for logs that had passed over Cameron Dam since the Dietzes took ownership of the adjacent property (despite the fact that their land title did not include control of the dam). Dietz resisted capture for years, and stood his ground in 1906 when the company purposely flooded the Thornapple and destroyed Cameron Dam. He was wounded by a Sawyer County posse that year, an incident that increased his support among newspaper editors already angered at the lumber barons' power. An Osceola editor described Dietz as "peaceable, quiet, law-abiding and liberty loving," arguing that if Dietz's true character were known, "his name would be emblazoned in Wisconsin's hall of fame as one of the greatest men this state has ever produced."

Weyerhaeuser sent a representative in 1907 who offered Dietz a settlement: in exchange for allowing removal of landlocked logs above Cameron Dam, the company would pay $1,717 in cash and Dietz could keep 300,000 feet of logs. Dietz accepted—then claimed he was still due $8,000 royalties from earlier log drives. He was finally caught in 1910, charged with murdering a member of the pursuing posse, and sentenced to twenty years in prison despite numerous petitions of support; one petition had 16,000 signers. A crowd of 500 cheered the Thornapple farmer as he was taken by train through Chippewa Falls to the state prison at Waupun. In 1921 Gov. John J. Blaine pardoned Dietz, who lived only three years longer. In editorials, magazine articles, books, and even a movie on "The Battle of Cameron Dam," Dietz was widely hailed as the little man who had stood up to Weyerhaeuser.

The End of the Logging Frontier

By then the frontier era in Wisconsin logging was virtually over, its end at least partly symbolized by the failure of the Weyerhaeuser interests to run their logs past John Dietz on the Thornapple. In earlier times lumbermen were thwarted mainly by nature when moving their logs; now a lone farmer had held their most powerful representative at bay. In the peak year of 1890, Wisconsin produced lumber worth $60,966,444, and two years later the Chippewa had its biggest drive, carrying some 3.5 million logs (632.3 million board feet). But that marked the zenith of log driving; declines came rapidly from that point on.

The northern forest was under attack in other ways by then. The loggers' slash and the sawdust excreted by sawmills (often dumped into swamps, used to fill Oshkosh's low-lying areas, discharged directly into Chequamegon Bay by Bayfield's busy mills) provided ready fuel for numerous fires. The Peshtigo fire of Oct. 8–9, 1871, killed between 1,000 and 1,500 persons and laid waste to portions of Oconto, Brown, Door, Shawano, Manitowoc, and Kewaunee counties, burning an area ten miles wide and forty miles long in four hours. In addition to virtually obliterating Peshtigo, the broad-ranging forest fire also destroyed Brussels, a Belgian community across Green Bay in Door County.

Finally the logging frontier was over. The era of "cut out and get out" had ended, and this crew near Suring in 1915 had only to look around them to see that the dream of "inexhaustible resources" was over. Northern Wisconsin had become a land of stumps and eroded earth, its slash and brush swept repeatedly by fires, the dead spars standing like bleached bones as remnants of a bygone era. COURTESY NEVILLE PUBLIC MUSEUM OF BROWN COUNTY, 34:1987.4.

Other blazes roared through portions of tinder-dry forest and cutover, sometimes taking out sawmills. These included fires at Oshkosh in 1872 and 1875, Marshfield in 1887, Iron River in 1892, Medford in 1893 and again in 1894, and a massive conflagration in 1894 that swept across parts of Douglas, Bayfield, Ashland, and other northern counties. In 1898 a forest fire ravaged the area around Cumberland and Turtle Lake, and the pattern continued into the new century, for logged-over districts were above all prime kindling. The impact of repeated fires on cutover lands left parts of the northland "as nearly desert as it can become in the climate of Wisconsin," a Wisconsin Forest Commission survey concluded.

Signs began to multiply that the easy times were over, the years when lumbermen were unimpeded and unchallenged as they cut white pine from "round forties" and moved the logs downriver with little concern for the natural or political environment. Daniel Shaw accepted nothing less than fifteen inches diameter at the small end of logs in 1860, and many other Wisconsin lumbermen took nothing under fourteen inches for years. But the acceptable minimum kept becoming smaller as the big trees were taken: it was twelve inches by the 1870s, and as the pineries dwindled the minimum reached a measure previously unimagined: five inches. By then the lumbermen were turning to hardwoods, trees once rejected as unfit. Now Southern and Pacific Northwest lumber was being sold everywhere, even in Wisconsin.

Just as many lumbermen had earlier migrated from the Northeast into Wisconsin and other Great Lakes states, now many moved on again. They invested first in Southern yellow pine, then in Pacific Northwest timberlands, most dramatically when Weyerhaeuser purchased 900,000 acres from the Northern Pacific in Washington State in 1900. Newspaper reports across Wisconsin's lumbering regions began to reflect this reality, as seen in a *Chippewa Herald* item in 1890: "It is understood that the Riggs & Rotch saw mill, at Bloomer, will, as soon as the logs are sawed, be dismantled, and the machinery shipped to Bucoda, Washington."

Milling began to decline sharply; by 1900 only three mills were left in Eau Claire, once called "sawdust city." The Chippewa itself sent its last logs downriver to the Mississippi in 1905. Four of Rhinelander's eight sawmills gave up in 1899 and the following year the final drive destined for a downstream mill passed through nearby Pelican Rapids. It was a tale told and retold across the north country.

The St. Croix was the last of the state's major rivers to run logs, and the final event there came June 12, 1914, when the boom master at Stillwater hitched the final log through the boom. Small-scale logging would go on—it is still going on today—and pulp mills would multiply across the northland to convert to paper the smaller trees now proliferating. But the massive attack on the northwoods forest was over.

It was perhaps the inevitable conclusion of what ecologist Aldo Leopold called "the epoch of cut out and get out" in northern

Wisconsin. One witness to the closing years wrote that "the desolation of much of the pine area in the 1920s and early 1930s is difficult to describe to anyone who did not see it"—giant stumps like bleached skeletons littered the landscape, which supported no trees beyond a few inches in diameter. With much of the forest destroyed and ground cover burned, floods became frequent and large, and, as a consequence of these sudden flows, year-round river levels fell sharply. Pine seed supplies declined and white pine blister rust arrived to attack younger trees, opening the way to invasion and proliferation of other species, especially aspen, a minor growth earlier. "Ecologically, no force since the glaciers has rivaled northern logging in either its immediate or long term effects," two forestry scientists have charged.

Perhaps it was all unavoidable, given the setting of the late nineteenth century in America's Gilded Age: settlement surging westward onto the treeless Great Plains, job-seekers drawn to the northwoods, trees in fantastic abundance, a national culture that exalted the successful businessman. Cheap land, cheap logs, rivers that seemed perfectly placed—these opened the way to progress, and one of the costs of that progress was deforestation. Neither the state of Wisconsin nor the federal government had any traditions against logging, nor were there any programs encouraging a forest's self-renewal.

If governments and businessmen had no pause, why should the lumberjack? The final word belongs to Louie Blanchard, who told of looking over the desolation left by a season on the "Chippeway":

> It seemed good business to cut down the pine. It give us jobs, and the lumber went down river to the sawmills and was used to build homes and cities. The government shouldn't have let them companies take off the little trees that wouldn't make anything bigger than a two by four. Us loggers thought the big woods would last forever. I guess we can't expect the government to be much smarter than us.

II.

LEGACIES

Close of the Frontier

Passenger pigeons streamed in masses through the Wisconsin skies, swooping down to clear forests of acorns and beechnuts, dropping their dung like pungent hail. Their speed and sheer dominance entranced the earthbound beings who watched below, engulfed by a roar like a waterfall. One amazed onlooker was Scots immigrant John Muir, who recalled seeing flocks "so large that they were flowing over from horizon to horizon in an almost continuous stream all day long, at the rate of forty or fifty miles an hour, like a mighty river in the sky, widening, contracting, descending like falls and cataracts, and rising suddenly here and there in huge ragged masses like high-plashing spray."

The passenger pigeon was one of the wonders of the frontier era, in Wisconsin and across the broad sweep of the Midwest and East where—according to some estimates—its numbers may have reached three billion birds, making up 25 to 40 percent of the bird population of the United States. The western extension of their principal nesting area was anchored over the southern two-thirds of Wisconsin, and stretched southward to Kentucky and eastward through most of Pennsylvania, New York, and New England. They were "bonnie, bonnie birds," Muir agreed, the male

The passenger pigeon swept over Wisconsin in flocks so extensive and thick that they blocked the sun for hours. Easy to hunt—with guns, nets, spears, dynamite—they were also tasty and brought a good price on the Chicago market. Habitat destruction, combined with increased hunting pressure and more potent firepower, finally brought the extinction of the bird that had once seemed as abundant as sunshine. COURTESY STATE HISTORICAL SOCIETY OF WISCONSIN, WHi (X3) 21076.

extending almost seventeen inches from its slatey blue head along its grayish blue back to its tail, standing up to twenty-two inches tall, with a rosy breast that changed along its sides to iridescent gold, emerald green and deeper crimson.

And they were tasty. Indians relied on the birds for food, later finding they could trade dried and smoked pigeons to the arriving Europeans just as they traded beaver pelts. Fur trade posts carried "pigeon shot," and as settlers came in numbers they looked forward to spring arrivals of this bird, described as "a boon to the poor" both for its abundance and its delicate taste.

Though largely forgotten today, the passenger pigeon was an apt representative of the Wisconsin frontier. It was one of the many riches awaiting those who traveled beyond the Lakes to build homes in the new land in the west. The spring of 1871 was especially bountiful in this regard for settlers in central Wisconsin, and the Black River Falls newspaper noted at the end of April that timber land between that city and Big Creek "is literally alive with pigeons from three to seven miles in extent in every direction. . . . This will be a rare chance for hunters to get all the shooting they want." By that decade the tasty meat was being sold widely in markets, first in nearby towns, then in Milwaukee, Chicago, and points east. "Six hundred and twelve barrels of pigeons have been shipped from five stations on the St. Paul R. Road this spring," the Stevens Point newspaper reported in May 1871. The totals sent from Kilbourn City (Wisconsin Dells) to eastern markets reached 30,000 birds daily that month. The 1871 Wisconsin nesting, one of the largest on record, was estimated to contain 136,000,000 passenger pigeons covering 850 square miles.

The pigeons were believed to be "inexhaustible." They became extinct nevertheless, victims of the frontier settler and his unfettered pursuit of nature's bounties, victims of the desire to reap financial rewards from such riches, but victims also of the frontier-bred confidence in an unending cornucopia of earth's natural wealth. As the pigeon moved rapidly toward its destruction at century's end, it provided a fitting seal, a capstone, for the frontier era in Wisconsin.

There were several key elements bringing the decline of the passenger pigeon. The cutting down of large hardwood forests from which it obtained acorns and beechnuts was a major setback, as was disease and several crippling storms which hit as its numbers were dropping sharply. The last major sale to city markets from Wisconsin occurred in 1882. There were no large nestings beyond 1887, and even smaller ones were often disturbed by hunters, who not only slaughtered the pigeons but also frightened birds away before eggs could be hatched and young squabs raised. Scientists have concluded that the pigeons were unable to mate unless in large flocks, but as they became fewer the hunters became ever more zealous in seeking them out, making worse a situation already inching toward disaster. An attempt by the legislature in 1877 to protect the birds proved ineffective, and an 1885 incident showed why: within an hour after a flock was spotted near Racine, 500 men were on their way with shotguns. It was a pattern repeated again and again across the shrinking domain of the passenger pigeon.

To those who grew up marveling at the unending, horizon-to-horizon flights, disappearance seemed impossible. Occasional small flocks were spotted in the 1890s, and the final report of a wild pigeon falling to a Wisconsin hunter's gun came near Babcock in 1899; four birds being raised in captivity in Milwaukee died in 1908–9. Some theorized that the main flock had flown south, perhaps to Chile, and rewards were offered to anyone who could find their hiding place. But the passenger pigeon was gone, a victim of shrinking forests and its own inability to reproduce in small flocks, but ultimately driven to extinction by the unceasing pursuit of hunters and netters after the $10 to $40 per day they could make from sale of the birds. The end finally came in 1914 when "Old Martha," the world's last remaining passenger pigeon, died in the Cincinnati Zoo.

Wildlife and the Fading Frontier

There were other disappearances during the frontier era— the buffalo, last killed in Wisconsin in 1832; the caribou, gone by 1840; the elk, by 1868. The beaver, for the early French the primary wealth offered by the Great Lakes region, was almost trapped into oblivion by 1900. Cougars, fishers, martens, and wolverines had virtually disappeared by the early decades of the twentieth century. Later efforts to bring back several of these— notably the beaver—have met considerable success.

Some animals changed location as well as numbers: deer had been numerous across southern Wisconsin, but became abundant in areas of the north as settlement surged from the south and brush—ideal for browsing—replaced mature forest throughout the northwoods. Deer reproduction rates also improved, because of shrinking numbers of the eastern timber wolf, which traditionally feasted on deer. But newly arriving farmers feared wolves were also feasting on their cows, and as a result bounties came early: in 1839 the territorial government offered $3 for each dead wolf, an offer extended in differing amounts over the next 92 years until the last wolf bounty was paid in 1957. The timber wolf was long gone from most parts of the state by then— disappeared from southern Wisconsin by the early 1880s and

from central Wisconsin by 1914. But it remained in pockets of LEGACIES
the north until the late 1950s, at which time restoration efforts
began.

The wild turkey, once abundant across the southern half of
Wisconsin, was hurt severely by the 1842–43 winter and the
spread of settlement; it soon vanished until modern efforts succeeded in bringing its reestablishment. Prairie chickens were
forced north, into competition with the sharp-tailed grouse which
were enjoying the new habitat left by abandoned fields and "post-
burn scrub." Jackrabbits, on the other hand, invaded the state
from the prairies as woodlots shrunk and the forest was logged.

Logging had an adverse impact on fishing, however, for the
increased runoff into streams brought silt which damaged trout
survival. But it was commercial fishing, supplying distant markets, that created problems on Lake Superior. New railroad connections to Duluth brought a massive expansion of commercial
fishing in Chequamegon Bay by 1870, when the Bayfield *Press*
reported 250 men "constantly employed in fishing" and 15,000
half-barrels of whitefish and trout exported by year's end. As
early as the 1880s complaints were multiplying that overfishing
was wiping out whitefish and lake trout. Like passenger pigeons,
Lake Superior's fish could not withstand the human assaults—of
large numbers of fishermen, modern boats and gear, and a waiting market with railroad connections. It would take the conservation efforts of a later period to restore the fish runs.

Government Protections

Starting with wolf bounties, politicians were drawn repeatedly into the debate over whether to protect nature's riches or
speed their exploitation. The first state legislature reacted to complaints of declines in deer populations by banning deer hunting
during late winter and spring, from February 1 to July 1, beginning in 1851. Variations on this appeared over succeeding years,
sometimes limiting deer hunting to five months a year, at other
times banning the use of set guns or dogs. The laws were widely
ignored.

As they attempted to restrict hunting and fishing, legislators were responding to a gradual change in public attitudes, evident in the increasing reports of community meetings to discuss the disappearance of fish and game. Fishing bans on specified lakes appeared from the early 1860s onward in an attempt to save breeding stock, and in 1866 a State Fishing Inspector was appointed; next came state programs to cultivate trout for transplanting. Restrictions began to be placed on the hunting of game birds. A State Association of Sportsmen was organized in 1874, aimed at improving game and fish laws and encouraging their support.

In response to growing market hunting of deer, the Legislature periodically tried to block shipping venison out of state; it also attempted to forbid the sale of venison after a certain period—six or eight days—beyond the close of hunting season. The disappearance of the deer herd no longer seemed impossible, and few could deny that—as one biologist later concluded—the 1890s deer decline "resulted almost entirely from over-shooting." Wisconsin's first bag limit for deer hunting was passed in 1897: two deer of either sex or any size, with a $1 hunting license required for the first time ($30 for out-of-state hunters). Some counties closed deer hunting entirely.

But as with pursuit of the passenger pigeon, market hunters showed little inclination to give up traditional practices, and Chicago and Milwaukee meat shops continued to overflow with illegal Wisconsin venison. The market men—who successfully lobbied for stepped-up campaigns against wolves because they believed these were reducing the size of deer herds—clandestinely shipped out illegal deer meat hidden in barrels under layers of partridges, secreted within loads of Christmas trees, and even packaged as butter, eggs, or veal. One Chicago man tried to evade the law by shipping out two deer carcasses in a coffin.

The public was stirring, but old ideas died hard. When Wisconsin's first State Forester met with a group in Rhinelander soon after taking office in 1904, he "took more abuse than I have ever seen a speaker take at any public meeting," a participant recalled. The idea of reforestation itself was condemned by editorial writers. By that time the Wisconsin cutover was being touted for the fact that the trees had already been cut, and land companies were luring would-be farmers to the north. Those who arrived found that stumps could be as formidable obstacles as trees. Most of the windfalls of the frontier were already taken.

These closing decades of the frontier era in Wisconsin were the formative years, the shaping environment, for two young men who would provide America with a much different view of the frontier experience. Born fourteen months and 100 miles apart at the start of the 1860s, Hamlin Garland and Frederick Jackson Turner had ample opportunities to consider what the frontier experience meant. Both knew lumberjacks and rivermen, and witnessed land yielding to the plow for the first time; both were on hand for the final subjugation of the Indians; and both left Wisconsin and the Mississippi Valley for a time, enabling each to reflect from afar on what he had seen. And when Garland and Turner burst upon the reading public in the early 1890s, America's view of the frontier was forever changed.

Hamlin Garland

Hamlin Garland was born September 14, 1860, on a farm clinging to the steep slopes of the coulee country near West Salem, not far from the Mississippi north of La Crosse. He was the product of pioneer families who converged on the state with thousands of other would-be settlers in the previous decades—his Yankee father coming from Maine, his mother accompanying her Scotch-Irish family's wanderings through Maryland, Pennsylvania, and Ohio.

Garland's father had worked in logging camps before the Civil War, driving log cribs down the "Wisconse" from Big Bull Falls through the Notched Rock in the Dells and eventually out onto the big river as far as Dubuque. The young boy spent many evenings before the fire as relatives from both sides of the family recounted tales of their westward treks.

But it was the unending severity of life on the farm; the settlers' struggles against weather, insects, railroads, bankers; and the sheer drudgery and isolation of their dreary existence—these

facts of life added a crueler cast to Garland's view of the frontier as he grew older. He saw there was nothing new or unusual
in his family's troubles, for his father was in most ways a typical
American pioneer: always moving, pulling along a reluctant family
as they left their coulee farm in 1868 and traveled west again,
moving every few years across Iowa and eventually into South
Dakota.

In 1884 Hamlin Garland left his own homestead in South
Dakota and headed not west but east—to Boston, where he im-
mersed himself in learning and writing. In 1891 he published
Main-Travelled Roads, and followed that in the next four years
with *A Spoil of Office*, *Jason Edwards*, *A Little Norsk: Ol' Pap's
Flaxen*, *A Member of the Third House*, *Prairie Songs*, *Prairie
Folks*, and *Rose of Dutcher's Coolly*. These formed the main body
of his fiction centering on the frontier experience; Garland's later
writing drifted into more romantic themes, much less acclaimed;
as one critic wrote, he was "at his best when he was most nearly
autobiographical."

Garland was caught up in the literary movement known as
Realism, a revolt against Romanticism and its use of heroic
types, happy endings, stilted speech and stereotyped actions aimed
at a genteel reading public. To Garland, it was essential that the
truth be told about "border life," as he termed it: "I know that
farming is not entirely made up of berrying, tossing the new-
mown hay and singing *The Old Oaken Bucket* on the porch by
moonlight." He later admitted he had "clearly perceived" that
"our Song of Emigration had been, in effect, the hymn of fugi-
tives!"

He told that story in his books and short stories, creating tales
out of memories of the coulee country. A repeated theme was of
opportunities lost—the desperation of those confined to farms in
an era of declining farm prices and unregulated railroads and
banking, when nature was no longer so bountiful and technology
had not yet eased the physical burdens of farmwork. Garland's
main characters usually had traveled to other parts and returned,
and this outside experience provided a different lens through
which to view farming in a "new country." In "Up the Coulee,"

Howard McLane comes home after an absence of ten years and finds his brother filled with bitterness and nearly crushed by unending labor and debt. His brother's wife unleashes an attack that contrasts sharply with the Currier & Ives picture of farming:

> "I hate farm life," she went on with a bitter inflection. "It's nothing but fret, fret and work the whole time, never going any place, never seeing anybody but a lot of neighbors just as big fools as you are. I spend my time fighting flies and washing dishes and churning. I'm sick of it all."

Garland demonstrated also a keen awareness of the place of immigrants who had rushed to settle this frontier, usually depicting their struggles as facing even greater odds. In "The Creamery Man," set in Molasses Gap near Dutcher's Coulee, the German girls labor in the fields, Norwegian girls do so occasionally but mainly work in town, and Yankee girls stay out of the fields. All are desperate to escape.

A New England family in *Jason Edwards* succumbs to the railway line's advertisements promising "Free farms for the homeless!"—only to fall victims to prairie disasters that finally force them to return to the East.

This picture of frontier life as not success but failure, not optimism but discouragement, was not welcome to some readers. Many were offended by Garland's raw depictions (as one sympathetic reviewer noted) in which "heroes sweat and do not wear socks," and "heroines eat cold huckleberry pie and are so unfeminine as not to call a cow 'he.'" Another writer agreed that, in contrast to traditional literary descriptions of farm life, Garland "put wrinkles and calluses on his men and made them sweat." His was also a world of coarse, unglamorous women; one reviewer said the long-suffering Agnes in "The Branch Road" was "such a farm wife as Mr. Garland has alone dared to draw."

Irruptions came immediately from publishers, many expressing doubts about the value of his work. One editor rejected a Garland story "where 'youp' is used for yes, . . . and where all sorts of vulgarisms occur." Garland would later recall that he was attacked by western critics as "a bird willing to foul his own nest," and statistics were trotted out "to show that pianos and Brussels carpets adorned almost every Iowa farmhouse." Farming, a critic claimed, was "not in the least like the pictures this eastern author has drawn of it."

Unfazed, Garland continued to urge young writers in the West to describe their region's logging camps, the mix of ethnic groups, Mississippi River life and its surviving French settlements, the rise of great cities and railroads. And in dealing with his critics, Garland perhaps took heart from the response of his own mother: "It scares me to read some of your stories—they are so true," she wrote. "You might have said more, but I'm glad you didn't. Farmers' wives have enough to bear as it is."

Frederick Jackson Turner

Frederick Jackson Turner, born November 14, 1861, in Portage, also spent his childhood and youth surrounded by frontier life. He left to study on the East Coast, and after his return developed a new interpretation of America's frontier experience which finally burst forth in his 1893 essay, "The Significance of the Frontier in American History." Like Garland, he wrote in response to eastern and European views of the frontier that clashed with the reality he had known.

Turner's parents were both from New York State, and met in central Wisconsin. But their life together did not revolve around the near-destitution of a frontier farm. Andrew Jackson Turner, his father, was an itinerant printer who bought into the *Wisconsin State Register* of Portage and soon became a major voice for Republicans in the area and state. The Turners were town-dwellers in a rising, if struggling, community.

Having an editor father who also possessed a deep interest in local history, the Turners' first child grew up with a keen awareness of the rough life about him. "There were still Indian (Winnebago) tepees where I hunted and fished," Frederick Jackson Turner later recalled, "and Indians came in to the stores to buy paints and trinkets and sell furs. The Indian ponies and dogs were familiar street scenes." They were part of life then, and he told of encountering them while canoeing, "hearing the squaws in their village on the high bank talk their low treble to the bass of our Indian polesman," and "feeling that I belonged to it all."

It was a world of the immigrant, too, as throngs of Europeans passed through, many stopping to establish farms in the area. A third of Portage's inhabitants were foreign-born, and when Fred Turner was eleven the City Council was made up of men born in Ireland, Baden, Prince Edward Island, Prussia, Württemberg, Holland, Wales, Massachusetts, and New York. Germans were especially numerous, and the newspaper reported in 1877 that sixty of them had joined "in purchasing a tract of 230 acres of land on the Wisconsin River bottoms," as common pasture for their cows—a joint activity somewhat at odds with Wisconsin pioneering. Eleven years later, just before leaving Wisconsin for graduate study, Turner wrote to his University of Wisconsin mentor that his native district was "becoming Germanized. . . . They (the Germans) are dispossessing whole townships of Americans and introducing the customs and farming methods of the fatherland."

Forests loomed to the north, and the lumberjacks rode logs down the Wisconsin River each spring, pausing for a spree in Portage after maneuvering through the nearby rapids. But the community soon had even closer connections with the pineries, when the Wisconsin Central Railroad which ran through town completed its line all the way to Ashland. Turner later recalled riding on "the first railroad into the pine forests of northern Wisconsin," and his editor father provided lengthy reports of that inaugural journey and a subsequent one for readers of the *Register*.

The first trip was made in October 1876, when the line was still short of Chequamegon Bay by some sixty miles; the next came in July 1877, and went all the way to Ashland. Fred Turner was then a high school student, apparently joining his father and a group of dignitaries (he is not mentioned in either of his father's reports). The locomotive pushed north through small towns and villages sprouting amid the forests—Auburndale, Marshfield, Mannville, Spencer, Unity, Colby, Phillips. This "howling wilderness" was now opened up by the railroad, and the editor exulted:

For the first 15 or 20 miles from Stevens Point one sees but little of interest except cut timber lands. A few years ago this was a dense forest, covered with stately pines and hardwood timber; but the pine has all disappeared before the ax of the lumberman, and farms are being opened up, here and there, by the pioneer. For 100 miles beyond a different aspect is presented. We might well call it all a wilderness, but the saw-mills that have been erected at all convenient points have led to clearings—the pine being removed to supply the mills, and "choppings" appearing here and there, where homesteaders and others have started in to open up farms and make homes.

The 1877 journey was made with an excursion party that toured Ashland, Bayfield, and the Apostle Islands, enjoying dances put on one evening by Chippewas from Bad River. Editor Turner's enthusiasm was stirred most, however, by the opportunities opened by the Wisconsin Central: ". . . probably no portion of Wisconsin offers as great inducements to actual settlers as the country bordering the Central road . . . the settler may go into these woods with a certainty of eventual success."

This was part of the shaping environment as young Fred Turner was growing up in Portage. "Is it strange that I saw the frontier as a real thing and experienced its changes?" he once asked a correspondent. Turner carried this background with him after graduating from high school in 1878 when he entered the University of Wisconsin in Madison. Stimulated there to take up the study of history, he eventually went on to graduate work at Johns Hopkins University in Baltimore, Maryland, in 1888. At Johns Hopkins, Turner benefited by working under men who had studied in Europe, but he was repelled by their arguments on the "Germ Theory"—the belief that American institutions developed from "germs" carried across the Atlantic as part of the European heritage. In addition, his professors' Eurocentric and Atlantic Seaboard biases repelled and frustrated him: "Not a man here that I know is either studying, or is hardly aware of the country beyond the Alleghanies," he complained to his professor back in Madison.

When Turner was hired to teach history by the university at Madison in 1889 he was suddenly presented with an opportunity to develop his views on the importance of the frontier. He took a

step on that road by offering a seminar on economic develop-
ment in the Old Northwest, while continuing to work on his Johns
Hopkins Ph.D. dissertation, "The Character and Influence of the
Indian Trade in Wisconsin, a Study of the Trading Post as an
Institution."

It was in a review he published in *Arena* magazine, in 1889,
that Turner first laid out some of the ideas which had been forming in his mind in response to his confrontations with the Germ
Theory at Johns Hopkins. He began by bluntly noting that "America's historians have for the most part, like the wise men of old,
come from the east; and as a result our history has been written
from the point of view of the Atlantic coast." What was needed,
Turner argued, was "a connected and unified account of the progress of civilization across the continent"—in other words, embracing different waves of settlement. The process was producing a "new composite nationality, . . . a distinct American people,
speaking the English tongue, but not English." But the exploration and settlement of the Mississippi basin had been ignored, he
told *Arena* readers; that important part of the nation's experience had "not found its historian."

Frederick Jackson Turner would become that historian. His
meteor-like rise to the forefront of the historical profession began four years later, in 1893, with a paper read before the American Historical Association in Chicago. That paper, "The Significance of the Frontier in American History," has been described
as "the most influential single piece of historical writing ever done
in the United States." A later historian explained one reason why:
it set forth "a unifying hypothesis" for organizing historical studies, so that historians working anywhere—even on local subjects—
could understand "how their work fit into the broader context of
American history."

Turner began his Chicago paper by asserting that an era had
closed with the Census Bureau's inability in 1890 to draw a line
marking off a frontier of settlement—an era that had been "in
large degree the history of the colonization of the Great West."
His basic premise: "The existence of an area of free land, its
continuous recession, and the advance of American settlement
westward, explain American development."

At the frontier—"the meeting point between savagery and civilization"—American institutions were repeatedly forced "to adapt themselves to the changes of an expanding people." Not only were institutions reshaped, but people themselves were changed when they arrived at the "hither edge of free land" and were forced to begin over, again and again. For Turner, one way to look at the concept of frontier was to study the changes as waves of settlers grappled with the Indian question, disposal of the public domain, relations with older settlements, political organization, and launching of religious and educational institutions. This frontier was a process as well as a geographic location.

Turner also looked closely at what was happening to the settlers, and argued that because of their struggles they themselves were changing. They were becoming a "composite nationality" as migrants from different regions and lands came together and jettisoned earlier loyalties. Individualism and democracy were promoted in the surge into new areas, as well as a practical, inventive nature, inquisitiveness, and materialism. Bonds of custom were broken when settlers were forced to depend upon themselves rather than on distant governments. (A student of Turner's later found that from 1840–60 in Trempealeau County, the lowest-ranking groups gained rapidly in land ownership and often rose to political leadership; even landless young farm workers were soon able to obtain land. Free land created opportunity for many in Trempealeau County, immigrants as well as the native-born.)

Such ideas may have "been floating around rather loosely," as Theodore Roosevelt observed when he wrote to Turner after receiving a copy of the 1893 paper. But Turner had combined these into a coherent theory, one that struck an instant chord with Americans who grasped the truth of his argument because they saw in it experiences they understood. They had no trouble believing that the settlement of various frontiers across succeeding generations—their families' collective pioneer past—was largely responsible for producing an America that was markedly different from what had arrived from Europe, both in human characteristics and institutions.

Turner would later argue that he had developed his frontier hypothesis with no overriding philosophy of history. But he brought something more than reading and research to the challenge of explaining American development: his Portage upbringing; his personal knowledge of the world of Indians and fur traders, settlers and loggers; his witness to the raw political conflicts that came with a new country; his understanding of the overriding optimism that led his father to exult in the pioneer's certainty of success (which Frederick J. Turner later summed up as "The West was another name for opportunity")—these were the primary building blocks of Turner's "Significance of the Frontier in American History."

Those probing for sources of his ideas have always come back to Portage. As one prominent historian concluded after a detailed examination of Turner's life, "those formative years not only equipped Turner for his professorial career but were a principal influence in shaping the historical concepts that revolutionized the study of our past."

Conclusion

Hamlin Garland and Frederick Jackson Turner arrived at the opportune moment to educate the public about the frontier. The frontier they knew was yielding rapidly to railroads and market hunters, its forests now sold off as "round forties" and sent downriver in massive armadas of logs. With the decline of the passenger pigeon, deer, trout, and other wild game and fish, worried citizens began to wonder about the fate of Wisconsin's "inexhaustible resources."

Both men had much they could draw upon to understand all this. Garland knew firsthand that the frontier had losers as well as winners—and he had known both types. Turner, able because of his studies to see the frontier in the context of human development, once wrote that "Wisconsin is like a palimpsest"—the palimpsest being a parchment or tablet written or marked upon several times, the previous writings still in view. Evidence of Wisconsin's past was visible in the modern state, he said: "The mound builders wrote their record and passed away. The state was occupied . . . by the most various peoples of the Indian race. Then came the French," followed by other fur traders, and eventually miners from the South, then New Englanders and New Yorkers, and finally Europeans.

Part of that palimpsest evident today might consist of Indian names—though these were usually mangled by translation first into French, then into English. The very name Wisconsin originated from such a tangle: Jolliet and Marquette interpreted their Miami guides' word for the river they reached at the portage as *Miskonsing* or *MesKousing* or *MisKous*—all three appear on their maps. In the French-English era it began to appear as Ouisconsin, sometimes Weeskonsan; the Americans eventually made it Wiskonsan, and finally Wisconsin. Potawatomis left their names on many southeastern Wisconsin communities, such as Milouaqui (Milwaukee), Waukesha, Mukwonago, Nashotah, Pewaukee, Oconomowoc. From the Chippewas came Menominee, Outagamie, Wausau, Wonewoc, and Namekagon, among others. The French added many, including Butte des Morts, Lac du Flambeau, Eau Claire, Des Moines Lake, Eau Pleine, Eau Galle, Lac Vieux Desert, and La Pointe—this last the oldest designation by the European newcomers still in use in Wisconsin. Many trading posts became the sites of later cities.[1] And numerous signposts across the state today bear the names of European nations and cities, fastened there by nineteenth-century immigrants.

Indian tribes were resilient through these transformations, showing great abilities of adaptation from the fur trade era onward. For them the Wisconsin frontier was generally not a battleground but more often a meeting place, where different cultures exchanged goods and ideas. The rise of the *métis* as an important group in many fur trade centers stood as testimony to the fact that for most of its participants, the early frontier represented a merger, not a defeat or victory. Indians were most tested when later waves of newcomers had less need to rely on native inhab-

---

1. The list of trading post sites now occupied by cities is a long one, and includes Milwaukee, Fond du Lac, LaCrosse, Eau Claire, Chippewa Falls, Oshkosh, Madison, Sheboygan, Manitowoc, Two Rivers, Kewaunee, Green Bay, Prairie du Chien, De Pere, Kaukauna, Neenah, Hudson, Portage, Menominee, Oconto, Peshtigo, Black River Falls, Rice Lake, Baraboo, and Shullsburg, as well as communities on the various Indian reservations.

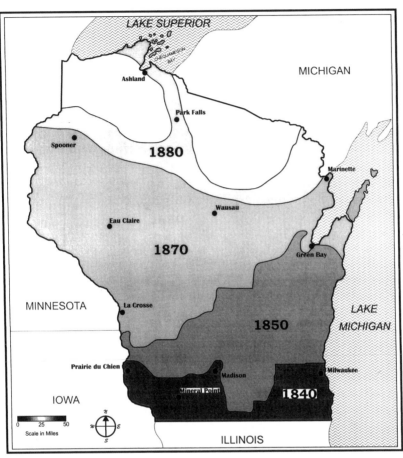

Wisconsin's frontier was generally northward-moving.
This map shows the frontier line at four censuses, the
line in each case setting off the region to the north with
less than two inhabitants per square mile, "excluding
Indians not taxed." The 1840 census revealed the
mining region of the southwest as the major
population center, with the lakeshore around
Milwaukee already adding many Yankees and York
Staters who had started west on the Erie Canal. Farm
settlement was behind the growth shown in the 1850
census, while the lumbering frontier drove the march
northward in the 1870 and 1880 censuses—the latter
marked by a lane of settlement poking through the
woods to Ashland along the Wisconsin Central
Railroad, completed in 1877. MAP BY JILL FREUND THOMAS
AND MICHAEL MAST.

itants and often considered them barriers to progress. This was increasingly the case as population soared from 3,245 in Wisconsin Territory in 1830, to 305,391 in 1850 after statehood was achieved, to 2,069,042 in 1900. Some Indians were moved west, some were given sharply reduced reservations in Wisconsin, and others assimilated into the white world.

Both Garland and Turner wrote in opposition to eastern notions about the frontier, but they also wrote during a time of rising interest in the pioneer past. Communities and states began to form historical societies and Old Settlers' Clubs, as they realized the speed with which a distinctive period, the frontier era, was passing. In 1874 a group of old *voyageurs* at Chequamegon Bay, including several who had arrived by canoe from Canada early in the century, were taken on a train ride from Ashland for a day of reminiscing as well as inspection of the Iron Horse: "Having lived in the wilderness all their years," the Ashland *Press* editor wrote, "they come at last just as their life sun is setting, to gaze in wonder upon the great civilizer, King Railroad." By the time young Fred Turner rode that train three years later, a passenger from Ashland could travel to the Atlantic Coast in just three days; two centuries earlier it had taken Father Claude Allouez almost two months to reach Chequamegon Bay by canoe after paddling away from Trois Rivières on the St. Lawrence.

The steam engine that brought about this revolution—driving lake boats, railroads, and sawmills—became the major agent of change in transforming the frontier of Wisconsin and the Upper Lakes into a settled part of the nation, integrated into its economy and government. In fact, most of the changes noted by Turner for his palimpsest rested on modes of transportation: the Indians' birchbark canoe, ideally suited to the network of streams and rivers, was adopted quickly by European traders; then came oxen, horses, the opening of the Erie Canal, the arrival of steamboats and railroads. All brought new groups to the frontier who in turn left their marks, both as tangible objects and as institutions and beliefs.

As the twentieth century opened, an editor with the *Engineering and Mining Journal* cited the steam engine and its "great cheapening of transportation" as constituting the crucial change in American life during the previous 100 years. This was undoubtedly the case for Wisconsin as it moved from frontier to settled state. The *EMJ* editor emphasized, however, that such opportunities for development would never—could never—return. No other country would ever match the record of the United States, he wrote, because "never again will a people of restless energy and a natural talent for mechanical devices be given the opportunity to develop at will a virgin country with wonderful natural resources."

He was right. Americans, in Wisconsin and elsewhere, had developed their frontiers "at will." Optimism, bred by success, had come naturally amid such surroundings, and many assumed this was a permanent condition, that such a world would exist forever.

But after the pioneer generations were gone, the frontier's wealth would have to be managed with care by men and women who could learn from the destruction of the forests and the passing of the passenger pigeon. For the 300-year excitement of chasing nature's windfalls "at will" now had to give way to acceptance of the fact that an era had closed.

There were signs that this was occurring. Aldo Leopold, Wisconsin's famous ecologist and naturalist, could complain some decades after the pigeons' demise that "There is as yet no social stigma in the possession of a gullied farm, a wrecked forest, or a polluted stream, provided the dividends suffice to send the youngsters to college." But the post-frontier conservation movement grew rapidly across Wisconsin, and when Leopold helped dedicate a monument to the passenger pigeon in 1947, he could observe: "For one species to mourn the death of another is a new thing under the sun." There was hope in this—in the mourning over the pigeons' extinction, rather than in the invention of nylon or the atomic bomb, Leopold concluded, "lies objective evidence of our superiority over the beasts."

The frontier era thus may have contained not only the seeds of its own destruction—but also of mankind's ultimate survival.

Essay on Sources

General

The starting point for any study dealing with Wisconsin's past is the State Historical Society of Wisconsin in Madison. The SHSW's library, manuscript room, and iconographic collections were all used extensively in preparation of this volume, as were many of its publications. These include the twenty-one volume *Collections of the State Historical Society of Wisconsin* (Madison: 1855–1915), cited hereafter as *WHC*; the *Proceedings of the State Historical Society of Wisconsin*, 74 vols. (Madison, 1875–1958); the quarterly *Wisconsin Magazine of History* (cited hereafter as *WMH*); and the society's History of Wisconsin series under general editor William Fletcher Thompson. The first three volumes in the series have been most useful for studying the frontier: Alice E. Smith, Vol. I, *From Exploration to Statehood* (1973); Richard N. Current, Vol. II, *The Civil War Era, 1848–1873* (1976); and Robert C. Nesbit, Vol. III, *Urbanization and Industrialization, 1873–1893* (1985). The society also brought out Nesbit's general survey, *Wisconsin: A History* (1973). Two of the society's earlier directors published general works that are also useful: Reuben Gold Thwaites, *Wisconsin: The Americanization of a French Settlement* (Boston: Houghton Mifflin, 1908), and Milo Milton Quaife, *Wisconsin: Its History and Its People 1634–1924* (Chicago: S. J. Clarke, 1924), 2 vols.

The Area Research Centers, linking regional history centers with the SHSW, provide researchers with the possibility of delving deeply into materials relating to different areas of Wisconsin. Centers at the University of Wisconsin–River Falls, University of

Wisconsin–La Crosse, University of Wisconsin–Green Bay, and University of Wisconsin–Eau Claire were extremely useful here.

The Milwaukee Public Museum's manuscripts and archives are especially good for material and photos dealing with Wisconsin's Indians, both in prehistoric and historic times. The Apostle Islands National Lakeshore center at Bayfield maintains an historical center which has materials on Chequamegon Bay and vicinity.

Historical collections in neighboring states are rich in materials relating to the Wisconsin frontier. This author relied heavily upon the Minnesota Historical Society, St. Paul, for some important nineteenth-century materials, and used publications of the Minnesota, Illinois, Iowa, and Michigan state historical societies.

Studies of Wisconsin's Indian tribes were relied upon for many portions of this study. These include Felix Keesing, *The Menomini Indians of Wisconsin: A Study of Three Centuries of Cultural Contact and Change* (Madison: University of Wisconsin Press, 1939, 1987); Patricia K. Ourada, *The Menominee Indians: A History* (Norman: University of Oklahoma Press, 1979); Paul Radin, *The Winnebago Tribe* (Lincoln: University of Nebraska Press, 1923, 1970); R. David Edmunds, *The Potawatomis: Keepers of the Fire* (Norman: University of Oklahoma Press, 1978, 1987); W. Vernon Kinietz, *The Indians of the Western Great Lakes* (Ann Arbor: University of Michigan Press, 1940, 1965); Harold Hickerson, *The Chippewa and Their Neighbors: A Study in Ethnohistory* (New York: Holt, Rinehart, and Winston, 1970); Edmund Danziger, Jr., *The Chippewas of Lake Superior* (Norman: University of Oklahoma Press, 1978); Walker D. Wyman with Kurt Leichtle, *The Chippewa: A History of the Great Lakes Woodland Tribe over Three Centuries* (River Falls: University of Wisconsin–River Falls Press, 1993). Also, the following chapters in William C. Sturtevant, gen. ed., *Handbook of North American Indians* (Washington: Smithsonian Institution, 1978), vol. 15, *Northeast* (Bruce G. Trigger, ed.): Lyle Stone and Donald Chaput, "History of the Upper Great Lakes Area," 602–9; Charles Callender, "Great Lakes–Riverine Sociopolitical Organization," 610–21; Callender, "Fox," 636–47; Callender, "Sauk," 648–55; Callender, Richard K. Pope and Susan M. Pope, "Kickapoo," 656–67;

Ives Goddard, "Mascouten," 668–72; Callender, "Miami," 681–89; Nancy Oestreich Lurie, "Winnebago," 690–707; Louise Spindler, "Menominee," 708–24; James Clifton, "Potawatomi," 725–42; Robert E. Ritzenthaler, "Southwestern Chippewa," 743–59; and Trigger, "Cultural Unity and Diversity," 798–804. A useful general survey is Carol I. Mason, *Introduction to Wisconsin Indians: Prehistory to Statehood* (Salem, Wis.: Sheffield, 1988). An excellent collection of maps and explanatory essays on regional Indian history is Helen Hornbeck Tanner, ed., *Atlas of Great Lakes Indian History* (Norman: University of Oklahoma Press, 1986).

Finding guides include Leroy Schlinkert, comp., *Subject Bibliography of Wisconsin History* (Madison: SHSW, 1947); Alice E. Smith, ed., *Guide to the Manuscripts of the Wisconsin Historical Society* (Madison: SHSW, 1944), and its supplements: Josephine L. Harper and Sharon C. Smith, eds., . . . *Supplement Number One* (Madison: SHSW, 1957), and Harper, ed., . . . *Supplement Number Two* (Madison: SHSW, 1966); and Donald E. Oehlerts, comp., *Guide to Wisconsin Newspapers 1833–1957* (Madison: SHSW, 1958).

Quotations from primary sources are reprinted using the punctuation and spelling of the original.

Chapter 1

Published and translated early French records offer an abundance of primary source materials on Wisconsin. Chief among these are vols. 23 and 50–51 of Reuben Gold Thwaites, ed., *The Jesuit Relations and Allied Documents—Travels and Explorations of the Jesuit Missionaries in New France: 1610–1791* (Cleveland: Burrows Brothers, 1899–1903); *The Works of Samuel de Champlain* (Toronto: The Champlain Society, 1922–36), 6 vols.; Louise Kellogg, comp., *Early Narratives of the Northwest: 1634–1699* (New York: Scribner's, 1917); Emma Helen Blair, trans. and ed., *The Indian Tribes of the Upper Mississippi Valley and Region of the Great Lakes . . .* (Cleveland: Arthur H. Clark, 1912), 2 vols.; and Joseph L. Peyser, ed., *Letters from New France: The Upper Country, 1686–1783* (Urbana: University of Illinois Press, 1992).

The major secondary study of the early French period is Kellogg, *The French Regime in Wisconsin and the Northwest* (Madison: SHSW, 1925); also see her "The Fox Indians during the French Regime," *SHSW Proceedings . . . 1907* (Madison: SHSW, 1908), 142–88. Good background on events elsewhere that affected Wisconsin is in George T. Hunt, *The Wars of the Iroquois: A Study in Intertribal Trade Relations* (Madison: University of Wisconsin Press, 1940); and the classic by Francis Parkman, *France and England in North America* (New York: Library of America, 1865, 1983), vols. I and II. On Indians, in addition to the chapters in Trigger, *Northeast*, see R. David Edmunds and Joseph Peyser, *The Fox Wars: The Mesquakie Challenge to New France* (Norman: University of Oklahoma Press, 1993), and Richard White, *The Middle Ground: Indians, Empires, and Republics in the Great Lakes Region, 1650–1815* (Cambridge: Cambridge University Press, 1991), a major new interpretation of Indian-French contact.

Early explorations are chronicled in Samuel Eliot Morison, *The European Discovery of America: The Northern Voyages—* A.D. *500–1600* (New York: Oxford, 1971), and W. J. Eccles, *The Canadian Frontier: 1534–1760* (New York: Holt, Rinehart and Winston, 1969).

On Etienne Brûlé, see Willshire Butterfield, *History of Brule's Discoveries and Explorations 1610–1626* (Cleveland: Helman-Taylor, 1898, 1974), and J. Herbert Cranston, *Etienne Brûlé: Immortal Scoundrel* (Toronto: Ryerson, 1949).

Chapter 2

On Aztalan, see especially S. A. Barrett, "Ancient Aztalan," *Bulletin of the Public Museum of the City of Milwaukee* (April 24, 1933), 8:1–602; and Joan Freeman, "Aztalan: A Middle Mississippian Village," *Wisconsin Archeologist* (September–December 1986) 67, n. 3–4:339–64; and the special Aztalan issue of *Wisconsin Archeologist* for March 1958.

On Indian prehistory, see Carol I. Mason, *Introduction to Wisconsin Indians;* Ronald Mason, *Great Lakes Archaeology* (New York: Academic Press, 1981); George Quimby, *Indian Life in the Upper Great Lakes 11,000* B.C.. *to* A.D. *1800* (Chicago: University of Chicago Press, 1960, 1971); Quimby, "Late Period Copper Artifacts in the Upper Great Lakes Region," *Wisconsin Archeologist* (December 1963) 44, n. 4 N.S.:193–98. The different periods of Wisconsin prehistory are examined in William Green, James Stoltman, and Alice Kehoe, eds., *Introduction to Wisconsin Archaeology: Background for Cultural Resource Planning* (special issue of *Wisconsin Archeologist* [September–December 1986]) 67, n. 3–4. The chapters in Trigger, *Northeast*, also cover prehistory for the different tribes.

On use of the land: Joseph R. Caldwell, "Eastern North America," in Stuart Struever, ed., *Preshistoric Agriculture* (Garden City, N.Y.: American Museum of Natural History, 1971), 361–82; and Gayle Fritz, "'Newer,' 'Better,' Maize and the Mississippian Emergence: A Critique of Prime Mover Explanations," 19–43, and James Gallagher, "Prehistoric Field Systems in the Upper Midwest," 95–135, in William Woods, ed., *Late Prehistoric Agriculture: Observations from the Midwest* (Springfield,: Illinois Historic Preservation Agency, 1992), 19–43. Gallagher, "Agricultural intensification and ridged-field cultivation in the historic upper Midwest of North America," in David R. Harris and Gordon C. Hillman, eds., *Foraging and Farming: The Evolution of Plant Exploitation* (London: Unwin Hyman, 1989), 572–84. Chandler W. Rowe, *The Effigy Mound Culture of Wisconsin* (Westport, Conn.: Greenwood, 1956, 1970). William M. Denevan, "The Pristine Myth: The Landscape of the Americas in 1492," 369–85, and William Doolittle, "Agriculture in North America on the Eve of Contact: A Reassessment," 386–401, in *Annals of the Association of American Geographers* (September 1992) 82, n. 3.

Chapter 3

Information on the Pageant of 1671 is drawn principally from Perrot's and La Potherie's accounts in Blair, *Indian Tribes of the Upper Mississippi Valley*, 1:220–25, and 2:340–47; *Jesuit Relations*, 4:105–15; and the official report reprinted in *WHC* 11:26–29.

The French push westward with the fur trade is followed in

Hunt, *Wars of the Iroquois*; Paul Phillips, *The Fur Trade* (Norman: University of Oklahoma Press, 1961), vol. 1; Thomas Elliot Norton, *The Fur Trade in Colonial New York 1686–1776* (Madison: University of Wisconsin Press, 1974); Eccles, *Canadian Frontier*; and Kellogg, *French Regime.* The French move into the Upper Lakes is also examined in Frederick J. Turner, *The Character and Influence of the Indian Trade in Wisconsin: A Study of the Trading Post as an Institution* (New York: Burt Franklin, 1891, 1970); Donald P. Heldman, "The French in Michigan and Beyond: An Archaeological View from Fort Michilimackinac toward the West," in John A. Walthall, ed., *French Colonial Archaeology: The Illinois Country and the Western Great Lakes* (Urbana: University of Illinois Press, 1991), 201–17; and Rhoda R. Gilman, "The Fur Trade in the Upper Mississippi Valley, 1630–1850," *WMH* (Autumn 1974) 58, n. 1:2–18.

Information on Indian involvement in the fur trade was also obtained from Jeanne Kay's 1978 University of Wisconsin dissertation, "The Land of La Baye: The Ecological Impact of the Green Bay Fur Trade, 1634–1836"; Charles E. Cleland, "Indians in a Changing Environment," in Susan L. Flader, ed., *The Great Lakes Forest: An Environmental and Social History* (Minneapolis: University of Minnesota Press, 1983), 83–95; and Thomas Vennum, Jr., *Wild Rice and the Ojibway People* (St. Paul: Minnesota Historical Society Press, 1988).

The controversy over whether maple sugaring was a major Indian activity before the Europeans' arrival is addressed by Carol Mason, "A Sweet Small Something: Maple Sugaring in the New World," in James Clifton, ed., *The Invented Indian: Cultural Fictions and Government Policies* (New Brunswick, N.J.: Transaction, 1990, 1994) 91–105. Hunting activities are traced in Kay, "Wisconsin Indian Hunting Patterns, 1634–1836," *Annals of the Association of American Geographers* 69, n.3:402–18. The roles of Indian women are studied in Spindler, "Menominee"; Keesing, *Menomini*; Vennum, *Wild Rice*; Carol Devens, "Separate Confrontations: Gender as a Factor in Indian Adaptation to European Colonization in New France," *American Quarterly* (1986) 38, n. 3; and Devens, *Countering Colonization: Native American Women and Great Lakes Missions, 1630–1900* (Berkeley: University of California Press, 1992). Lacrosse is examined in Thomas Vennum, *American Indian Lacrosse: Little Brother of War* (Washington: Smithsonian, 1994).

Father Marquette's account of his journey across Wisconsin and into the Mississippi is in *Jesuit Relations* 59:87–163. Other missionary accounts are reprinted in Kellogg, *Early Narratives;* and Louis Hennepin, *Father Louis Hennepin's Description of Louisiana* (St. Paul: University of Minnesota Press, 1938).

On the canoe and its use in the trade, see Eric Morse, *Fur Trade Canoe Routes of Canada: Then and Now* (Toronto: University of Toronto Press, 1969, 1979); Edwin Adney and Howard Chapelle, *The Bark Canoes and Skin Boats of North America* (Washington: Smithsonian, 1964); Jacqueline Peterson, "Many Roads to Red River: Métis Genesis in the Great Lakes Region, 1860–1915," in Peterson and Jennifer S. H. Brown, eds., *The New Peoples: Being and Becoming Métis in North America* (Lincoln, Neb.: University of Nebraska Press, 1985); Robert E. Bieder, *Native American Communities in Wisconsin 1600–1960: A Study of Tradition and Change* (Madison: University of Wisconsin Press, 1995). Peter Kalm's description is from *Peter Kalm's Travels in North America* (New York: Wilson-Erickson, 1937) 2:551–568; Elizabeth Therese Baird's is from *WHC* 14:61. The best study of portaging is Douglas Birk, "When Rivers Were Roads: Deciphering the Role of Canoe Portages in the Western Lake Superior Fur Trade," in Jennifer S. H. Brown, W. J. Eccles, and Donald P. Heldman, eds., *The Fur Trade Revisited* (East Lansing, Mich.: Michigan State University Press and Mackinac State Historic Parks, 1994).

Chapter 4

On the changing fur trade as the British challenged the French in the region, in addition to earlier works cited on the trade see the following: Louise Kellogg, *The British Regime in Wisconsin and the Northwest* (Madison: SHSW, 1935); Ida A. Johnson, *The Michigan Fur Trade* (Grand Rapids, Mich.: Michigan Historical Commission, 1919, 1975); Arthur Neville, "La Baye," *Green Bay Historical Bulletin* (April 1925) 1:1–10; Peter Scanlan, *Prairie du Chien: French-British-American* (Menasha, Wis.: George Banta, 1937); John Boatman, "Historical Overview of the Wisconsin Area: From Early Years to the French, British, and Americans," in Donald L. Fixico, ed., *An Anthology of Western Great Lakes History* (Milwaukee: University of Wisconsin–Milwaukee, 1987), 40–43.

Archeological findings are used to trace historical events in Susan Branstner, "Tionontate Huron Occupation at the Marquette Mission," 177–201; Lenville J. Stelle, "History and Archaeology: The 1730 Mesquakie Fort," 265–307, and John Walthall and Thomas Emerson, "Indians and French in the Midcontinent," 1–13, in Walthall and Emerson, eds., *Calumet & Fleur-de-Lys: Archaeology of Indian and French Contact in the Midcontinent* (Washington: Smithsonian, 1992). Also, Robert Birmingham, "Historic Period Indian Archeology at La Pointe in Lake Superior: An Overview" (draft paper, SHSW, n.d.).

John Lawe's letter is reprinted in *WHC* 20:351–53. The mixing of peoples is analyzed in Jacqueline L. Peterson, "The People in Between: Indian-White Marriage and the Genesis of a Métis Society and Culture in the Great Lakes Region, 1680–1830" (University of Illinois–Chicago dissertation, 1981); Olive Patricia Dickason, "From 'One Nation' in the Northeast to 'New Nation' in the Northwest: A Look at the Emergence of the Métis," in Peterson and Brown, *New Peoples*, 19–36.

On Indian changes during the French and British fur trade era, see the tribal histories cited earlier, and John Douglass, "Cultural Changes among the Wisconsin Indian Tribes during the French Contact Period," *Wisconsin Archeologist* (March 1949) 30:1–21; John Holzhueter, "Wisconsin's Indians since 1634," Addendum to vol. I, SHSW, *Wisconsin's Historic Preservation Plan* (Madison: SHSW, 1976); Nancy Oestreich Lurie, "Winnebago Protohistory," in Stanley Diamond, ed., *Culture in History: Essays in Honor of Paul Radin* (New York: Brandeis-Columbia, 1960), 790–808; Peyser, *Letters from New France*; Edmunds and Peyser, *The Fox Wars*. The *Journal of Joseph Marin* has been translated and edited by Kenneth Bailey (published by author, 1975).

On French struggles with the Foxes, also see Kellogg, "The

Fox Indians during the French Regime"; S. S. Hebberd, *History of Wisconsin under the Dominion of France* (Madison: Midland, 1890); and Warren Wittry, "The Bell Site, Wn9, an Early Historic Fox Village," *Wisconsin Archeologist* (March 1963) 44, n. 1:1–57. Augustin Grignon's recollections are in *WHC* 3:195–295; the quotation is on 204.

On the French and Indian War, see Kellogg's accounts of the *French Regime* and the *British Regime;* Clarence Alvord and Clarence Carter, eds., *The Critical Period 1763–1765* (Springfield, Ill.: Illinois State Historical Library, 1915), vol. 10; Jack Sosin, *Whitehall and the Wilderness: The Middle West in British Colonial Policy, 1760–1775* (Lincoln: University of Nebraska Press, 1961); and documents from the war reprinted in *WHC* 1:24–48 (Lt. James Gorrell's Journal), and 18:221–22, 263–68. Alexander Henry was present at the Mackinac attack; his account is in Milo Quaife, ed., *Alexander Henry's Travels and Adventures in the Years 1760–1776* (Chicago: Lakeside, 1809, 1921), 78–85. Carver's experiences are related in his *Travels through the Interior Parts of North America, in the Years 1766, 1767, and 1768* (London: 1781; reprint 1956), 19–20.

Sources on the American Revolution include James A. James, ed., *George Rogers Clark Papers* (Springfield: Illinois State Historical Library Collections, 1926); Lyle Stone, *Fort Michilimackinac 1715–1781: An Archaeological Perspective on the Revolutionary Frontier* (East Lansing: Michigan State University Press, 1974); and "Papers from the Canadian Archives, 1778–1783," *WHC* 11:97–212.

Chapter 5

The fur trade wars of the late eighteenth century and early nineteenth century are described in many studies cited for the fur trade in chapters 3 and 4. Chief among these are Peterson, "The People in Between"; Kay, "Land of La Baye"; Gilman, "Fur Trade in the Upper Mississippi Valley"; and Kellogg's *French Regime* and *British Regime.*

Fur trade journals used are George Nelson, *A Winter in the St. Croix Valley: George Nelson's Reminiscences, 1802–03* (St. Paul:

Minnesota Historical Society, 1948); Jean Baptiste Perrault, "Narrative of the Travels and Adventures of a Merchant Voyageur in the Savage Territories of Northern America Leaving Montreal the 28th of May 1783 (to 1820)," *Historical Collections and Researches Made by the Michigan Pioneer and Historical Society* 37:508–619; Michel Curot, "A Wisconsin Fur-Trader's Journal, 1803–1804," *WHC* 20:396–471; and François Victor Malhiot, "A Wisconsin Fur-Trader's Journal, 1804–05," *WHC* 19:163–233. Also useful was Theresa Schenck, "The Cadottes: Five Generations of Fur Traders on Lake Superior," in Brown, et al., *Fur Trade Revisited;* and John Denis Haeger, *John Jacob Astor: Business and Finance in the Early Republic* (Detroit: Wayne State University Press, 1991). Archeological work at the Yellow River site where Nelson and Curot wintered is described in Edgar Oerichbauer, "Archeological Excavations at the Site of the Northwest and XY Company Wintering Post (47Bt–26)," *Wisconsin Archeologist* (September 1982) 63, n. 3:153–236.

On Indian women, see Peterson, "People in Between"; Devens, "Separate Confrontations"; and Nancy Shoemaker, "Introduction," 1–25, Kathleen Brown, "The Anglo-Algonquian Gender Frontier," 26–48, and Lucy Eldersveld Murphy, "Autonomy and the Economic Roles of Indian Women of the Fox-Wisconsin River Region, 1763–1832," 72–89, in Shoemaker, ed., *Negotiators of Change: Historical Perspectives on Native American Women* (New York: Routledge, 1995).

On American-British confrontations over the region, see Kellogg, *British Regime;* Royal Way, "The United States Factory System for Trading with the Indians, 1796–1822," *Mississippi Valley Historical Review* 6:n. 2 (September 1919), 220–35; R. David Edmunds, *Tecumseh and the Quest for Indian Leadership* (Boston: Little, Brown, 1984); Alec Gilpin, *The War of 1812 in the Old Northwest* (East Lansing: Michigan State University Press, 1958); and three reports on the British Army's final days at Prairie du Chien, in *WHC* 13: Alfred Edward Bulger (son of the British commandant), "Events at Prairie du Chien Previous to American Occupation, 1814," 1–9, and "Last Days of the British at Prairie du Chien," 154–62; and Andrew H. Bulger, "The Bulger Papers," 10–153. Nicolas Boilvin's letter of July 28, 1809 (trans.

Marian Scanlan), is in SHSW manuscript collections. Zebulon
Pike's account is from Elliott Coues, ed., *The Expeditions of*
Zebulon Montgomery Pike (New York: Harper, 1895), vol. 1.

Chapter 6

Information on early Green Bay is drawn from many sources, including the city's early newspapers, the *Intelligencer* and the *Wisconsin Democrat*; Henry S. Baird, "Recollections of the Early History of Northern Wisconsin," *WHC* 4:197–221; James McCall, "M'Call's Journal of a Visit to Wisconsin in 1830," *WHC* 12:170–215; Elizabeth Thérèse Baird, "Reminiscences of Life in Territorial Wisconsin," *WHC* 15: 205–263; Henry R. Schoolcraft, *Narrative Journal of Travels through the Northwestern Regions of the United States . . . in the year 1820* (East Lansing: Michigan State College Press, 1821, 1953). On Prairie du Chien, and the world of the mixed-breeds, see Alfred Brunson, "Early History of Wisconsin," *WHC* 4:223–51; Scanlan, *Prairie du Chien: French-British-American*; Jacqueline Peterson, "Ethnogenesis: The Settlement and Growth of a 'New People' in the Great Lakes Region 1702–1815," in Fixico, *Anthology of Western Great Lakes History*; 111–77; Peterson, "The People in Between"; and Kay, "Land of La Baye." The French land system is described in Carl Ekberg, *Colonial Ste. Genevieve* (Gerald, Mo.: Patrice Press, 1985); Mary Antoine de Julio, "The Vertefeuille House of Prairie du Chien: A Survivor from the Era of French Wisconsin," *WMH* (Autumn 1996) 80:36–56. John Lawe's report is in *WHC* 20:174–75, 351–53. Also see Daniel Durrie, *Early Out-Posts of Wisconsin. Green Bay for Two Hundred Years, 1639–1839. Annals of Prairie du Chien* (Madison: no pub., 1873). The collection of documents on "The Fur-Trade in Wisconsin 1812–1825," *WHC* 20:1–395, contains much information on Green Bay, Prairie du Chien, and other Wisconsin trading centers. Juliette Kinzie's memoir, *Wau-Bun: The Early Day in the Northwest* (Menasha, Wis.: Colonial Dames of Wisconsin, 1856, 1948), provides helpful information also.

Lead mining sources include Herbert Kuhm, "The Mining and Use of Lead by the Wisconsin Indians," *Wisconsin Archeologist* (June 1951) 32:25–37; Janet D. Spector, "Winnebago Indians and Lead Mining: A Case Study of the Ethnohistoric Approach in Archaeology," *Midcontinent Journal of Archeology* (1977) 2:131–37; Joseph Schafer, *The Wisconsin Lead Region* (Madison: SHSW, 1932); Moses Strong, *History of the Territory of Wisconsin, from 1836 to 1848* (Madison: Democrat Printing Co., 1885); Kellogg, *French Regime;* Moses Meeker, "Early History of Lead Region of Wisconsin," *WHC* 6:271–96; Morgan L. Martin, "Narrative of . . .," *WHC* 11:385–415; Louis A. Copeland, "The Cornish in Southwest Wisconsin," *WHC* 14:301–34; Theodore Rodolf, "Pioneering in the Wisconsin Lead Region," *WHC* 15:338–89; Works Progress Administration, Wisconsin Writers Program, *The Story of Mineral Point* (Mineral Point: Mineral Point Historical Society, 1979); Dale Fatzinger, "Historical Geography of Lead and Zinc Mining in Southwest Wisconsin 1820–1920: A Century of Change" (Michigan State University Ph.D. dissertation, 1971); William Peterson, "The Lead Traffic on the Upper Mississippi, 1823–1848," *Mississippi Valley Historical Review* (June 1930) 17:72–97.

On the settlers in the lead region, see also John Reynolds, *My Own Time: Embracing also the History of My Life* (Chicago: Chicago Historical Society, 1879); Daniel M. Parkinson, "Pioneer Life in Wisconsin," *WHC* 2:326–64 (includes quote on dugouts); Arthur Cecil Todd, *The Cornish Miner in America* (Glendale, Calif.: Arthur Clark, 1967); Louis Pelzer, *Henry Dodge* (Iowa City: State Historical Society of Iowa, 1911); S. U. Pinney, "Eulogy on Henry Dodge," *WHC* 5:173–77,

On the Red Bird or Winnebago War, see Pelzer, *Henry Dodge;* Col. Thomas McKenney's account in *WHC* 5:178–204; also see Agent Joseph Street's report in *WHC* 11:366–67; "Early Days at Prairie du Chien and Winnebago Outbreak of 1827," *WHC* 5:123–53; Louis B. Porlier, "Narrative by . . .," *WHC* 15:439–47. Also, Strong, *History of Wisconsin Territory;* Francis Paul Prucha, *American Indian Policy in the Formative Years: The Indian Trade and Intercourse Acts 1790–1834* (Cambridge, Mass.: Harvard University Press, 1962), 178–80.

The Black Hawk War has received abundant attention from historians. Major sources used here include Donald Jackson, ed., *Black Hawk: An Autobiography* (Urbana: University of Illinois

Press, 1833, 1990); Roger Nichols, *Black Hawk and the Warrior's Path* (Arlington Heights, Ill.: Harlan Davidson, 1992); Nichols, "The Black Hawk War in Retrospect," *Wisconsin Magazine of History* (Summer 1982) 65:239–46; William Hagan, *The Sac and Fox Indians* (Norman: University of Oklahoma Press, 1958); Anthony Wallace, *Prelude to Disaster: The Course of Indian-White Relations Which Led to the Black Hawk War of 1832* (Springfield: Illinois State Historical Library, 1970); recollections of the Black Hawk War by various participants, most already cited, are published in *WHC* volumes 2:365–414; 5:285–90 and 315–20; 10:178–212; 11:385–15; 12:217–65. Also used were the collections of hour-by-hour accounts of the war gathered in several volumes by Crawford Thayer, ed., including *Hunting a Shadow: The Search for Black Hawk—An Eye-Witness Account of the Black Hawk War of 1832* (1981), *The Battle of Wisconsin Heights: An Eye-Witness Account of the Black Hawk War of 1832* (1983), and *Massacre at Bad Axe: An Eye-Witness Account of the Black Hawk War of 1832* (1984), all privately printed in Ft. Atkinson, Wis.

Chapter 7

The opening Vermont incident is recalled in Elisha Keyes, *The Founding of Lake Mills* (Lake Mills: Lake Mills Aztalan Historical Society, 1894, 1986). Other early letters describing the rush into Wisconsin are in "Wisconsin Territorial Letters, 1837–1852," in SHSW. Also see Joseph Schafer, *Four Wisconsin Counties: Prairie and Forest* (Madison: SHSW, 1927); Ebenezer Childs, "Recollections of Wisconsin since 1820," *WHC* 4:154–95. Green Bay *Intelligencer* quotes are from April 9, 1835, July 20, 1835, and March 2, 1836. The quote, "if there is no way," is from John Lakin to Major Henry B. Brevoort, Dec. 5, 1827, in Henry B. Brevoort papers, SHSW.

County histories often reprint summaries of treaties; the following were used here: Western Historical Company, *History of La Crosse County, Wisconsin . . .* (Chicago: Western Historical Company, 1881), and Western Historical Company, *History of Waukesha County, Wisconsin . . .* (Chicago: Western Historical

Company, 1880), 214–18 in each. Also see Smith, *History of Wisconsin;* Clarence Carter, ed., *Territorial Papers . . . Michigan* 12:916–18; Joseph Schafer, *The Winnebago-Horicon Basin: A Type Study in Western History* (Madison: SHSW, 1937), 138–39; as well as separate volumes on the affected tribes. The quote by the Menominee leader, "We are ignorant," is from George B. Porter diary, Oct. 13, 1832, in SHSW. The *plus* system in Indian trading is explained in John Porter Bloom, ed., *Territorial Papers . . . Wisconsin* (Washington: National Archives, 1975) 28:96–97.

The New York Indians are discussed in Albert G. Ellis, "Advent of the New York Indians into Wisconsin," *WHC* 2:415–49; Thwaites, *Wisconsin: The Americanization of a French Settlement;* Frank Merrill, *The Church's Mission to the Oneidas* (Oneida Reservation, Wis., 1899; no pub.); Keesing, *Menomini;* Smith, *History of Wisconsin;* the events were covered extensively in the Green Bay *Intelligencer.*

Inclusion of the *métis* in treaties is examined in James L. Hansen, "'Half-Breed' Rolls and Fur Trade Families in the Great Lakes Region—An Introduction and Bibliography," in Brown et al., *The Fur Trade Revisited,* 161–69; Francis Paul Prucha, *The Great Father: The United States Government and the American Indians* (Lincoln: University of Nebraska Press, 1984), 247. Major documents used are from Bloom, *Territorial Papers . . . Wisconsin* 28:12–18, 131–33, 528–29, 561, 577, 601. Alfred Brunson's comments are from his letter book, 37–39, in SHSW.

Indians, annuities, and the trade are examined in James Tripp, "The Impossible Role of the Indian Agent: Joseph M. Street at Prairie du Chien and Rock Island: 1827–1840" (University of Wisconsin–River Falls thesis, 1981); Gilman, "Fur Trade in the Upper Mississippi Valley"; and Francis Paul Prucha, *Broadax and Bayonet: The Role of the United States Army in the Development of the Northwest 1815–1860* (Madison: SHSW, 1953). The Francis Desnoyers Indian account book, 1844–49, is in University of Wisconsin–Green Bay Area Research Center; Gustave de Neveu's account, "A Menominee Indian Payment in 1838," is in SHSW *Proceedings . . . 58th Annual Meeting . . . 1910* (Madison: SHSW, 1911), 153–64.

Broad issues of Indian removal are examined in three books by Prucha, *Great Father, Broadax and Bayonet,* and *American Indian Policy in the Formative Years;* also see Thwaites, *Wisconsin: Americanization of a French Settlement;* and *History of Waukesha County.*

The fur trade's decline is treated in Kay, "Land of La Baye"; Gilman, "Fur Trade in the Upper Mississippi Valley;" and Grace Lee Nute, "The American Fur Company's Fishing Enterprises on Lake Superior," *Mississippi Valley Historical Review* (March 1926) 12:483–503.

On the French system of agriculture and landholding, see Carl Ekberg, "Agriculture, *Mentalités,* and Violence on the Illinois Frontier," *Illinois Historical Journal* (Summer 1995) 88:101–16; Arthur Neville, "French Land Claims at Green Bay," *Green Bay Historical Bulletin* (November–December 1926) 2:1–8; Frederick Trowbridge, "Confirming Land Titles in Early Wisconsin," *WMH* (March 1943) 26:314–22. Documents are in *American State Papers* (Washington: Gates & Seaton, 1860) 5:271; Carter, *Territorial Papers . . . Michigan* 11:209, 507; the Dousman case is Dousman and wife *v.* Hooe (1854) 3 *Wisconsin Reports* 416–46.

The process of surveying and selling the land is covered in Joseph Schafer, *A History of Agriculture in Wisconsin* (Madison: SHSW, 1922); Schafer, *Four Wisconsin Counties;* Malcolm Rohrbough, *The Land Office Business: The Settlement and Administration of American Public Lands, 1789–1837* (New York: Oxford, 1968); Hildegard Binder Johnson, *Order upon the Land: The U.S. Rectangular Land Survey and the Upper Mississippi Country* (New York: Oxford, 1976); Ingolf Vogeler, *Wisconsin: A Geography* (Boulder, Colo.: Westview, 1986); *History of Waukesha County,* 222–25, 471; Paul Wallace Gates, *History of Public Land Law Development* (Washington: Public Land Law Review Commission, 1968); and Benjamin Hibbard, *The History of Agriculture in Dane County Wisconsin* (Madison: University of Wisconsin Economics and Political Science Series, 1905).

The statehood process has been extensively covered and so is only touched on here. I leaned heavily upon Smith, *History of Wisconsin,* chs. 11–12; and the U.S. Census.

Sources on women are scattered. See Lillian Krueger, *Mother-hood on the Wisconsin Frontier* (Madison: SHSW, 1946); Mrs. John Weaver's story is recounted in *History of Waukesha County*, 477–85; also see 355–57. On farm beginnings, see Joseph Schafer, "The Yankee and the Teuton in Wisconsin," *WMH* (1922–23) 6:125–45, 261–79, 386–402, and 7:3–19, 148–71; Schafer, *Four Wisconsin Counties*; Schafer, *History of Agriculture*; John Thompson, *The Rise and Decline of the Wheat Growing Industry in Wisconsin* (Madison: University of Wisconsin Bulletin, 1909); Hibbard, *History of Agriculture in Dane County*.

Early roads and transportation are covered in H. E. Cole, "The Old Military Road," *WMH* (1925) 9:47–62; Vogeler, *Wisconsin: A Geography*; Thwaites, *Wisconsin: Americanization of a French Settlement*; Balthasar H. Meyer, "A History of Early Railroad Legislation in Wisconsin," *WHC* 14:206–300.

Chapter 8

The Unonius memoirs are published as *A Pioneer in Northwest America: 1841–1858—The Memoirs of Gustaf Unonius* (Minneapolis: University of Minnesota Press, 1950). The community Unonius helped form is treated in Mabel Hansen, "The Swedish Settlement at Pine Lake," *WMH* (1924) 8:38–51.

Wisconsin's ethnic mix is covered in Fred Holmes, *Old World Wisconsin* (Eau Claire, Wis.: E. M. Hale, 1944); La Vern Rippley, *The Immigrant Experience in Wisconsin* (Boston: Twayne, 1985); and Mark Wyman, *Immigrants in the Valley: Irish, Germans, and Americans in the Upper Mississippi Country, 1830–1860* (Chicago: Nelson-Hall, 1984). The architectural legacy of immigration is exmined in Allen G. Noble, ed., *To Build in a New Land: Ethnic Landscapes in North America* (Baltimore: Johns Hopkins University Press, 1992); see especially chapters on Wisconsin's Belgians (by William G. Laatsch and Charles F. Calkins), Norwegians (by William H. Tishler), and Finns (by Matti Enn Kaups).

On immigrants from the British Isles: Louis Copeland, "The Cornish in Southwest Wisconsin," *WHC* 14:301–34; Brian Birch, "From Southwest England to Southwest Wisconsin: Devonshire

Hollow, Lafayette County," *WMH* (Winter 1985–86) 69:129–49; John Muir, *The Story of My Boyhood and Youth* (Madison: University of Wisconsin Press, 1965); Alan Conway, ed., *The Welsh in America: Letters from the Immigrants* (Minneapolis: University of Minnesota Press, 1961); Schafer, *Wisconsin Lead Region*, 162–83.

On Norwegians: Consul General Adam Løvenskjold, "An Account of the Norwegian Settlers in North America" [1847], *WMH* (1924) 8:77–88; Søren Bache, *A Chronicle of Old Muskego: The Diary of Søren Bache, 1839–1847* (Northfield, Minn.: Norwegian-American Historical Association, 1951); Jon Gjerde, *From Peasants to Farmers: The Migration from Balestrand, Norway, to the Upper Middle West* (New York: Cambridge, 1985); Jane Marie Pederson, *Between Memory and Reality: Family and Community in Rural Wisconsin, 1870–1970* (Madison: University of Wisconsin Press, 1992). On Danes: William Orr, "Rasmus Sorensen and the Beginnings of Danish Settlement in Wisconsin," *WMH* (Spring 1982) 65:195–210; Thomas Christensen, "Danish Settlement in Wisconsin," *WMH* (1928) 12:19–40. On Germans: Schafer, "Yankee and Teuton," and *Wisconsin Lead Region;* Louis Frank, comp., *German-American Pioneers in Wisconsin and Michigan: The Frank-Kerler Letters, 1849–1864* (Milwaukee: Milwaukee County Historical Society, 1971); Kate A. Everest, "How Wisconsin Came by Its Large German Element," *WHC* 12:299–334; Kate E. Levi, "Geographical Origin of German Immigration to Wisconsin," *WHC* 14:341–93. On Swiss: John Luchsinger, "The Swiss Colony of New Glarus," *WHC* 8:411–49; Luchsinger, "The Planting of the Swiss Colony at New Glarus, Wis.," *WHC* 12:335–82; J. Jacob Tschudy, "Additional Notes on New Glarus," *WHC* 8:440–45; Jane Eiseley and William H. Tishler, "The Honey Creek Swiss Settlement in Sauk County: An Expression of Cultural Norms in Rural Wisconsin," *WMH* (Autumn 1989) 73:3–20.

On Belgians and Poles: Xavier Martin, "The Belgians of Northeast Wisconsin," *WHC* 13:375–96; Michael Goc, *Native Realm: The Polish-American Community of Portage County, 1857–1992* (Stevens Point, Wis.: Worzalla, 1992); Rev. Leo Rummel, *His-*

tory of the Catholic Church in Wisconsin (Madison: Knights of Columbus, 1976). On Icelanders: Harry White, "The Icelanders on Washington Island," *WHC* 14:335–40.

Recruitment attempts are detailed in Rippley, *Immigrant Experience in Wisconsin*, and Strong, *History of the Territory of Wisconsin*. Trempeleau County's immigrant–native born relations were studied by Merle Curti, *The Making of an American Community: A Case Study of Democracy in a Frontier County* (Stanford, Calif.: Stanford University Press, 1959).

United States maps showing the frontier lines from 1840 to 1890 are reprinted in U.S. Department of the Interior, 11th Census (1890), *Report on Population of the United States . . . Part I* (Washington: GPO, 1895).

John Solon's unpublished "Reminiscences" of 1911 are in the UW–River Falls ARC; William Lalor's 1868 letter is in the Arnold Schrier Irish emigrant collection, University of Cincinnati. Comments on the Swedish settlements appear in George Brown, ed., "A Swedish Traveler in Early Wisconsin: The Observations of Fredrika Bremer," *WMH* (September 1978) 61:300–18.

New England missionary efforts are best followed through *The Home Missionary*, magazine of the American Home Missionary Society (AHMS), and copies of the AHMS Letters from Wisconsin in SHSW. The AHMS' work is examined in Colin Goodykoontz, *Home Missions on the American Frontier: With Particular Reference to the American Home Missionary Society* (New York: Octagon, 1939, 1971); Charles Kennedy, "The Congregationalists and the Presbyterians on the Wisconsin Frontier" (University of Wisconsin Ph.D. dissertation, 1940); William Warren Sweet, ed., *Religion on the American Frontier—1783–1850*: vol. 3, *The Congregationalists* (Chicago: University of Chicago Press, 1939); and Jeremiah Porter, "First Home Missionary Labors in What Is Now the State of Wisconsin" (Prairie du Chien, 1868, unpublished), in SHSW. Specific AHMS-member churches are examined in Ethel S. Cady, *A History of Union Congregational Church 1836–1955* (Green Bay: Union Congregational Church, 1955); and records of the First Presbyterian Church of Green Bay for 1835–1876, in UW–Green Bay ARC.

On Methodism: Rev. P. S. Bennett, *History of Methodism in*

Wisconsin (Cincinnati: Cranston & Stowe, 1890); Elizabeth Wilson, *Methodism in Eastern Wisconsin* (Milwaukee: Wisconsin Conference of Methodist Episcopal Church, 1938); Sweet, *Religion on the American Frontier*: vol. 4, *The Methodists* (Chicago: University of Chicago Press, 1946); and Rev. C. Wesley Boag, "One Hundred Years of Methodism in Green Bay," *Green Bay Historical Bulletin* (September–October 1926) 2:3–15. On Baptists: Sweet, *Religion on the American Frontier—The Baptists, 1784–1830* (New York: Henry Holt, 1931).

Roman Catholic activities are chronicled through Father Samuel Mazzuchelli's *Memoirs . . .* (Milan, Italy: 1844; trans. and reprint, 1967); Rummel, *History of the Catholic Church in Wisconsin*, and several broad studies of Catholic missionary activities that include material pertaining to Wisconsin: Gerald Shaughnessy, *Has the Immigrant Kept the Faith? A Study of Immigration and Catholic Growth in the United States 1790–1920* (New York: Arno, 1925, 1969); Rev. Theodore Roemer, *The Ludwig-Missionsverein and the Church in the United States (1838–1918)* (Washington: Catholic University, 1933); Edward John Hickey, *The Society for the Propagation of the Faith—Its Foundation, Organization and Success (1822–1922)* (Washington: Catholic University, 1922). The letters of Father T. J. Van den Broek [trans. Gerlof Homan] are in the William de Haan Papers, SHSW.

European Protestant denominations: John Philipp Koehler, *The History of the Wisconsin Synod* (St. Cloud, Minn.: Protestant Conference, 1970); Carl Schneider, *The German Church on the American Frontier: A Study in the Rise of Religion among the Germans of the West* (St. Louis: Eden, 1939). The 1848 German Methodist complaint is in John Konrad Meidenbauer papers, SHSW. Scandinavian religious controversies are treated in Robert Ostergren, *A Community Transplanted: The Trans-Atlantic Experience of a Swedish Immigrant Settlement in the Upper Middle West, 1835–1915* (Madison: University of Wisconsin Press, 1988); Bache, *Chronicle of Old Muskego;* and a Norwegian minister's diary, *A Pioneer Churchman: J.W.C. Dietrichson in Wisconsin 1844–1850* (New York: Norwegian-American Historical Association, 1973).

Conflicts and controversies between church groups are covered in various degrees in the works cited above; also see Sister M. Hedwigis Overmoehle, "The Anti-Clerical Activities of the Forty-Eighters in Wisconsin 1848–60" (St. Louis University dissertation, 1941). The 1858 dispute in Barton is reported in *Home Missionary* (February 1859) 31:237. Wood River Baptist Church records are in the UW–River Falls ARC.

Chapter 9

The Winnebago removal story is drawn from Moses Paquette, "The Wisconsin Winnebagoes," *WHC* 12:407–18; *Badger State Banner* (Black River Falls), Jan. 4, 1873–July 17, 1875, and Jacob Spaulding's obituaries in issues of Jan. 29 and Feb. 5, 1876; and Current, *Civil War Era*, 558–59. On Winnebagoes, also see two later Indian accounts: William L. Clark and Walker D. Wyman, comps., *Charles Round Low Cloud: Voice of the Winnebago* (River Falls: University of Wisconsin–River Falls Press, 1973), and Nancy Oestreich Lurie, ed., *Mountain Wolf Woman, Sister of Crashing Thunder: The Autobiography of a Winnebago Indian* (Ann Arbor: University of Michigan Press, 1961).

See individual tribal studies for removal information, as well as the chapters on Wisconsin tribes in Trigger, ed., v. 15, *Northeast.* Also, Prucha, *Great Father*; U.S. Commissioner of Indian Affairs *Reports* for 1870–89 (Washington: GPO, each published the year after date of report); Lurie, *Wisconsin Indians;* and Holzhueter, "Wisconsin's Indians since 1634."

On the controversial attempts to move the Chippewas in 1850–51, see James Clifton, "Wisconsin Death March: Explaining the Extremes in Old Northwest Indian Removal," *Transactions of the Wisconsin Academy of Sciences, Arts and Letters* (1987) 75:1–39. Also, Ronald Satz, "Chippewa Treaty Rights: The Reserved Rights of Wisconsin's Chippewa Indians in Historical Perspective," *Transactions of the Wisconsin Academy* (1991) 79:1–251. Menominee removal attempts are covered in Stephen J. Herzberg, "The Menominee Indians: From Treaty to Termination," *WMH* (Summer 1977) 60:267–329.

Life on reservations is covered in the individual tribal histories; the yearly Commissioner of Indians Affairs *Reports* provide agents' reports on conditions of their charges. Also see John Nelson Davidson, "Missions on Chequamegon Bay," *WHC* 12:434–52. Local newspapers are also abundant sources on the topic, including the Bayfield *Press* and Ashland *Press*, for the northern Chippewas (the Ashland "half-breed" incident is from the Ashland *Press* [May 24, 1873, 3]), and the *Shawano County Journal* (Shawano), for the Menominees. On schooling, see the Commissioner of Indian Affairs *Reports* and Suzanne E. Moranian, "Ethnocide in the Schoolhouse: Missionary Efforts to Educate Indian Youth in Pre-Reservation Wisconsin," *WMH* (Summer 1981) 64:243–60.

In addition to coverage in local newspapers, civilizing the Indians is discussed in Commissioner of Indian Affairs *Reports* and individual tribal sources listed above; in Bieder, *Native American Communities in Wisconsin;* and Richard Morse, "The Chippewas of Lake Superior," *WHC* 3:338–69. A broader view is shown in Francis Paul Prucha, ed., *Americanizing the American Indians: Writings by the 'Friends of the Indian' 1880–1900* (Cambridge: Harvard University Press, 1973).

Sources on the Dream Dance include the studies of the Menominees and Chippewa; see also Robert Ritzenthaler, "Southwestern Chippewa"; James Slotkin, *The Menomini Powwow* (Milwaukee: Milwaukee Public Museum, 1957); S. A. Barrett, "The Dream Dance of the Chippewa and Menominee Indians of Northern Wisconsin," *Bulletin of the Public Museum of the City of Milwaukee* (1911) 1:351–407; Walter J. Hoffman, "The Menomini Indians," U.S. Bureau of Ethnology, *14th Annual Report, 1891–93* (Washington: GPO, 1896), 157–61. The St. Paul *Pioneer Press* reports were reprinted in the *Burnett County Sentinel*, June–August 1878; also see Ashland *Press*, June 29, 1878.

The Menominees' fight to save their timber is presented in the Menominee tribal histories noted above, the *Shawano County Journal*, and Duncan Harkin, "The Significance of the Menominee Experience in the Forest History of the Great Lakes Region," in Susan Flader, ed., *The Great Lakes Forest: An Environmental and Social History* (Minneapolis: University of Minnesota Press, 1983).

Chapter 10

Information on lumbering in Wisconsin is drawn heavily from Robert Fries, *Empire in Pine: The Story of Lumbering in Wisconsin 1830–1900* (Madison: SHSW, 1951); Dale Arthur Peterson, "Lumbering on the Chippewa: The Eau Claire Area, 1845–1885" (University of Minnesota Ph.D. dissertation, 1970); William Rector, *Log Transportation in the Lake States Lumber Industry 1840–1918* (Glendale, Calif.: Arthur H. Clark, 1953); A. R. Reynolds, *The Daniel Shaw Lumber Company: A Case Study of the Wisconsin Lumbering Frontier* (New York: New York University Press, 1957); Charles E. Twining, *Downriver: Orrin H. Ingram and the Empire Lumber Company* (Madison: SHSW, 1975); Ralph Hidy, Frank Ernest Hill, and Allan Nevins, *Timber and Men: The Weyerhaeuser Story* (New York: Macmillan, 1963); and Frederick Kohlmeyer, *Timber Roots: The Laird, Norton Story, 1855–1905* (Winona, Minn.: Winona County Historical Society, 1972).

C. H. Cooke's trip on the Chippewa is recorded in his diary, which is included in pages 43–55 of the unpublished, undated manuscript by William Bartlett, in the Bartlett Papers, Box 5, Folder 3, University of Wisconsin–Eau Claire ARC. Broad changes in the industry are described in Charles Twining, "Plunder and Progress: The Lumbering Industry in Perspective," *WMH* (Winter 1963–64) 47:116–24; also see Dopp, "Geographical Influences in the Development of Wisconsin," and Thwaites, *Wisconsin: The Americanization of a French Settlement*, 281–83. Statistics from the end of the logging frontier are taken from above volumes and two state reports: Alfred Chittenden and Harry Irion, *The Taxation of Forest Lands in Wisconsin* (Madison: Wisconsin State Board of Forestry, 1911); and *Report of the State Forester, 1907–8* (Madison: included in *Governor's Message and Accompanying Documents, 1907–8*, vol. 44[7]). Compare with an earlier, ignored warning: J. A. Lapham, J. G. Knapp, and H. Crocker, *Report on the Disastrous Effects of the Destruction of Forest Trees, Now Going on so Rapidly in the State of Wisconsin* (Madison: Atwood & Rublee, State Printers, 1867).

Additional sources on early logging include John Vogel, "The Round Lake Logging Dam: A Survivor of Wisconsin's Log-Driving Days," *WMH* (Spring 1983) 66:171–91; Augustus Easton, ed., *History of the Saint Croix Valley* (Chicago: H. C. Cooper, Jr., 1909), 1:18–22, 2:974–77; *History of La Crosse County*, 187–88; Frederick Merk, *Economic History of Wisconsin during the Civil War Decade* (Madison: SHSW, 1916, 1971); Frederick Kohlmeyer, "Northern Pine Lumbermen: A Study in Origins and Migrations," *Journal of Economic History* (December 1956) 16:529–38; and Richard Current, *Pine Logs and Politics: A Life of Philetus Sawyer 1816–1900* (Madison: SHSW, 1950). On Chequamegon Bay lumbering, see Charles Twining, "The Apostle Islands and the Lumbering Frontier," *WMH* (Spring 1983; reprint by Apostle Islands National Lakeshore) 1–16.

On timberland acquisition, see Raleigh Barlowe, "Changing Land Use and Policies: The Lake States," in Flader, *The Great Lakes Forest*, 156–76; and James Hurst, *Law and Economic Growth: The Legal History of the Lumber Industry in Wisconsin: 1836–1915* (Cambridge: Belknap Press, 1964). James Holden's account is in Bartlett ms., 30–31.

Louie Blanchard's story is told in Walker D. Wyman, ed., with Lee Prentice, *The Lumberjack Frontier: The Life of a Logger in the Early Days on the Chippeway* (Lincoln: University of Nebraska Press, 1969). Other sources on logging camp operations include Eldon Marple, *The Visitor Who Came to Stay: Legacy of the Hayward Area* (Hayward, Wis.,: County Print Shop, 1971); Goc, *Native Realm*; Tim Pfaff, *Settlement & Survival: Building Towns in the Chippewa Valley, 1850–1925* (Eau Claire: Chippewa Valley Museum Press, 1994); George Engberg, "Lumber and Labor in the Lake States," *Minnesota History* (March 1959) 36:153–66; *Chippewa Union & Times; Wisconsin Pinery; Shawano County Journal; Badger State Banner.*

The Wisconsin Supreme Court case is Stevens Point Boom Company *v.* Reilly and another, 44 *Wisconsin Reports* 295, 302. Additional information on log drives is in William G. Rector, "From Woods to Sawmill: Transportation Problems in Logging," *Agricultural History* (October 1949) 23:239–44; and R. K. Boyd, "Up and Down the Chippewa River," *WMH* (March 1931) 14:243–61. The account of breaking up a log jam appeared in the Oshkosh *Northwestern*, May 18, 1882, reprinted in Fries,

Empire in Pine, 46–47. The Norwegian pastor's letter is in Theodore Blegen, *Land of Their Choice: The Immigrants Write Home* (Minneapolis: University of Minnesota Press, 1955), 377–78.

On improving rivers and making log rafts, also see *Daily Journal 1882–1890 Little Falls Dam (Holcombe)* (Chippewa Falls: Chippewa County Historical Society, n.d.); Vogel, "Round Lake Logging Dam," 176–80; Walter Blair, *A Raft Pilot's Log . . .* (Cleveland: Arthur H. Clark, 1929).

The Beef Slough controversy and Weyerhaeuser's rise are drawn from Peterson, "Lumbering on the Chippewa," 296–335; Bartlett ms., 83–86; Hidy, *Timber and Men*, chaps. 1–6, esp. 44–66; Twining, *Downriver*, 106–14; Fries, *Empire in Pine*, Ch. 9; Kohlmeyer, *Timber Roots*, 81–112; Agnes Larson, *History of the White Pine Industry in Minnesota* (Minneapolis: University of Minnesota Press, 1949), 125–53. See interview with Weyerhaeuser in *Chippewa Herald*, Nov. 4, 1887, 5.

Dewitt C. Clark's letter is included in Bartlett ms., 27–30; the Winona reporter's 1868 comment on French and Canadians was reprinted in *Chippewa Union & Times* (July 11, 1868), 1.

Information on John Dietz is taken from Malcolm Rosholt, *The Battle of Cameron Dam* (Rosholt, Wis.: by the author, 1974); James Kates, "A 'Square Deal' for a 'Primitive Rebel': Alfred E. Roese and the Battle of Cameron Dam, 1904–1910," *WMH* (Winter 1995–96), 83–108. On the rise of cut-over farms, see Vernon Carstensen, *Farms or Forests: Evolution of a State Land Policy for Northern Wisconsin 1850–1932* (Madison: University of Wisconsin College of Agriculture, 1958); Arlan Helgeson, *Farms in the Cutover: Agricultural Settlement in Northern Wisconsin* (Madison: SHSW, 1962); and Robert Gough, "Richard T. Ely and the Development of the Wisconsin Cutover," *WMH* (Autumn 1991) 75:3–38.

The decline of lumbering and increase in forest fires are described in contemporary press acounts and John T. Curtis, *The Vegetation of Wisconsin: An Ordination of Plant Communities* (Madison: University of Wisconsin Press, 1959); Kris Beisser Olson, comp., "The Great Fire of October 1871: A Nation Responds," *Voyageur* (Winter/Spring 1997) 13:10–17; T. V. Olson, *The Rhinelander Story* (Rhinelander, Wis.: Vocational School,

n.d.). On their impact, see Aldo Leopold, *A Sand County Alma-*
nac (New York: Ballantine, 1949, 1966); and Clifford E. and
Isabel F. Ahlgren, "The Human Impact on Northern Forest Eco-
systems," in Flader, *Great Lakes Forest*, 33–51.

Chapter 11

On the passenger pigeon, see A. W. Schorger, *The Passenger Pigeon* (Madison: University of Wisconsin Press, 1955); Schorger, "Extinct and Endangered Mammals and Birds of the Upper Great Lakes Region," *Transactions of the Wisconsin Academy* (1942) 34:23–44; Muir, *Story of My Boyhood and Youth*, 128–31; *Badger State Banner* (April 29 and May 13, 1871); *Wisconsin Pinery* (May 18, 1871).

On other animals, see Schorger, "Extinct and Endangered Mammals," and "The White-Tailed Deer in Early Wisconsin," *Transactions of the Wisconsin Academy* (1953) 42:197–247; Hartley H. T. Jackson, *Mammals of Wisconsin* (Madison: University of Wisconsin Press, 1961); Otis Bersing, *A Century of Wisconsin Deer* (Madison: Wisconsin Conservation Department, 1956, 1966); Richard Thiel, *The Timber Wolf in Wisconsin: The Death and Life of a Majestic Predator* (Madison: University of Wisconsin Press, 1993); Aldo Leopold, "The Distribution of Wisconsin Hares," *Transactions of the Wisconsin Academy* (1945) 37:1–14; D. John O'Donnell, "A History of Fishing in the Brule River," *Transactions of the Wisconsin Academy* (1944) 36:19–31; Apostle Islands National Lakeshore, *Special History Study: Family-Managed Commercial Fishing in the Apostle Islands during the 20th Century, with Background Information on Commercial Fishing on Lake Superior* (Washington: National Park Service, 1985).

On early beginnings of forest conservation, see F. G. Wilson, "Past Planning and Present Realities," Wisconsin Silver Anniversary Forestry Conference *Proceedings . . . 1953* (Evansville, Wis.: published by the conference, 1954), 73–74; F. G. Wilson, *E. M. Griffith and the Early Story of Wisconsin Forestry (1903–1915)* (Madison: Wisconsin Department of Natural Resources, 1982).

Hamlin Garland's writings used here include *Trail-Makers of the Middle Border* (New York: Macmillan, 1926); *Crumbling Idols* (Chicago: Stone and Kimball, 1894); *Son of the Middle Border* (New York: Macmillan, 1917); *Jason Edwards, An Average Man* (New York: Appleton, 1897); and *Main-Travelled Roads* (New York: New American Library, 1891, 1962).

Other information on Garland is drawn from Charles Silet, Robert Welch, and Richard Boudreau, eds., *The Critical Reception of Hamlin Garland, 1891–1978* (Troy, N.Y.: Whitston, 1985); James Nagel, *Critical Essays on Hamlin Garland* (Boston: G. K. Hall, 1982); and Jean Holloway, *Hamlin Garland: A Biography* (Austin: University of Texas Press, 1960).

Frederick Jackson Turner's writings have been published in a variety of editions. His works used here include *The Frontier in American History* (New York: Henry Holt, 1920), which includes "The Significance of the Frontier in American History"; "The Winning of the West," *The Dial* (August 1889) 10:71–73; *The Character and Influence of the Indian Trade in Wisconsin: A Study of the Trading Post as an Institution* (New York: Burt Franklin, 1891, 1970); and Martin Ridge, ed., *History, Frontier, and Section: Three Essays by Frederick Jackson Turner* (Albuquerque: University of New Mexico Press, 1993). Evaluations of his work are numerous; I have consulted those collected in George Rogers Taylor, ed., *The Turner Thesis Concerning the Role of the Frontier in American History* (Lexington, Mass.: Heath, 1949, 1972); Wilbur Jacobs, ed., *The Historical World of Frederick Jackson Turner: With Selections from His Correspondence* (New Haven: Yale University Press, 1968); Ray Allen Billington, *Frederick Jackson Turner: Historian, Scholar, Teacher* (New York: Oxford, 1973); Billington, *The Genesis of the Frontier Thesis: A Study in Historical Creativity* (San Marino, Calif.: Huntington Library, 1971); O. Lawrence Burnette, Jr., comp., *Wisconsin Witness to Frederick Jackson Turner: A Collection of Essays on the Historian and the Thesis* (Madison: SHSW, 1961); and Ridge, "The Life of an Idea: The Significance of Frederick Jackson Turner's Frontier Thesis," *Montana: The Magazine of Western History* (Winter 1991) 41:2–13.

His father's newspaper, the *Wisconsin State Register* (Portage), is a good source on Turner's home environment. The railroad journeys are reported in the issues of Oct. 28, 1876, 2; June 9, 1877, 2; and July 28, 1877, 2.

The Trempealeau County study was directed by Merle Curti: *The Making of an American Community: A Case Study of Democracy in a Frontier County.* Sources of Wisconsin's names are examined in Virgil Vogel, *Indian Names on Wisconsin's Map* (Madison: University of Wisconsin Press, 1991). The Ashland *Press* account of the voyageurs' train ride appeared on July 11, 1874, 3. The *Engineering and Mining Journal* toasted the new century (Jan. 13, 1900) 69:42. Leopold's most famous essays are collected in *A Sand County Almanac;* his 1947 dedication speech "On a Monument to the Pigeon" is 116–19.

Index

Alcohol: French policy on, 57; in fur trade, 104, 106, 109–11; and immigrants, 210–11; and Indian violence, 57; Menominees seek, 86–87; priest attacks, 56–57; Shawnee prophet and, 121; at treaty payments, 168–69; U.S. bans, 118

Algonquians, 2, 8, 10. *See* individual tribes

Allouez, Fr. C.J., 6, 15, 39, 48, 51, 55; at Chequamegon Bay, 1–2, 54; and Fox complaints, 79; notes canoe use, 61; speech to Indians, 64–65

American Fur Co., 101, 135, 172–73

American Home Missionary Society, 202–3; criticizes immigrants, 209–10; leads schools, 212–13. *See also* Congregationalists; Presbyterians

American Revolution, 91–96

Americans: arrivals of, 116–20; and Indan lands, 147; and *Métis*, 272–73

André, Fr. Louis, 47, 55

Animals: decline of, 172–73, 282–83; prehistoric, 24–25; protection of, 283–85

Ashland, 231, 243; fires at, 276

Ashland County, 271

Astor, John J., 101, 135

Atkinson, Gen. Henry, 148, 149

Atwater, Caleb, 133

Aztalan, 18–20

Bad Axe, Battle of, 152–53

Bad River Reservation, 232–33; allotments on, 236; traditions in, 237; women on, 242–43

Badgers: as name, 139

Baird, Elizabeth T., 63–64, 148

Baptists, 203, 213

Baraga, Fr. Frederick, 228–29

Baraboo, 190

Barton, 210

Bayfield, 175, 231, 251; citizenship debate at, 235; fires at, 276

Beaumont, Dr. William, 128

Beaver: decline of, 98–99, 282; profits in, 40–41. *See also* Fur trade

Beecher, Rev., Lyman, 201

Beef Slough War, 247, 267–68

Belgians, 195, 196, 197

Berlin, 183

Black Hawk: background of, 147–48; in Black Hawk War, 149–55; at British evacuation, 125; in captivity, 155

Black Hawk War, 145–56

Black River: drives on, 261; improvement of, 264; logging on, 256; logging trespass on, 252

Black River Falls, 220; Indians' produce in, 241; and passenger pigeons, 280–81; sawmills, 250, 251; and Winnebago removal, 215–20

Blacks, 113–14

Blanchard, Louis: and clearcutting, 255; describes camps, 254, 258–59; at drive's end, 263; and end of era, 278

Bloomer, 277

Blue Mounds, 140, 150, 152

Bohemians, 198

Boilvin, Nicolas, 118–19

Bois Brule River, 63

Bremer, Frederika, 196–97

Britain: U.S. opposes traders of, 118–19, 120. *See also* British

British: in American Revolution, 94–95; and Black Hawk, 148; and blacks, 113; early policies of, 85–88, 89; evacuate Prairie du Chien (1815), 124–26; in French and Indian War, 83–85; gifts for women, 111–12; Indians support (1812), 121–26; Iroquois oppose (1763), 87–88; occupy Wisconsin, 85–

87; oppose U.S. traders, 97; payments to supporters, 95–96; policies opposed, 89–90; Proclamation of 1763, 89, 92; retain Indian ties, 117–18; refuse to evacuate posts, 97–98; seek buffer state, 117–18, 123–24; trade with Iroquois, 79

Brothertown Indians, 164. *See also* New York Indians

Brûlé, Etienne, 8–10

Brunet, Jean, 272

Brunson, Alfred, 213; defends *Métis*, 166

Buffalo, 282

Buffalo, Chief, 225

Bulger, Capt. Alfred, 124–25

Burnett County, 189, 213, 271; and dream dance, 239–41; and railroad, 271

Cadotte, Jean Baptiste, 75–76, 100

Cadotte, Jean Baptiste, Jr., 100, 101

Cadotte, Michel, 100–1, 108

Cahokia, 19, 94

Cameron Dam, Battle of, 274–75

Canoes: Americans and, 97; French use, 59–64; fur traders and, 62–64; Indians and, 61; manufacture of, 60–62; moose skins for, 103; routes of, 60, 62–63; types of, 61–62

Caribou, 282

Carver, Jonathan: and Chippewa-Sioux warfare, 77; sees female chief, 50, 112; travels of, 90–91

Cartier, Jacques, 4–5

Cass, Gov. Lewis, 132, 143, 165

Champlain, Samuel de, 7–12; and canoes, 59–60; and torture, 50

Chequamegon Bay, 22, 237; and dream dance, 240; fishing in, 283; log rafts on, 265; lumbering around, 251; missionaries at, 1–3; old voyageurs meet, 296; reservations on, 226–29; sawdust dumped in, 275; Turner's visit to, 289–90. *See also* Ashland, Bayfield, La Pointe, Bad River Reservation, Red Cliff Reservation

Chicago, 100, 118; black trader at, 113; British seize (1812), 122; railroads, 183; treaty of 1833, 160; Wisconsin lumber in, 251

Chippewa Falls, 100; and Beef Slough War, 267–68; land values, 158; and logging, 263

"Chippewa Pool." *See* Chippewa River Logging Co.

Chippewa River, 246–47, 269, 275, 277; drives on, 261; improvement of, 264; and logging, 249, 250, 251; logging accidents, 258; pinelands on, 249. *See*

also Beef Slough War; Logging drives; Logging camps

Chippewa River Improvement Co., 268

Chippewa River Logging Co., 269

Chippewa-Sioux warfare, 114–16

Chippewas, 2, 15, 39, 112, 230; in American Revolution, 92, 93–95; attack black traders, 114; battle Foxes, 80; battle Sioux, 76–78; Carver visits, 91; and churches, 229; citizenship of, 234–35; in Civil War, 233–34; and civilizing attempts, 232–33; described, 34; and dream dance, 238–41; employment of, 243; and farming, 241–42; and gifts, 72, 86; housing of, 48; influence on names, 294; and *métis*, 165; and Midewiwin Society, 237; movements of, 42–44, 74; population (1768) of, 91–92; and removal attempts, 223–26; reservations for, 225–26; and schooling, 229; and sports, 231; support Pontiac, 88; support Tecumseh, 121; and traders, 104–9; treaties (1679 and 1695), 43–44; (1829), 145; (1837 and 1842), 161–63, 223, 250; (1854), 225–26; 236; and wild rice, 45, 47. *See also* Bad River, Lac Courte Oreilles, and Red Cliff reservations

Churches: adapt to frontier, 204–8; diversity of, 212; friction between, 207–11; and reformers, 209–11; and reservations, 228–29. *See also* Missionaries; Religion; and individual denominations

Circuit riders, 205–6

Citizenship of Indians, 233–36

Civil War, 233–34

Claims associations, 176–77, 198

Clam River, 262

Clark, George Rogers: meets with Indians, 93–94; helps repel British, 95

Clark, Gov. William, 122–23

Colonial settlements, 188

Columbia County, 188

Columbus, 182

Congregationalists, 202–3, 204, 229. *See also* American Home Missionary Society

Corn: and Hopewellians, 27; prehistoric spread of, 32, 36; unsuitable for north, 34. *See also* Food

Cornell University lands, 252

Cornish, 190; as miners, 140; as Methodists, 203

Coureurs de bois, 57–58, 67, 71

Cooke, C. H., 246–47, 268, 272

Copper, 7, 25–27

Cumberland, 276

Curot, Michael: life as trader, 106, 110, 111, 112, 115–16
Cut-Nose, 167–68

Dablon, Fr. Claude, 6
Dakota tribe: *See* Sioux
Danbury, 104, 105n
Dane County, 181, 182, 188
Danes, 188, 189, 195
Dawes Act (1887), 237
Deansburg, 164
Deer: decline of, 282, 284; protection of, 283–84
Delafield, 190
De Neveu, Gustave, 168–70
De Pere, 55, 69, 250
Desnoyers, Francis, 167–68
Detroit, 67, 85, 88, 95, 98, 117, 118, 122, 130; battle at (1712), 79–80
Dickson, Robert, 134–35
Dietz, John, 274–75
Disciples of Christ, 203
Diseases, 75–76
Dodge, Henry: background, 140–41; in Black Hawk War, 150–51, 153, 155; in Red Bird War, 143–44; and squatters' rights, 178; and Treaty of 1836, 161; and Winnebago lands, 145–46
Dodge County, 179, 188, 190
Dodgeville, 140, 145
Doty, James, 134, 166
Douglas County, 249–50, 276
Dousman, Hercules and Jane, 174
Dream dance, 237–41
Dreams: importance to Indians of, 49
DuBuisson, Charles Regnault, Sieur, 80
Dubuque, Julien, 136
Dubuque mines, 95
Dulhut (Duluth), Daniel Greysolon, 41, 43
du Sable, Jean Baptiste Point, 113
Dutch, 189, 195

Eagle River, 273
Eau Claire, 176; and Beef Slough War, 267–68; rafts from, 265; sawmills, 251, 277; workers protest, 273
Eau Claire County, 271
Eau Claire Lumber Co., 256
Eau Claire River, 110, 247
Effigy Mounds, 29–30
Elk *v.* Wilkins (1884), 235–36
Embarrass River, 262
English immigrants, 188, 189, 190, 212
English. *See* British
Erie Canal, 130
Exploration: European beginnings of, 3–7; French routes for, 2, 14–15; fur trade propels, 41

Factory system, 118–19, 135
Fallen Timbers, Battle of (1794), 117
Farming: by Indians, 228, 241–42; contrasting American and French, 180–81
Fever River. *See* Mining region
Fillmore, President Millard: and Chippewas, 225; and Menominees, 221–22
Finns, 189
Fires, forest, 275–77
Fishing: by American Fur Co., 173; commercial, 283; by Indian women, 47, 49; by Indians, 47; regulation of, 284
Flambeau River: protest on, 273; Shaw farm on, 263
Folle Avoine (post), 100, 104–6. *See also* Yellow River
Fond du Lac, 158, 251
Food: shortages of, 129–30; types used by tribes, 44–48. *See also* Indians, prehistoric; and specific foods
Forests, 24, 249
Forsyth, Thomas, 137
Fort Edward Augustus, 86, 88
Fort Howard, 132
Fort Mackinac, 92; seized by British (1812), 122; medical research at, 128. *See also* Michilimackinac
Fort Madison, 118
Fort Shelby, 123
Fort Snelling, 120
Fort Winnebago, 128, 151, 152
Fox River, 63–64, 195; travel on, 128
Fox-Wisconsin Canal, 190
Fox-Wisconsin portage, 55–56
Foxes (tribe), 2, 15, 39, 61, 74, 86, 119, 136; in American Revolution, 93–95, 96; attack Winnebagos, 51; background of, 34, 42; flight of, 81–82; harry travelers, 79; join Sacs, 82; population (1768) of, 92; and warfare, 78–82. *See also* Sacs and Foxes
France: builds forts, 69–70; claims of, 39, 41, 83; trade controls of, 67, 69–70. *See also* French; New France
French, 189; adapt to Indian ways, 59, 70–71; and disease, 75; and canoes, 62; and Foxes, 79, 80–82; at Green Bay and Prairie du Chien, 132–34; influence on names, 294; and lead mining, 136; persist in fur trade, 100. *See also* France; New France
French & Giddings Co., 268
French and Indian War, 83–85
French-Canadians. *See* French; *Métis*
Frontier: close of, 297; definitions of, 3; impact of, 16–17, 282–85, 296–97; Turner theory on, 291–93

Fur trade: beginnings, 5, 11, 40–42; British in, 66, 67, 89; British control of, 97–120 passim; canoes in, 62–64; changes in, 66–67; *coureurs de bois* in, 57–58; declines, 135; European goods in, 53–54; foreigners barred in, 135; French in, 40–41, 53–54, 57–59, 64, 70; gifts in, 72–73; impact on animals, 172–73; and War of 1812, 123; and Indians, 42–44, 53; "jack-knife" posts in, 99–100; lives of traders in, 102–9; new companies in, 101; North West–X Y competition in, 101, 104–6, 108–9; post locations, 294n; production, 98–99, 173; profits, 40–41, 70; store's records of, 167–68; treaty payments and, 166–67; U.S. regulates, 134–35; women in, 111–13

Galena, Ill., 144
Garland, Hamlin: criticism of, 287–88; early years, 285–86; and frontier, 286–87, 293; writings of, 286–88
General Co. of Lake Superior and the South, 101
Germans, 188, 189, 192–93, 196, 197
Gifts, British policies on, 85–88; by French, 50; French policies on, 87; by traders, 103–4, 106–8; U.S. factories and, 119
Ginseng, 243
Glaciers, 21–24
Gordon, 110
Gorrell, Lt. James, 85–87
Grand Portage, 104
Gratiot's Grove, 140
Great Britain. *See* Britain; British
Great Lakes: fishing in, 46; glaciers' impact on, 21. *See also* individual lakes
Green Bay, 22, 134, 195, 237–38; British at, 85–86, 122; Carver visits, 90; Catholics in, 201; church discipline in, 213; contrasts in, 128; and *coureurs de bois*, 58–59; dependence on shipping, 129–30; diseases at, 75; Fort Howard built at (1816), 132; in French and Indian War, 84; French fort at, 69; French land claims at, 173–74; and fur trade, 70, 98–99, 100, 102; growth of, 158; Indians pass through, 172; and Indian wars, 77–78; land system in, 132, 159–60, 175; logging at, 250; Marquette and Jolliet at, 55; merchant records of, 167–68; New York Indians and, 164–65; Nicolet in, 12–14; Protestants in, 201–3; Schoolcraft visits, 132; slaves in, 114; and United States laws, 134. *See also* French; Winnebagos

Grignon, Augustin, 114, 121; in attack on Prairie du Chien, 123; describes Chippewa wars, 78; describes Foxes' acts, 81
Grignon, Pierre, 102
Grignon family, 100
Groseilliers, Medard Chouart de, 41

Half-breeds: *See Métis*
Hall, James, 141–42
Hamilton's Diggings, 138
Harrison, Gov. William H., 120, 146
Haugean movement, 208–9
Hayward, 256, 263
Hazel Green (Hardscrabble), 140
Helena, 140, 152
Hennepin, Fr. Louis, 21, 34, 48, 49, 64; attitude toward Indians, 56; and canoes, 61, 62; and Indian religion, 48; notes women's roles, 49
Henry, Alexander: Indians seek alcohol from, 109, 114
Henry, Gen. James, 152
Ho-Chunk Nation: *See* Winnebagos
Holcombe: *See* Little Falls
Holden, James, 253, 259
Hopewell Culture, 27–29
Horicon, 183
Housing: as civilizing factor, 233. *See also* by individual tribes
Hudson's Bay Co., 67
Hunting: by Indians, 47. *See also* Fur trade
Hurons, 1–2, 8, 10, 11, 15; battle Foxes, 80; and European goods, 73

Illiniwek: *See* Illinois (tribe)
Illinois Country, 67; and fur trade, 98
Illinois (state): miners from, 139; sawmills in, 267; soldiers from (1831), 144, 148–50
Illinois (tribe), 2, 15, 34, 39, 76; attack Winnebagos, 51
Immigrants: assimilation of, 198; difficulties of, 196; discord between, 197; and dream dance, 239–41; and Indians, 197–98, 239–41; recruitment of, 189; reformers criticize, 209–10; separate churches for, 204–5; and women's roles, 196–97. *See also* individual groups
Indian reservations: churches on, 228–29. *See also* individual tribes and reservations
Indians: assimilation of, 164; and canoes, 61; citizenship of, 233–36; civilizing attempts for, 230–33; criticized by whites, 216–17; debts of, 166–70; defended by whites, 218–19, 221, 225; destroy sawmill, 250; employment of,

241–44; and European goods, 73–74, 104, 166–67; and farming, 228; fear settlers, 87, 92; flee northward, 171–72; housing, clothing of, 233; and immigrants, 197–98; and land ownership, 236–37; locations of, at European contact, 33–35; locations in 18th century, 74; logging by, 244; religious beliefs of, 48–49; removals of, 170–71; seasonal moves by, 47–48; as slaves, 113, 114; strike by, 243–44; and traditional beliefs, 237–38; tribal power ends, 236; unsanitary practices of, 105; and voting, 179. *See also* Fur trade; individual tribes' names. [Brief mentions not indexed.]
— population: at contact, 33–35; in 1650, 44; in 1768, 91–92; in 1770, 241; in 1856, 226
— prehistoric: Archaic, 25–27; burial mounds of, 28, 29–30; early trade by, 25, 28–29, 36; foods of, 25, 27–28, 36; landscape changed by, 36–37; Late Woodland, 29–31; Middle Mississippian, 31; Oneota, 31–32; Paleo-Indians, 24–25; pottery of, 19, 27, 32; tools of, 25–26; women's roles, 31; Woodland, 27–29
Ingram and Kennedy Co., 267, 268
Iowa (state): sawmills in, 267
Iowa County, 188
Iowas (tribe), 86, 94
Irish, 189, 190, 197, 198
Iroquois, 2, 8; drive toward west, 15; obtain guns, 51; and treaty of 1700–1, 78–79
Ixonia, 188

Jackson, President Andrew, 155
Janesville, 183
Jay's Treaty (1794), 117
Jenny Bull Falls, 264
Jesuits (Society of Jesus), 2, 38, 54–57. *See also* individual missionaries
Jim Falls: and logging, 256; in Beef Slough War, 268
Johnson, Col. James, 137
Jolliet, Louis, 55–56
Juneau, Solomon, 158

Kalm, Peter, 6–7, 62
Kaministikwia, 69, 85, 106
Kaukauna, 164
Keokuk (Sac), 147, 155
Kickapoos, 15, 34, 39, 42, 55, 61, 74; in American Revolution, 94; battle Foxes, 80; population (1768) of, 92
Kilbourn, Byron, 158
Kilbourn City, 281

Kinzie, Juliette: comments on miners, 138; and Indian removal, 171; and river travel, 128
Knapp, Stout and Company, 251, 263, 267, 271
Koshkonong, Lake: lead mining at, 136; in Black Hawk War, 150–51; settlement near, 157

Lac Courte Oreilles Reservation, 100, 236, 244; Carver visits, 91; dream dance at, 238–39; women, children work at, 242
Lac du Flambeau: portage to, 63; posts at, 100, 107–9, 112
La Crosse (city), 183, 203
Lacrosse (sport), 52–53, 119
Lac Vieux Desert, 100, 103
Land system: French, 132, 173–74; Indian ownership of, 236–37; rising values of, 158; sales of, 175–78; and squatters, 176–78; surveys of, 174–78; variations in, 181–82
Langlade, Charles de, 83–84, 95–96
Language: Chippewa, 42–43; and courts, 187; English, requirement, 232–33; Indians use European, 73–74
La Pointe, 69, 100, 223, 233, 294; *métis* at, 165–66; vote fraud charged at, 235
LaSalle, Robert Cavelier de, 6–7, 41, 64
Law: issues in, 134, 139
Lawe, John, 100, 135
Lead Miners: and Red Bird War, 143–44. *See also* Lead mines; Mining region
Lead mines: early growth of, 135–40; regulation of, 137–38. *See also* Mining region
Leopold, Aldo, 277–78, 297
Le Sueur, Pierre, 43, 71
Linctot, Daniel, 94
Little Falls Dam, 264, 269, 273
Little Lake Butte des Morts, 80
Lockwood, James, 133–34, 251
Log cabin, 198–200
Logging, 263; accidents in, 257–58; booms, 264–65; business combinations in, 247, 263–64, 268–69; buying systems, 251–52; camp life, 252–54, 258–59; dams built, 264; decline of, 277; and downriver mills, 266–69; drives, 259–63, 264, 268; employment in, 244, 272; extent of, 249–50; on Menominee Reservation, 244–45; rafts, 265–66; size of operations, 256; trespassing in, 252; wages, 258; work described, 254–55; workers organize, 273–74
Logjams, 262
Long, Maj. Stephen, 133
Louisiana, 69–70

Lumber: from east, 128–29, 250; production, 275; rafts, 265–66; and saw improvements, 266. *See also* Sawmills; Logging
Lutherans, 204, 208–9

Mackinac: blacks at, 113; British evacuate (1815), 124; U.S. factory at, 118; U.S. takes over (1796), 117. *See also* Fort Mackinac; Michilimackinac
Madeline Island, 100–1, 102
Madison, 182; in Black Hawk War, 151; capital moved to, 158; Norwegian drinking in, 211–12
Malhiot, Franois: life as trader, 106–10
Manitowoc, 266
Maple sugar, 47, 103
Marathon County, 196
Marin, Joseph, 70, 72
Marin, Pierre Paul, 70
Marinette, 251
Marquette, Fr. Jacques, 6; canoe used by, 61; journeys to Mississippi, 55–56; at La Pointe, 54–55; and Winnebagos, 11–12
Marsh, Rev. Cutting, 201, 202–3
Marshfield, 276
Mascoutins, 15, 39, 42, 50, 55, 74; in American Revolution, 94; battles with Foxes, 80; population (1768) of, 92
Mazzuchelli, Fr. Samuel, 202, 204, 207, 228; criticizes Irish drinking, 210
McDouall, Col. Robert, 123
McKenney, Col. Thomas, 144–45
Ménard, Fr. René, 45, 55
Menasha, 175, 251
Mendenhall, Cyrus, 225
Menomonie, 251
Menominee, Mich., 251
Menominee River: blacks at, 114; drives on, 261; logging on, 251
Menominees: and agent, 228; in American Revolution, 95; attack black traders, 114; avoid allotment, 237, 245; block removal, 221–22; and Catholic Church, 204; and citizenship, 235; in Civil War, 233–34; and civilizing attempts, 233; criticize Americans, 142; and disease, 75; and dream dance, 239; at French contact, 34; hunting by, urged, 74; and land issues, 163; and logging, 257; and Marquette and Jolliet, 55; and *métis*, 165; and New York Indians, 164, 221–22; obtain reservation, 222; payment to (1838), 168–69; population (1768) of, 92; receive gifts, 72, 86–87; support Tecumseh, 121–22; trade records of, 167–68; treaties of 1831 and 1836, 160–61; treaty of

1848, 163, 221; treaty of 1854, 222; and wild rice, 45–46; win prizes, 231
Menominee Reservation: logging in, 244–45; "Pagan party" in, 237
Mesquakie: *See* Foxes
Methodists, 204; use circuit riders, 205–6; criticism of, 207; criticize immigrants, 211; and Indians, 229; send missionaries, 203
Métis: and Americans, 272–73; and Catholic Church, 204; described, 71–72; in fur trade, 100; at Green Bay and Prairie du Chien, 132–34; increase of, 71; as issue in treaties, 161, 165–66; prejudice against, 231; significance of, 294–95; strike by, 243–44; voting by, 235
Miamis, 2, 15, 34; in American Revolution, 94; battles with Foxes, 80
Michigan, Lake, 21; and logging, 250, 265–66
Michigan Territory, 131, 132
Michilimackinac, 69, 100; in American Revolution, 92, 94; British post at, 85; diseases at, 75; excavations at, 53–54; in French and Indian War, 84; fur trade at, 98; Jesuits at, 56; placed within U.S., 95; post overthrown (1763), 88. *See also* Mackinac; Fort Mackinac
Michilimackinac Co., 101
Midewiwin Society, 237–38
Military Road, 182
Militia, 149–55
Milwaukee, 182, 282; early settlement of, 158; fur trade at, 98; Germans in, 192; Indians from, 86, 93; land sales at, 175; Presbyterians in, 203; and railroads, 182–83; squatters at, 177; Swedes in, 185–86
Mineral Point, 175; Cornish in, 140; editor attacks Winnebagos, 171; food shortages in, 129; hanging in, 139; Methodists in, 203
Mining region: churches in, 203; contrasts in, 127, 138–39; Cornish in, 190; described, 136, 138; housing in, 139; and Indian removals, 221, 223–25; rush to, 137–38; shortages in, 130; towns in, 139–40. *See also* Lead mining; Miners; Mineral Point
Missionaries: concern for west by, 200–2; as circuit riders, 205–6; explorations by, 55–56; French, 54–57; leave Wisconsin, 69; and New York tribes, 164; and revivals, 206–7. *See also* Churches; and individual denominations and missionaries
Mississippi River: early tales of, 14; in fur trade, 89, 90; glaciers' impact on, 21
Missouri, 267

Mixed-bloods: *See Métis*

Mole Lake, 116

Montreal, 4, 6, 8; controls fur trade, 97–99; diseases at, 75; and treaty of 1700–1, 75, 78

Montreal River: portage on, 63, 106, 107

Mormons, 203

Morse, Rev. Jedediah, 164, 171

Mountain Wolf Woman, 217, 233, 241

Muir, John, 191, 197–98, 279

Munsees, 164, 232–33, 236. *See also* New York Indians

Muscoda (English Prairie), 140

Muskego, 194

Muskrat, 172–73

Names: carried from east, 181; European, 187; Indian and French origins of, 294

Necedah, 217

Neenah, 251

Negroes: *See* Blacks

Nelson, George: life as trader, 104–6, 110, 115–16

Neopit (Menominee), 244

New Diggings, 140

New England: settlers from, 157–59, 179

New France, 38–40, 43. *See also* France; French

New Glarus, 193

New Orleans, 99

New Richmond, 271

New York, 159, 179

New York Indians, 163–64

Nicolet, Jean, 9–14, 41

Nipissings, 2, 10, 11

North West Co.: operations of, 101–9 passim; post on Yellow River, 105–6

Northwest Ordinance, 178

Northwest passage, 5–7, 14

Norwegians, 189, 194–95, 196, 198, 212; churches of, 201, 208–9, 210–11; and drinking, 210–11; and logging, 263

Nye, Bill, 258–59

Oconomowoc, 186

Ojibwas: *See* Chippewas

Oneida Reservation, 236

Oneidas, 163–64; in Civil War, 233; civilizing attempts with, 233; land ownership among, 236; and missionaries, 229; and schools, 229–30. *See also* New York Indians

Osages, 93

Oshkosh: fires at, 276; sawdust in, 275; sawmills at, 251; workers' protest in, 273–74

Oshkosh, Chief, 221

Ottawas, 1, 7, 11, 15, 34, 75; in American Revolution, 93–94; battle Winnebagos, 51; battles with Foxes, 80; and canoes, 62; divisions among, 42–43; and fur trade, 53; receive gifts, 72, 86; support Tecumseh, 121; and treaty of 1829, 145

Ottawa River, 1, 9

Ouiatanon, 85

Oxen, 181

Passenger pigeon, 279–82

Pecatonica, Battle of, 151

Pepin, Lake, 67, 69, 70; Carver plundered at, 91; Chippewa-Sioux fighting at, 77; Perrot's fort on, 41

Perrault, Jean Baptiste: life as trader, 102–4, 110, 111, 115

Perrot, Nicolas, 41, 43, 50, 51; at pageant of 1671, 38–39; sees lacrosse game, 52; trades with Sioux, 53

Peshtigo Fire, 275

Peshtigo River, 262

Pewaukee, 180

Pike, Lt. Zebulon: expedition, 119–20; and Julien Dubuque, 136; sees lacrosse game, 52

Plants: exotic, arrive, 183–84

Platteville, 140, 203

Polish, 195, 198; in logging, 256, 262

Pond, Peter, 99

Pontiac's Conspiracy, 87–89

Population: census lines, 295; totals for 1830, 1850, and 1900, 296; territorial, 131–32

Porlier, Jacques, 100

Portage, 63, 100, 288; Marquette and Jolliet at, 55

Portaging: canoes and, 63; on Montreal River, 106; on Ontonagon River, 103. *See also* individual rivers; Canoes

Potawatomis, 2, 15, 34, 39, 42, 61, 74, 75; in American Revolution, 93–94; battles with Foxes, 80; and dream dance, 239; influence on names, 294; and medicine dance, 238; population (1768) of, 92; (1870s–80s), 221; removals of, 220–21; treaty of 1829, 145; treaty of 1833, 160, 171

Pottersville, 188

Pottery, Indian, 19, 27, 32

Poygan, Lake, 251

Prairie du Chien, 52, 130, 182, 213; in American Revolution, 95; in Black Hawk War, 152–53; Carver visits, 91; Catholics in, 201; contrasts in, 128; French land claims in, 173–74; fur trade at, 99; land system in, 132; lead arrives at, 136; Pike expedition visits,

119–20; in Red Bird War, 143; Sioux parade in, 148; slaves at, 114; traders at, 102; treaty payments at, 166; U.S. licensed trader in, 118; in War of 1812, 122–26
Presbyterians, 202–3, 204, 229; discipline by, 213. *See also* American Home Missionary Society
Protestant Episcopal Church, 202, 228–29
Prussians, 198

Quebec, 3, 4, 8

Racine, 266, 281
Radisson, Pierre Esprit, 41, 45
Railroads: beginnings, 182–83; and fishing, 283; impact on Indians, 243; importance of, 296–97; in logging, 271–72
Ramsey, Gov. Alexander (Minn.), 223
Recollets, 9, 54
Red Bird, 143–45
Red Bird (or Winnebago) War, 142–45
Red Cedar River: in Beef Slough War, 268; Chippewa-Sioux warfare on, 115; logging on, 249; traders at, 102, 103, 114
Red Cliff Reservation: allotments on, 236; farming success in, 228; logging on, 244
Reformers: and allotment plan, 236–37; criticize immigrants, 209–10
Religion: freewill doctrines in, 207–9; of Indians, 48; lack of, criticized, 212; value to frontier, 211–14
Revival meetings, 206–7
Reynolds, Gov. John (Ill.), 138, 149
Rhinelander, 277, 284
Rivers: channel work on, 264; logging use of, 247, 249. *See also* Logging drives; individual rivers
Ritzenthaler, Robert, 101
Roads, 182
Roman Catholics: and dream dance, 239; fear for west, 201, 203–4; and reservations, 229; send missionaries, 202, 203–4
Roosevelt, Theodore, 292
Round Low Cloud, Charles, 216–17
Rudolf, Theodore, 139

Sacs, 2, 15, 39, 74; alliance with Foxes, 42; in American Revolution, 93–95; Carver visits, 90; foods of, 44; at French contact, 34; housing of, 44–45; population (1768) of, 92; receive gifts, 72, 86. *See also* Sacs and Foxes

Sacs and Foxes: buildup to Black Hawk War, 147–48; land cession by, 120, 146–47; and miners, 137; moves in 18th century, 74; removal of, 171; support Tecumseh, 121, 124; treaty of 1825, 148
St. Croix River: Carver meets Indians at, 91; first sawmill at, 161–62, 250–51; land office at, 175; last drive on, 277; log rafts on, 266; logging on, 249; portages on, 63; sawmills on, 265; steamboats on, 130
St. Ignace (Mich.), 73
St. Louis (Mo.), 267; British attacks on, 94–95, 124–25; and lead mines, 136–37; Sacs' cession at, 120
St. Lusson, Simon Franois Daumont, Sieur de, 38–39
St. Martin, Alexis, 128
Sauk City, 151
Saukenuk, 147–48
Sauks: *See* Sacs
Sault Ste. Marie, 38–39, 56
Sawmills, 249, 266; decline of, 277; worker protests at, 273–74. *See also* individual towns
Sawyer, Philetus, 252, 264
Sawyer County, 274
Scandinavians: *See* Danes; Norwegians; Swedes
Schoolcraft, Henry, 132
Schools: for Indians, 229–30
Schullsberg, 140, 190
Scots, 189, 191, 198, 212. *See also* John Muir; British
Settlement: census shows, 189; rapidity of, 157–59
Seven Years War: *See* French and Indian War
Shaw, Daniel, 247, 263
Shawano, 235, 257, 263
Shawnee Prophet (Lalawethika), 121–22
Shipping, 129–30
Siggenauk (Chippewa/Potawatomi), 93, 95
Sioux, 6, 34, 43; in American Revolution, 94–95; in Black Hawk War, 155; Carver visits, 91; play lacrosse, 119; population (1768) of, 92; support British (1812), 122; treaties (1679), 43; (1825), 148; (1837), 161; and wild rice, 47. *See also* Chippewa-Sioux warfare
Slaves, 113, 114, 142
Spanish, 136
Spaulding, Jacob, 218–19
Speculators, 177
Squatters, 176–78

Steamboats, 130
Stevens Point, 175, 195; and logging, 262, 264; and passenger pigeons, 281
Stillman's Run, Battle of, 149–50
Stillwater, 277
Stockbridges, 203; in Civil War, 233; and civilizing attempts, 230, 232–33. *See also* New York Indians
Stockbridge Reservation, 236
Strang, James Jesse, 203
Street, Joseph, 143, 166
Sun Prairie, 176–77, 182
Superior, Lake, 1, 9–10, 22; glacial impact on, 21; sailing vessels on, 101–2. *See also* Chequamegon Bay
Swedes: and Indian "uprising," 185–86, 189, 197, 240–41; and "readers" movement, 208. *See also* Unonius, Gustaf
Swedish Baptist Church, 208, 213
Swedish Mission Covenant Church, 208
Swiss, 189, 193

Tanneries, 243
Tecumseh, 121–22
Thames, Battle of the (1813), 122
Thornapple River, 274
Timber wolf, 282–83
Tippecanoe, Battle of (1811), 122
Tomah, 217, 220
Tools: in fur trade, 53, 73. *See also* Indians; Indians, prehistoric
Totagatic River, 262
Traders: *See* Fur trade
Trading posts: modern sites of, 294n. *See also* Fur trade
Trapper River, 256
Treaties: *See* individual tribes
Treaty of Ghent (1814), 124
Trempealeau County, 28; immigrants in, 198; land issue in, 292; Lutheran divisions in, 209
Trois Rivières (Canada), 1, 8
Turner, Andrew Jackson: background, 288; praises Northwoods, 290, 293
Turner, Frederick Jackson: 288–93 passim
Turtle Lake, 276

United States: Army of, in American Revolution, 93–94, and Battle of Fallen Timbers, 117; boundaries of, 95; and citizenship requirements, 234; creates factory system, 118–19; land laws of, 174, 178; opposes British traders, 118–20
— Commissioner of Indian Affairs: on aid for women, 243; and Chippewa removal, 223; and civilizing Indians, 230,

232; and land issue, 236; and Potawatomis, 220–21
— Congress: backs Menominees' logging, 245
Unonius, Gustaf: builds cabin, 198–200; and drinking, 210; immigration of, 185–86, 188; and Indians, 197; at land meeting, 198; and religious beliefs, 214; and work requirements, 194–95
University of Wisconsin, 290–91

Van den Broek, Fr. T.J., 207–8
Vermont, 157
Voyageurs. *See Coureurs de bois*

Walworth County, 182
War of 1812, 120–26; Black Hawk in, 147
Warfare: Chippewa v. Sioux, 76–78; Fox Wars, 78–82; Indian traditions of, 50–52; prehistoric Indians and, 30–31, 36
Watertown, 182
Watrous, John S., 223–25
Waukesha, 158, 220
Waukesha County: colony in, 188; land issues in, 177; New Englanders in, 179–80
Wausau, 175, 220
Weapons, 24–25, 31
Webster, 105n
Welsh, 188, 189, 190, 212
West Bend, 209
West Salem, 285
Weyerhaeuser, Frederick, 267–71 passim; blocked by Dietz, 274–75; moves to Pacific Northwest, 277
Wheat, 183–84
Wheeler, Rev. Leonard, 225
White-Indian attitudes, 141–42
White pine: logging importance of, 255. *See also* Logging; Lumber
Whitewater, 183
Whitman, Walt, 218
Wild rice: at Folle Avoine post, 106; Indians' reliance on, 45–47; traded for alcohol, 110; traders purchase, 112
Williams, Rev. Eleazer, 164
Wilson, William, 251
Winnebago, Lake, 136, 266
Winnebago Prophet, The, 148, 155
Winnebago War: *See* Red Bird War
Winnebagos: agriculture of, 34; in American Revolution, 93; annuities for, 220; attacks weaken, 15; battle Foxes (1729), 81; block removal, 215–17; clothing of, 233; criticized by editor, 171; and disease, 75; farm production of, 241–42, 244; foods and housing of, 44; homesteads for, 220; mining by,

136, 137; and New York Indians, 164;
and Nicolet, 12–14; population (1768)
of, 92; and Pike, 119; play lacrosse,
119; protest payment, 244; receive
gifts, 72, 86; and prehistoric tribes, 33–
34; removals of, 171; support Tecumseh, 121–22, 123; treaties (1829,
1832, 1837), 160–61; (1829, 829),
145; (1837), 171; warfare by, 51–52;
woman chief of, 50, 112

Winneconne, 168–69, 251, 267

Wisconsin: climatic zones, 22, 24; eastern
tribes in, 171–72; ethnic groups in,
189; lures immigrants, 188; origin of
name of, 294; population (1830,
1840), 131–32; (1850), 179; statehood
(1848), 178–79; topography of, 22–
23;

— Constitution: and Indian voting, 234

— State Government: and Indian removal,
216; protects game and fish, 283; protects passenger pigeons, 281

— State Supreme Court, 174, 260

— Territory: created (1836), 161; land
sales in, 175; legislator shot, 127; lumber for capitol building, 250; population (1840, 1846), 159; seal of, 130–
31, 230

Wisconsin Central Railroad, 271–72

Wisconsin Dells: See Kilbourn City

Wisconsin Heights, Battle of, 151–52

Wisconsin Rapids, 220

Wisconsin River: drives on, 259, 261, 262;
improvement of, 264; logging on, 251;
Marquette and Jolliet on, 55–56; name
of, 55, 294; sawmills along, 249;
strikes on, 273

Wittenberg, 220

Wolf River: drives on, 261; improvement
of, 264; logging on, 249, 251; logging
accidents on, 257

Women: in church services, 205; immigrant, roles of, 196–97; lack of, in
French posts, 71; roles on farms, 179–
81;

— Indian: aid for, urged, 243; in fur trade,
111–13; in prehistoric tribes, 31; roles
in tribes of, 49–50; and trade goods,
167–68; work by, 242–43

X Y Co., 101–2, 104–6

Yellow River: Chippewa-Sioux warfare on,
115–16; portage on, 63; posts on, 104–
6, 112–13

MARK WYMAN

born and educated in Wisconsin, has written on the far West and more recently on immigration in the Midwest. Among his best known works are *Hard-Rock Epic: Western Miners and the Industrial Revolution, 1860–1910* (1979), *Immigrants in the Valley: Irish, Germans, and Americans in the Upper Mississippi Country, 1830–1860* (1984), *DP: Europe's Displaced Persons, 1945–1951* (1989), and *Round-Trip to America: The Immigrants Return to Europe, 1880–1930* (1993). He is presently Professor of History at Illinois State University in Normal, Illinois.